The B-45 Tornado

The B-45 Tornado

An Operational History of the
First American Jet Bomber

JOHN C. FREDRIKSEN

McFarland & Company, Inc., Publishers
Jefferson, North Carolina, and London

LIBRARY OF CONGRESS CATALOGUING-IN-PUBLICATION DATA

Fredriksen, John C.
The B-45 Tornado : an operational history of the first
American jet bomber / John C. Fredriksen.
p.   cm.
Includes bibliographical references and index.

ISBN 978-0-7864-4278-2
softcover: 50# alkaline paper ∞

1. Tornado (Jet bomber) — History.
2. Aerial reconnaissance — History — 20th century.
3. United States — History, Military — 20th century.
4. United States. Air Force — History — 20th century.   I. Title.
UG1242.B6F27   2009
358.4'283 — dc22   2009026356

British Library cataloguing data are available

On the cover: B-45A Tornado, 1948 ©2009 Boeing;
background ©2009 Shutterstock

Manufactured in the United States of America

McFarland & Company, Inc., Publishers
Box 611, Jefferson, North Carolina 28640
www.mcfarlandpub.com

To the men of the Tornado

Table of Contents

Preface

History, as a discipline, remains subject to the vagaries of human memory and exhibits unfortunate tendencies towards unsightly, even inexplicable, gaps. Important events, viewed by contemporaries as commonplace or unimportant at the time of occurrence, can be ignored, insufficiently recorded, or even overlooked altogether. Such fate certainly applies to the North American B-45 Tornado, a historically significant machine apparently little known to the aviation community at large. Some facets of this neglect are easy to understand: chronologically, this aircraft has always labored in the shadow of its highly successful contemporary, Boeing's magnificent B-47 Stratojet. Also, in the course of a lengthy operational life, the Tornado fulfilled a number of critical tasks such as nuclear strike or strategic reconnaissance, both of which were and remain highly classified activities. These facts, plus the relatively small number of aircraft manufactured, all conspire to render the B-45 a little-appreciated commodity, misunderstood, or contemptuously deemed unworthy of attention. This unhappy status, however, bespeaks a disservice to the flight and ground crews who spearheaded jet bomber operations and whose accomplishments — and sacrifices — deserve the recognition and approbation of posterity. Their untold story is a glaring gap in aviation and Cold War historiography that begs redress in an objective and scholarly fashion to finally set the record straight. The story that emerges, happily, is fascinating, fulfilling, and illustrative of this first generation of American jet pioneers. I consider myself privileged to pay them homage that is long overdue.

The book you hold is the first-ever attempt to chronicle the B-45 Tornado and subject it to the rigors of historical scrutiny. I intended from the onset to compose a definitive treatise, and the final product represents fruits of two decades of excruciating work. Little did I know at the time that this would develop into an arduous trek, one Xenophon himself may have found daunting. My methodology is comprehensive and employed relevant documents and unit histories, the declassification of heretofore restricted materials, and interviews with over one hundred pilots and ground crew associated with this aircraft. Assembling such a mountain of empirical evidence was challenging and is by no means complete, given the secretive nature of nuclear and reconnaissance activities and their concomitant inaccessibility. Yet, from those materials unearthed and examined, a reasonably accurate picture emerges about the B-45 and the various caps it wore over a decade of continuous service. In presenting my case, I eschew the usual analytical synthesis in favor of a straightforward Rankean discourse, namely, letting the story tell itself. My emphasis on oral history also lends human perspective to what might have otherwise ended up as simply another dour recital of flights, airfoils, and crashes. I sought to closely

1

examine the interaction of man and machine from the earliest days of jet bomber aviation and vicariously reconstruct a forgotten chapter of American aviation. As such, the overall tone was kept narrative by design, and I forego lengthy technical discussions of avionics, subsystems, and national policies. I am, to the extent that this endeavor finally and objectively tells its tale, satisfied with the results. May readers find it as fascinating and informative.

Another brief word concerning my methodology: I aspired to compile the most meticulously researched and documented airplane study ever written. As such it should satiate the curiosity of even the most demanding aviation buff, while remaining accessible to lay readers less versed in the nuances of aeronautics. My approach to the topic is inclusive by nature, hence the final product is something of a hybrid, part scholarly inquiry and part oral history — a rich tapestry of empirical evidence woven together in an engaging format. Through this expedient it is now possible to explore the B-45 in all its operational facets, more often than not in the words of those who were actually there. More than anything else, I posit this book as the fitting tribute to a magnificent body of men, long neglected in aviation annals, whose story is both compelling and worth reciting. Its scope of inquiry and breadth of documentation should finally place the North American B-45 Tornado, its success and its failures, in a more deserving historical context. In sum, a landmark book about a landmark aircraft.

Uncovering this plethora of data has proved to be a difficult undertaking over these past 20 years, and I extend gratitude to the following individuals, without whose cheerful and persistent cooperation I could not have prevailed. Foremost among them are Archie DiFante and Dick Gamma of the Air Force Historical Research Agency, Maxwell AFB, whose patience and tact with my many and impossible requests is truly remarkable. No less vital were the labors of David A. Giordano and Herbert Rawlings-Milton of the National Archives, College Park — real declassification troopers. I also extend gratitude to Drs. Raymond L. Puffer and Craig W. Luther; Air Force Flight Center historian Grant M. Hales; Air Combat Command historian John D. Weber; Air Materiel Command historian Lori S. Tagg; Aeronautical Systems Center, Deborah L. Barone of the Albert Simpson Library; Air University Library, John Sheehan, for a peek at his unpublished B-45 manuscript; R. Cargill Hall of the National Reconnaissance Office, Jim Baldwin, of England for information on RAF Sculthorpe; John K. Mott, renowned B-45 collector; John W. Conners for help with Pratt and Whitney; Wai Yip for his blurb on RB-45Cs used in British overflights; Dr. Gerhard Moroff of Germany for help in locating articles; and Fritz Krag of Denmark for his translated essay on RB-45C stopovers. Thanks also to Paul Lashmar, UK, for sharing his many interviews and documents on Cold War overflights, and Randall Bergmann of the Defense Technical Information Center (DTIC) for help is acquiring technical documentation. Finally, nods accrue for Maury Seitz, *recce raconteur* and B-45 cheerleader extraordinaire, for his help and boundless encouragement over the years, and Merle Sollars, Las Vegas, for constant and valuable input relative to Detachment A in Korea. Kudos are further due to my indefatigable manuscript reviewer William V. Menkevich for his insightful critique, Bob Gordon for keeping me abreast of the latest publications, Pat Chapman Meder and Julie Hendrickson for access to their fathers' papers, and to that affable avatar of all things Air Force, Dave Menard. A special nod also goes to Mat and Vicki Le Croix for leasing me that little slice of heaven by the sea, Point Judith's A-frame, where I labored over the winter of

2005–2006. Finally, the author expresses heartfelt appreciation towards all members of the 47th Bomb Wing, the 91st Strategic Reconnaissance Wing, and the 19th Tactical Reconnaissance Squadron, without whose assistance and input this book might have ended up an afterthought. Rarely has a historian enjoyed such a buoyant, enthusiastic support system. Gentlemen, the privilege has been mine alone.

In pursuing this project, my endeavors were expedited by receipt of a short-term research grant from the National Air and Space Museum, Smithsonian Institution, along with a research grant from the Air Force Historical Research Agency, Maxwell AFB. My indebtedness to Dr. Michael J. Neufeld and Dr. A. Timothy Warnock for their assistance in these matters is freely and gratefully acknowledged.

John C. Fredriksen, PhD
Narragansett, Rhode Island

CHAPTER ONE

Wild Blue Wonder

"As you know, there is almost a fist fight involved any time the relative merits of jet and propeller aircraft are discussed."
— Major General Alden R. Crawford.[1]

By summer 1944, the allied air offensive in Europe was inexorably advancing the cause of victory. Eighth Air Force bomber streams appeared daily in German skies with metronomic regularity, leaving death and tangled destruction in their wake. Their efforts coincided with an equally determined night campaign waged by the Royal Air Force, and together this relentless rain of bombs systematically dismembered Hitler's vaunted *Festung Europa* from on high. Resistance from the highly skilled and well-equipped Luftwaffe was predictably fierce and occasioned heavy losses among bomber crews, but such attrition was acceptable in light of massive American bomber production and the appearance of North American's redoubtable P-51D Mustang in 1944. German aerial losses increased exponentially and there was general agreement on both sides that it was only a matter of time before the Luftwaffe yielded control of its own airspace. Allied planners then received a distinct jolt in August 1944 when the Germans unveiled their nascent jet-fighter technology. Nazi aviation prowess had reached its highest expression in the Messerschmitt Me-262 Schwalbe, a deadly Dervish sporting unmistakably shark-like lines, swept-back leading edges, a bomber-killing armament and, most important, a 100 mile-per-hour speed advantage over contemporary allied designs. Its capacity for upending bomber streams was underscored in February 1945 when a force of sixty Me-262s scythed through heavily armed B-17 formations, knocking down twenty-five of the lumbering giants with ease.[2] This was a chilling portent of things to come and highlighted the passing of propeller-driven aircraft in aerial combat. Naturally, the U.S. Army Air Force (AAF) high command viewed such developments alarmingly and, given the potential for prohibitive losses, they pondered whether or not daylight bombing operations were still desirable, or even feasible.

It was against this military setting that the genesis of America's jet bomber program began in the summer of 1943. Officers of the AAF's Air Material Command (AMC) were increasingly aware of German developments in jet aviation, and they approached General Electric for a more capable successor to the British-inspired TG-100 axial-flow turbojet engine. GE engineers complied and a year later they bench tested their small-diameter TG-180 (J35) turbojet, which yielded improved fuel efficiency and 4,000 pounds of thrust. This compact and relatively lightweight engine was a great improvement

5

over existing devices. Moreover, the promise of greater thrust, coupled with the perceived necessity for similarly powered aircraft to penetrate German air defenses, arose in April 1944 when AAF officers issued specifications for the first U.S. jet bomber. The machine in question was expected to weigh between 80,000 and 200,000 pounds and to be capable of hoisting four tons of ordnance at speeds approaching 500 miles per hour. The combat radius was set at 1,000 miles and the bombing capacity was revised upwards to 22,000 pounds to accommodate British-designed "Grand-slam" weapons. High speed was also envisioned as the best protection against fighter interception, hence only a single tail turret would be required. Considerable research supported this seemingly drastic decision, and several military authorities agreed that "defensive guns and gunners on bombers were not worth what we were paying for them even at the low cruising speeds of World War II bombers."[3]

The ensuing bomber program set extremely ambitious objectives for itself, considering the primitive nature of jet propulsion and its attendant aerodynamics, but AMC officers waxed so optimistic that they announced a competition in December 1944 with these specifications intact. Specifically, AAF officials were pushing for a crash program that could field a prototype as quickly as possible, despite the fact that the requisite technology was either poorly understood, problematic, or, in many instances nonexistent. Still, as Colonel Bruce K. Holloway cogently penned in a postwar essay, "We must build our bombers to operate in the immediate vicinity of sonic speed, or they will probably have great difficulty in reaching future targets."[4] Recent events had only underscored what would one day prove a perilous reality for military aviation. Consequently, the acquisition of a new jet bomber would push the envelope of aviation knowledge beyond existing limits. Many aviation companies found these futuristic demands far too daunting; consequently only four established firms, North American, Martin, Consolidated, and Boeing, rose to the challenge.

In January 1944 it fell to James H. "Dutch" Kindelberger, president of North American Aviation (NAA), to proffer one of the earliest jet-bomber proposals to the AAF. He did so by drawing upon a legacy of designing and constructing outstanding military aircraft, as his P-51 *Mustang* fighter and B-25 *Mitchell* medium bomber attest. As company chief executive, he was also renowned for a willful approach to getting things done. George Gehrkens, a long-time North American employee, neatly summed up his attitude: "Kindelberger did things his way — and *you did* them his way, but he'd let you know nicely." Construction of the new jet bomber was in capable hands, for Kindelberger had previously broached the subject with Army officials, as early as November 1943, and, within weeks, he laid the groundwork for a comprehensive study program. This endeavor was North American's 130th aircraft design and it received the company designation NA-130; it turned out to be another example of Kindelberger's engineering and business savvy. Kindelberger believed that the war would end before a prototype could be airborne, yet he still resolved to beat out the competition despite that possibility.[5] His staff drew upon a largess of company innovation, abetted by their boss's practical streak. Kindelberger, characteristically, next pursued a conservative design approach utilizing existing construction techniques to save time, while gradually phasing in newer technologies. His approach was calculated to minimize the risks associated with cutting-edge research and development, and, hopefully, minimize any prospective "Gordian knots" awaiting to be untied. Moreover, experience gained here would invariably yield new information for designers and help develop even more advanced construction and operational techniques.[6]

The new aircraft appeared at the confluence of several new streams of thinking in aviation engineering, for the application of jet technology was in its relative infancy as the NA-130 took shape. Under Kindleberger's aegis, it gradually emerged as a high-shoulder, straight-wing design incorporating four jet engines in two wing-mounted pods. At first glance, the proposed design looked like a conventional, World War II–style aircraft, upon which jet propulsion had been arbitrarily grafted. This decision also stemmed from the company's unfamiliarity with the latest German swept-wing technology, which eluded American scrutiny until after 1945. The ensuing design did not present North American with undue challenges in terms of aeronautical engineering, being far more grounded in present, than future, exigencies. With this outline in hand, technical direction of the bomber program reverted to First Vice President J. Lee Atwood, who delegated design-study responsibilities to Harold E. Dale, a guiding spirit behind the superlative B-25 Mitchell. Dale was tasked with harnessing and harmonizing the collective ingenuity of an army of engineers, described by one AAF liaison officer as 239 draftsmen and administrative draftsmen, 71 master lines and loftsmen, 22 stress analysts, six weight analysts, and two aerodynamists, in addition to the teams tasked with power-plant, hydraulics, and electrical concerns. "I confess that all this put our production scheduling people to quite a task," Dale emoted, "and it's a good thing our engineering staff and their representatives get along so famously together. We used to shake hands practically every day."[7] George Gehrkens, who gained appointment as assistant chief project engineer, had previously helped vanquish gremlins associated with the P-51's famous belly air scoop. Now his thorniest issue was resolving cooling problems associated with the J35's lengthy tailpipe, and designing proper insulation and its fitting. Moreover, like most North American employees, Gehrkens demonstrated North American's unique esprit de corps and close teamwork throughout the prototype's gestation. "The B-45 was the product of an ongoing engineering development organization and we had lots of good people and they knew what they were doing. We were progressive in that it was a follow on to other projects. Lots of good people and the B-45 was the product," he beamed.

With a preliminary layout finalized on paper, the next phase involved constructing wooden mock-ups for scrutiny by company engineers and military representatives. AMC officials proved sufficiently impressed by Kindleberger's achievements and on August 25, 1944, they authorized procurement of preliminary engineering data, wind tunnel models, and a full-scale,

A preproduction wooden model of the XB-45 demonstrates its highly streamlined nature, despite the conventional straight wings (John Mott).

wooden mock-up of Model NA-130. On September 8, 1944, a formal Letter Contract
(W33–038-ac-5126) authorized the payment of $226,311.90 to cover company expenses.[8]
Given the technological challenges encountered, World War II ended long before the
United States could field a viable jet bomber prototype, as Kindelberger predicted. Nevertheless, AMC officials were convinced that NA-130, above all competing designs, held
a promise for the least-troubled gestation and, on February 5, 1946, they authorized construction of three flying prototypes under the experimental bomber designation of XB-
45 with serial numbers 45–59479 through 45–59481. Military leaders remained favorably
impressed by the practical viability of Kindelberger's brainchild and the promise of expediency in acquiring it. Concurrently, AAF officials closely scrutinized and evaluated competing bids submitted by Consolidated, Boeing, and Martin, which received the
designations XB-46, XB-47, and XB-48, respectively. It was at this precise juncture that
Kindelberger's conservative approach paid immediate dividends in terms of design, production and acquisition. Senior officials monitoring the progress of Consolidated's XB-
46 had already judged it inferior in performance to the XB-45 owing to its greater weight.
Boeing's XB-47 and Martin's XB-48 prototypes were also at least two years away from
flight testing and, coupled with mounting Cold War urgencies to obtain a jet bomber
quickly, AAF officials elected to forge ahead with North American's simpler design. Consequently, on July 18, 1946, a recommendation was forwarded to Air Force headquarters
for the procurement of an initial batch of 54 production models — even before the prototype had flown. Their endorsement noted that "The B-45, since it possesses the fewest
unconventional components, can be made available in production in approximately one
year. Such components as the wing section, wing and tail planforms, landing gear, etc.
are of proven design on the B-45 airplane and should, therefore, present few development problems.... [T]he Army Air Force having seemingly committed itself to jet-powered planes to fill future requirements, it would seem imperative that a substantial quantity
be placed in operation at the earliest possible date to provide for service testing of the
airplane and the training of Air and Ground crews."[9] On October 30, 1946, Contract
No. W33-038-ac-15569 was issued authorizing an expanded purchase of 96 production
models, now labeled NA-147, along with requisite tools and spare parts, for
$73,977,632.00. The military anticipated that these aircraft, numbered 47–001 through
47–096, would enter service two years later as the B-45A.

   In constructing the XB-45 prototype, North American capitalized upon its prior
experience in designing and fielding multiengine medium bombers. As it emerged, the
new design incorporated several advanced features from the XB-28 high-altitude bomber,
which was successfully tested but never accepted by the AAF. The new craft utilized an
orthodox planform with a conventional shoulder-mounted wing, a single vertical tail,
and fuselage-mounted horizontal stabilizers. The latter possessed a strikingly high dihe-
dral to clear the jet efflux emanating from the engines. The broad wings, spanning 89
feet, possessed a low-drag, high-lift laminar airfoil and, like the horizontal stabilizers,
exhibited North American's trademark, squared-off tips. The wings also housed 19 self-
sealing fuel bladder cells, mostly arrayed outboard from the engines. Their total capacity was 3,400 gallons of JP1 to fuel the four thirsty J35s, whose combined thrust of 16,000
pounds would, it was to be hoped, push the craft along in excess of 550 miles per hour.
The handsomely streamlined pods housing the engines were underslung on both wings,
ahead of the leading edge, and opened along the bottom centerline for ease of maintenance.

The first XB-45 prototype under construction at the North American Long Beach facility in late 1946 (History Office, Air Force Flight Test Center).

The XB-45, being configured with tricycle landing gear, also possessed a nose wheel which enfolded under the nose, while the mains raised into accommodating wells near the wing roots. The craft sat on newly engineered, high-pressure rubber tires which, having to fit a rather thin wing, were five feet tall yet only 19 inches in width. Their apparent thinness belied the fact that the aircraft was three times heavier than a B-25. The XB-45's empennage also rose to 25 feet from the ground.[10]

The pressurized fuselage, 74 feet in length, utilized a system developed for the XB-28 and was the epitome of streamlined design at the time. Smooth and flush-riveted, it employed an elliptical cross section and was bereft of all protuberances or turrets, save for a fighter-style bubble canopy. Consistent with company philosophy, the fuselage was constructed from four distinct components — the forward pressurized crew compartment, the bomb bay, the aft fuselage, and the pressurized tail compartment — each of which were brought together on the assembly line. This approach allowed large numbers of skilled production personnel to work simultaneously and efficiently on each section before the whole body was joined together. "Design breakdown has another advantage," engineer Dale opined, "although it is far removed from the production line. It is to be found, in fact, on the distant maintenance line — the point where the crew chief reigns. For ease of maintenance can be traced easily to logical aircraft construction — and conversely, illogical construction can cause all manner of maintenance difficulty."[11] The most conspicuous feature of the fuselage was a cavernous bomb bay, divided into two compartments. It could hold 22,000 pounds of bombs (five times the amount carried by World War II "heavies") or two rubber bladders dubbed "Tokyo tanks" with an internal fuel capacity of 5,600 gallons. Thus augmented, the XB-45 possessed a ferry range of 2,921 miles.[12]

A crew of four was required to operate the craft. Pilot and copilot sat in tandem under the streamlined, teardrop-shaped, Plexiglas canopy, well in front of the wing's leading edge. The canopy itself was fixed in place to aid pressurization and could be jettisoned only for escape purposes. Once strapped in, the pilot confronted an array of sixty instruments and sixteen indicator lights. These were displayed on a console laid out with ergonomics in mind. Flight panels on either side of the main array were canted 15 degrees inboard, towards the pilot, to optimize his "cone of vision" and thereby facilitate ease of operation. With all major instrumentation positioned along a single focal point, the pilot could readily monitor his craft's performance without constantly shifting and fatiguing his eyes.[13] The aerial observer/bombardier (AOB) was likewise perched in a latticed Plexiglas nose compartment, also pressurized. AAF officials had chosen to dispense with optical bombing altogether in favor of eventual installation of the new APQ-24 radar bombing system; however, until this complicated unit became available, the famous Norden bombsight would be installed on production models as an interim measure. In addition, design engineers intended to mount an Emerson Electric-designed, radar-directed tail turret on the XB-45 but, when this failed to materialize, a pressurized manned station was substituted in its place. Provisions were also made for tail gunners to operate a pair of .50 caliber M3 Browning machine guns on a powered mount. Significantly, the XB-45's onboard electric generators produced 60,000 watts of energy, conducting it through five miles of wiring exclusive of radios and other electrical devices.[14]

High speed flying produced flight-control surface loads far too strong to be handled by human muscle, so the XB-45 featured hydraulically-boosted control surfaces, including ailerons, rudder and tailplane, and flaps, powered by a high pressure 3000-psi system. The latter provided 95 percent of the energy required to move control surfaces at high speed, with the pilot providing the final five percent. The trim tabs, however, remained electrically driven. For crew comfort, hot air could be bled from the engines to provide cabin pressurization and heating. The plane also utilized a powerful and adjustable air conditioning capable of maintaining the cabin environment 30 degrees below outside temperatures. Creature comforts aside, crew survival remained a somewhat hazardous proposition. The aircraft's high speed flight envelope convinced AAF officials that only newly developed ejection seats afforded the pilot and copilot a realistic means of escape; these were not installed in the first prototype, however. The aerial observer/bombardier faced even more daunting prospects. His emergency egress required him to bail out of the cabin door, directly into a high-speed slipstream, a perilous undertaking that risked striking a nacelle or tail surface. The tail gunner's task was easy by comparison; he simply unstrapped himself, kicked open his access panel, then vaulted into the ether.

The emergent prototype of beautifully streamlined, dutifully arrayed metal weighed in at 87,000 pounds and, by World War II standards, would have been considered a heavy bomber. Yet, under new classifications adopted after the war which were predicated on range, not weight, the XB-45 was officially termed a "light bomber." The first machine rolled out in September 1946, and the handiwork of North American's design team was immediately apparent. The XB-45 was at once both strikingly modern, functional and, even parked, exuded potentiality. In fact, it possessed the air of a scaled-up fighter plane. Nor is it an exaggeration to say that, by merging jet engines with conventional straight wings, the XB-45 had one foot in both the future and the past. Swept-wing bombers were still an unknown commodity at this point, so the issue never arose. Kindelberger, justifiably pleased with his newest creation, adamantly determined to beat his nearest competitor, the Consolidated XB-46, into the air.[15]

No sooner had the XB-45 been declared functional in March 1947 than it was disassembled at the Inglewood facility, mounted on a flatbed truck and, for security reasons, hauled beyond the San Fernando Valley over an obscure mountain route to Muroc Dry Lake, some 90 miles distant. This facility, home of the Air Force flight testing, had hosted strange shapes on its ramp of late, but nothing like this. On March 17, 1947 — St. Patrick's Day — aircraft number 45–59479 was swarmed over by an army of technicians, like so many worker ants doting on their queen. The preflight itinerary was intensive, for the prototype had been fitted with a bewildering array of photo recorders, oscillographs, manifold pressure gages, and Selsyn transmitters capable of monitoring over 28,000 instrument readings every minute.[16] Once readied for flight, a crew consisting of 29-year-old North American test pilot George E. Krebs and flight engineer Paul E. Brewer clambered in past the cabin door, wended their way up to the cockpit, and began flipping innumerable switches to begin the preflight process. Brewer, who had joined North American in July 1936 as a radio installer, had advanced through the ranks in the B-25 and XB-28 test programs as a technical representative and transferred to the Muroc facility only in January. Naturally, he was elated by participating in the XB-45 project. "We were all overwhelmed, it was the first big jet," Brewer beamed. "It was faster than the prop fighters and it was just a real thrill to be involved with anything new and different." Leo Hunt, a youthful NAA mechanic also assigned to the program, shared this enthusiasm: "This B-45 sounded so alluring to me — jets were kind of rare anyhow — and having a bomber! So they sent me to Muroc."

Previously, minor difficulties appeared in the landing gear uplock system, but company officials decided against replacing them, for the process was overly time-consuming. Krebs then wound up his four J35s, which shuddered to life with an ear-splitting scream. After a few more final checks, he advanced the throttles and gingerly nursed this steely chimera down the ramp and onto the runway, making three test taxi runs to check brakes and flight controls before taking the plunge. Brewer, carefully monitoring the situation from the back seat, declared all systems functional, so Krebs advanced the throttles and released the brakes. "On the third run I lifted the nosewheel off and found that the elevators, rudder, and ailerons were very effective," he explained. "After that it was just a matter of letting the airplane fly itself and keep going."[17] The XB-45 whined down the runway and leapt like an eagle released from its cage, rocketing upward with a deafening roar. Inky streaks of black smoke marked its wake as America's first jet bomber tore its way into the sky — and aviation history.

The test flight of the XB-45 proved short and relatively uneventful, even though the uplocks malfunctioned and the left nacelle landing doors failed to close correctly. Krebs, his airspeed restricted to 250 miles per hour, simply completed his test hop with the main gear extended. One hour later, he eased 45–59479 back onto the tarmac and taxied in, enthralled by his charge. "Anyone who can fly a multi-engine airplane can fly the B-45,"

Krebs later explained. "The B-45 is very easy to fly and very maneuverable. It handles more easily than many smaller airplanes, and flies very well with two engines out on either the port or starboard side. The stalling characteristics are excellent, with no tendency to roll or pitch. I used to do a lot of gliding and even there you get a lot of wind noise. There is actually less noise in the B-45 than there is in a glider, although the plane has the same smooth, effortless flight. Paul Brewer, my flight engineer, and I talked back and forth easily. We could even hear a propeller-driven plane flying off to one side There is no engine noise or vibration in the cabin at any power setting, which gives you a weird sensation when adjusting the throttles — nothing seems to change except for the tachometer needles moving up or down." Repairs were subsequently made to fix the balky landing gear doors and the XB-45 sortied again on March 26, 1947, flying two hours and hitting top speeds of 516 miles per hour.[18]

Like any experimental aircraft, the XB-45's impressive debut was offset by unexpected deficiencies. Time, coupled with some hair-raising incidents, exposed numerous problems begging immediate redress. Chief among these was the realization that the prototype's lack of ejection seats meant a perilous egress for the flight crew through the cabin front door. At high speed, this placed them perilously close to the engine nacelle and in the midst of a high-speed slipstream. The time required to clamber down from the cockpit to the cabin further impeded their chances for survival. Tests were subsequently run

The XB-45 prototype unveiled for the public at North American. Note the line of Navions and the F-82 Twin Mustang in the immediate background (John Mott).

to check the possibility of exiting down through the open bomb bay doors. Brewer, who left the copilot seat in mid-flight to conduct the exercise, recalled the results with trepidation: "I stood by the bomb bay and threw three dummies and sandbags down to see if they cleared the back end — which they didn't. So our main avenue of escape got closed off to us that day. You'd throw in a 25-pound sandbag, it would go down into the stream and back up, so that told us that either we're going to have to use the ejection seat or get out the front door." At length engineers decided to install a slipstream baffle that popped out when the cabin or gunner's door opened in flight to deflect the slipstream and facilitate their escape.[19] At best, this ramshackle arrangement only underscored the dire necessity for keeping the XB-45 airborne — for the crew's sake.

Recurring problems also arose with the XB-45's powered flight controls. These units had been engineered as separate left and right wing hydraulic systems, which meant that a partial failure left the pilot grappling with a 40-ton aircraft whose controls were non-functional on one side. The solution, it turned out, was cross-connecting the entire system so, in the event of a system breakdown, both sides would be affected equally and the aircraft could be controlled manually.[20] Krebs and Brewer continued putting 45–59479 through its paces, contending with minor problems as they arose and rectifying those difficulties where possible. By August 1, 1947, the prototype had reliably logged 28 flights and was returned to Inglewood for a major rework. Their flight-test experiences resulted in 250 engineering changes or modifications, such as strengthening the wing and landing gear doors, enlarging the horizontal stabilizers, and replacing the control cables with new ones made from stainless steel. After a brief flight check on October 1, 1947, the XB-45 returned to Muroc for additional testing. Flight number 50, completed on December 6, 1947, formally concluded Phase I of the test program and also served to familiarize Air Force pilot Major Robert L. Cardenas for Phase II, or Air Force acceptance, testing.[21]

Eventually two more prototypes, 45–59480 and 45–59481, emerged and were added to the XB-45's stable. The former machine completed its first flight on December 10, 1947, and was transferred to the Air Force on August 1, 1948. The original prototype subsequently made its way to Wright Patterson AFB, Ohio, where it fell under the purview of Colonel Albert Boyd, the "Tennessee Mountain Man"— already a legendary figure in the Air Force test program. Possessing a mind like a steel trap — with a disposition to match — Boyd literally invented the practices and procedures of his department from the ground up and is regarded as the "father of American flight testing."[22] He also bent back many ears in the process and George Gerkhens, who had been transferred to North American's Columbus division, was unsentimental about his encounters: "Al Boyd, of course, was the head guy, everybody knew him — you couldn't avoid him. If you had a problem you heard from him — and I heard from time to time from Al Boyd. He also made it a practice to fly every airplane that was under his operation."[23] As vice commander of the Wright-Patterson Aeronautical Development Center, no aircraft, pilot, engineer, or mistake ever escaped Boyd's intense scrutiny. Consequently, by the time he retired from the Flight Test Division in 1957 as a major general, he had amassed an unbelievable 23,000 hours flying 723 different types of aircraft. Such was Boyd's reputation that between 1945 and 1957, the Air Force reputedly did not acquire a single machine that did not bear his personal stamp of approval.[24]

Boyd, who candidly admitted that a "test pilot's life is never an easy one," threw himself into wringing out the XB-45 with gusto. On June 28, 1949, he took number

NAA Flight Engineer Paul Brewer in front of the first XB-45 prototype. Note the heat-reflective windows to lessen cockpit temperatures (John Mott).

45–59479 aloft to test the effect of precipitation static on equipment — and nearly lost his life. Boyd recalled the incident:

Immediately after take-off the gear failed to retract; it retracted only about a quarter of its travel and it jammed in that position. We flew at an altitude of about 13,000 feet for quite a while attempting to extend the gear. In the meantime the pressurization cooling system had failed, and so had the electrical system and the number four engine. We were suffering from heat and we couldn't communicate with anyone. The only choice we had was either bailing out or crash landing.

We didn't have ejection seats then, and bailing out wasn't a simple thing because we had to go out through an exit in the nose. So I elected to come down and bounce the airplane on the runway, striking the gear and attempting to lock it in place. But this didn't change the position of it so we decided to make a crash landing on the runway. As I came around and turned on final for the landing, the right inboard flap failed at the inboard hinge at an indicated airspeed of 150 M. P. H. and at an elevation of 400 feet. When this big flap failed and rotated around the top of the wing it caused the airplane to roll violently, practically on its back. At this low altitude, and with the other conditions being what they were, I knew this was the end. I didn't think there was a possible way of recovery but I did all I could, as anyone will, to survive.

I applied full power on the three good engines and took advantage of what altitude I had to recover. I rolled out over the trees, just missing them, and then we staggered all the way around the field but still keeping full control. It required all the aileron and all the rudder to maintain level flight. I asked the co-pilot and flight engineer if they didn't want to bail out once we were back up to about 1,500 feet and they said no, they'd stay. So we made it around the field without even enough control to align the airplane on the runway. We were about thirty degrees off. Just as soon as we got over the fence we touched down on the sod. Any flat place looked wonderful — just to get it on a piece of flat ground. As I closed the throttles and we touched down, the gear folded right away and the airplane started skidding across the field, taking runway lights with it. We were going over that runway just as if we were going through a wheat field. We skidded a mile and toward the end of the skid we saw a big ditch ahead, and it looked as though the airplane would skid into it; again, we thought we had it. But we slid practically up to the edge of that ditch and stopped. That was about as close as one can come.[25]

The XB-45 prototype was written off as scrap, but the still-intact canopy and nose section were subsequently placed on a movable display by the Air Force Orientation Group (AFOG) to assist recruiting purposes. It functioned in this capacity until 1961, when a fire destroyed the hangar housing it.[26]

Back at Muroc, Phase II testing of the second XB-45 prototype passed into the hands of Major Robert L. Cardenas, another accomplished flier. He is best known for piloting the B-29 that carried Chuck Yeager's Bell X-1 on October 14, 1947, when the sound barrier was broken. Previously, Cardenas had flown B-24 Liberators with the 506th Bombardment Squadron over Europe and was shot down over Germany in March 1944. Escaping to France, he transferred stateside as a pilot assigned to the Flight Test Division

A goggle-eyed apparition, the Douglas XB-43 was, technically, America's first jet bomber, but only two were built (History Office, Air Force Flight Test Center).

at Wright Field, flying captured examples of the Arado Ar-234 Blitz, Germany's first jet bomber. Cardenas enjoyed a well-deserved reputation as a highly skilled and motivated individual, and in 1946 he became chief of the division's Bomber Operations Section and was assigned to the XB-45 project. Once 45–59480 was handed off to the Air Force on August 1, 1948, Cardenas completed 22 Phase II flights to certify the design's perform-ance, stability, and control.[27] Generally, he looked askance at the XB-45 and was not overtly impressed by it. "It was not a spectacular aircraft and, in fact, I remember when I wrote my report, on the final page I put down 'This aircraft will make a good training aircraft, but operationally its range is limited.' There were several things, as a bomber, I didn't feel were much of an improvement, you might say. Boyd then called me into his office and said, 'Bob, I'm going to strike out the last part. Operational requirements are up to another phase, that's up to the operators to comment on that.'" The J35-powered prototype was, in fact, a somewhat anemic performer, but it would be retrofitted with more powerful General Electric TG-190s (J47s) once they became available.

North American had scored some contractual successes with the XB-45, but the contest to build America's first jet bomber remained far from decided. In fact, by 1947 no less than four futuristic aircraft were vying for that privilege. The ensuing "47 Fly-off" remains legendary in the annals of military aviation, given the stakes involved and the garish technical innovations it occasioned; hence it remains the only such contest of its kind. Moreover, the competition occasioned high levels of collaboration between the Air Force, the National Advisory Committee for Aeronautics (NACA) and several air-plane manufacturers, which was unprecedented at the time. Little-heralded today, this multi-bomber program was trumpeted in aviation circles as "a radical departure from tra-ditional military development techniques and produced a flying prototype of new type aircraft less than 28 months after it was begun on the drawing board."[28]

In a strictly historical sense, the first jet-powered American bomber to fly was not the XB-45, but rather the Douglas XB-43. This was an outgrowth of its bizarre XB-42 turboprop pusher creation, the appropriately labeled "Mixmaster." As early as 1943 the AAF had broached the subject of jet bombers with Douglas over the possibility of redesigning the XB-42 to be outfitted with two General Electric TG-180 engines. The initial design study looked propitious on paper; as a consequence, on March 31, 1944, AAF officials authorized construction of a flying prototype, 44–61508. This machine became available for flight testing a little over two years later and first flew on May 17, 1946. Like its predecessor, the new XB-43 was ungainly but possessed sleek lines, a straight wing and straight tail surfaces. Its most distinctive feature, two fully blown teardrop canopies sitting side by side for the pilot and copilot, projected a bug-eyed mien straight out of a 1950s science-fiction movie. Nonetheless, the XB-43 cruised at 503 miles per hour with a bomb load of 4,000 pounds and possessed a range of 1,100 miles. These figures were a vast improvement over German jet designs preceding it only two years ear-lier. However, the AAF had since decided that a minimum of four engines were neces-sary to achieve the performance desired, and the XB-43 never entered production. The two prototypes labored and lingered at Edwards Air Force Base (Muroc) for several years as test beds for the J47 engine before finally retiring in 1953.[29]

North America's closest competitor was the Consolidated XB-46, which AAF officials had found wanting long before it flew. Consolidated engineers nevertheless forged ahead with a flying prototype to possibly salvage its fortunes. The ensuing aircraft was one of the cleanest designs to grace a draftsman's board. In fact, the XB-46 remains one of the most attractive aircraft ever assembled and exhibited beautifully attenuated lines. The crew of three was housed in the front of the aircraft, with pilot and copilot seated beneath a long, fighter-style bubble canopy, while the bombardier worked from behind a beautifully shaped Plexiglas nose dome.[30] The cockpit layout proved so efficient that the AAF held it up as an example to other manufacturers. Another of the aircraft's most conspicuous features was the large, streamlined jet pods, housing two engines apiece, which had been designed in conjunction with NACA authorities. Consolidated's beauty performed its maiden flight on April 2, 1947, exhibiting viceless characteristics at low speed. The craft, however, was also one-third larger than the XB-45 and five tons heavier, while employing identical power plants. Consequently, the XB-46 was slower than its competitor, and its delightfully gracile planform conferred no real advantages in flight. It also encountered problems at high speed when harmonic dissonance emanating from the elaborate flap system caused the wings to shake. Another serious drawback was that svelte fuselage cross section, so pleasing to the eye, was deemed insufficiently roomy to hold necessary radar and radio equipment. Army officials, apparently satisfied with the XB-45, never requested a second prototype to be built. The sole prototype machine languished several years as a test bed aircraft at Eglin AFB, Florida, before being scrapped in February 1952. Perhaps the most fitting epitaph was penned by aeronautical historian Walter J. Boyne when he wrote, "The XB-46 set no records, but it did set a few pilots' hearts aflame, as any good looking aircraft will."[31]

The third contender, at the extreme opposite as far as appearances are concerned, was Martin's Model 223, or XB-48, which made aviation history as the world's first six-engine jet bomber. From a design standpoint, it was an ungainly alliance of curves and angles that gave Martin's "monstrosity" the impression of a malevolent pipe organ. Otherwise, the XB-48 was relatively conventional, with straight wings and a crew of three housed on a pressurized front section. A noted exception was the large, squarish engine nacelles, each housing three J35s. During development, Martin engineers hit upon the idea that the large, contoured cooling passages between the engines would improve airflow around the engines and act as a lifting body. Preliminary wind tunnel testing seemed to corroborative their beliefs. When the XB-48 first flew on June 22, 1947, it displayed pleasant handling characteristics, but the unsightly engine arrangement created enormous drag.[32] Consequently, the XB-48's overall performance fell short of both the XB-45 and XB-46, despite the thrust of two additional engines. At the time, the Martin Company was too absorbed in constructing seaplanes for the Navy and experimenting with its own two-engined line of civilian transports to take on the challenges of a complicated jet bomber. The XB-48, in fact, was never a company priority; and skilled engineers were steadily siphoned off for other projects. Consequently, the end product became increasingly slipshod. The first prototype emerged 12,000 pounds overweight and a second one had to be "picked clean" on the assembly line to reduce weight. However, a major innovation was the tandem, bicycle-like arrangement of the landing gear, assisted by wheeled outriggers on the engine nacelles. This aspect of the XB-48 proved truly innovative and was ultimately adopted by its main competitor, Boeing. Otherwise, Martin's Model 223 was completely outclassed by the more futuristic XB-47 once it emerged.[33] The first XB-48 was ultimately cannibalized to keep the second one flying until it too was scrapped at the Aberdeen Testing Grounds, Maryland, in September 1951.

Svelte as Convair's XB-46 was, its attenuated lines failed to impart any performance advantages (History Office, Air Force Flight Text Center).

Every contest has a winner and Boeing's seminal Model 450, the futuristic XB-47, heralded a jet-bomber monopoly for years to come. The design originated in January 1944 as Model 424, essentially a straight-winged B-29 with jet engines. AAF officials were unimpressed and directed company engineers back to the drawing boards. Fortuitously, NACA had finished computations on the theoretical advantages of swept-back wings, which were further validated by German engineering data obtained after the war. The ensuing delays meant that Boeing was not firmly wedded to a straight-winged arrangement beyond the paper stage and, with Army Air Force urging, it began sounding the prospect of swept wings. The most daunting challenge proved to be the placement of six engines; various configurations were tried before Model 450 finally emerged in October 1945. This daring leap broke all aviation precedents to date. The new craft consisted of a long, slender fuselage, thin wings employing 35 degrees of sweep, a bicycle landing gear arrangement with outrigger balance wheels at the wingtips, and six J35 engines arrayed in four, pylon-mounted pods below the wing. The prototype exuded modernity and would appear comfortably posed at an airport today.[34]

When the XB-47 finally debuted on December 17, 1947 — the forty-fourth anniversary of the Wright brothers' pioneering flight — Boeing had obviously cornered the jet bomber "fly off" by default. Its potent design reached 578 miles per hour at 15,000 feet

Top: Boeing's futuristic XB 47 prototype, which set the standard for jet bombers throughout the 1950s (U.S. Air Force Museum); ***bottom:*** The ungainly Martin XB-48, which flew as badly as it looked (San Diego Air & Space Museum).

and was capable of hauling ten tons of bombs over 2,650 miles. These performance statistics virtually assured a production contract; Boeing ultimately manufactured more than
2,000 Stratojets over the next decade. Up through 1965 they formed a mainstay of the
Strategic Air Command's (SAC) retaliation capabilities and constituted a significant Cold
War weapons system — one that helped maintain the peace. Success here, unfortunately,
was not without implications. At the time of rollout, the XB-47 represented cutting-edge
aeronautical technology whose intrinsic pratfalls required several years of testing and
engineering to resolve. Consequently, the first combat-capable Stratojet, the B-47B, would
not become operational until 1953, six years later. The nascent Air Force still required a
viable jet bomber to secure meaningful experience and expand its body of knowledge
respecting combat operations, flight safety, and future aeronautical developments. Thus
Air Force planners also acquired B-45s, if only as an interim expedient. It is not without
a little irony that the two "fly off" winners were such dramatic counterpoints to each other.
They represented diametrically opposed solutions to the problem of designing a large jet
bomber, with the B-45 being as conventional as the B-47 was revolutionary. The former, while overtaken by newer technology at the design stage, nonetheless marked a great
advance over propeller-driven designs and fulfilled Air Force needs until more capable
Stratojets arrived. In sum, it was a practical solution. Yet, rarely has a new weapon system been so marginalized before even reaching operational status, and its future as a standard Air Force type remained questionable. And while the XB-45 had weathered an
inauspicious debut, this was the first of many obstacles surmounted before its progeny
proved their value to a service that scarcely acknowledged them.[35]

CHAPTER TWO

New Bomber for a New Air Force

"By some hook or crook, the AAF has managed to scrape together enough
money to order ninety-six four-engined jet bombers, the first such order
placed anywhere in the world, so far as is officially known."
— Anonymous.[1]

From the onset, developments in other spheres militated against the B-45 from ever
becoming a major player in America's air arsenal. The principal issue was money. In fact,
ever since the United States Air Force become an independent entity on September 18, 1947,
the service grappled with shrinking defense appropriations. Fortunately, Air Force Secretary W. Stuart Symington, a hard-nosed corporate executive, was determined to adminis-
ter his charge along business lines to maximize the yield of every dollar spent. He also
believed that air power had reached unprecedented levels of military significance it heretofore had never enjoyed; therefore, its new-found preeminence ought to be reflected in
national budgeting priorities. Accordingly, Symington proposed no less than an all-jet Air
Force of 9,000 planes in fifty-nine groups, to be slowly expanded to 70 groups by 1952.[2]
His ambitions, however, ran counter to President Harry S Truman's insistence on fiscal
austerity to balance the budget and pay down the national debt with postwar surpluses.
He held this belief despite the fact that the Soviet Union had already orchestrated the
overthrow of Czechoslovakia and aggressively imposed a land blockade of Berlin in 1948.

Regardless of these facts, the budget ax fell hard in the spring of 1949, and the fledg-
ling Air Force found itself with barely sufficient funding to operate 48 groups, far below
what Symington envisioned as his "bedrock minimum" to insure national security. The
secretary was disillusioned by this tight-fisted entrenchment, confessing, "We are more
shocked at this decision of the Bureau of the Budget than at anything that has happened
since we came into government."[3] The Air Force, moreover, was now forced to compete
for scarce dollars in the postwar environment, and a three-way fight erupted with the
Army and Navy for their slice of a shrinking budgetary pie. A contentious debate also
ensued over how best to deliver the all-important atomic bomb, either by Consolidated
B-36 Peacekeepers or carrier-based aviation. This unleashed an interservice contretemps
of seismic proportions, and it dominated the appropriations agenda throughout
1948–1949. Congress eventually appeased both sides, allowing the Navy to keep its
autonomous air arm, while the Air Force was allowed to procure its fleet of giant bombers.
To do so, however, meant drastically curtailing other new weapon systems, even as B-
45s began surging through procurement pipelines.

Truman's fiscal policies boded ill for the Air Force in general and the B-45 in particular. In the fall of 1948, a board of U.S. Air Force officers convened to determine how
best to pare down aircraft acquisitions for fiscal year 1949, with the least detrimental effect
to national security. Symington and the Air Staff had resigned themselves to the 48-group
structure by eliminating 51 B-45Cs (the follow-on tactical version), 118 of the still-exper-
imental North American F-93 penetration fighters, and 30 Northrop C-125 assault transports. The development of Northrop's controversial B-49 "Flying Wing" also reached its
terminus, as did Boeing's B-54, a final attempted upgrade of the aging B-29. This $269
million in savings was immediately shunted towards additional B-36B intercontinental
bombers, now a centerpiece of General Curtis E. LeMay's reinvigorated Strategic Air
Command (SAC).[4] Such prioritization came at the expense of the Tactical Air Command
(TAC), previously slated to operate five light bomber groups in the 70 Group Plan, unceremoniously reduced to one. The Aircraft and Weapons Board had previously questioned
the tactical viability of B-45s, owing to their excessive takeoff and landing distances.
Upon further reflection, the board believed that "immediate curtailment of the B-45 air-
craft program was necessary in July 1948. This resulted in cancellation of fifty-one (51)
B-45s from planned procurement."[5]

In sum, the new bomber became a victim of fiscal retrenchment and reordered pri-

**A production B-45A being assembled in 1948 with a line of Navions under construction to
the rear (San Diego Air & Space Museum).**

orities. This reduction from 190 to 139 units also sent ripples through North American Aviation, which laid off 2,600 workers at three plants; payroll losses totaled $18 million.[6] Curiously, "Dutch" Kindelberger had anticipated the shortfall for some time. He had been called to testify before the House Armed Services Committee during the B-36 controversy. He spent several minutes educating inquisitors about the aircraft, which was a good indicator of the B-45's penchant for slipping into obscurity. "I knew for some time there was some question of the continuity of the bomber as a type," Kindelberger explained. "With the emphasis, which I believe to be a correct one, on strategic bombing, if the Air Force were reduced from the 70 groups which were then being planned when this work was given to us ... it was pretty obvious that there would not be use any longer for the tactical bomber, and possibly a reduction would be in order." The congressmen, while having approved large sums of money to acquire B-45s, candidly confessed that they knew nothing about them.[7]

As Air Force leaders busied themselves with procurement matters, hoping to fiscally torpedo as many prospective Navy carriers as possible, manufacture of B-45As continued apace at North American. Construction of the new F-86 Sabrejet had monopolized the company's Inglewood facilities, so bomber production shifted to the former 375,000-square-foot Douglas facility at nearby Long Beach, California. Of 4,800 personnel employed, 4,100 worked on the B-45 assembly line. The first A-model was inspected and test flown by Krebs and Nick Piccard on February 28, 1948, without incident. Aircraft continued rolling out of the factory at a rate of three units a month throughout spring, with an expected rise to 10 units by the following June. The first production block of 23 B-45A-1 aircraft (47–001 through 47–022) were destined to be fitted with Allison-built J35 engines, and were slated for testing and target-towing duties only. Significantly, the A-model incorporated refinements brought about by testing the prototypes, which included enlarged tailplane and stabilizer surfaces and a redesigned "greenhouse" nose running parallel to the fuselage instead of canting upwards. The new machine also landed on a dual-wheeled nose gear with slightly smaller wheels. Other modifications included the addition of ejection seats for the pilot and copilot, wind deflectors on the bombardier and tail gunner's escape hatches, an E-4 autopilot, provisions for the advanced APQ-24 radar bombing system, and an Emerson A-1 fire control system for the tail guns. Difficulties arose while procuring the radar bombing system, which was also being installed in the B-36, while the A-1 turret proved unworkable and was ultimately cancelled. Consequently, none of the B-45A-1s could be considered operational combat aircraft. The remaining 73 B-45A-5 units (commencing with number 47–024) were scheduled to be fitted with the more powerful General Electric TG-190 engine — the ubiquitous J47 — with 5,200 pounds of thrust. This upgraded configuration made it possible for B-45s to serve in bombardment units.[8]

During the preoperational testing phase, the new jets weathered the usual spate of "gliches" inherent in all advanced technology. Among the most innocuous was the plane's conspicuously vibration-free flight, which allowed many instruments to freeze in place. North American engineers countered this problem by installing a vibrator in the control panel to keep them working at high altitude.[9] More serious was the B-45's extremely aerodynamic shape, resulting in low drag and high landing speeds. In fact, the aircraft decelerated so slowly that controlling air speed and flight-path angle while descending proved somewhat challenging. No provisions for air brakes or drag parachutes were made; con-

The 11th production B-45A being flight-tested over the California desert. The broad wing and cleanly aerodynamic planform are very apparent at this angle (Wright State University Special Collections).

sequently, pilots soon hit upon the expedient of opening the main wheel doors, each twice the size of a dining room table, which worked as improvised speed brakes before being snapped back into place upon touchdown.[10] Landing speeds nonetheless remained high, around 130 miles per hour, which resulted in brake-squealing rolls of 4,700 feet before taxiing became possible.

Yet, the biggest obstacle vexing the B-45 program remained the lack of funding. So adroitly had government officials reduced Air Force funding that, having acquired a fleet of ultramodern jet-bombers, it could not scrape up the money to operate them. Therefore, as new B-45s rolled off the assembly line at Long Beach, they were either cocooned at Los Angeles International Airport or flown to the Air Materiel Depot at Norton AFB, San Bernardino, and mothballed there. The cash-strapped Air Force had little choice but to inter their shiny bombers and the practice occasioned protests from within the organization. "The Air Materiel Command does not concur in the storage of 34 modern and expensive B-45A airplanes while keeping in service less effective [Douglas] B-26 airplanes," one agonized AMC communiqué read. "It is recommended that the B-45A be utilized in tactical units without the A-1 Fire Control system to gain valuable experience in maintaining and operating jet bombers."[11] Without appropriations from Congress, little could be done. However, a handful of B-45A-1s still managed to reach various testing concerns, from which a reliable body of flight data began accruing.

Having procured a smaller number of B-45s, Air Force officials began exploring the various ways they would ultimately be deployed and operated. Three years after World War II, large-scale jet operations remained problematic, largely because the issue of high fuel consumption lay unresolved. Officials feared that heavy use of jet aircraft might drain existing fuel stocks and compromise routine operations for propeller-driven craft. On July 11, 1947, Colonel Leslie O. Peterson, of the Air Staff's Requirements Division, authorized the Air University to pinpoint future problems and possible solutions. "With the advent of jet aircraft, the problems connected with ground and low altitude operations have increased tremendously due to the high fuel consumption of jet engines at low altitudes and on the ground," Peterson warned. "It is not difficult to envision a mileage loss as great as ¼ or ⅓ of the combat radius if too much time is spent getting a bomber formation assembled and on course." The Air University study, when it emerged later that year, confirmed Peterson's apprehensions and further noted that if B-45s were expected to consume "10-15 gallons per minute ... the range reduction at 30,000 feet will be approximately 7 miles for each minute spent taxiing."[12] Cognizant of this tendency, another board of officers convened at the behest of General Muir S. Fairchild in 1948 to put the B-45 on a crash diet and possibly extend its range. Among the various weight reduction options under review were elimination of both the copilot's crew position and the aircraft's tail bumper, which would shave off 700 pounds.[13] When neither expedient proved practical, the board hoped that the forthcoming block of B-45A-5s, powered by more efficient J47 engines, might ameliorate high fuel consumption.

The B-45 was originally envisioned as a high-speed, high-altitude bombing platform capable of delivering up to ten tons of ordnance from altitudes approaching 40,000 feet. While its 800-mile combat radius failed to meet the old AAF range requirement of 1,000 miles, the aircraft's sparkling performance occasioned serious discussion of its possible use as an all-weather interceptor. In fact, at high altitude the B-45 outstripped both the Lockheed F-80 Shooting Star and the Republic F-84 Thunderjet, mainstays of the new jet Air Force. On September 28, 1948, Secretary Symington made a tantalizing, if cryptic, reference to the B-45 by announcing that it "ran away from jet fighters."[14] In light of such a heady performance, and a possibility that Air Force officials seemed ready to dispense with light bombardment aircraft altogether, the idea of a heavy jet fighter gained traction. Air University researchers investigated the possibility of converting all 96 B-45s into all-weather interceptors to replace marginally effective propeller-driven F-82 Twin Mustangs. Their study, eager to protect the $200 million already invested, found that while the B-45 narrowly missed performance parameters outlined in the official *Military Characteristics of an All Weather Fighter* for speed and altitude, it exhibited fine handling characteristics combined with a useful loitering time and combat radius. Moreover, the sheer size of the bomb bay facilitated a wide variety of bomber-killing combinations, including 5-inch HVAR and 2.75-inch folding fin rockets. Suggested modifications included eliminating the copilot and the tail gunner to save weight, plus utilization of two 5,000-pound rocket-assisting takeoff units; all these entailed only minor engineering changes. The writer concluded that "the basic B-45 configuration can be adapted with relatively little change to a heavily armed all weather fighter, offering the USAF proved high performance with excellent handling characteristics, economical procurement, and a high degree of flexibility for alternate load installation. The utilization of the tooling, worker experience, and existing facilities now devoted to the ground support version is consistent with the desire of the USAF to get maximum value for its procurement dollar."[15] Documentation on this intriguing facet of B-45 development is sketchy, but apparently little action materialized beyond the concept stage.

In 1948 Air Materiel Command staff officers also broached the possibility of converting B-45As into night fighters, since continuing shortages of fire control systems and visual aiming precluded bombing activities for at least two years. In a hypothetical match-up against the still experimental Curtiss XP-87 Blackhawk (never deployed), the larger B-45 came out ahead, prompting one official to declare, "Since the role of a night fighter does not call for high maneuver loads, it is believed the B-45A factors will be acceptable." This new configuration, if adopted, called for a solid nose mounting no fewer than twelve 20mm cannons, an A-1 Sight tie-in with APG-3 radar, and speed brakes.[16] Again, no action was taken on the proposal. On May 24, 1950, the director of Procurement and Engineering again resurrected the interceptor scheme, with preliminary evaluation of the B-45A fitted with the following modifications:

> Install three hundred sixty 2.75" rockets in the bomb bay.
> Add a 1,200 gallon non-sealing tank in the bomb bay.
> Replace the APQ-24 bombing radar with a Hughes 250 KW All-Weather Radar and Rocket Fire Computer.
> Delete the tail turret.
> Add dive brakes.
> Reduce the crew to a pilot and a copilot/radar operator.

These suggested changes entailing outlays of $222,000 per plane for a fleet of 70 aircraft might have appeared excessive during a period of austerity. Still, discounting its relatively sluggish 21-minute climb to 37,900 feet, the B-45A could nonetheless perform intercept missions 3.5 hours in duration and, once at altitude, it handled nearly as well as the new F-95A (F-86D) then under development. In this vein, one official noted how "The B-45A can satisfactorily intercept a B-50D at 25,000 feet and at 10,000 feet without exceeding the structural limit load factor of 2.50g at any time, provided the bomber flies at a reasonable speed above the speed for minimum turn."[17] Nevertheless, the surviving documentation fails to indicate any specific reason for rejecting the B-45 as a night fighter. The root cause was probably cost-related, and Air Force officials most likely felt that the same mission could be performed more cost-effectively with smaller, cheaper aircraft like Northrop's new F-89 Scorpion.

Whatever official disdain existed for B-45 interceptors, money was occasionally available for tinkering with and testing them along these lines. Bill Crowley, a North American Aviation technical representative, labored at Eglin AFB, Florida, "before 1950," for that express purpose. He recalled pitting B-45 number 47–026 up against early variants of the Lockheed F-94 Starfire after some relevant modifications:

> We put dive brakes on it and they were huge. It took about four men to lift them and get them up on the side. We were competing against the F-94, the so-called interceptor at that time, and the F-94 was equipped with English radar and also an English pilot. We were being tested to start at the end of the runway, take off and climb to altitude next to each other. I had the job of wiring the airplane so that the pilot pressed one switch and all four engines started at one time, and he had a gang throttle that was fixed so that he could pull up all four at once.

He hit the switch and I tell you those C-22 (ground power unit) cables went *straight out,* just like that. We got started, yanked them out, didn't even get the door closed when he started rolling and, of course, the air pressure would keep the door closed anyway — it didn't matter. The F-94 got off just slightly ahead of us at about 35,000. The Englishman comes on and goes, "I say, where is that old *lumber wagon*?" We next heard this voice, just as calm as ever — it was Major Minor —"*Right on your tail, old boy!*"

At the other end of the tactical spectrum, the Air Force also expended considerable thought about employing B-45s as low-level, close-support aircraft. Preliminary studies undertaken by the Air University seemed encouraging, especially when the jet was contrasted against the prevailing tactical aircraft, the Douglas B-26 Invader. At first blush it appeared to be no contest. The report highlighted that B-45s could deliver three times the bomb load, in train, over a given target. They also could carry large quantities of heavier ordnance, like 1,000 pound bombs for the reduction of masonry dams, railroad tunnels, and other fortified targets. Up to 22,000 pounds of bombs could also be delivered in a single throw, if necessary. Moreover, the B-45's high speed made it less vulnerable to antiaircraft fire — long the bane of low level work. So, in strictly operational parlance, the B-45 theoretically functioned four times more effectively in these tactical profiles than the World War II-era Invader. The study declared, "It seems very conservative to estimate that one wing of B-45s is equal to four wings of B-26s when calculations are based upon combat effectiveness. One wing of B-45s will not require the amount of logistical support that four B-26 wings will. More engines, fuel, and fuel storage facilities will be necessary but the saving in other categories more than cancel this out."[18]

Close-up shot of the canvass tarpaulin designed to shield the cockpit from solar rays. Excessive cabin heat while on the ground dogged the B-45 throughout its career (John Mott).

These tactical assessments proved attractive but overly optimistic, unfortunately. After more realistic operational considerations were factored in, officials realized that heavy jets were impractical in this niche. In fact, the B-45A, specifically conceived as a high-altitude, level-flight bomber, proved structurally unsuited for the rigors of close support missions. These deficiencies were underscored in a study commissioned by Headquarters, Tactical Air Command, in May 1950, once the bombers had been operational for a year. The study's basic premise held that tactical air support inherently requires machines with exceptional maneuverability at low altitude, combined with physical robustness. In this context, the B-45 could not be adequately stressed or equipped for such wrenching activity as air-to-ground rocket operations.[19] Moreover, the aircraft's aerodynamics were somewhat inefficient at very low altitudes, exacerbating its already high fuel consumption. On this basis the study projected that, over a one-hour period, 125 Republic F-84E Thunderjets could operate on the fuel quantities necessary to run thirty-two 32 B-45s. Furthermore, the necessary bomb-delivery equipment for tactical strikes, once installed, completely negated the B-45's ability to conduct high level bombing, its raison d'etre. Worst of all, the requisite reengineering of B-45 airframes to withstand the stress of low-altitude maneuvering would set the taxpayers back $1.4 million per plane for the entire fleet. "Even at this tremendous investment," the study summarized, "the military establishment would not have suitable configuration to perform the proposed mission." Therefore, under this increasingly demanding tactical regimen, better results could be achieved by larger fleets of smaller, tougher fighter-bombers like the Thunderjet. This report concluded its findings on a cautionary note: "Certainly the employment of the B-45 in ground attack does not appear to be in the best interests of the country, or the military establishment, when the costs involved to perform the mission could be well directed to obtaining and providing aircraft types that are cheaper and capable of performing the tasks to a degree of effectiveness that is considered necessary by the Army and the Tactical Air Command."[20] This negative assessment terminated any further consideration of B-45s for ground support operations.

Months before tactical employment of the B-45A became moot, North American pursued design studies for several follow-on models. The B-45B was intended to employ upgraded electronics and a radar-directed fire control system, in addition to more powerful J47 engines. Yet, "since the B-45 with the J35 engine installation was underpowered, it was later decided to convert all B-45A airplanes to the J47 engine installations by modification when these engines became available. This decision eliminated the requirement for a B-45B model designation."[21] Hence, none were built. However, on October 17, 1947, Contract AC-18000 stipulated the design and construction of NA-153, the B-45C, an improved level-flight bomber. The prototype first flew on May 3, 1948. While outwardly similar to the A-model, it was structurally a different aircraft. Both the airframe and wings had been beefed up for low-altitude work and crew member canopies sported conspicuous reinforced braces not unlike a birdcage. The new craft was powered by four J47 jet engines with 5,200 pounds of thrust apiece, to which disposable 214-gallon water tanks of water/alcohol injection were fitted under both nacelles to provide 90 seconds of injection-augment thrust during takeoff. The B-45C also featured single point fueling in the bomb-bay compartment, so that the previously time-consuming practice of ground refueling could be accomplished in 30 minutes instead of three hours. The Air Force initially held out high hopes for the design, whereupon Major General Joseph T.

McNarney assured superiors that "the B-45C offers greater flexibility than the B-45A since, through structural reinforcements, it is capable of carrying larger bomb loads for the same combat radius as the B-45A airplane."[22]

The C-model's most conspicuous departure from the B-45A was the addition of oversized wingtip drop tanks that measured 22 feet in length, carried 1,200 gallons of fuel, and weighed 7,500 pounds apiece when fully loaded. Further refinements, including broadened tailplane surfaces, also manifested to rectify earlier instability problems. This new configuration increased the plane's gross weight from 80,000 to 112,000 pounds, while also raising its top speed to 579 miles per hour at sea level and extending the ferry range up to 2,610 miles. Under combat conditions, the B-45C could carry a ten-ton bomb load across 1,100 miles, finally meeting the range requirement for jet bombers established five years earlier. However, the added weight lowered the maximum combat ceiling to 37,500 feet–5,000 lower than the B-45A. As FY 1949 approached, Air Force officials anticipated another severe budget pinch and realized that another round of production cuts were inevitable, especially among those deemed marginal. In the words of Colonel N.T. Perkins of the Requirements Division, "The added performance of the B-45C is not significant enough to warrant its purchase over the replacement of the B-45s in the contemplated tactical groups."[23] Consequently, the programmed order of 51 B-45Cs was cancelled by the Fairchild Board in favor of purchasing additional Consolidated B-36s. Nonetheless ten C models were acquired (numbered 48–001 through 48–009), with the final unit being accepted in the spring of 1950. These machines were never intended for combat operations and were berthed in testing assignments.[24]

The final run of B-45 production coincided with the growing realization that Air Force reconnaissance capabilities in future wars were being seriously compromised by technical obsolescence. Unarmed and propeller-driven RB-29s and RB-50s, standard photo aircraft of their day, were increasingly viewed as imperiled in a world of jet fighters; yet, several years would elapse before a high-performance reconnaissance workhorse, the RB-47, took to the skies in 1952. Requirements for the comparatively new and steadily advancing field of radar photography were equally pressing. On January 30, 1948, Colonel R.B. Landry outlined to Air Force Chief of Staff Carl Spaatz their predicament: " I believe it is absolutely essential that we do have a specialized type aircraft to accomplish radar photographic reconnaissance of potential enemy objective. The aircraft must be a high altitude, high speed aircraft capable of at least, and preferably greater, speed than any potential intercept type aircraft. Any possible future enemy will expect us to conduct radar photographic reconnaissance of their vital points and will, just as the Germans did, do everything possible to destroy our aircraft engaged in this type of mission.... As I see it, we have a requirement second to none that we do have a radar reconnaissance force made ready at the earliest possible time in order to provide us with the information that is going to be required and necessary for the successful operation of the bombers."[25] The B-45 thus represented the best possible interim solution until RB-47s materialized. On July 30, 1948, preliminary specifications and minimum requirements were issued to North American for changing the 33 B-45C airframes then on the production line into reconnaissance aircraft. The test model received the designation RB-45C, while the company referred to it as NA-162.[26]

After extensive testing and engineering, the first RB-45C finally flew at Long Beach, California, in December 1949. Outwardly, the most conspicuous change was the metal-skinned "duck snout" replacing the bombardier's Plexiglas station. Greater changes were internal, as the craft now housed ten cameras at five different stations along the fuselage. Among them were three new K-17C metrogon cameras (the term refers to a lens ground to permit the same degree of focus at each corner as at its center). As the name Trimetrogon implies, this station employed three cameras combining vertical and oblique-angle photography, in which one lens was aimed directly below the plane's flight path, while the other two viewed either side. The pieced-together film strip provided wide-angle, horizon-to-horizon photographic coverage of sequential areas. Another optical masterpiece was the S-7A, or Sonne camera used for high-speed, low-level missions. This device lacked a lens but exposed a continuous, 900-foot-long film strip through an adjustable slit which compensated for high speeds and low altitudes. It was theoretically capable of taking a photographic strip of the entire United States coast to coast on a continuous reel of film, with a viable 3-D effect for discerning the topography.[27] A 16mm motion picture camera could also be located behind clamshell doors in the extreme nose of the plane. Once closed, the doors exhibited a distinctive bulge, which was usually decorated as a giant, blood-shot eye. This Cyclopean motif gave the entire craft a humorous, if surrealistic, mien. From the time the first RB-45Cs began arriving in April 1950, it was the

Conceptual sketch of the Tornado 8, a proposed high-speed, high-altitude version of the B-45 that was never built (Patricia Chapman Meder).

world's most adept reconnaissance platform, being fast, extremely smooth in flight, and capable of photographing 30,000 square miles from nine miles up. Moreover, the RB-45C could execute a variety of flight profiles, including day and night reconnaissance, along with charting and mapping. Flying at sustained speeds of 500 miles per hour, the RB-45C was much more survivable in hostile environments than vulnerable RB-29s and RB-50s; crew members, taking stock of its prodigious mapping proclivities, unofficially dubbed it the "Flying Cartographer."[28]

High-speed flight also produced surface temperature variations outside the RB-45C, ranging from 120 degrees Fahrenheit near sea level to well below zero at high altitudes. The need to maintain strict environmental conditions inside the fuselage to preserve delicate film and cameras was achieved through a large refrigeration system. This device drew hot air directly from the inboard jet engines, cooled it rapidly, and piped it where needed. It approximated 100 home refrigerators in terms of energy output and was capable of producing 550,000 ice cubes a day. Another important aspect of the RB-45C was its high fuel capacity. It could carry an additional 1,200-gallon bladder tank in its bomb bay for a total of 8,133 gallons, in addition to the 1,200 gallon wingtip tanks. More significantly, this was also the first jet aircraft capable of in-flight refueling through a nozzle receptacle located atop of the fuselage, just behind the wing's trailing edge. This configuration could theoretically extended the aircraft's range indefinitely, subject only to crew fatigue. The crew itself had been reduced from four members to three: a pilot, a copilot, and a radar operator/photographer, the latter being completely sealed off in his darkened nose compartment. The tail gunner's position was deleted and his small compartment stripped of guns and sealed off. Events in Korea highlighted the necessity of reversing this practice; but at the time, Air Force leaders believed that the RB-45C flew higher and faster than any opposition it would likely encounter. It also enjoyed the same fine flying attributes of the bomber model, although a poorly designed nose gear steering system could complicate takeoffs.[29] The RB-45Cs, designated by sequential numbers from 48–010 through 48–043, began phasing into Strategic Air Command service by late summer 1950.

By December 1950, more than a year into the actual service life of the B-45, engineers at North American Aviation formulated a final design study to possibly secure a new production contract. Labeled the "Tornado 8," this new craft featured lengthened fuselage and wings and was to be propelled by four Wright J65 (Armstrong Siddeley Sapphire) jet engines of 7,220 pounds thrust apiece. The design drew its name from the 8 percent wing thickness intended to facilitate faster speeds at higher altitudes. This B-45 variant was expected to achieve transonic speeds of 590 miles per hour (Mach .90) at 40,000 feet, possess a combat radius of 1,325 nautical miles, and be capable of handling either bombing or high altitude reconnaissance tasks. It was also the first version specifically designed to be fitted with speed brakes and an on-board rocket assist take-off system (RATO), consisting to two Aerojet YRL63-AJ-1 rocket units, each with its own, built-in fuel supply. Once fired, these units provided 10,000 pounds of additional thrust for 40 seconds into liftoff. Other design considerations were a tail turret borrowed from the Convair B-36, which mounted two 20mm cannon, and a drag parachute for reduction of landing run. In another conspicuous departure, the copilot's position had been eliminated altogether, and both pilot and navigator were provided with ejections seats. The tail gunner, however, was still required to egress through his utility hatch. It is intriguing to think what performance the "Tornado 8" might have achieved but, insomuch as the Air Force was already deeply committed to Boeing's swept-wing B-47, no action was taken on procurement.[30]

The Air Force severely curtailed the B-45 construction program, but Muroc-based test pilots continued intensive flight testing with the second prototype, number 45–59480. The test article first flew on December 10, 1947, and was declared airworthy; it was accepted by the service on August 1, 1948. By then the day of committing B-45s to field service was fast approaching, and Air Force test officials fell under increasing pressure to verify its utility as a warplane. "The B-45 airplane will, within the very near future, be allocated to operational units," General L.C. Craigie, director of research and development at AMC Headquarters warned. "It is extremely important that these aircraft be capable of accomplishing the mission for which they have been designed."[31] A systematic bomb-testing program consequently started in January 5, 1948, and consisted of 14 flights utilizing 100-, 250-, 500-, 1000-, 2000- and 4,000-pound bombs. These weapon shapes were released at speeds of up to 500 miles per hour, both singly and in train. Projectile ballistics were recorded by cameras installed on the plane's wingtip, in the bomb bay, and in a nearby chase plane. Initial results were mixed, with some 100 and 250 pounders actually tumbling in the bomb bay slipstream at 350 miles per hour. After the initial series

A B-45 releases a string of 500-pound bombs during a high-speed run. Considerable engineering was required to prevent ordnance from tumbling in the slipstream (John Mott).

of test drops was concluded on March 3, 1948, number 45–59480 was transferred from the program for cabin heating and pressurization tests.[32]

The result of the high speed bombing runs with the XB-45 stimulated much discussion and some apprehension in Air Force R&D circles. "The high speed capabilities of the jet bomber have created problems in bomb sighting and bomb release that have heretofore been of relatively minor concern," one official wrote. "Current standard bombing equipment, both optic and radar, will not suffice for an aircraft with the speed and altitude capability of the B-45."[33] Other high ranking leaders, sensing an urgency to resolve this most basic of bombing problems, evinced similar concerns. "Until new bombs are developed, or as a matter of fact even proposed, and until we find some new method of carrying and releasing our bombs so that they will not be affected by the turbulence now experienced in our bomb bays, we must know what to expect from the material we have and will have to use in the next few years," a classified report read.[34] In light of the dire necessity of rendering B-45 high-speed bomb runs as accurate as possible, with a view towards resolving similar problems on future aircraft, the drop testing program was upgraded to a 1-A priority.[35]

Phase II bomb testing temporarily shifted from Muroc to AMC headquarters — Wright-Patterson AFB — by the late summer of 1948. AMC director of research and development General F.O. Carroll wrote, "This command recognizes the importance of the subject tests and will lend every effort consistent with its capabilities toward the early resolution of the bombing problems induced by high speed flight." He further noted that "The entire subject of high speed bombing from high altitude is a formidable one. Solution of the manifold related problems is of vital concern to the future operation of the USAF."[36] Accordingly, XB-45 No. 2 arrived at Wright-Patterson on August 1, 1948, to receive Shoran equipment, along with additional cameras and flight instrumentation. AMC intended to test drop for accuracy, safety of release, and fuse-arming calibrations twenty-five kinds of bombs, new types of chemical weapons, and various naval munitions. In October the prototype aircraft returned to Muroc to resume bomb drops. Two B-45As — 47–012 and 47–014 — were also diverted to Wright-Patterson for instrumentation refits before rejoining the prototype in California. Further relevant documentation vanishes at this point and it is not known with certainty when the Air Forced resolved bomb release problems at 500 miles per hour. Nevertheless, another historic milestone had been reached and, according to one official, "It is believed that the XB-45 was the first airplane to drop bombs from an internal bomb bay at such high speeds." Given the secrecy surrounding tests, Air Force officials did not publicly announce the result of their bomb drop tests until the fall of 1950.[37]

The B-45 bombing program at Muroc employed flight test techniques ranging from sophisticated to downright primitive. NAA Flight Engineer Paul Brewer recalled that during "the one bomb dropping test I participated in, we flew up over Lake Tahoe and back to San Clemente Island, where there was a bombing range. We were well up there at 39,000 feet. I climbed out of my seat, got down in the crawlway and opened the door leading to the forward bomb bay. From that point I could toggle the bombs and observe their action on the way out." Captain Robert "Bob" Hoover, renowned as one of America's leading acrobatic pilots, recalled a more daunting incident when his bomb bays were opened at 550 miles per hour:

Conducting this type of test was dangerous because the doors under pressure from the high wind velocity could separate from the plane. If the doors came off they could take part of the tail with them. That's exactly what happened on the B-45 test flight where I was the copilot behind Joe Lynch in my checkout flight. Just prior to opening the doors, Joe said, 'Bob, put your hands on the next of kin [ejection-seat] handles.' I braced myself and got ready to eject if disaster occurred. When Joe opened the doors, that B-45 shook like a dog excreting a peach seed. Seconds later one of the doors snapped off with a whoosh and headed straight for the tail. It clipped the top edge and then zipped across the sky. The plane continued to shake, but Joe kept it under control. We landed safely, but another airborne pilot took a picture of the damaged B-45 that I still have today.[38]

Few of the B-45s engaged in test bombing at Muroc possessed APQ-24 radar sets due to endemic parts and supply shortages. Most aircraft had to make do with aiming devices from World War II, which were better than nothing. NAA Technical Representative Bill Crowley relates a surprising incident arising more from mirth than malfunction: "We were checking out the Norden bombsight and your parallel lines have to be adjusted just right to make their runs, and we had a huge window up front that was probably three feet by eighteen inches — no radome. We were lining up on the breakwater at Long Beach, that's where we did the check on it, and I kept trying to stay with it and it seemed to be moving all the time. I said to the pilot 'Something is wrong here — I can't keep this thing on at all.' He said: 'Look over your head.' I looked up and there was the breakwater — we were doing a slow roll!"

Less dramatic than the bombing testing was the mundane but essential task of wringing out unforeseen "bugs" in B-45s before declaring the planes operational. NAA mechanic Leo Hunt, assigned to work on hydraulic and fuel systems at Muroc, vividly recalled some of the misadventures he experienced during those early days:

> [NOISE] As many as three B-45s running at full power at once. The noise was amplified by a nearby building. The company was concerned about ear damage, so they had an audio tech measure the sound volume. We fired up two B-45s and the audio gauge went off the scale. He was amazed as this never happened before. We did use ear plugs and headsets with foam inside. I don't think they helped as I have hearing aids now.
>
> [MUFFLERS] After the flight line was set with new blast fences someone came up with the idea of large portable mufflers to cut down jet engine noise. So we wheeled them in back of the tailpipes. The engines were fired up and blew them to pieces, blowing fiberglass all over the flight line. So much for the mufflers.
>
> [CANOPY] We were testing the pressurization of the cockpit while an inspector was inside watching the gauges. We were at 5 lbs when suddenly the canopy exploded with a loud bang. Pieces of canopy buzzed in all directions. We were surprised that 5 lbs of pressure at a large volume made such a big explosion. This called for fiberglass reinforcing. We had a shook-up inspector. We never did find his hat.[39]

Recurring canopy cracks were also potentially dangerous malfunctions and required immediate attention. As the second block of J47-powered B-45As came from the factory they received new, multi-framed canopies and reinforced nose window glazing to preclude any chance of a high altitude blowout. This refitting process began with number 47–034, and earlier numbered aircraft were gradually retrofitted as time and resources allowed. The original bubble canopy was highly attractive and fighter-like, but it was also disturbingly prone to in-flight failures. Repairs were also expensive and time-consuming. As "Dutch" Kindelberger candidly admitted, "We had a similar one to change at

Muroc which took 125 hours. This is a lot of time, but the sealing and air-tightening job is quite a tricky one and, as I told you, the canopy carries a test pressure equivalent to 64,000 pounds, which is working to blow it off."[40] Fortunately, the reinforced canopies functioned perfectly and the problem was resolved.

On January 29, 1949, shortly before the B-45As deployed operationally, number 47–015 was dispatched to Ladd AFB, Alaska, under Captain Louis S. Stokes for cold weather testing. The aircraft, resplendent in high visibility Arctic markings, performed well under excruciating Arctic conditions and experienced shorter takeoff rolls due to the higher density of frigid air, which resulted in greater thrust. The B-45's top air speed also received a concomitant boost, and Stokes reported that "While at 30,000 feet, the critical mach was inadvertently exceeded by 10 mph, and as a result of severe buffeting the tail gunner's windshield cracked and the elevator trim tabs shorted out and became inoperative." Another mishap occurred during simulated bombing runs when the pilot's salvo switch was not wired in accordance with the wiring diagram and, once activated, "the [bomb bay] doors opened and closed continuously until the plane landed."[41] Ground crews, however, were found to be proficient at removing and replacing heavy J47 engines in as little as fifty minutes, despite the necessity of wearing heavy gloves. Captain Stokes capped his assignment by inadvertently chalking up another of the B-45's many unofficial records during the return leg of the mission. On March 1, 1949, while flying at 16,000 feet between Ladd AFB, Stokes and Elmendorf AFB, Anchorage, Stokes and copilot Colonel Charles Overstreet touched down after only 24 minutes. Their flight had apparently been assisted by an estimated 150-mile tailwind, boosting their ground speed to 675 miles per hour.[42] Another active center for testing B-45s at this early date was Eglin AFB, Florida, site of the Air Force's Climatic Hangar. Captain Stokes, now a full-time project officer, subjected aircraft number 47–013 to the full rigors of extreme temperatures as low as minus 65 degrees. Various deficiencies appeared in the craft's electronic and hydraulic components, which resulted in a list of twenty suggested modifications. The most worrisome problem was the pilot windshield, which sustained an eight-inch crack after being frozen and then exposed to warm air for several minutes. Until such changes were incorporated, Stokes concluded, "the B-45 is not satisfactory for operation at low temperature."[43]

The appearance of such high-performance aircraft as the B-45 at Eglin was naturally a cause for celebration among younger test pilots. Captain Vernon "Mac" Greenamyre, a former P-38 jock, took readily to his first test hop in the new craft: "It certainly wasn't scary by any means, very easy to handle, very easy to land — you could just touch it down like a damn feather. One of my missions was to go up, come in on an approach and shut off one engine to see how we could make it in. Then we'd shut off two engines to see how we could make it in. Then we'd go and shut off two engines, one on each side, and see how we could make it in. I don't think we ever shut off three, as I recall." As word of the B-45's superlative handling qualities spread, abetted by its celebrity status as the first jet bomber, many of the Air Force's top brass came to Eglin for a first-hand view. "It was the first jet that would take more than one person," Greenamyre emoted. "So damn near every general that came down to Eglin wanted to ride in a jet. Guess who took them up?"

A young B-26 pilot, Lieutenant Robert H. Clark, also received his first orientation flight at Eglin and walked away singularly impressed. "I couldn't believe it," he said. "It

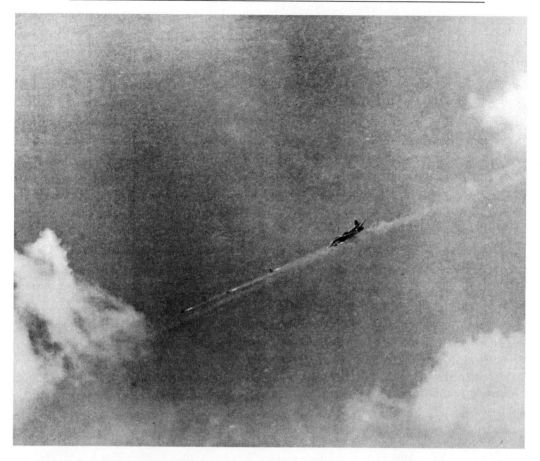

Over Eglin AFB, Florida, a heavily modified B-45A releases a salvo of air-to-ground rockets from its bomb bay. However, the aircraft was deemed insufficiently braced for such low-altitude work (Harry S. Truman Library)

was so quiet and so smooth, it was as though the earth was turning beneath us — that we weren't even moving at all. We had no sensation of movement in flight." Another eager flyer at Eglin was Captain Donald S. Lopez, a former P-40 pilot who enjoyed a distinguished career with the 14th Air Force in China. Shortly after the first B-45 arrived for flight testing, the squadron commander and his operations officer departed for Muroc to undergo a familiarization course. They intended to be the first pilots at Eglin to fly B-45s before checking out other pilots in the squadron. "Things did not work out as planned," Lopez noted. Once the two senior officers departed, "the group commander and the squadron's assistant operations officer could not bear to see it parked forlornly on the ramp, unflown." The two men proceeded to scrutinize the flight manuals, then proceeded to check themselves out in the B-45. They flew it several times before the senior pilots returned from California, "prepared to bask in the glory of being the first to fly the first jet bomber at Eglin, and instead found that it had been flying regularly since a few days after they left. It was a bitter blow. They probably would have taken some disciplinary action had the prime culprit not been the group commander. Rank is a most effective armor in the military."

Fortunately, Lopez, with some clandestine assistance from "Mac" Greenamyre, finally managed to steal aboard for his first flight in a B-45: "I found it easy to fly and much more responsive to the controls than other bombers I had flown. Also, it felt more like flying a fighter because the seats were in tandem rather than side-by-side."[44] Events at Eglin climaxed on April 22, 1950, when the Air force showcased all their newest equipment during an air show that drew 1,500 spectators, including President Harry S. Truman, Secretary of Defense Louis Johnson, and Canadian minister of defense Brooke Claxton. A spectacular display of firepower ensued, with everything from F-86s to B-36s dropping a wide variety of ordnance for the benefit of their enthralled audience. According to one reporter, "Virtually every mission involved strafing, rocket firing, and high explosive bombing that rent the air and the earth." At one junction a lone B-45 appeared and tore apart a mockup tank column with a rippling salvo of 35-inch rockets fired from its belly. Truman subsequently toured local hangars with his entourage, pressed the flesh with several local officials, and commended all involved for such an impressive expenditure of taxpayer's money.[45]

The United States by this time had achieved cordial working relationships with Great Britain's aeronautical industry, and British pilots at American testing facilities were relatively common. The practice made sense considering that the British, having pioneered jet flight, were openly regarded as leading authorities in the field. On May 20, 1948, celebrated pilot Roland Beaumont accompanied George Krebs on a test hop of XB-45 No. 3, which had been fitted with dual controls in the back seat. He quickly conceded that, "For an airplane the equivalent in weight and bomb load to the (Avro) Lincoln, the B-45 breaks new ground in that its handling qualities compare it more with aircraft of the Mosquito class." The insufferably British Beaumont, while not exactly damning the B-45 with faint praise, still couched his flattery with a caveat: "The North American Tornado was a very advanced aeroplane for its time; but it was immediately apparent that if our B3/45 Canberra fulfilled its design potential, it would outclass the Tornado, and anything else then under development in the USA, by a handsome margin."[46] The indomitable Canberra, was, in fact, a superb design when it finally emerged, yet that versatile craft did not nose its way down a tarmac in RAF service until 1951; by then B-45s had been plying the skyways for two years.

The development and maturation of any cutting-edge technology, particularly in aviation, is inherently fraught with peril. Flight testing the B-45 throughout most of 1948 had been spectacularly successful, since it had become routine and unattended by serious mishaps. Nevertheless, it was only a matter of time before a major accident occurred. Back at Muroc, number 47–001, the first production B-45A, had its original J35 engines retrofitted with J47s. On September 20, 1948, George Krebs and Paul Brewer were scheduled to take it up for stress testing in a series of shallow dives. Fate intervened at the last moment when Brewer was bumped from the mission by 31-year old flight engineer Nicholas G. Pickard, who required more experience. Krebs eased the craft down the runway at 10:17 A. M., while Brewer went off to lunch, unaware of what would transpire next. An hour later he returned to the flight tower to check on events: "When I got back the guy was sitting there kind of stone-faced and he said, 'I can't reach them.' So then we got a phone call, and somebody in the air had seen a plane go down by Fresno — we were pretty sure what it was. We got in a Navion and landed in a rice field right next to where we found the crash." Engineer George Gehrkens was among the first to survey the

For many years the salvaged nose-section of the first XB-45 prototype was mounted on a flatbed and trucked around as a recruiting device (David Menard).

crash site, two miles south of Alpaugh, California, and 110 miles northwest of Muroc. He immediately began vicariously reconstructing the accident from an engineer's stand-point: "We started finding the first things along the flight path, these little piece of fiber-glass insulation, so that gave us the clue with what the problem was as that was the first thing we found. I called Ray Rice and said 'Ray, we had a tail failure.' Ray was prima-rily a structures guy and he said, 'Impossible, keep looking!' and turns out it was not a tail failure, it was tail destruction."

This first fatal crash of the Air Force's new jet bomber triggered a formal investiga-tion to determine the cause. An army of investigators combed through the metallic con-fetti, remnants of a once-proud craft, seeking clues and incriminating evidence. As days passed and more of the wreckage was retrieved for examination, a grim picture of num-ber 47–001's final moments emerged; Ray Rice had correctly discounted structural fail-ure as the cause. "The problem basically was the insulation that we had put around the tailpipe to keep the heat in," as Gerhkens, who eventually headed the crash investigation, explained, "The engine compartment simply exploded and blew the heavy doors, which were the flak protection around the engine. They were about a quarter-inch thick alu-minum and, say, three and a half yards long, and one of these came off, went back, and hit the tail. It chopped off the tail at that point so the airplane pitched over and they were about 500 feet off the ground making a high speed run. It nosed over and hit the ground upside down, so they didn't have a chance."[47] This last point was dramatically under-scored when oscillatorgraph data salvaged from the wreck indicated an airspeed of 505 miles per hour upon impact. Subsequent investigations concluded that the tailpipe insu-lation, consisting of aluminum foil and glass wool, had worked itself free, lodged tightly in the nacelle, and facilitated a build up of leaking jet fuel. The volatile mix then ignited, ripping the left nacelle apart and destroying enough of the horizontal stabilizer to nose the jet over. High G-forces then ripped off both wings past the outboard engines and the "main wreckage, consisting of the fuselage and partial wing and tail surfaces, crashed in an inverted position with the nose approximately 180 degrees from the original line of flight."[48] The loss of the aircraft and two crew members led to improved maintenance procedures, and no further B-45s were lost to insulation-related failures. Still, a down payment for progress had been paid in lives.

Five years after its inception in 1944, America's jet bomber program found itself on shaky but steadily solidifying ground. The B-45s had undergone intensive flight testing and modifications over the prior two years, and in the spring of 1949 they were being groomed for their operational debut. One disillusioned Air Force writer, bemoaning postwar cutbacks in men and machines, hoped that with its arrival, "a faint tinkle of hope has been sounded — a tinkle which to the optimistic ear indicates that perhaps with a little luck, we may once again aspire to the position of aerial eminence."[49] The ensuing decade witnessed more capable and glamorous jet bombers entering and leaving the Air Force inventory, but the B-45 remains sole claimant to the title of first. As such, it transcended theoretical paradigms and cut the template from which large-scale jet bomber operations gradually arose. In this respect the B-45 is a significant link in a continuous chain of high-performance aircraft. Equally important, as the deaths of Krebs and Piccard attest, was a singular reality that both the promise — and perils — of jet aviation had arrived with it.

CHAPTER THREE

The Dawn of Jet Bombardment

"Although it might be highly desirable that a nation await technical perfection prior to the employment of new weapons, weapons systems, and doctrines, such a course of action would, in fact, be suicidal. Technical perfection is a condition which, from a military point of view, is impossible of attainment."

—Major General E. M. Powers.[1]

The deployment of America's first jet bomber was a momentous occasion for the U.S. Air Force and for the unit assigned new B-45s which, by necessity, had to be among the best in service. The honors fell upon the 47th Bomb Group, then based at Biggs AFB, Texas, and to whom the distinction was well-merited. The unit had been constituted at McChord Field, Tacoma, Washington, on November 20, 1940, to fly Douglas B-18s and Consolidated LB-30s on antisubmarine patrols in the early days of World War II. Thirteen months later the 47th was refitted with fast Douglas A-20 Havoc light bombers and began training for close ground-support work. In November 1942 it assembled in North Africa where, between February 15 and 19, 1943, the group won its first Distinguished Unit Citation (DUC) for outstanding service during the Battle of Kasserine Pass. That spring the unit's mission changed to medium-altitude bombardment; in this capacity it fought well throughout the Sicilian Campaign.

On September 2, 1943, the 47th Bomb Group made history by landing at Taranto, Italy, becoming the first allied bomber unit stationed on the European continent.[2] Subsequent operations carried it northward up the peninsula, where it also flew missions from the island of Corsica during the invasion of Southern France. The unit then moved back to Italy where, in January 1945, it was reequipped with speedy new Douglas A-26 Invaders, the best light-attack bomber of World War II. The 47th Group used this lethal aircraft effectively throughout operations in the Po River Valley, where it interdicted supply lines and hounded fleeing German units. The crews also performed exceptionally well in bad weather from April 21 to 24, 1945, whereupon a second DUC was conferred. By the time hostilities ceased in Europe, the 47th Group had flown 1,442 missions and 16,654 sorties. They were subsequently shipped to Seymour Johnson Airfield, North Carolina, in preparation for transferring to Okinawa, but the war ended before this move was effected. Following a brief stay at Lake Charles Army Air Field, Louisiana, the 47th Group finally put down postwar roots at Biggs Field, El Paso, Texas, on October 26, 1946.[3] There it assumed night-attack duties flying all-black (and redesignated) B-26 Invaders of the 84th, 85th, and 86th Bombardment squadrons.

Exceptional combat performance demands exceptional military leadership; Air Force leaders chose Colonel Willis Fred Chapman, a man well-suited by experience and temperament to usher in the age of jet bombardment. Born in Jackson, Michigan, on November 15, 1912, Chapman graduated from the U.S. Military Academy, West Point, New York, in 1935. Two years later he received his pilot's wings at Kelly Field, Texas, and fulfilled various staff and flying assignments during the buildup to World War II. Chapman initially drew administration and flight training duties, but chafed under the yoke of military bureaucracy and sought a combat command. He then ventured to North Africa as Chief of Combat Operations under Colonel Lauris Norstad, acquitting himself well. On March 16, 1944, Chapman finally received his wish with an appointment as commander of the 340th Bomb Group, Pompeii Air Field, Italy, flying North American B-25 Mitchells. Before Chapman could distinguish himself in combat, nature

Colonel Willis Fred Chapman. More than any other individual, Chapman's determination to make the B-45 operations viable ushered in the age of jet bombardment (National Archives).

rudely intervened on March 22, 1944, when nearby Mt. Vesuvius erupted, damaging or destroying some 85 bombers parked on the airfield. After some delays to refit his group, Chapman and the 340th blazed a trail of glory across the skies of northern Italy with well-delivered strikes against German targets in the Northern Apennines Mountains, the Brenner Pass, and Yugoslavia. In 3,000 hours of flying, the hard-charging colonel also accrued two Distinguished Flying Crosses, the Air Medal with Oak Leaf Clusters, the Bronze Star, a Presidential Unit Citation with two clusters, and a European-Middle Eastern Campaign Ribbon with ten battle stars.[4]

In essence, "Fred" Chapman proved himself a commander in the classic mold, invariably first over a target and the last one out. General Robert M. Lee, when recommending him for a brigadier's star, dwelt upon his secret for handling aviation units: "In addition to being a leader of men, he is one of few commanders I have seen who is a complete master of the weapon which his unit uses. He makes it a point to know everything about the supply, maintenance, and operation of aircraft and associated equipment in his units.... [H]e has a pleasing personality and gets along well with others. In my opinion he will go far in any field for which he is chosen." Chapman also indelibly impressed many subordinates under his command. Joseph Heller, author of the antimilitary diatribe *Catch 22*, had served with the 340th in Italy and parodied his former CO by modeling self-centered Colonel Cathcart after him. "Col. Cathcart was conceited because he was a full colonel with a combat command at the age of only 36," Heller wryly penned, "and Col. Cathcart was dejected because, although he was already 36, he was still only a full colonel."[5]

Like any ranking combat officer, Chapman was perhaps a tad full of himself, yet his amicable demeanor belied a singularly determined nature: he demanded — and received — the best performance from his charge, regardless of rank or station. The colonel brooked no nonsense, but he unhesitatingly mingled with lower ranks and addressed many on a first-name basis. In turn, fifty years later, many airmen recalled him with a mixture of respect and affection. "A great big, robust man and he carried himself real well," supply sergeant Jim Sharpe beamed. "I don't think he had an enemy anywhere." Sgt. Claude Riddell also spoke effusively, insisting, "He was an enlisted man's officer. Everybody liked him."[6] To such a figure was entrusted America's first jet bomber.

Chapman rotated home in the fall of 1945, where he assumed temporary command of Hunter Field, Savannah, Georgia. Following the 340th Group's disbandment, he held several intermediary assignments, including a year at the Armed Forces Staff College. Chapman next served at Biggs Field, El Paso, where he took charge of the 47th Bomb Group on October 10, 1947. That desert base, 3,700 feet above sea level and saddled with a mile-long runway, poised problems for men and machines alike. "Biggs was kind of primitive, especially for a bachelor officer," Captain Bruce Deakin reflected. "We lived in old World War II barracks and when we had sand storms out there, we would hang wet sheets in the room just to catch the sand that passed through. It was pretty grim." Sergeant Sharpe was equally pensive about this harsh environment, especially after, in his own words, "A pile of sagebrush blew up against me, wrapped around my leg, and it scared me to death!" Headquarters, Tactical Air Command, similarly expressed reservations about Biggs for, under prevailing conditions there, J35 engines failed to develop sufficient thrust to lift off from the relatively short runway. With the jet-bomber program accelerating and the day of operational status dawning, one report cautioned that "Take off and landing characteristics of the B-45 preclude the use of Biggs Air Force Base due to field elevation, temperature, and runway lengths."[7] Headquarter officers consequently began searching for a new and better venue for the 47th Bomb Group before jet aircraft began arriving, or so they hoped, by the summer of 1948.

While Air Staff officials wrestled with the problem of suitable bases, the men and officers at Biggs underwent a carefully phased introduction to the world of jet technology. Progressive training was carried out by the new B-45 Mobile Training Unit (MTU) which had arrived on base in December 1947 and begun processing trainees the following January.[8] For many, it was their first inkling of things to come and generated almost giddy anticipation. The MTU training system consisted of a dozen types of demonstration devices, mock-ups, and models intended to supplement technical manuals and class instruction. These included a cutaway J35 engine that revealed all its working parts. It also weighed 2,400 pounds and required a reinforced floor to stand upon. The entire setup also required ten medium-sized rooms in order to function successfully.[9] "Of course there was a lot of hoopla and we were all excited because this was the first one," Major James Story recounts," We did have a mobile training unit, the MTU, and that's the first we had ever heard of it. I guess that this was the first ever formed. But it was very interesting and a good way of doing it. The aircrew went through it and of course our maintenance people also went through it. We at least had a head start on the airplane."

One unusual student passing through the six-week MTU class at Biggs AFB was Lieutenant Gordon Cremer, an RAF exchange officer who enjoyed a long association with the B-45. "Personally I thought it was a very fine course," he intimated. "I experienced a little difficulty at first, not with the assimilation of knowledge, but getting used to the hot climate after the much cooler latitudes of the British Isles. To review the course in more detail, the breaking down of the various sections and allocating of one instructor to individual sections led to a very thorough explanation and demonstration of that particular phase. The mocks ups, expensive though they might be, more than compensated for the cost by the amount of instruction they afforded. The instructors I found to be most useful and altogether the course was a most enjoyable time." Cremer also confided how accommodating his Texan hosts had been and how much he had enjoyed his tour, but, he confessed, "It may sound a little strange that two English-speaking communities have such different ways of living, but three thousand miles of ocean makes a lot of difference."[10]

The first jet bomber touched down at Biggs on June 28, 1948, for preliminary flight testing and training, which prompted the unit historian to note: "Everyone watched the B-45 making these load/runway tests, and are eagerly looking forward to receiving the B-45 soon."[11] Piloting this aircraft was Major Robert L. Cardenas, who had been temporarily relieved of duties at Muroc for testing and instruction purposes at Biggs. Once there, Colonel Chapman imposed a little favor on him. "I remember the bomb wing that was going to get it was down in El Paso, Texas, so I flew down from Muroc to let them see what they were going to have," Cardenas reflected. "Of course, they were impressed because they had been flying the B-26. On the way home the wing commander asked me if he could send his wing navigator on board and we took off at night and headed for Muroc. Shortly after takeoff the navigator called up and said, "Major, you know I've flown this area quite a bit — that looks like Phoenix down there but it can't be.' 'No,' I said, 'its Phoenix.' 'Jesus Christ!' was his comment, so they were impressed with the aircraft." The B-45 made a second official appearance at Biggs on September 18, 1948, heading up a cast of eighteen different aircraft displayed during celebrations marking Air Force Day. "This was the first time the B-45, the Air Force's first jet bomber, had been available for first hand inspection by the public," the unit history observed. "Advantage was taken by all to have the chance to inspect the plane."[12]

As ground crews trained at Biggs, a steady trickle of pilots also cycled through Muroc for orientation and their first hops in a B-45. For men long familiar with propeller-driven craft, it proved a radical departure from what they had previously known as flying. Major Cardenas, the principal instructor pilot, was careful to stress proper landing techniques, given the plane's high approach and landing speeds. "With the B-45 you got off a mile or so, pull it back to idle, and float in," he said. "I checked out, I believe, it was five aircrews out of Muroc, [with] Danny Forbes and I was showing them that the difference to a B-26 pilot was the landing." One of the 85th Squadron's first pilots to master the B-45 was Captain Louis Carrington, the maintenance officer, who recalled, with a laugh, "My first flight was in the backseat. My next flight was in the front seat, checking somebody else out and I buzzed the ramp at 575, which was the limiting mach. It was so smooth in flying, quiet and all, and to me it was one of the best pilot's airplanes I've ever flown in my life. It was just a *beautiful* airplane." Another student was Captain Edward "Sandy" Sanderson, who touted himself as only the third pilot checked out at Muroc, and perhaps his opinion best typifies the 47th Group's reaction to the B-45. "I wanted to fly it," he beamed. "The last time I flew it I was equally happy with it."

As flight crews acquired proficiency, they were allowed to ferry brand-new jet bombers from the Long Beach facility to Norton AFB, San Bernardino, for further modifications and tests. Yet, as B-45 numbers increased, the problem of where to ultimately base them lay unaddressed. Biggs' soaring temperatures, wispy air, and short (5,200-feet) runway were deemed unfeasible for safe operations — particularly for an aircraft with long takeoff and landing rolls under normal circumstances. As Major James Story, base safety officer and accident investigator, noted, "First we got the early models that had the J35 engines in it — getting them off a 5,000-foot runway was no good. You'd have to get up at three in the morning and get that mother up while it was still cool or else your weren't going to make it until the next day." For this same reason, Lieutenant Donald Orr found his first flight from Biggs most memorable. "Well, we revved it up and headed down the runway, and it rolled and rolled and it rolled," he shuddered. " When the end of the runway came up we pulled back at the controls and went into the air and slowly we went out across the desert, milking the flaps a little bit at a time." It

was painfully apparent that the 47th Bomb Group required a new home with more accommodating runways, and soon.

On November 8, 1948, the 47th Bomb Group finally received orders to transfer all B-45 operations to Barksdale AFB, near Shreveport, Louisiana. A bomber facility with a 10,000-foot runway, it was also under the jurisdiction of the Air Training Command and the shift made for awkward operational relationships. "We were a tenant unit, that's never good," Major Story declared. "Training Command owned it so we had to do what they said." Proof of this status manifested in the cramped facilities accorded the newcomers. Whereas at Biggs all squadrons received their own hangar, each capable of housing three planes apiece, all that Barksdale could spare was two smaller hangars sheltering two planes each. The all-essential MTU, which required a minimum of ten rooms to operate, was marooned for lack of space and ceased functioning until Jan-

Colonel Chapman beams as he addresses the Shreveport Chamber of Commerce during welcoming ceremonies for the 47th Bomb Wing. On the podium is the large wooden B-45 model presented to him by North American Aviation (Patricia Chapman Meder)

uary 24, 1949, when it relocated to buildings previously reserved for prisoners of war.[13] Nevertheless, Colonel Chapman orchestrated the laborious procedure by departing with his staff on November 8 and setting up shop ten days later. The group's B-26s were also flown directly to their new home, although eighteen ended up mothballed at Smyrna AFB, Tennessee, to lighten the maintenance load and give ground crews more time for B-45 orientation. On November 19, 1948, the 47th Bomb Group was again declared operational, with Chapman receiving the new designation of wing commander.[14]

Once settled in their new abode, the wing resumed running pilots and crews through the jet training program at Muroc. Previously, that facility had qualified 20 pilots and 84 ground crew on B-45s, in addition to the 500 support personnel already trained on the MTU at Biggs. Yet, one essential factor in the equation remained curiously absent: jets. "When this training was completed there followed many months of waiting for our first B-45," the unit historian conceded. Colonel Chapman flew to Tinker AFB, Oklahoma, in December to check on the impending delivery of aircraft. He was duly informed that production snags and other unforeseen difficulties would keep his B-45s from arriving at Barksdale anytime soon. So, nine months after becoming the nation's first jet bomber unit, the 47th Bomb Wing possessed none of its fifty-three aircraft.[15] The case of the missing B-45s could not be resolved until the following spring.

March 23, 1949: Colonel Chapman emerges from 47–027 as the B-45 begins its operational tour at Barksdale AFB (Patricia Chapman Meder).

The lack of jet bombers did not dampen public relations with authorities in nearby Shreveport who, in true Southern fashion, extended cordial hospitality towards their new neighbors. On January 18, 1949, the local chamber of commerce feted the 47th Bomb Group with a banquet held at the Washington Youree Hotel. Colonel Chapman, the guest of honor, was regaled by master of ceremonies Mr. Thad Andress, and received further accolades from Carl J. Hansen, assistant chief engineer at North American Aviation, who presented him with a large wooden model of the B-45. Over 500 officers and civilians attended, including General Robert W. Harper, commander of Air Training Command, and Colonel A.C. Strickland, commander of Barksdale AFB. In his after-dinner address the affable Chapman heartily thanked his hosts and admitted that the banquet "was the first such welcoming for any air force unit he knew of." He also expressed his gratitude towards the citizens of Shreveport for helping to house 500 families recently relocated from Texas. "The jet business is in its infancy," Chapman declared in his closing remarks. "Here you see the nucleus of officers for the jet force of the future. Here is the heart and beginning of the big business of jet operation."[16]

In January 1949, Captain James L. Louden, 47th Wing's public information officer (PIO), devised a contest to officially name the B-45. He received a total of 348 entries, from which a panel of eight judges selected the three best names: Apache, Challenger, and Tornado. According to Captain Louden, "North American Aviation made the airplane and they had a policy; they would let the first bomb group to get their airplane to name it. Me being the first public relations officer for the first and only jet bomber group at that time, I ran a contest and I had hundreds of names submitted to me. I had a committee help me pick the names and some master sergeant submitted the name 'Tornado.' So North American wanted me to send them what me and my committee hoped were the three most appropriate names for that aircraft. They liked the name Tornado and they gave the master sergeant who submitted that name a beautiful model of the B-45 and gave us a lot of publicity in aviation magazines." The winner, Master Sergeant Clyde N. Parker, also received an Emerson FM radio from radio station KWKH, Shreveport, on January 27, 1949.[17]

The first B-45 finally touched down at Barksdale on January 15, 1949, piloted by Captain Robert A. Robinson. Its appearance set off flurries of expectations but 47th Wing personnel were "in for a slight let down" since Robinson was simply passing through on other duties. The next attempt to acquire a Tornado also proved futile. On February 16, 1949, Colonel Chapman was notified by authorities at San Bernardino that number 47–006, a J35-powered aircraft, was certified for delivery. Accordingly, he took Major George B. Thabault, the B-45 project officer, and navigator G.B. Kubicek to California and ferried it back. After they departed San Bernardino on March 1, a section of the bombardier's nose blew out at 39,000 feet over Phoenix, Arizona, causing the navigator's change of clothes to be explosively blown out the hole. Chapman, instantly concerned for Kubiek's safety, relates what happened next: "Here we are with an 80 or 90 degree minus factor up there, and the thing is you had to get him down as fast as you can to 20,000 feet or he's not going to last long. So I pulled the engines back, but I'm still up around 39,000 feet and there's no drag, particularly up there. What happened was that I could not get the aircraft to slow down, even though the engines were throttled back. And every time you stick the nose down a bit the airspeed would run up past the allowable max. So I cut one engine, and that did not do a Helleva lot of good, so I cut another one. Now I have two engines off and I'm getting some nose down on it , and I was just getting ready to cut a third engine, but we finally made it below 20,000 feet." Kubicek was shaken but unharmed, thanks to his commander's quick actions. Chapman then turned around and safely returned to the San Bernardino Depot for repairs.[18]

Unfazed, the colonel was determined to try again the moment another B-45 became available. March 23, 1949, became enshrined as a momentous date for the 47th Bomb Wing for, at 3:30 that afternoon, number 47–027 appeared over Barksdale, circled the field twice, and proceeded on a long landing approach. Chapman was again at the controls, seconded now by Captain Charles McDonough and navigator Captain Harold Berman. The trio departed San Bernardino without incident and only stopped briefly at

Biggs to refuel. They then cruised along at 84 percent power over the final 748 miles, covering it in one hour and 35 minutes at an average speed of 498 miles per hour. Chapman maintained an altitude of 25,000 feet until passing over Fort Worth; he then began descending 1,000 feet per minute until Barksdale hove into view. Lieutenant Don Orr witnessed the Tornado's arrival: "Everybody went out to the flight line, to the edge of the ramp, so they could see the runway, which was 500 feet wide and 10,000 feet long. [The bomber] landed right on the beginning of the runway and rolled all the way to the far end before it taxied to the ramp, a big crowd all around it." Once Chapman and his crew clambered outside, Orr noted, "work stopped as the entire wing assembled on the ramp to greet the colonel and his aircraft." Chaos ensued as the colonel was mobbed by newsmen and photographers, while spectators flocked around his burnished bird with unconcealed delight. Craft and crew alike received a full court press and a local radio reporter managed to corral Chapman for a broadcast interview. Basking in the moment, he matter-of-factly declared, "We will receive 15 jet bombers from San Bernardino in the next two months. After that we will receive approximately two each week from other B-45 factories." A *Shreveport Times* reporter also noted how Chapman, when asked if B-45s could carry atomic weapons, circumspectly declined to answer.[19]

Two days later balky number 47–006 zoomed into Barksdale with Lieutenant Colonel Sherman R. Beatty at the controls. On June 4, 1948, Major John J. Ruettgers claimed the latest B-45 distance and time record by arriving nonstop from California, a flight of 1,400 miles, which he covered in only three hours and fifteen minutes. "It was a cruise control flight and not an attempt at any speed record," Ruettgers announced. "The ship handled beautifully and we had no mechanical trouble whatsoever." Finally, after months of interminable waiting, the 47th Bomb Wing finally possessed a handful of jet bombers, which were handed off to pilots and crews of the 85th Bombardment Squadron. Meanwhile, pilot training continued apace at Muroc and new jets were being readied for delivery to their new home. "We were bringing different crews out from Barksdale, giving them a quick checkout and back to Barksdale they'd go," Captain Carrington recalled. "I forget how long I stayed, probably a month. I don't know how much time, but I got in quite a few flights while I was there — I'd check some of the other guys out — do anything to get into the air with the thing because it was such a joy to fly." So, after what seemed to be interminable delays, the 47th Bomb Wing had finally morphed into the nation's premier bomber outfit, and expectations naturally ran high. "Thus started our jet operations," the wing historian beamed. "At this writing it is too early to know what trials and triumphs are in store for us but they will be faithfully recorded in future issues of this history."[20] Unbeknownst to all, the tribulations encountered, when they arrived, proved almost daunting beyond endurance.

The spring of 1949 proved heady days at Barksdale as the deafening whine of J47s resonated up and down the flight line. The 84th Squadron historian reported unaccountably buoyant spirits for the month of April and attributed it to the arrival of more Tornados. "Most all rated personnel are very eager to fly in the B-45 and the airmen have expressed desires to work on them. It is uncertain as to where this present rise in morale will stabilize but it is expected to remain above its present level."[21] Far from being intimidated by the big airplane, pilots came to love the B-45 by virtues of sweet handling and its predictable disposition. "It was what we called an honest airplane," Lieutenant Colonel Raymond Fitzgerald explained. "If you did this, you knew what was going to happen.

If it stalled you'd know ahead of time — like the B-25.... Where you could kick the tires and pretty much jump into a B-26, this was a little more involved and you knew you had to do it because there was a lot more to the airplane." Captain "Sandy" Sanderson, another convert from the Muroc days, maintained it was "One Hell of a fine airplane. It flew well, had good altitude capability, it had good range capability, particularly after we got the 500-gallon drop tanks.... [L]eave it alone and it would land itself."[22]

Naturally, pilots of 47th Bomb Wing were eager to demonstrate what they could do with their shiny new mounts. During an early demonstration flight staged on April 26, 1949, harmonica-toting Captain Louden, known throughout the command as "Big Jim," arranged his Tornado to perform a high-speed pass over neighboring Shreveport: "We were coming in hot, but we had permission from the FAA to do that. Here I am in the cockpit, describing this on radio to an NBC station on the ground in Shreveport and they were playing it nation-wide on stations throughout America. It was quite an assignment for a twenty-eight year old captain!"[23] Captain Charles McDonough, a senior pilot with 56 hours at the controls of the B-45, also spoke enthusiastically about his plane: "The only unusual experience I've had was landing one without the hydraulic aileron boost. Even then it was just like landing an ordinary plane with stiff controls." Soon after, Colonel Chapman clamped down on excessively high-speed flying for reasons of econ-

omy, as well as safety. "Pilots must become much more fuel conscious," he lectured. "When you're tearing along at better than eight miles a minute you must realize those four jets are burning up a lot of fuel." It finally devolved upon safety officers at Headquarters, 12th Air Force, to curtail some of the excesses — and most of the fun — at Barksdale. Higher-ups grew concerned about young men operating a hot ship without receiving systematic training beforehand. No such program existed for jet bomber crews, so one would have to be designed, literally, from the ground up. Operations were therefore scaled back until comprehensive plans for standardized training procedures could be worked out, vetted, and approved. The unit historian concurred, noting, "It must be taken into consideration, however, that before an unlimited transition

Famed test pilot Robert Cardenas was also one of the earliest B-45 instructor pilots (John Mott). program for pilots in this aircraft can be initiated, more specific information concerning the operational characteristics of this aircraft must be determined by the more experienced pilots."[24]

Word consequently arrived from on high that, for the meantime, all B-45s at Barksdale would be utilized for rechecking the first batch of 21 pilots, men who had previously qualified at Muroc. Moreover, all training now fell under the positive control of the group's director of operations and training to ensure that this systematic approach was enforced. Headquarters, 12th Air Force, was taking no chances with the potentially fatal combination of young pilots and jet bombers. This apprehension was not unfounded. As the 47th Wing settled into its routines at Barksdale and B-45s continued arriving, all hands faced the implications of what new technology had wrought. Pilots loved the aircraft; however, from a maintenance perspective, keeping it safely aloft was distinctly uncharted territory. As Sergeant Terry Little perceptively reasoned, "The B-45 was a quantum leap in aviation technology at the time. It had high pressure hydraulics, boosted flight controls, and there was very little experience-generated data available to aid in either flying the airplane or maintaining it. There was no Dash-2 maintenance manual with any experience generated for trouble-shooting procedures. So that factor alone seriously affected flying and maintenance of the airplane for several years." In sum, high-tech troubles were in the offing and the accumulated wisdom needed to fix them could be obtained only through costly trial and error.[25]

The hazards of working around such complex machinery cannot be understated. For example, the Tornado sported bomb bay doors that snapped open and shut with lightning rapidity to minimize problems associated with high-speed drag. "The B-45 had a 3,000 pound hydraulic system," Sgt. Little recalled. "Everything moved faster and with more force." Claude Riddell, another 84th Squadron mechanic, mentions his first encounter with such potentially dangerous equipment: "The bomb bay doors, the first time I saw them close — I happened to bat my eyes that instant — it shut while I blinked. So I'd watch them occasionally and sure enough they'd go *clunk!*–3,500 pounds of hydraulic pressure. And if you were standing in the bomb bay, they would close just about where your hips would be. Well, some guy put a 4 × 4 in the bomb bay doors, and when someone went goofing off and closed the doors, splinters fell down on the hangar floor."

The mounting litany of grievances included unreliable avionics, breakdowns in bomb bay equipment, and the occasional engine fire during startups. Captain Carrington, the 85th Squadron maintenance officer, declared, "We got back into the business of checking out a bomb group — we had all kinds of trouble. Sometimes we'd open up the electrical compartment and find it would be full of water from rain. The canopies would crack. The heating system, with its fish oil in it, failed almost every flight. And in the heat down there, we had a deal that if you were scheduled to fly the airplane they'd put a canopy over it, and they'd actually let you taxi to the end of the runway and hold, then take that off." As B-45s continued operating, unsatisfactory reports (URs) began "flying like bullets." The usual maintenance headaches were further compounded by chronic shortages of parts and qualified personnel to install them. Improvisation and innovation thus became essential bywords throughout the B-45's tenure at Barksdale. In April 1949, the 84th Squadron mechanics reported that stripping combustion chamber linings from J47s, an essential part of mandatory engine inspections, was almost impossible because "a special tool for removing the chambers is not at hand. A tool was manufactured locally that appears to be more satisfactory than the one authorized."[26] It is a time-honored axiom among ground personnel that, while they make the headlines, flight crews could never get airborne save for the skill, tenacity, and technical imagination of the crew chiefs and their men. The Tornado, as events unfolded, taxed those abilities to the utmost. "They hated it," mechanic Merle Sollars unequivocally asserted, "it was a tough airplane."

Tragedy interrupted the 47th Bomb Wing's happy routine on June 9, 1949, less than two month after receiving its first Tornado. The accident also spawned one of the most harrowing survival stories in aviation history.[27] On that clear and cloudless morning, public information officer Captain James Louden lost a coin toss prior to his third flight on a B-45, number 47–033. Twenty-seven year-old Captain Ralph L. Smith, a Shreveport native and the wing's air inspector, won the honor of sitting in the co-pilot's seat while it was flown by 31-year old instructor-pilot Captain Milton O. Costello, of Chicago. Costello, a senior pilot, was something of a memorable character in the group's annals. Major Story noted, "He was a very strong man [who] he always smoked his cigarette on a stick like FDR, it was kind of comical. He was well thought of as a commander and I got to know him real well. And we did skits one time imitating him — with that cigarette holder — at the club in Barksdale." Having lost the toss, Louden resigned himself to climbing into the bombardier's station for a front-row seat. After two hours of practice stalls and touch-and-go landings, he would trade perches with Smith for his own turn in the cockpit.

"Then it was time for Smith's last landing," Louden recalled, "after which we were going to taxi onto the tarmac, but I never got the opportunity to switch seats with him. We were coming down the down wind leg of the traffic pattern about 3,000 feet off the ground and got into our final approach. We were coming in about three or four miles out from the runway and we were cleared for Number One to land. About this time the torque tube on the right wing flap broke which meant that we had one flap full up and one flap full down. Costello didn't realize what the problem was so he poured on the coal to all four engines trying to get that wing back up and when he did not we screwed into the ground. They estimated we were going close to 300 miles per hour completely out of control with me, Jim Louden, in the nose. We had 16,000 pounds of JP-1 in the fuel tanks at that time and the airplane blew like a bomb, killed the other two guys instantly — blew them into a million pieces and they were sitting just a few feet from me behind the firewall. The explosion blew me 150 yards from the impact point through a barbed wire fence and I have scars all over my body to prove it. I woke up seventeen days later."

At 10:20 A.M., the stricken bomber smashed into the ground six miles north of Barksdale with a resounding explosion that alerted the base. Fire trucks and other rescuers then raced to the crash site to behold wreckage strewn across an alfalfa field, and one nacelle resting 150 feet away from the main impact. The tangled remains burned furiously for two hours, despite the best effort to extinguish them. Among the first persons on the scene was 19-year old supply sergeant Sharpe, who started scanning the vicinity for survivors amidst the twisted, smoldering remains. "We didn't expect to find anyone alive; there was fire everywhere, and there wasn't enough of the plane to even recognize. I'd never experienced war, and this was the worst scene I had ever laid eyes on," Sharpe reflected. "I spotted a busted up helmet beneath a clump of trees. I hesitantly rolled it over, with an almost eerie expectation that I would find the remains of a human skull." It was a sickening experience for many of the rescuers. Amazingly, Captain Louden was blown 500 feet clear of the explosion and landed in a clump of trees. He was dangling from the branches, bleeding profusely, when local taxidermist Ned Touchstone discovered him there. Crewmen hastily evacuated him to the nearest medical facility but, considering the injuries sustained, which included broken bones and internal ruptures, Loudon's mere survival was miraculous. He spent the next two-and-a-half years in therapy relearning to talk, walk, and take care of himself while his faithful wife, Peggy, stood vigilantly in attendance. More impressive still was the fact that "Big Jim," a strapping, harmonica-playing optimist, resumed active duty with the 47th Bomb Wing in 1951 and flew an additional twenty-one years before retiring in 1971. All in consequence of a coin toss he allegedly lost![28]

Colonel Chapman launched an immediate investigation into the crash of number 47–033 and its two crew members. Early on he had resigned himself to some inevitable tragedies and he recalled "speaking to the group after our first B-45 crashed and saying that we must expect to lose a few aircraft by malfunctions." However, the colonel determined that their "No. 1 objective is to never lose a second aircraft to the same cause."[29] As much wreckage as could be salvaged was then trucked into a hangar and painstakingly reassembled. The remains were thoroughly analyzed by board members, who divined that "the accident was primarily caused by failure of the right torque tube assembly, resulting in a left-flap-down and right-flap-up condition." Their conclusion was promptly forwarded to Headquarters, Twelfth Air Force, whose commander dutifully grounded all B-45s on June 16, 1949, pending inspection of all aircraft. The search uncovered several defective torque tubes. The requisite repairs were made and the Tornados were again declared operational, although now restricted to only four hours of flight time per month, per aircraft. This did not stop five B-45s being dispatched to Langley AFB, Virginia, on June 26 and 27 to partake of Operation Blackjack, a cooperative mission with the Air Defense Command's Eastern Seaboard Warning Net.[30] No accidents or malfunctions occurred and the bombers returned safely, but an important precedent had been set: hereafter, repeated groundings were a galling reality in the B-45 program.

The wing continued rebounding throughout July as deliveries of nine more B-45s brought the total number of jets at Barksdale up to twenty-five. Pilot training procedures had also solidified to the point where oversight of this vital activity reverted to squadron authority. Flight crews were now obligated to successfully conduct twenty-two instrument missions with various profiles, including forty hours of formation flying, and to complete the rigorous program established for aerial observer/bombardiers (AOB) to be judged proficient. Once this curriculum was accomplished, the entire unit was expected to conduct twenty-four wing strike missions annually, at altitudes ranging from 10,000 to 40,000 feet. As proficiencies improved, B-45s were occasionally culled for activities in the public sphere. On July 3 and 4, 1949, two Tornados departed Langley AFB for flight and static display duties at Chicago's Orchard (O'Hare) Airport, one of the nation's great air shows, where they were viewed by an estimated 300,000 people.[31]

The hot and hazy Louisiana summer ground on through August as training activities intensified at Barksdale. B-45s were repeatedly grounded for a host of recurring problems, including canopy cracks, defective elevator sections, tailpipes, turbine wheels, and engine-mount bolts. One complaint became an infamous, recurring theme throughout B-45 operations. "There was one annoying feature that was amplified by being stationed at high temperature air bases such as Langley and Barksdale," Lieutenant Bruno M. Larsen asserted. "The canopy was fixed and could not be operated for cooling or circulation.

There were times — before TAC could obtain external air conditioning units — during preflight and engine start, that rivulets of perspiration ran down the pilot and copilot's forearms and hit the overheated floor with a hiss and immediately evaporated. There was a good chance that your flight suit changed color before all the engines were started and the air conditioning became effective." Deliveries of new aircraft continued, and by August the 47th Bomb Wing boasted thirty-one jet bombers. Public viewing demands also increased, and three Tornados were dispatched to Philadelphia, Pennsylvania, for the American Legion Convention, to Detroit for the International Air Fair, and to Cleveland for a showy overflight at the national air races. On the 24th of August Colonel Chapman led two B-45s to San Marcos, Texas, where they jousted with some F-51 Mustangs of the Texas National Guard. In two low altitude fly-bys at 1000 and 3000 feet, it was duly noted how "F-51 type aircraft were unable to stay with the flight of B-45 type aircraft and demonstrated that the present conventional air force fighters would be very inefficient and ineffectual in combating jet type bombers."[32]

Despite all the precautions observed and the modifications undertaken, accidents continued taking their toll. On August 12, 1949, number 47–037 took off from Barksdale on a routine training flight with pilots Captain Joseph F. Sneed, Lieutenant Alvin R. Heslep in the cockpit, and Captain John Gailen in the nose. Shortly before landing Sneed noticed that his right main landing gear would not lock down and radioed the tower for assistance. Technical experts relayed flight manual procedures for an emergency lockdown and, when he flew by the tower, the landing gear appeared to be secured in place. However, it collapsed immediately after touching down, whereupon Sneed pushed the throttles forward for an emergency go-around. Suddenly, flames trailed from the number four engine on the right and CO_2 fire suppressant canisters failed to extinguish them. Sneed ended up pancaking his Tornado in a cotton field three miles northwest of the base, resulting in back injuries to both him and Heslop. Wreckage analysis pointed to a defective main-gear-position lock. On August 18, Headquarters, Twelfth Air Force, ordered all B-45s grounded until sheer-resistant steel pins were installed.[33]

The loss of number 47–044 and its entire crew on August 31, 1949, was a further blow to the 47th Wing. The aircraft departed Barksdale at 10:22 A.M. to perform routine instrument and transition training. Four minutes later, it inexplicably smashed into a cotton field fourteen miles northwest of Barksdale. Major Paul B. Neafus, the 85th's Squadron's assistant group operations officer, and Lieutenant Donald A. Paulson perished in the fiery wreckage, parts of it scattered over a wide area. Eyewitnesses reported seeing the aircraft's right side on fire when the pilot, apparently attempting to land, lost control and cartwheeled. "The plane hit the ground and then turned over," D.M. Powell told the press. "I didn't hear an explosion but a big puff of flame enveloped the craft." Once the fires were doused, anxious crash investigators picked through the sprawling debris for clues among the ruins. Preliminary indications highlighted defective thermocouples in the tailpipe assembly, after which all B-45s were grounded once again. Crash authorities subsequently deduced that vapors from an apparent fuel leak exploded in flight and blew off the right nacelle structure. All B-45 tailpipe assemblies were accordingly stripped, inspected, and repaired as necessary, and the jets resumed flying by mid–September 1949. Still, the loss of an experienced pilot like Neafus was serious and considered "immeasurable not only to the 47th Bombardment Wing, but also deprives the United States Air Force in a critical period of advance of a devoted and able commander."[34]

The unkindest cut of all occurred on September 17, 1949, when Order No. 93 arrived from Headquarters, Twelfth Air Force, announcing the 47th Bomb Wing's deactivation. The full extent of President Truman's FY 1950 budget cuts now manifested in the new Department of Defense Economy Program. Consequently, the 84th and 85th squadrons were reassigned to the 363rd Tactical Reconnaissance Group, 4th Fighter Wing, at Langley AFB, Virginia. The 86th Squadron was disbanded outright, with planes and personnel absorbed by the remaining two formations. Facing an inactivation date of October 2, 1949, Colonel Chapman worked to effect a smooth transition to his new clime, where he would also assume command of the 363rd Group. He announced the changes at a massed meeting and urged hardship cases to prepare their arguments thoroughly before requesting to remain at Barksdale. The colonel then bid farewell to all hands, unequivocally declaring that the 47th Wing was "the best organization he had ever served with." Sufficient time was still found to dispatch six B-45s to Brookley AFB, Alabama, to participate in Air Indoctrination Course II, where another round of cannibalization ensued to keep them aloft.[35] Meanwhile, preparations were underway at an already crowded Langley to receive their new guests. The 363rd Group historian cryptically commented on one obvious problem. "If B-45's descend upon us, the ceilings of the hangars we have are much too low to accommodate the high tail of the B-45," he wrote. "Solution to that should be interesting."[36]

The 47th Bomb Wing's tribulations would have discouraged a lesser man and Colonel Chapman's friends, concerned about his future, offered him a way out. General Herbert B. Thatcher, Air Force Deputy for Operations, sympathized with the colonel's plight and suggested a possible transfer to the Continental Air Command headquarters at Mitchel Field, New York, rather than working to unravel the knotty problems awaiting him at Langley. Chapman thanked him for the offer, but he respectfully declined and his response is indicative of the man: "Langley Field offers no personal attractions to me except the satisfaction of driving this jet bomber program through to an effective and logical completion. I feel more or less like the daddy of the project right now and I don't want to leave it half done.... From my viewpoint at this level, I frankly believe that I can be of more value to the Service by remaining with the jet bombardment project during this very critical period."[37] Chapman, despite the loss of lives an a vexing litany of problems, bought wholeheartedly into the Tornado program; as was typical of him, he remained doggedly fixed upon seeing it through to a successful conclusion.

On a lighter note, aviation writer Joseph Stocker arrived at Barksdale on September 12, 1949, intending to ride in a B-45 and recount his experiences for *Boy's Life* magazine. Stocker waited nearly a week for obliging weather before accompanying Colonel R.D. Sampson and Captain Ralph W. Mitchell aboard number 47–045 — which he characterized as "a monstrous mechanical cat preparing to spring" — for a brief test hop. He was utterly transfixed by what followed. "We were a blob of shimmering silver arching swiftly and steeply in the sky, with two black trails of smoke swirling out behind, for all the world like a locomotive that sprouted wings. Ah, but this was flying. Not flying as I had always known it, with the roar of engines, and the vibration, and the circular pencil line of spinning propellers. An entirely new kind of flying. Quiet, almost mystically quiet. Effortless. There was no sensation of being pulled through the air by powerful engines. Rather there was one of being wafted over the earth on a magic carpet, or of being suspended at the end of a great wire hung down from the ceiling of the sky." The

impressionable Stocker distilled the essence of jet flight for youthful readers with elo-
quence and verve.[38]

The Tornado's debut at Langley augured ill for, as the 363rd Group historian predicted, they proved too large for facilities assigned to them. "When the B-45s arrived at
Langley and were towed to their designated hangars for maintenance, behold! We had
more of the B-45 vertically than we had of the hangar," he wrote. "It was patently impossible to raise the hanger roof, so we did the best thing and cut holes in the ceiling to
accommodate the tall B-45 tails." Even more challenging was towing the hulking jets in
and out past low hangar doors for maintenance, an act requiring dexterity that Houdini
himself might envy. The solution hit upon was practical, but also dangerous: a dolly
would raise the nose of the plane several feet off the ground, while simultaneously lowering the tail, whereupon the bomber was gently nudged inwards. It nonetheless took
eight to ten men over an hour to safely berth a Tornado, lest, it was noted, "one slip,
bingo! A B-45 with only part of a tail." Furthermore, the Base Supply proved unequal
to the task of procuring sufficient spare parts to keep the jets operational. "You can't supply that which doesn't exist," the historian bemoaned. "Indeed it was necessary to can-
nibalize B-45s flown to Langley in order to find parts needed to ferry in B-45s
AOCP-grounded at Barksdale." More headaches arose when an entire series of J47 engines

**Back at Los Angeles, aspiring actress Julie London emblazons a B-45A with its new name.
That's test pilot Chuck Yeager in the front seat (Patricia Chapman Meder).**

were found with defective 12th-stage compressor seals. All 23 B-45s present were grounded pending new engine replacements, possession of which had already been prioritized by Langley's F-86 squadrons. By now such travails had become routine for Colonel Chapman, who focused more upon smoothly integrating his old outfit into the new one. "October left but one problem and that was all important," he cheerily declared, "the welding of these diverse elements into a unit which for spirit, discipline and accomplishment could be nowhere paralleled."[39]

Chapman's optimism proved misplaced, unfortunately, for B-45 operations reached their nadir shortly afterwards. Taking a leaf from Murphy's Law, everything that could go wrong at Langley did so with a seeming vengeance. An onslaught of mechanical difficulties, coupled with strict economy measures, hampered the ability of the 363rd Group to get jets aloft. Consequently, the unit historian lamented how "November brought falling temperatures, falling leaves, and a definite fall in flying time to the 363rd Tactical Reconnaissance Group." Previous difficulties due to part shortages were further aggravated by faulty fuel regulators and starter generators, which again grounded the entire fleet, now risen to 42 machines. Nor had any progress been made in devising better methods of getting B-45s in and out of hangars designed for fighter craft. "Three separate jacking operations raise the nose gear nearly a meter onto a mobile dolly; in this position the aircraft is extremely unstable and the tail skid is depressed approximately six inches," the historian recorded. "The damage which could result from a fall from this height is hard to imagine." The unit also struggled with a growing lack of ramp space, whereupon the increasing numbers of B-45s were arrayed in staggered lines, with new aircraft sandwiched between them. Consequently, if a jet in the rear-most row was to taxi to the runway, the two aircraft in front had to be towed out of its way first.[40]

On the brighter side, the six B-45s previously detached to Eglin AFB for Air Indoctrination Course II returned with glowing reviews from Major General Willard R. Wolfinbarger, who wrote, "The pilots, even through initially hampered by the lack of formation experience in the B-45, demonstrated exceptional ability in adapting themselves to the proper formation technique applicable to this aircraft.... Their devotion to duty is commendable." Chapman, meanwhile, grappled with even bigger priorities on hand. He had been ordered to hone flight crew proficiencies with 1,296 radar bombing sorties and the dropping of 10,044 bombs annually. Unfortunately, wing activities were stymied by a continuous lack of suitable bombing ranges. "Without such a range, combat proficiency in bombing cannot be achieved," the unit history reads. "If we are to pioneer radar bombing with the AN/APQ-24 set from the only operational jet bomber the USAF possessed, we must have the necessary elbow room." Nobody realized this better than Chapman himself, and he implored superiors to take immediate action. "Yearly and semi-yearly access to a bombing range provides indoctrination training, but is not a substitute for day-to-day training in attaining and maintaining combat proficiency," he advised.[41]

The 363rd Group weathered a difficult two months at Langley, but flight and ground crews continued laboring energetically to rectify the flurry of technical difficulties. As more Tornados resumed operational status, longer hours could be flown and, in the words of a finally happy unit historian, "B-45s aloft became no longer a subject of wonder and speculation." An influx of new fuel regulators and starter generators cured most of the J47's ills, and engine life, previously computed at seven hours, gradually increased. The historian attributed this success to the overworked ground crews, whose efforts resulted in fourteen aircraft in commission — a record for the unit — and 188 hours in flight time achieved. This new level of productivity proved no walk in the park, given endemic part shortages, a lack of viable manuals, and maintenance personnel's unfamiliarity with the aircraft. "They are actually pioneering where the manufacturer left off and are constantly unearthing and documenting unsafe conditions that will some day make the B-45 as safe and dependable as the outmoded C-47," a unit historian wistfully wrote.[42]

This seemingly endless workload notwithstanding, crew chiefs and ground crews remained undiminished in their professionalism. Sergeant Terry Little declared, "We were really enthused about the first jet bomber. Most of us were ex—B-17 people. Hell, we were fired up—it was an honor to work on it, but it was a bugger to maintain. Everybody in the aircraft maintenance business depends on experience-generated data—this guy had this problem, here's where he finally gets the solution, and that goes on records and goes in papers somewhere and comes out in the manual. There was no such thing on the B-45 or for flying it either. All we picked up were the three or four months' service testing at Edwards. We learned a lot out there, but we were trouble-shooting our own new problems."

The turnaround took time and effort, but by December Colonel Chapman's persistence and methodical approach to troubleshooting began paying dividends. "At year's end the Group found itself comfortably situated at a new location and resolved that the coming year was to mark an era of greater achievement in the operation of multi-jet aircraft," he stated. Many subordinates, undaunted by crashes and debugging problems, shared their commander's unshakable faith in their aircraft and themselves. "There was a lot of excitement," Captain Deakin recalled of the early days at Langley. "I think that B-45 crews had a pretty good bit of confidence in the airplane—we had some bad mishaps, that's true, but in all they were very enthusiastic about making this thing work." Important progress had been made and valuable lessons learned, but Chapman reflected on his past nine months with blunt and professional ambivalence. "It should be understood that various situations which affected operations were not isolated things that temporarily halted normal operations," he informed superiors. "These situations have occurred with such frequency that normal operations have never been possible."[43] More work—and greater support—was required.

Happily, the new year found the 363rd Group acquiring still more flight time. Two major problems, the lack of parts and a shortage of replacement J47 engines, had finally subsided to the point where regular aircraft maintenance was increasingly possible. Consequently, more Tornados were airborne longer and cross country flying resumed to give flight crews more experience at cruise control and high-speed navigation. Support facilities at Langley nonetheless languished, and bombers were still being jacked up by the nose and backed into undersized hangars, a hazardous and time consuming process. For expediency, many crews preferred working outside in the cold rather than manhandling jet bombers in and out of buildings. Still, "It is believed that prolonged maintenance, particularly in weather extremes, is best performed indoors where personnel are more comfortable and where engines and systems are not exposed to the elements when protective coverings are removed," a unit historian concluded. Work, when carried on indoors, was also complicated by inadequate lighting, described by one irate crewman as "so poor you have to light a match to see if the bulb is lit." Overcrowding on the ramp still vexed

The biggest remaining piece of 47–033 after it slammed into the ground during a high-speed run. Miraculously Captain James Louden survived and rejoined the unit two years later (LSU Shreveport-Noel Memorial Library).

the flight line, which only promised to worsen once the group's 162nd Squadron obtained RB-45Cs in the near future. Another serious deficiency was Langley's short runways, the longest being 6,999 feet long, which aggravated the Tornado's perilously long takeoff roll. "It has been necessary on first transition rides with trainee pilots to find a 15-20 knot wind in order to approximate another one thousand (1000) feet of runway," the history cautioned. "The B-45 is too big and too expensive to allow any errors of judgement."[44]

The group's routine still remained punctuated by operational accidents, although fewer than had been experienced at Barksdale. On January 24, 1950, a Tornado was running up prior to take off when a J47 suddenly exploded, damaging its nacelle. No cause for the failure could be discerned, so the remaining aircraft were not grounded. The only major mishap for this period occurred on February 3, 1950, when number 47–040 suffered a complete loss of power during its landing approach. Instructor pilot Captain Hubert M. Blair held his speed at 190 miles per hour as long as possible, but all four engines failed to restart. Gliding in, Blair discovered that his landing gear and flaps were likewise nonfunctional. He then careened down the runway and crash landed; no injuries resulted but 47–040 was written off. A thorough investigation followed, but the cause of the crash was never pinpointed. "No material failure of the engine or its related aircraft systems is indicated," the report stated, "These facts, however, do not preclude engine phenomena such as flame out." Another engine-related accident occurred on February

14, 1950. Lieutenant Edward J. Sanderson suffered a compressor explosion in his number three engine while returning from MacDill AFB, Florida. Sanderson quickly doused the flames using onboard CO_2 canisters and landed safely at Langley. General Ennis C. Whitehead subsequently commended him for his cool-headed reactions.[45]

The spring of 1950 marked the one-year anniversary of the Tornado's debut as the nation's first jet bomber. It had been a particularly harrowing experience for the 363rd Tactical Reconnaissance Group, but strides had been made in safety, flight worthiness, and in-commission rates per month. By June, both the 84th and 85th squadrons were flying double the number of hours that had been flown the previous February. The percentage of B-45s in commission had also soared to 78 percent, which elicited giddy exuberance from the unit historian. "This happy condition and the ability to maintain this high percentage differed so greatly from the early days of Louisiana that the humorous remark was heard to the effect that 'When we had three B-45s in commission at Barksdale, a legal holiday was declared.'" Accidents during this period remained a major source of concern, but had declined proportionally given the overall number of hours flown. The most serious incident occurred on May 28, 1950, when number 47–032 crashed on landing. Loud noises had been heard in the left wing nacelle when lowering the main gear, which refused to indicate fully locked. When the aircraft touched down, the unsecured landing gear collapsed, spinning the plane completely around and snapping off both main landing gears. No injuries resulted but the Tornado was unsalvageable. Impact damage was also sustained by number 47–052 when "a large seagull disputed the right-of-way in the traffic pattern during the last few days of March. Although the gull came out second best in the dispute, a great deal of sheet-metal work was required to affect [sic] repairs." Finally, on June 21, 1950, number 47–055 experienced a compressor explosion during an instrument training flight. The aircraft landed safely, after which the faulty unit was removed and shipped to General Electric for disassembly and inspection.[46] So, despite a variety of accidents and engine-related malfunctions, operations with the B-45s displayed an overall improvement.

Tornados were also tapped to participate in Operation Swarmer, a combined forces maneuver involving ground support actions. On April 18, 1950, the group operations officer, Major James S. Kale, advised Colonel Chapman of the unsuitability of the Tornado for low-altitude work, reiterating the conclusions of previous Air University studies. He opined that the whole scheme of close support was extremely unsound when considering "high fuel consumption, great susceptibility to enemy fighter attack, low weight of explosives carried, high cost of the aircraft ($1,200,000), and doubtful accuracy of release is weighed against the fact that a great weight and variety of munitions can be satisfactorily and economically employed by release at high altitudes."[47] Other work highlighted the difficulties of B-45s in formation bombing, which called for the development and refinement of automatic formation bomb-release mechanisms to better synchronize ordnance delivery. The numerous problems associated with simultaneous bomb-release testing proved detrimental to the Tornado's primary functions and required immediate resolution.[48]

While the B-45s grappled with operational-readiness at Langley, they nonetheless performed admirably in a series of mock attacks against Navy carriers off the Virginia coast. In fact, they embarrassingly upstaged their naval competitors. During the first week of June 1950, Air Force planners conferred with Admiral M.E. Curtis, commander of the

Operational Development Force, over simulating attacks upon capital ships to test radar equipment, picket positions, and fighter interception techniques. Soon after, such raids were conducted against the carriers USS *Saipan* and *Coral Sea* while Combat Air Patrol interceptors (CAP) were vectored by the onboard Combat Interception Control (CIC) to stop them. The results proved embarrassing to naval commanders. Although early radar warnings from the picket craft alerted the carriers and vectoring techniques likewise proved effective, the Grumman F9F Panthers and McDonnell F2H Banshees could not keep pace with Tornados at low altitude. An official report readily conceded that "on-the-deck attacks could not be detected until it was too late to prevent an attack on the Task Force Target." In mid–July, the Navy switched over to high altitude attacks, which yielded similar results. The B-45s bored in at 35,000 feet and 500 miles per hour, and were detected by radar 155 miles out, but once again the CAP interceptors failed to protect the ships.[49] A top secret naval study concluded the following:

> Actual attack of such a high speed target, if accomplished at all, was made at the cost of long tail chases at military power.
> Skillful air controllers can direct successful high speed interceptions, although the margin for error is critically small[50]

Navy officials were anxious that potential attacks by Soviet-built Ilyushin IL-28 Beagles and Tupolev Tu-14 Bosuns might wreak havoc on carrier tasks forces *despite* the presence of jet combat air patrols. The results from these exercises confirmed the validity of these apprehensions. Moreover, it became clear that naval fighters, tasked with protecting these floating airfields, could only surmount jet bombers through a combination of increased speed, greater armament, or both. The 363rd Group threw itself wholeheartedly into the joint exercise and savored a few chuckles at the Navy's expense, which added "to the growing collection of data concerning operational use of the relatively new and untried jet bomber, the B-45."[51] Nor was the Navy beyond cushioning the rout, perhaps as a sop to the *Coral Sea*'s pride. As the ship's command history cryptically noted, "These tests proved satisfactory in that the information desired was obtained. The evaluation of CGA equipment revealed certain deficiencies in flying the present patterns and deficiencies in the equipment."[52] Present throughout these proceedings was Captain Zack Ryall, who thoroughly enjoyed handing the Navy its comeuppance: "The initial missions were airspeeds, altitudes, and then for the final phase the Air Force had *carte blanche*— and it didn't make any difference. Anything above 35,000 feet, the Navy *Panthers* could not get up to us. I remember the Navy controller saying 'Do you see him?' 'Yes, he's above us.' 'Can you intercept?' 'I can't even get up there.' Even when they were programmed ahead of time. I never knew what kind of aircraft they were trying to intercept us with because the only time I ever saw them was when we cranked over the wing, which you could do at 40,000 feet, and you could see the little spots down below."

Despite this striking success, senior Air Force officials began pondering the B-45's ultimate employment. In 1948, prior to President Truman's fiscal cuts, they had envisioned that the 47th Bomb Group would be deployed at Yokota, Japan, as part of the Far East Air Force (FEAF) and replace the B-26-equipped 3rd Light Bomb Group. Clearly, the A-model B-45 lacked the range to fly nonstop, or to stage out of Hawaii, so the possibility of shipping them across by boat was considered. The idea was abandoned after it was found that B-45s were too large for conveyance on Liberty or Victory ships, unless

Engines still smoldering, 47–037 rests in a cotton field after a perilous belly landing (LSU Shreveport-Noel Memorial Library).

ten feet were somehow removed from each wing. Moreover, the Tornados already deployed still lacked fire-control equipment and other important systems. By 1949 the plan to deploy bombers abroad was abandoned after the USAF director of Requirements reviewed their combat readiness. Colonel R.W. Puryear observed, "B-45 aircraft are being received from production which are unsuitable for tactical operations either in the Zone of the Interior or overseas. This tactical unsuitability is attributed to a lack of any bombing equipment on the aircraft and to an insufficient supply of jet engines."[53] Adding to the short supply of J47s was their unreliable nature. Field experience had revealed a service life of only seven-and-a-half hours before inspections or replacement became necessary. Moreover, the small stock of readily available J47 engines was claimed by F-86 fighter units, which enjoyed equipage priorities over the B-45. This situation angered Major General Ennis C. Whitehead, commander of the Continental Air Command, who remained unhappy with either aircraft. "We are still having H — with F-86s," he complained. "One day we may have 75 percent of the F-86s in commission at Kirtland. The next day they are all grounded. There must be some better way to place new types in service in units."[54] Nobody said the transition to jets would be easy.

Events at Barksdale and Langley certainly lent credence to the old aviation saw to "Never fly the A-model of anything." This rang painfully true with early Tornado bombers but, in fairness to the 47th and 363rd groups, test units operating B-45s also experienced losses. On September 20, 1948, as B-45C number 48–003 attempted to land at Long Beach Municipal Airport, California, it suddenly caught fire in midair. Onboard were Colonel Arthur W. Schmitt, pilot, and three North American Aviation officials who were riding along as observers. NAA mechanic Leo Hunt, working in the cockpit of another B-45C nearby, related what happened next: "I looked across the Long Beach runway as our new B-45C was coming in for a landing. I then saw a flash of fire coming out of the right engine nacelle, and then more flames as the right wing dipped, and it looked like it was heading in my direction. I went out the escape hatch into space as the inspector had used our ladder to check intakes before engine runs. Then it flew over our heads. It bounced across a golf course and then across a busy street into a stand of large trees with a huge explosion of rolling black smoke and flames.... Amazingly, the left wing had hit the trees and exploded while the fuselage continued forward and all the crew was safe." Less fortunate was the crew of another C-model, number 48–006, operated by the All Weather Flying Division. The aircraft had just completed a series of touch-and-go landings when the pilot reported an engine fire; then his jet suddenly exploded over Dayton, Ohio, on February 24, 1950. One crewman parachuted to safety but two others died, including the pilot, Royal Air Force Wing Commander Derek S. Pain, a high-ranking exchange officer.[55] This incident highlights the close working association that RAF personnel enjoyed with the Tornado from its earliest days.

One year into its service life, the B-45, like most jet aircraft in the Air Force inventory, remained tenuously employed, with little prospect for expanded operations. Overseas deployment was also deemed impractical but, within months, unforeseen events in Asia dramatically altered that conclusion. For the time being, just keeping the 363rd Group's Tornados airborne proved challenging enough. Lives and planes had been sacrificed, yet the Air Force was coping with its temperamental new bombers, in spite of seemingly endless difficulties. In fact, it was during the aircraft's tenure at Langley that many gremlins, once deemed insurmountable, were finally exorcized. One perceptive group historian, buoyed by their progress, concluded, "A great deal of experimental work remains to be done before promulgation of tactical jet bombardment doctrine.... [Yet] work in this field opens up a vast new area for exploration in military aviation." Equally sanguine, if more effusive for his youthful audience's sake, was writer Joseph Stocker's assessment following his fleeting tryst with a B-45: "Here, I realized, is the beginning of what will some day be America's all-jet bomber force. And these men who fly the Tornado are the pioneers — as truly pioneers as the Wright brothers, and Bleriot and Billy Mitchell."[56] To Willis F. Chapman and his Spartan band, truer words were seldom uttered.

CHAPTER FOUR

To the Yalu — and Beyond

"As you can see, we in air intelligence don't put much stock in the idea that, what we can't get openly, we simply ask the CIA to get it with spies, then sit back and wait for it."

— Major General Charles P. Cabell[1]

On 4:00 A.M., June 25, 1950, the Cold War's prevailing winds blew a lot hotter once armored columns of the North Korean People's Army crashed southward across the 38th parallel and into South Korea. Nearly a decade had passed since Pearl Harbor; yet, for a second time, the United States found itself unprepared militarily. For the Air Force, which had atrophied under the cut backs and false economies of the postwar period, its deficiencies were immediately and painfully apparent. "In the period beginning with the end of World War II, the U. S. Armed Forces suffered from malnutrition," General Charles P. Cabell, director of Air Force Intelligence, lamented. "We had watched helplessly the head-long rush to destroy the great military machine which had won that war. It was not until late 1948 that even military authorities really began to see, rather than vaguely feel, that there was a force loose in the world that was dangerous in strength and purpose. Even then there were those in the Department of Defense who were still more concerned with economizing than with the building of an adequate military force."[2]

Consequently, when the Korean War erupted, American reconnaissance capabilities in the Far East were virtually nil. Even basic information about North Korean topography proved lacking, while target dossiers were nonexistent. In-theater assets consisted of two squadrons of aging RB-29s, two flights of photo-mapping RB-17s, and a handful of jet powered RF-80As with the 9th Photo Reconnaissance Squadron at Yokota, Japan. Moreover, the personnel, equipment, and organizational infrastructure for rapidly conveying photographic intelligence to where it was needed most also proved sadly deficient. General George E. Stratemeyer, commanding the Far East Air Forces, dutifully scrambled to make up the shortfalls, but initial results proved slapdash and only underscored the inadequacies of American reconnaissance. The North Korean juggernaut continued rolling south and Cabell, in a highly-charged missive to Stratemeyer, urged a redoubling of efforts. "This situation must be corrected by an all-out effort in reconnaissance which gives us the information we require," he insisted.[3]

Unknown at the time, the Tornado would figure prominently in Korean War reconnaissance, and then at the highest levels of classified operations. No sooner had President Truman committed the United States to a massive "police action" than orders were cut

62

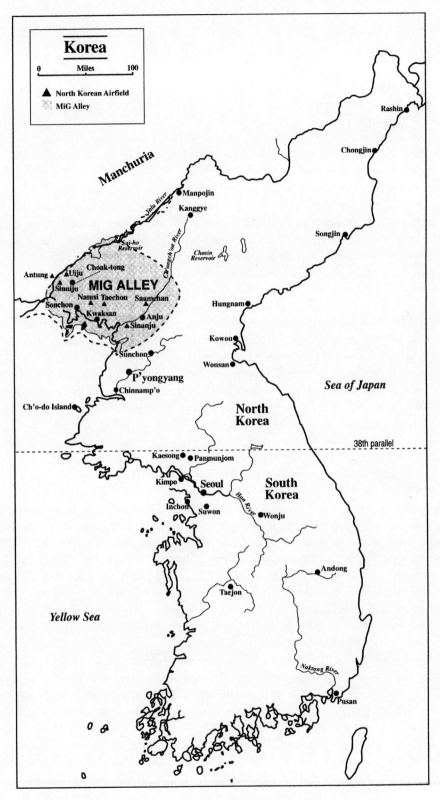

The Korean theater of war (Air Force History and Museums Program).

to cobble an RB-45C detachment together for "reconnaissance suitability tests" overseas. The Air Materiel Command prepared a comprehensive scheme for supplying said endeavor under the code name Operation Hold Off. However, an immediate snag arose for, while RB-45Cs had been entering the Air Force inventory since April 1950, neither the Strategic Air Command nor the Continental Air Command (ConAC) mustered a combat-ready crew between them.

Pilots and ground personnel from the 323rd Reconnaissance Squadron, 91st Strategic Reconnaissance Wing, were already at Langley AFB undergoing training on the B-45 MTU; however, they were months away from being qualified.[4] By default, it fell upon the 363rd Tactical Reconnaissance Group, Tactical Air Command, to provide pilots with any B-45 proficiency — despite their own unfamiliarity with reconnaissance. It was decided that volunteers culled from the 84th and 85th Bombardment squadrons at Langley would deploy back to Barksdale for a 30-day crash course in photographic techniques. This mixing of TAC crews with SAC or ConAC machines may have ruffled feathers in certain quarters, but it proved the only practical expedient for getting Tornados in theater as quickly as possible. This new, top-secret unit received the official designation of Detachment 4149A, 84th Bombardment Squadron — more simply known as Detachment A.

Documentation remains spotty as to this highly classified assignment, but certain key figures are known. Detachment commander was 31-year-old Captain Charles E. McDonough, of New London, Connecticut. Previously he had flown B-25s in North Africa and Italy and was now one of the most experienced B-45 pilots at Langley. McDonough's presence here did not surprise those who knew him, for he was a six-foot, three-inch daredevil by nature. "Charlie was a character," Major Joseph Story recalls. "I just want to compare him to a Robert Mitchum type. He smoked cigars, nothing was too hard, he could do it. Charlie just volunteered to go — and away he went."[5]

McDonough was seconded by another imposing individual, 30-year-old Captain Louis H. Carrington of Cleburne, Texas. A soft-spoken, burly individual, Carrington was temperamentally the mirror opposite of McDonough, but he was a fine maintenance officer. According to Lieutenant Earl Huggins he was popularly known as "The Bear" and "one of the best."[6] The final member of the team was Captain Albert D. Simmons of Timmonsville, South Carolina, of whom little is known and who functioned as operations officer.[7] Sometime in July Detachment A's ground personnel reached Barksdale to initiate their reconnaissance training. Meanwhile, ConAC flight crews were sent to Long Beach to pick up new, factory-fresh RB-45Cs. The crews returned to Barksdale on July 29, 1950, with aircraft numbers 48–013, 48–014, and 48–015, eliciting some jealousy from the SAC personnel training there to receive them. "The boys of the 323rd were both elated and disappointed at the same time," the historian dejectedly noted. "We had hoped to claim these planes." The new craft were promptly transferred over to the Continental Air Command, while the TAC crews underwent reconnaissance instruction.[8] Continued bureaucratic infighting resulted in some wrangling, but Carrington relied on Captain McDonough to calm the waters. "He did all the work with higher headquarters and everybody else, keeping people off our backs so that we could do our work," Carrington explained, "We finally got out of there — the main reason is that we had direct communication with Continental Air Command, and anytime we'd ask for something they'd say 'Sure!'" A year following its troubling debut, the Tornado suddenly found itself accorded priority status.

On August 22, 1950, orders arrived from ConAC instructing Detachment A, 84th Bombardment Squadron, to embark on a 90-day TDY at Yokota AB, Japan. McDonough's command had completed its thirty-day training period on August 25 and passed a readiness inspection held by Headquarters, ConAC, three days later.[9] It now faced the immediate problem of actually deploying overseas. Initially, the three aircraft flew to the Sacramento Air Materiel Area on September 15 for their eventual transit by aircraft carrier to Japan. Captain Carrington describes what happened next:

> They were arguing how we were going to get there, to the Far East. No airplane had ever flown it before and at those high altitudes. They had no knowledge of the winds. The Navy wanted, I think, one million dollars apiece to haul them over and the Continental Air Command couldn't afford it. I worked outside, Mac worked inside, and he would tell me what was going on. Anyway they had quite a hassle. And finally we convinced them that we could fly it, so we moved up to Fairfield-Suisan [Travis AFB] and sat there for a couple of weeks. There I decided that if we lost cabin pressure like we normally had been losing it in the older models we wouldn't have enough oxygen to stay up high enough to get there, so they let me modify the airplanes and we added extra tanks. And then Mac and Simmons would talk to airline pilots coming back and forth from Honolulu — what they could tell us about the upper winds.

In contrast to the no-nonsense Carrington, 29-year old Captain Jules P. Young of East Rochester, New York, evinced a pragmatic air about the entire matter. A former P-47 jock and a golfing fanatic, Young informed his parents, "It will be the first time that jet aircraft have crossed the Pacific. I have my golf clubs and I hope we break down for a week of so in the islands. They have some beautiful courses out there."[10]

A departure date from the Zone of the Interior (ZI) was established at September 20, 1950, whereby the three RB-45Cs would be preceded by a C-54 transport carrying ground crews and 30 days' worth of spare parts to Hawaii. An additional 90 days' worth of parts traveled concurrently by water.[11] The RB-45C's range was a constant source of concern because of anticipated 50-knot headwinds; final calculations for maximum range were abetted by including a one-hour fuel reserve as insurance. RB-45Cs were capable of in-flight refueling, but Air Force officials involved in the project felt that "air to air refueling is not considered necessary and is not recommended without prior training in the Zone of the Interior."[12] For keeping such large, complex, and temperamental aircraft like the RB-45Cs functional, a premium was also placed on forwarding spare parts and supplies to Japan, resulting in a superabundance that would have been unimaginable at Barksdale or Langley.

No effort was spared by AMC or any other agency to secure the means of keeping the planes aloft. "We supposedly, and I am sure we did, leave the United States with 120 days of parts, or any conceivable parts that we needed for that aircraft," Sergeant Merle Sollars says. " I took ninety gallons of hydraulic fluid with me, which is a Hell of a lot of hydraulic fluid." North American Aviation was also represented by a B-45 technical expert, Jack Waite. Six months later, when Waite filed his official report, he attributed the detachment's ability to keep their aircraft in commission to two distinct factors. The first was "fly away" kits requisitioned directly from North American Aviation, which completely bypassed the labyrinth of Air Force supply channels. The second factor, Waite wrote, "has been the never tiring efforts of all officers, airmen, and civilian technical representatives assigned to re-work, substitute, or do whatever should be done to use what was available."[13] Compared to events elsewhere, it was an impressive and effective effort.

The three RB-45s departed Fairfield-Suisun AFB on September 20, 1950, and let down onto Hickham Field, Hawaii, following a five-hour transit. According to Major Carrington, "The day came and we decided to try it. We filled our tanks and we lined up on the runway, cut down, and filled them all up again — put in every pound that would go in there. And we all took off in formation for Honolulu using JP1." The flight itself was uneventful, but highlighted the fact that "aircraft could use more navigational aids, especially celestial navigation provisions."[14] Secrecy surrounding the detachment was also closely maintained and security remained tight. Sergeant Walter Dackson, a camera repairman, related that "We were segregated from the rest of the base and they had armed guards around us in the barracks, and we were marched, as I remember, over to the mess hall and back. Couldn't go to the PX, couldn't go to the movies, couldn't do anything. We kind of wondered what was going on and the master sergeants and those people, they knew but they wouldn't say anything — and we wondered 'What the Hell's going on?'" Two days later Detachment A departed for the next leg of their journey, Midway Island.

The RB-45Cs dropped down on Midway on September 23 and made preparations to refuel before finally proceeding onto Yokota AB, near Tokyo. Thus far, good planning

Number 48–014 shortly upon arrival at Barksdale for transfer from the Continental Air Command (CAC) to the Tactical Air Command (TAC). Note the complete absence of unit markings, which persisted until the late spring of 1951 (8th Air Force Museum, Barksdale AFB).

and adroit flying had kept the operation functioning smoothly, save for a near disaster with Carrington's mount, number 48–015. Midway was short of just about everything needed for jet operations, including stocks of jet fuel but, given the urgency of the situation, it was decided to improvise and press on as quickly as possible. Sgt. John Mangum, crew chief of 48–014, recalled that "We were putting in 115–145 [octane avgas] fuel — they didn't have any jet fuel. We ran it through a water separator and there's about as much gas leaking out as water." Then came 48–015's turn. Sgt. John Wilkerson was working with Sgt. Oscar E. Hager on the wing as the plane was being refueled. "Hager had a Ronson cigarette lighter in his pocket and, as he stooped over to pick up the water separator and it hit the wing and sparked. The fumes from the jet fuel were all over the place and then one big 'boom!'" The fire started burning along 48–015's wing as the startled ground crews pulled back, but only Jack Waite retained the presence of mind to act decisively. "We heard somebody hollering Hell," Sgt. Mangum recalled, "so we turned around and there's Jack Waite upon the wing putting that fire out — all the rest of them were gone. And so we got every fire extinguisher we could and threw them up to him and he put it out." Waite's quick thinking saved the million-dollar warplane, which sustained relatively light damage save for a tear in its leading edge. Unhappy at being detained longer, Captains McDonough and Simmons decided to forge ahead; Carrington could catch up to them at Yokota. A thorough search of the island was conducted for aluminum, but none turned up. Carrington then resorted to the only source of sheet metal available. According to Sergeant Sollars, "The crew stayed on requisitioning parts which were not forthcoming, so they decided to patch this airplane with beer cans, which they did. That undoubtedly must have been Carrington because he was the type of guy who would do that." This tacky but eminently practical improvisation worked fine, and number 48–015 eventually rendezvoused with the other two RB-45s at Yokota a few days later.

Sergeant Price also mentioned an incident on Midway Island not recounted elsewhere. He had been called upon to check number 48–015 for any possible damage to its electrical systems and was performing a preflight of the APQ-24 navigation system:

> I really can't remember the sequence of switches except for one that I'll never forget. The last switch controlled the ship's converter that produced 400 cycle (hertz) AC, mainly for the APQ-24. When I threw the switch, both wing tip fuel pods ejected!
> I ran outside to see the starboard pod laying on the ground with some fuel leaking out. The port side pod was dangling from one bolt. The ground crewmen that had been lying around waiting for me to finish were on the other side of the tarmac, having done the hundred-yard dash in eight seconds! I yanked the cable from the engine nacelle and grabbing the towing tongue in the power unit, I started pulling it away from the aircraft. I was pleasantly surprised to see Captain Carrington run up to help me. Later I was told that another cable ran out to the wing tips that was further back in the wing and apparently there was a short in this cable that carried signals to the wing tip pods, including, I assume, eject signals. As far as I know, nothing else was ever made of the incident.[15]

Two RB-45s of Detachment A roared into Yokota AB on September 28, 1950, and awaited Carrington's appearance shortly thereafter. Staff Sergeant Robert Stadille, working with the intelligence section of the 91st Strategic Reconnaissance Squadron, was awestruck by the gleaming visitors. "They were the sleekest-looking things that I'd ever seen," he said. "The pilots were young guys in their 20s — nice guys. They talked to you, they were young and eager and excited about flying that B-45. And, of course, every RB-

29 jockey was envious of those guys. They flew some missions for us over Korea, and they did in three and-a-half hours what took a B-29 eight — nine — ten hours to do — and were flying at 40,000 feet."

Mechanics, who had previously endured systemic shortages at Langley and Barksdale, also found their new abode a literal spare-parts heaven. "When we first got over there we had all kinds of support in the world," Sgt. Wilkerson beamed. "We had the North American rep, the G.E. Rep, and the electronic rep, and we got an engine over there in a matter of a week. We had some pretty good priority when we first got there."[16] Crew and airplanes alike began prepping for active service in theater, but they were immediately sidelined for four weeks after it was discovered that their 263 equipment (cameras) had yet to arrive. Bill Crowley, the NAA technical representatives at Long Beach, understood why. "One of the problems was that the program was so damn secret that nobody knew it was there except those that were working on the problem," he reasoned. "Jack Waite was our lead representative and we had John Spielman over there, and they would have difficulty going through their own supply circles of getting parts and it would take so long. So they were using me as a funnel, especially for the Land camera parts."[17]

Devoid of essential camera parts, Detachment A simply marked time and did not conduct its first mission until November 2, 1950, five months into the war. Men and machines performed suitably over North Korea, although a bureaucratic lapse nearly caused a disaster during the return leg of the mission. The Tornado had been apparently dispatched without prior clearance from Center of Combat Operations, Fifth Air Force, nor the director of operations, FEAF headquarters. Consequently, four flights of F-80s scrambled from South Korea to intercept what appeared to ground radar as a fast moving intruder. "Only tentative recognition of the RB-45 (which was new to this theater) by one of the fighter pilots prevented the F-80s from making attacks," it was noted. Henceforth, orders directed future Detachment A flights to be cleared in advance with Combat Operations for their own safety. By now the RB-45C's unsavory ditching characteristics were also appreciated, and necessitated deploying a mission-designated SB-29 over the Sea of Japan. The rescue bomber orbited in place until the jet bomber safely returned from the north. Their presence was considered essential because a Tornado crew would likely succumb after 20 minutes' exposure in the frigid waters, even with their rubberized, anti-exposure suits.[18]

Over the ensuing two months, Captains McDonough, Carrington, and Simmons performed weekly missions over the Korean peninsula. The exact nature of these flights is not recorded; yet, at this stage of the conflict, these probably consisted of target-gathering information, bomb damage assessment (BDA), and Trimetrogon mapping of the rugged peninsula. Detachment A was demonstrating its worth and Captain Fred Sager, photo interpreter of the 548th Reconnaissance Technical Squadron at Yokota, who was responsible for discerning every shred of information captured by the Tornados, felt "Every mission where they were able to get over the target, they always brought back good results." The FEAF operational history records twenty-four reconnaissance missions between November 2 and December 31, 1950, with little commentary, save that Headquarters, Fifth Air Force, assumed operational control of all flights as of November 3. Henceforth, operations came under the purview of Major General Earle E. Partridge, who emphasized proper mission profiles, careful evaluation of all reconnaissance equipment extant, and development of evasive tactics to negate enemy air defenses.[19]

   This last factor was of increasing relevance to Detachment A following the debut of Soviet-manned MiG-15 interceptors on November 1, 1950. Their arrival had been detected by an RB-29 flight on October 18, 1950, which photographed 75 swept-wing fighters arrayed along Andong (Antung) airfield, Manchuria. In fact, the Russian 151st and 28th Fighter Air divisions had only recently deployed there, astride the Yalu River, which subsequently became their air operations center for the war. The MiGs were not only superb combat aircraft, they were manned by veteran pilots capable of engaging their American counterparts on equal terms. The introduction of crack Soviet pilots and their high performance interceptors also dramatically skewed the balance of air power above North Korea. At a stroke, every airplane in the Fifth Air Force was immediately outclassed, and the death-knell of lumbering, propeller-driven bombers was sounding. Moreover, the Russians were especially keen to bag an RB-45C, which until then operated with near-impunity around the northwest corner of Korea, a region soon to gain infamy as "MiG Alley." Their unwelcome presence certainly upped the ante for Tornado missions and, as Lieutenant General Georgy Lobov crowed, "When the MiG was introduced, a quiet life for the reconnaissance crews ended."[20]

   To the specter of MiGs must be added the crushing onslaught of Chinese Communist forces in November 1950, whose startling success radically altered the nature of RB-45C activity. Emphasis now shifted from topographical mapping, bombing pre-reconnaissance, and bomb damage assessments to daily monitoring of enemy troop movements along the Yalu. "When it became apparent, that the Chinese were intervening," Sager explained, "the major mission of the RB-45s in Korea was to photograph the bridge at Andong to see what the bridge traffic was, the number of Chinese troops crossing, and where they were going." In Carrington's words, "We had our wings sticking over in China because we were photographing the river every day.... After the Chinese invaded, we photographed the river every day so they could count the footprints in the snow to see how many came over."[21] Continuous proximity to Andong also brought the Tornados within easy reach of Soviet jets stationed there. The threat they posed further underscored their utter lack of tail defenses, long considered a major deficiency in RB-45Cs. The aircraft did, in fact, possess a gunner's compartment, but this had yet to be fitted with twin .50 caliber machine guns as in the bomber variant.

   The Tornado's vulnerability did not skirt Captain Carrington's vigi-

356-2 G 6161st ABG 3 Dec.50 Broken Wing Rivets + Beer Can Patch

The famous "Beer-can patch" on the leading edge of 48-105 (John Mott).

lance for long; once alerted to the presence of MiGs, he approached Sergeant Price to try to jury-rig a radar-warning device for the tail section. The resulting device proved worthy of "Rube Goldberg" himself. Price said:

> When all was installed, I took a portable field strength meter to check the radiation field pattern. It was supposed to be a cone like pattern of 45 degrees with the apex at the tail. Unfortunately the damn thing was radiating everywhere. I suspected that the large metal mass represented by the tail stabilizer was creating interference patterns. The AN/APS-13 was designed for fighter aircraft and I think that the massive metal structure of the RB-45C was interfering with the transmit/reception abilities of the AN/APS-13. Finally we had a local fighter fly behind the RB-45C and crisscross in and out of the tail area. You might have guessed it; I was lying in the tail gun position with a screw driver, tweaking the receiver sensitivity control, trying to find an optimum point where the interference was minimized while still detecting the intruder flying into the tail transmitter pattern. Alas, our efforts were in vain because at low altitudes, where most needed, the combination of fouled-up transmission and ground clutter would give continuous false alarms and I could just imagine that *school bell* going off in that small cockpit space![22]

The Tornado's vulnerability was further compounded when superlative North American F-86 Sabrejets, the only American fighters capable of tangling with MiGs, were absent from Korean skies for another month.

On November 20, 1950, less than a month after RB-45C operations commenced, Detachment A officials issued a report to Headquarters, Air Force, recommending immediate installation of a tail warning radar or a tail gunner's position, along with identification friend or foe (IFF) transponders, an auxiliary scope for photography at the copilot's position, and a voice recorder for logging camera operations. "It is hoped that these recommendations can be carried out, so that future operations using this type of aircraft may be improved," the unit historian wrote.[23] Photographic problems also arose, especially in the low-level Sonne system, which proved particularly troublesome. Captain Carrington related the following: "We found out that the photo cameras that we had couldn't keep up with our speed and we ripped a lot of film that way, going too fast. The Fairchild people worked with us — everybody came over and worked with us — then we got it all squared away and were doing really well." Speaking of his own contributions to flight activities, Captain Young, who had flown P-47s during World War II, informed his parents, "We have taken some good pictures and some of them have been quite valuable, of course you don't know the satisfaction that I used to get when I could blast a bunch of enemy troops with 8 fifties on my old 'Jug'— this is a different job but every bit as important as the shooting."[24]

The perils of unarmed, unescorted reconnaissance missions tragically hit home on December 4, 1950, when Detachment A suffered its first and only loss. On that fateful day, Captain Charles E. McDonough inexplicably commandeered Carrington's aircraft (48–015) to fly a mission northward with copilot Captain Jules E. Young and navigator Captain James J. Picucci. According to the only information available, this was a routine photo mission from Sinuiji eastward to Hoeryeng along the North Korea–Manchuria border.[25] Routine radio contact had been maintained as they coasted into Korean airspace, but thereafter McDonough failed to call in as scheduled. Orbiting SB-29s search and rescue aircraft did not detect any distress call or observe any floating debris. The reason is clear: McDonough's Tornado had been successfully intercepted by a *sveno* (flight) of four MiG-15s from the 523rd Fighter Aviation Regiment near Andong. According to

Starshi Lieutenant Aleksandr F. Andrianov, the Russians scrambled jets around noontime to engage American F-51s that had been active near the river. Flying at low altitude, the Russian pilots noticed a set of contrails above them and, after reporting their sighting back to headquarters, they were ordered to intercept the high-flying intruder. The MiGs rapidly climbed to 30,000 feet in trail of McDonough who, lacking either a tail gunner or tail-mounted radar, remained unaware of their approach. The RB-45C still enjoyed an advantage of distance over its pursuers and forced the MiGs to chase it for 50 miles (80 kilometers) before firing could commence. The Soviets gradually worked themselves to within a few hundred yards of their quarry, then cut loose with heavy cannon and fatally stitched the Tornado in two passes. "As a result of the engagement, the right engine caught fire and the aircraft began losing altitude," Andrianov explained in 1995. "At approximately 3,000 meters or lower, I saw one parachute deploy from out of the plane.... I followed the aircraft in its descent down to 1,000 meters, but there were hilltops at 1,200 meters. When I noticed that one of the hilltops was at a higher altitude than my aircraft, I broke off my pursuit. However, I clearly saw the aircraft crash and explode.... I am not sure if the pilot of the aircraft made an error or not, but if he had not gone into a turn we would still have been chasing him over Korea."[26]

Back at base, the four MiG pilots, flushed with victory, drew cards to received credit for downing 48–015. Andrianov picked the jack of clubs and won a 3,000-ruble bonus for his effort. Many years elapsed before the facts were finally known, but the presumed loss of an expensive jet and its crew to MiGs did not go unheeded at Yokota. Two days after the shoot-down, FEAF historians noted that "RB-45 missions were scheduled with regular TOTs (times over target) which invited enemy interception. It was decided that immediate action be taken to assure staggered target times on all such missions."[27]

Exactly where the crippled Tornado impacted remains speculative and various sources pinpoint the site as either near Sinuiju, on the Korean side of the Yalu, or several miles north of Andong, inside Manchuria. McDonough was apparently the sole surviving crew member and was severely burned when he parachuted into the burning wreckage. The injured pilot lost his boots while extricating himself and spent several days in the freezing snow before being apprehended by Korean authorities. McDonough was in terrible physical condition when brought before Soviet authorities for interrogation. Afterwards, he relayed his plight to Captain Hamilton Shawe, a fellow prisoner who, after being exchanged, informed Air Force debriefers that McDonough was removed from his unheated cell by North Koreans guards, placed on an ox-cart, and never seen again. Shawe believed that McDonough's health appeared so impaired that he did not expect him to live much longer. Thus perished one of the B-45's most memorable personalities whose daring spirit, along with those of Young and Piccuci, reposes in the ghostly court of the Great Khans.[28]

The mystery surrounding the shoot-down of number 48–015 intensifies, however, for there was apparently a fourth passenger on the ill-fated flight. Colonel John R. Lovell, a high-ranking Air Force intelligence officer, apparently accompanied McDonough for reasons that remain unclear. Like McDonough, Lovell was a professional officer with an appetite for danger. Born in Ottuma, Iowa, he graduated from West Point in 1927 and had functioned with Army intelligence during World War II. Lovell remained in the army after the war and developed a flair for espionage. In 1948, while serving as air attaché at the American embassy in Bucharest, Romania, he was arrested, accused of spying, and expelled the following year. Lovell then transferred to the Air Force, where he found welcome work in the Directorate of Intelligence under General Charles P. Cabell. The successful Chinese offensive of November 1950 appreciably alarmed Cabell, who undoubtedly wanted to know why state-of-the-art reconnaissance aircraft missed the presence of 300,000 Communist troops. On Thanksgiving Day, Lovell left his family and boarded a plane bound for Japan. His sudden appearance at Yokota, as Cabell's personal representative, is easily comprehended. The general demanded answers — and Lovell was just the officer to get them. Still, his presence on number 48–015 is surprising since "full bird" colonels were not expected to fly combat missions. When they did, it was usually for the purpose of adding additional medals or ribbons to their collection. Such flights were not uncommon, even in a top secret unit such as Detachment A, and Captain Carrington had carried several such officers on his sundry forays. "A lot of people would come over and want to go riding with us and they'd pin themselves a DFC and all this — higher headquarters people — so we saw a lot of people in the back seat," he recalled. "I say a lot, maybe a handful."

However, the RB-45C lacked arrangements for a fourth passenger. With no seats available, and the bomb bays crowded with swollen bladder tanks, Lovell would have flown the entire mission hunched over in the cabin walkway. Perhaps discomfort was no obstacle to Lovell, a former Olympic boxer and athlete, who possibly prevented the installment of creature comforts to avoid garnering unwanted attention. Sergeant Merle Sollars, Carrington's eagle-eyed mechanic, worked constantly on 48–015 and remains skeptical as to how Lovell positioned himself in flight. Years later he composed a detailed letter to his former commander:

Copilot Captain Jules E. Young, a former P-47 pilot during World War II (Julie Hendrikson).

There are certain things I know about carrying a passenger in a B-45. The man could have flown in the tail gunner position but that was highly unlikely owing to the fact that position had been previously been [*sic*] modified to contain the radar-operated guns you experimented with and the seat had been removed along with oxygen equipment necessary for a passenger. My memory says neither of the three airplanes could have carried a passenger in the tail before doing a lot of restoring. Also, it seems quite unlikely a high-ranking intelligence officer would ride in such an isolated position where his viewing area was limited until after passage.

The only other available position, and the most likely, would be the cabin walkway, but that, too, presents problems. To carry a passenger in the walkway, you will remember a temporary seat had to be installed. Then a seat belt had to be installed and then oxygen lines had to be installed to supply the passenger. Also, my memory seems to say one additional oxygen bottle had to be installed to compensate for the passenger for each two hours of flying. Because of the location of the oxygen bottles, it was no easy task to secure extra bottles.

All of these things had to be done by the ground crew in advance of carrying a passenger. As I recall, it was about a four to five hour job so the ground crew would have to had known in advance that a passenger was going on a flight. Due to unusual takeoff times in the morning, the job would have to have been done the previous day which means that, in a very small and compact unit such as ours, every man would have known in advance about a passenger.... I did, in fact, preflight 015 that day and I was in the cockpit just prior to takeoff. There was no provision for a passenger.[29]

Equally perplexing is Lovell's alleged fate after he jumped from the plane. Fragmentary evidence provided by Russian authorities after the Cold War suggest that he was rounded up by Korean or Chinese officials and interrogated by the Soviets, who were delighted to secure such a high-ranking prize. The officer directing the interrogation, Lieutenant Colonel Pavel Vasilyevich Fironov, found Lovell haughty and arrogant, and watched as a North Korean general ordered him paraded through a local town bearing a placard reading "war criminal." Conscious of his value to the Russians, perhaps Lovell deliberately sacrificed himself by antagonizing irate locals, who then beat him to death. If, in fact, he met his fate in such a truly reprehensible manner, Lovell's demise represents a terrible loss to Soviet military intelligence; it is even more unworthy for a such brave individual.[30] Nonetheless, the murkiness attending Lovell's presence on 48–015 will probably never be resolved. This author concurs with Nancy Lovell Dean, the colonel's daughter, who feels that he was on a classified mission to evaluate the RB-45 program, or to relay personal impressions of intelligence-gathering in the region for General Cabell. Given the gravity of Korean events at this time, either scenario seems plausible.[31] Sergeant John Magum, Captain Simmon's crew chief, noticed an unusual memento left behind at headquarters by Colonel Lovell. "He was from the Pentagon and that's all us enlisted dogs knew," Mangum stated. "There was a bird colonel's cap hanging up there, and it stayed there—I don't know how long."

Chinese intervention also spurred an entirely new chapter in the Tornado's operational history. On November 30, 1950, with Communist hordes bearing down on UN forces, President Harry S. Truman hinted at using nuclear weapons to stop them. He was also gravely concerned that massed Chinese or Soviet air power, launched from bases in Manchuria or Siberia, might irretrievably tip the balance of power in favor of the Communists. If this attack developed, Truman threatened to retaliate by bombing "every airfield in sight" out of existence.[32] The Chinese onslaught and heightened fears of war with the Soviet Union also sparked intense debate as to the RB-45's continuing presence in Korea, specifically, what kind of missions—and where? In light of the ongoing crisis, the aircraft was discussed in the highest military circles for possibly trespassing into "denied territory," namely, Manchuria or the Soviet Union.

As early as October 1950, the possibility of RB-45 overflights figured prominently in discussions held at the Office of Air Force Intelligence. A reconnaissance study commissioned by Colonel William A. Adams openly endorsed violating Soviet airspace with Tornados, then the only aircraft capable of surviving a jaunt through Communist air space. The scheme, however, was quickly sandbagged by a reluctant Cabell. "My forecast is that it would not get by either the A.F. front desk, the Joint Chiefs of Staff (JCS), Defense, or State," he cautioned, so the plan remained on hold for the time being.[33] Air Force leadership in theater, being much closer to the Chinese threat, appreciably embraced an immediacy of action that bureaucrats in Washington lacked. FEAF commander General George E. Stratemeyer pushed strongly for Tornado overflights in a top secret telex dated November 30, 1950. "Furthermore," he warned, "if we are attacked in force by the Communist Chinese Air Force we must be ready to deliver effective counter air effort. If this is to be effective, I feel it is imperative that we be authorized to utilize our RB-45s for reconnaissance of airfields in Manchuria. I feel that the RB-45 reconnaissance of airfields can be accomplished at high altitude, 40,000 feet, without positive identification and probably without detection."[34] Given the relative helplessness of RB-29s and RB-50s in the face of determined MiG opposition, Tornados represented the only viable alternative for securing desperately needed intelligence.

Documents pertaining to overflights are nearly nonexistent, leaving readers to speculate as to how and when FEAF, the Joint Chiefs of Staff, and the White House finally orchestrated Detachment A's secret missions on a regular basis. Fragmentary evidence suggests that initial efforts were undertaken without proper sanction — and in apparent hopes that government officials, recognizing a fait accompli, would simply go accept them. "Early in the war," General Cabell wrote, "I had a discussion with Lieutenant General George E. Stratemeyer, Commander of the Far East Air Force. I suggested, and he agreed, that it was unthinkable that there should be no air reconnaissance beyond the Yalu into Manchuria. The information was vital for theater purposes as well as for use in Washington. We both suspected that if specific permission should be sought from either his superior, General MacArthur, or my superior, General Vandenberg, it would put each of them on the spot. They might, in turn, feel obligated to ask the President and that would put him in a difficult political position. The only solution was to proceed on our own responsibility."[35] A preliminary step for RB-45C overflights happened on February 1, 1951, when operational control of Detachment A transferred from Fifth Air Force to Bomber Command and under General Emmett "Rosie" O'Donnell. Administrative matters were likewise delegated to the 91st Strategic Reconnaissance Squadron at Yokota. Two days later, on February 3, an RB-45C flew the first recorded "special mission," with a follow-up flight on February 19.[36] No mention is made of either objective but, given the course of events in Korea, the crews were most likely photographing airfields in Manchuria. Only after this information was in hand, and at great peril to those obtaining it, could potential Chinese threats be assessed and countered.

In April 1951, a new UN commander, General Matthew Ridgway, voiced concern over the possibility of Chinese air strikes launched from the Shantung Peninsula, then off-limits to American air power. On April 27, 1951, he dispatched an urgent message to the Joint Chiefs, requesting prior authorization for both retaliatory and preemptive action against Chinese airfields as tactical matters warranted: "I have further concluded that I should at once be authorized to conduct air reconnaissance of enemy air bases in Manchuria and the Shantung Peninsula, as an essential preliminary to the effective attack on such bases, if this should be ordered." Discarding their usual reticence, the JCS concurred with Ridgway's assessment and replied, "You are authorized to use the United States Forces assigned to the Far East Command to conduct air reconnaissance of the enemy air bases in Manchuria and the Shantung Peninsula. Such reconnaissance should, if possible, be made at high altitude and as surreptitiously as possible." General Stratemeyer, however, was not content to simply nibble around the periphery. On May 11, 1951, he attended a conference with General Ridgway and pressed his case for detailed radar photography of Manchurian airbases. "Both General Craigie and myself urged approval of the three short missions and the B-45 mission and stated that the remaining two would have to wait for the arrival of the tanker due on or about June 1. After asking if there were any further comments, and there were none, General Ridgway then directed the chief of staff, FEC, to approve my recommendations, to wit: fly the three short missions and the B-45 mission (for scope photography) at my discretion, depending upon the weather."[37] The Tornado was on the cusp of making aviation history again, this time as the first large jet aircraft committed to clandestine, strategic reconnaissance missions on a regular basis. These transpired a full year prior to the first RB-47 Stratojet overflight of Siberia, two years before the English Electric Canberra's strolls above Kaputstin Yar, and five years before the appearance of Lockheed's legendary U-2.

Detachment A's temporary duty assignment had drawn to a close in the previous December (1950), but, as the unit historian chronicled, "the first 90-days had expired with no sign of an extension of orders recalling the detachment to Langley."[38] Until this happy occurrence, the two surviving RB-45s under Captains Carrington and Simmons continued their work load without interruption. FEAF records note that on February 14,

Thnaksgiving Day at Yoktota AAB, 1950: Detachment A pilots Louis Carrington (left) and Al Simmons (right), the man in the center is unidentified (Julie Hendrikson).

1951, an RB-45C flight over North Korea was approached "by three unidentified fighters while flying at 30,000 feet." Thereafter orders arrived to conduct all theater missions from 40,000 feet to preclude any chance at interception. In January RB-45Cs were also directed to assist in air defense tests as intruder aircraft to determine the capability of the Japanese radar net and Air Force F-86 interceptors.[39]

In return, the Sabrejets were also tapped to counter MiGs scouring the skies above Sinuiji. Captain Carrington recalls how the impetus behind escorts originated during a routine flight along the Yalu: "I photographed it from one end of it to the Suiho reservoir and the MiG base at Andong was just across the river. We'd usually start there because the wind was always 250 miles an hour at 270 degrees, so we'd always go east with that big tail wind, plus our speed — those guys would take off and I'd watch them scramble, and they'd catch me before I got to Suiho reservoir — eighty miles. Fantastic speed. I had a Navy captain in the back seat one day when this happened, and I don't know what his job was at Far East, but they said, 'You guys won't go up here anymore without escort.'" Accompanying the high-flying Tornados could represent a problem for the more nimble F-86s. Carrington noted that, "At 40,000 feet, which was where we wanted to be, they couldn't turn, they were heavy with fuel and they'd just spin right out. So they said, 'Okay, we'll escort you — you come down to 30 or you can go up to 40 and go by yourself. Send us a postcard.' So we said, 'We'll be right down to 30!'"[40]

Despite the recent loss of a Tornado, and ongoing struggles at FEAF headquarters to commit its two remaining RB-45Cs to strategic reconnaissance, Air Force officials remained highly pleased by Detachment A's performance over the previous six months. They extolled how both men and machines had acquitted themselves well under trying circumstances and how "the RB-45s have photographed several important targets such as the airfields at Pyongyang, the cities of Chongju, Rashin, and Chongjin plus strip photography of all marshaling yards and sidings along the main rail line between the North Korean capitol [sic] ... and their huge communication hub and supply center at Kanggye." Another glowing assessment proclaimed, "The RB-45 has proved to be an excellent photo reconnaissance aircraft. Detachment A of the 84th Squadron has completed over six months of combat operations and has met FEAF's photo requirements with little trouble."[41]

Naturally, due to the increasingly clandestine nature of Detachment A's activities, its aircraft remained tightly under wraps and off-limits to other units. Staff Sergeant Stadille was struck by the constant security attending Tornados on the airfield. "You couldn't get near the 45s, you could not photograph them," he recalled. "We could go inside 29s and that type of thing, but we couldn't get anywhere near the 45s." Detachment personnel were also increasingly conscious of their elite status, evinced by the new uniforms they received. Sergeant John Mangum maintains that before they left Barksdale they had loaded up "all us enlisted dogs into a Gooney Bird and flew us to Langley field to put us in the blue uniform. And when we got to Japan we were the only people over there in blue uniforms." Sergeant Dackson was also surprised by the reaction to his new blue attire and the resulting confusion. "Up until we got to Japan we were still using the olive drab uniform," he recalls. "Everything was still Army until we got the blue uniform — we were the first outfit to have the blue uniform and when we wore it into town the first time the MPs said 'Who are you?' and 'What are you?' You know they asked for identification and we pulled it out."[42]

Another reason for Detachment A's exceptional performance arose from its hand-picked crews and the greater emphasis on discipline enacted at Yokota. "Prior to that," Sergeant Sollars reflected, "we could call anything up to a major by his first name. That was at Barksdale and it carried over to Langley until we got to Detachment A, and things changed. Everybody liked it. Everybody knew what they were doing. Everybody on Detachment A was qualified in his job; there were no misfits, no one that you were afraid to trust on an airplane to get the job done." In light of their special status, Detachment A also received numerous perks not available elsewhere. According to Sergeant Dackson, "I think there were about fifty people in Detachment A, and the enlisted men in that detachment on that base were the only ones that had a Class A pass, where we could go into town every night." The distinctive uniforms and privileges represented proof of a job well done. On the other hand, the young men of Detachment 2 were in for some bald-faced culture shock during off-duty hours. Sergeant Price recalled when his friend, then dating the mayor of Kofu's daughter, invited him to spent the weekend at a swank hotel. "After a strenuous night of fun we staggered down to the hot springs and dove in. About five minutes later a side door opened and out popped a bevy of young Japanese girls in their birthday suits. To this day I can't explain our reaction. We hollered until a manager came and said something to the girls who in turn giggled all the way out of the Hot Springs area. Unisex bathing was the custom over there, but even at twenty years of age I don't think I could have handled it."[43]

By March 23, 1951, plans for Detachment A and its RB-45Cs had been finalized at Yokota, whereupon the unit was redesignated Detachment 2 and formally transferred to the Strategic Air Command. Furthermore, it now operated under the aegis of the 91st Strategic Reconnaissance Wing, which had originally been slated to receive Tornados when the war broke out. The parent unit was currently at Barksdale training crews who, in turn, would be rotated to and from Japan on a regular basis. The transfer to SAC reflects the expanded role in which RB-45Cs were to play for the rest of the war. "This move should prove well-advised as it appears that most of the effort of this detachment had been primarily strategic in nature," one official wrote.[44] The 91st Wing historian also trumpeted how "The morale of the Detachment is still quite high, and discipline has been excellent, since the transfer into SAC has been accomplished." A somewhat contrarian assessment to all this is proffered by Sergeant Dackson: "We became Detachment 2 and we were told, very matter of factly, 'Your new commanding general is Curtis E. LeMay,' The general response was 'Well ... we're *doomed!*'"[45]

Concurrent with plans for expanded theater reconnaissance at Yokota was growing anxiety that a Tornado might fall into Russian hands. One authority predicted that, "next in priority to the F-86 and F-94, the Soviets would have a primary interest in obtaining technological data on the RB-45." Another study warned, "Special interest would stem from the Soviet's own endeavors to produce successful light jet bombers and from the fact that during any war in the immediate future, the bomber version of their aircraft would understandably be used as a tactical weapon." To this end, Air Force inspectors remained concerned over the lack of tail armament or a warning radar to preclude interception. "The enemy knows the B-45 is unarmed," the study declared. "On one mission, while the F-86s were heavily engaged to the rear, two MiG-15s flew wing-tip formation with the RB-45 before peeling off to make firing passes. So critical do the RB-45 pilots regard their inability to defend themselves that, as an interim measure, fixed .50-cal machine guns are being installed in the tail."[46] This acknowledged vulnerability had little dampening effect on plans being drawn up for Detachment 2 and their Tornados.

March proved to be the latest productive period for the RB-45Cs. In concert with the RB-29s of the 91st Squadron, they obtained continuous coverage of all bridges along the Manchurian border from Hyesanjin to Sinuiji, characterized as "330 miles of winding turns very difficult to photograph." There also seems to have been a lull in MiG activity at this time, for the only sighting happened on March 31, 1951, when unidentified fighters shadowed a Tornado for 150 miles but did not close. Soviet Captain Victor Abakumov, 324th Fighter Air Division, insisted, "Some of our group met enemy aircraft even before landing at our home field, Andong. One of our pilots even attacked an RB-45 American reconnaissance aircraft, but he had forgotten to charge his cannons and 'fired' on it with his gun camera. The target did not wait for the MiG's cannon to place fire on it, but headed south quietly."[47]

Enemy air activity suddenly spiked the following April, when captains Carrington and Simmons were performing their most active duty along the Yalu River. This month produced a bumper crop of MiG interceptions, as if the Soviets were bidding Detachment A crews a fond farewell before they rotated back to Barksdale. On April 8, 1951, Russian pilots broke through the F-86 escort and aggressively boxed in Captain Simmons.

Dare-devil Captain Charles E. McDonough (left) parties with his men on Thanksgiving Day 1950. He and his crew were shot down by MiG-15s a few days later (Julie Hendrikson).

"During the course of the attack, two MIGs flew abreast of the RB-45C at approximately 300 ft away for about 30 seconds, apparently studying the aircraft for defensive armament," the historian recorded. As the MiGs maneuvered into firing position, Simmons quickly salvoed his tip tanks and commenced violent, evasive turning that brought his altitude down from 40,000 to 21,000 feet. He ultimately escaped unscathed, but the critical shortage of wing tanks complicated future missions. "I think it was Simmons who dropped his tip tanks one day, and that created a problem for us in that we had to switch tanks to the airplane that was going to fly," Sergeant Wilkerson mused. "We were still doing that when we rotated."[48]

On April 9, 1951, Simmons and Carrington waged what was probably Detachment A's most celebrated scrape in North Korean skies. According to Carrington, "One day, over Andong, and right along the bridge that the B-29s bombed all day, a flight of MiGs caught us. Al Simmons had decided that I would fly co-pilot for him; when I looked back there were two MiGs sitting there firing at us. We did not know their exact armament, but I knew it was cannon. I turned around in my seat and was up on my knees with my movie camera. I tried to pull it back but it was hooked on the throttle. As Al would push the throttles and I'd jerk back — I never did get a picture of them. But anyway I told Al, 'Don't move — they're locked on and they'll never hit us from where they are now. *Don't you make a move.*' So the first guy was firing by himself— two F-86s went by him and he yonked up, went back, and bailed out. Then his wingman started firing — same thing, I told Al again, '*Don't ... move ...*' and the navigator could see the tracers going down the centerline of our aircraft. But he exhausted his ammunition and two F-86s made a pass at him and he never let up on the trigger — they didn't hit him. So we went down the river photographing and I think the F-86s were out of fuel — the MiGs also turned back. We finished the mission and went on home. But that was the only time they bothered us." Still, Carrington could not believe the abysmal marksmanship of MiG pilots. Once back at Yokota, he inspected the aircraft closely for possible damage. Sergeant Mangum recalled Carrington's reactions all too well. "I had to get a huge aero stand and roll it around that airplane for him to look, and Carrington declared 'They had to hit us,' but we didn't find one mark."[49]

Sustained combat invariably strained flight crew nerves to the breaking point. Sergeant Price reflected once on how it was "our job was to see off and greet the aircraft before and after each mission. We would check for redline items entered by the crew and schedule maintenance for repairs. After one particular flight, the hatch door opened and there was one frightened navigator. I greeted him and I noticed a cigarette dangling between his lips. He was fumbling without much luck in his flight suit. Finally he said, 'Sergeant, gimme a light.' I reminded him we were on the flight line, a no smoking area. He gave me a look that reminded me that I was a lowly E-5, so I gave him a light and he damn near inhaled the whole stick in one drag. We found out later that they had been jumped by MiGs and barely escaped into a cloud layer."[50]

More than anything, Carrington's encounter demonstrated the Tornado's acclaimed maneuverability in a high altitude turning contest with jet fighters. "Four separate firing passes were made on the RB-45C by the MiGs," the historian wrote. "The RB-45C was flown on this occasion at speeds up to 20 to 25 mph above its Mach number and violent evasive turns were necessary to get out of the stream of cannon shells which were in close proximity of the fuselage."[51] Carrington, while grateful for poor Soviet marksmanship, remained nonetheless perplexed by it. "I have been thinking for fifty years why they couldn't hit us," he mused. "I can take any airplane and turn inside someone else and shoot him —*I learned that in a bomber.* You never shoot at a guy, and the only thing I can think of is that they would not give the Chinese their sight. That's the only thing I've come up with that makes any sense at all because these pilots were Russian. But why they couldn't hit us in a standard rate turn is beyond me, because any American pilot would *kill* them." No further flights over Sinuiju were scheduled that week as the Russians were clearly intent upon bringing down one of the remaining RB-45Cs still in the theater. Moreover, even the heavy screen of F-86s could not prevent them from trying.[52] Happily, a handful of other missions concluded without serious injury and, despite some close calls, the unit historian chortled that "so far the MiGs have failed to hole the RB-45C."[53]At this juncture Detachment A passed its torch to Detachment 2, whose escapades in "restricted airspace" proved equally laudable.

CHAPTER FIVE

Atomic Interlude

"Implementation of this program will give the TAC a limited bomber force capability which they do not have now and will not have for approximately twenty-four months unless the B-45s are utilized to the fullest extent."
— Major General Roger M. Ramey.[1]

More than anything, the Korean War revitalized moribund American defense spending, and the Air Force proved one of the biggest beneficiaries. This sudden influx of funding dovetailed with mounting concern over Soviet conventional superiority in Western Europe, namely, fear that a sudden, overpowering attack might occur while the United States remained preoccupied in Asia. Consequently, the Air Force's response to the problem of Soviet conventional superiority was to develop a new family of nuclear weapons with direct battlefield applications. As early as 1949, the Air Force Office of Atomic Energy (AFOAT) investigated the potential for designing smaller, more versatile fission devices. Previously, notions of atomic warfare centered upon strategic bombing, since existing weapons weighed five tons apiece and required very large aircraft to deliver them. However, AFOAT officers believed that the ultimate defense of Western Europe against communist aggression required a widespread application of tactical nuclear weapons; hence they urged Air Force Special Weapons Center (AFSWC) officials to begin planning for that contingency. Concurrently, another agency, the Weapons System Evaluation Group, compiled a study in November 1949 which listed probable nuclear targets behind the Iron Curtain. It gradually dawned on many military officials that air-delivered tactical nuclear weapons were the most cost-effective way of countering Soviet numerical superiority.[2] This new emphasis on atomic weaponry within Tactical Air Command doctrine completely and irrevocably redefined the B-45's operational history.

The atomic device indelibly associated with the Tornado was the Mark 5 bomb, the first attempt to devise lightweight nuclear weapons for tactical purposes. Work on the design commenced in 1947 when the Atomic Energy Commission (AEC) began casting about for a smaller, more efficient device than the cumbersome Mark III "Fat Man" (Nagasaki–type) bomb then in use. Its size and weight (60-inches in diameter and 10,900 pounds) precluded delivery by anything smaller than a B-29. The Mark 5 weapon was designed to counter this; it was a capsule–fission-implosion device measuring 128 inches long and 43 inches in diameter and, at 3,175 pounds, it weighed less than a third of the "Fat Man." The greatest weight savings came from redesigning the casting, which utilized aluminum instead of steel and employed fewer conventional and nuclear materials in its explosive process. The Mark 5 also contained a 92-point detonation system, as opposed to the 32- and 60-point detonation systems of earlier weapons, which was much more efficient and yielded 40–50 kilotons of explosive force — roughly twice that of the Mark III. The new weapon was originally labeled TX-5, with the X standing for experimental and the "T" (in the design paper's words) for "'tentative' or 'tiny' or something.'" The Mark 5 was first successfully detonated during Operation Greenhouse in the spring of 1951, entered mass production shortly thereafter, and began reaching Air Force stockpiles in November1952. TAC anticipated that its upcoming deployment on jet aircraft would "immeasurably increase the flexibility with which atomic energy can be applied in warfare." The Mark 5 proved itself to be a useful design and it remained in the Air Force weapon inventory for more than a decade before being phasing out in 1963. During this period it was carried by B-29s, B-36s, B-45s, and B-50s but, owing to violent oscillations arising from turbulence in its bomb bay, Boeing's ubiquitous B-47 was rejected as a Mark 5 carrier.[3]

The Mark 5 was also unique for safety and security reasons, since the fissionable core was stored separately under all but combat conditions. Once airborne, a plutonium canister ("baseball") would be manually inserted into the casing through two open panels in the nose; later versions employed an electromechanical device for in-flight insertion (IFI) and arming purposes. The blunt-nosed bomb was also exceedingly squat and Lieutenant George Roos, a pilot with the 4925th Test Group (Atomic), felt "It was an ugly thing. Ballistically, I don't know how that darn thing fell or came close to the target, but it did." To prevent in-flight wobbling, no less than twenty-eight different tail configurations were tested in wind tunnels, after which a large, double-wedge fin tail finally emerged on production models. As the bomb fell, the tail induced a spinning motion which maintained a proper trajectory. The Mark 5 also lacked a parachute retarding system, which meant that it could be safely dropped only between 5,000 and 40,000 feet, while fusing options were restricted to airbursts against soft targets.[4]

Mark 5

Throughout the late 1940s and early 1950s, the basic design and construction of nuclear weapons represented few technical or scientific challenges, yet a multiplicity of overlapping civilian and military agencies complicated their acquisition. Given the large size of prevailing weapons and the general consensus surrounding their use in strategic warfare, few complaints arose prior to 1949. Nevertheless, the process was less than perfect owing to bureaucratic politics, turf

Squat, ugly, and lethal, the Mark 5 bomb was designed to be armed in flight through mechanically actuated doors in the nose section (National Atomic Museum).

wars, and the extreme secrecy surrounding atomic issues. Consequently, Los Alamos Scientific Laboratory scientists, who designed the weapons, did so without consulting military authorities in advance. Air Force officials were therefore denied technical design specifications for new weapons produced, and had little recourse but to reconfigure bomber aircraft to fit the atomic ordnance they were issued. It is no exaggeration to state that a distinct, bureaucratic disconnect existed between designing atomic bombs and delivering them.[5] The B-45 is a typical example. Having originating in 1944, the bomber was constructed with bomb bays too small for accommodating over-sized Mark III and Mark IV weapons which appeared several years later. Figures of the size and weight of these weapons had never been made available to North American engineers. As early as July 21, 1948, an official memorandum warned that "the B-45 aircraft in its present configuration will not carry the main type atomic bomb. It is not feasible, nor practical to modify the B-45 to carry this main type bomb as it will require a redesigned center fuselage center."[6] The first successful test of a Soviet A-Bomb in 1949, the onset of the Korean conflict, and a looming specter of outright war with Russia lent urgent impetus towards more coherent policies that rendered bombs and bombers more compatible. Greater emphasis was placed on promoting more rational discourse between civilian and military agencies involved in the manufacture of either commodity and, consequently, both were now treated as integrated weapons systems.[7]

For the Strategic Air Command, this new policy culminated in Project On Top, tasked with converting all B-29, B-36, B-47, and B-50 aircraft to atomic status, which conversion was pursued by SAC with greater urgency than fighting the Korean War. The Tactical Air Command, a relative newcomer to this business of atomic weapons, also experienced a similar metamorphosis. In August 1950, Air Staff officers drew up preliminary requirements to modify 60 B-45s into tactical nuclear bombers for use in three 16-plane squadrons, with 12 aircraft remaining as spares. This decision evolved through simple recognition that "the B-45 is the only bomber type aircraft available to TAC which is capable of carrying atomic weapons."[8] On October 6, 1950, Headquarters, TAC, alerted the Commanding General, ConAC, that the Air Force Office of Atomic Energy had decreed that mass production of tactical nuclear weapons was imminent. Moreover, both F-84G Thunderjets and B-45 Tornados were chosen as delivery vehicles.

The ability for B-45s to deliver special weapons nonetheless required extensive modifications to be accomplished in a program subsequently christened Project Back Breaker. Preliminary work began in December 1950 when the Air Materiel Command began converting nine B-45As into test aircraft for developing and refining operational techniques. These machines would be outfitted with APQ-24 radar bombing and navigation systems, Norden M9C bombsights, and AN/APN-3 Shoran in pursuit of this mission. The Tactical Air and Special Weapons Commands also obtained two TX-5 prototype bombs apiece for testing and evaluation purposes. Because of extended delays in the manufacture of the Mark 5 weapon, Major General Willard R. Wolfinbarger, commander of Ninth Air Force, proposed modifying a handful of B-45s to carry heavier Mark 4s and Mark 6s, through the simple expedient of fielding atomic bombers as soon as possible. "If the modified B-45s were assigned to TAC," he reasoned, "this command could have a tactical atomic weapons capability well in advance of availability dates of smaller weapons." Wolfenbarger was overruled, and on July 14, 1951, Headquarters, Air Force, formally announced the Back Breaker program, which received a priority second only to SAC's Project On Top.[9]

Back Breaker consisted of two distinct but interrelated phases. The first entailed retrofitting thirty-two B-45As with Mark 5, Mark 7 and Mark 8 bomb-carrying capabilities, along with navigation, radar, and defensive equipment (AN/APQ-24, Shoran, Emerson A-1 tail turrets, various defensive and tail warning radars), and a fuel flow totalizer to maximize consumption rates under the increased weapons load. These machines were to be refurbished and in operating condition no later than April 1, 1952, whereupon the second part of Back Breaker began. This phase, called Project Fandango, created the new 49th Air Division as the only dedicated atomic strike force within TAC. This organization was the brainchild of General John K. Cannon, the new commander of TAC, who envisioned it as a foil to any Soviet drive towards the English Channel. As such, the 47th Bomb Group, which had been resurrected on March 12, 1951, would be accompanied by atomic-armed F-84Gs of the 20th Fighter Bomber Wing and deployed at forward bases in the United Kingdom. For six years they performed as one of the North Atlantic Treaty Organization's (NATO) most potent deterrents against Soviet aggression. The 49th Air Division was also the world's first large jet-bomber force to be deployed outside the United States — another record for the Tornado. How ironic that this aircraft, originally acquired as a training vehicle and continually derided for lack of range and speed, suddenly thrust itself to the forefront of American nuclear deterrent strategy.[10]

Over the following months, B-45s began shuttling to the San Bernardino Air Materiel Area, California, for atomic modifications. North American Aviation was contracted to provide the necessary kits but, as Back Breaker unfolded, it became apparent that electronic subsystems intended for in-flight arming and fusing of the bomb were in short supply. These could only retrofitted to the planes when they became available. Simultaneously, TAC competed with SAC for limited supplies of the highly complicated

The first B-45C — 48-001 — was also the first jet bomber to test drop a live nuclear weapon. Note the cut-out glass pane on the lower chin sections, possibly to accommodate a Norden bomb sight (Phillips Laboratory History Office, U.S. Air Force).

AN/APQ-24 radar system, which occasioned further setbacks and delays. The biggest shortfall proved to be the all-important fuel flow totalizer, intended to maximize range and minimize consumption, which only became available long after the program officially ended. In July 1952, Air Staff officials initiated a new program, Second Call, to enlarge its pool of atomic-capable B-45As available. Consequently, fifteen Tornados serving as trainers with the 91st Strategic Reconnaissance Wing were outfitted with atomic delivery gear and transferred directly to TAC. Despite incipient delays, parts shortages, and technical glitches, the program culminated in yet another major refinement: once the Mark 5 weapon carriage support mounts were relocated to the forward bomb bay area, the aft section received a 1,200 gallon fuel tank. This additional fuel capacity increased the B-45's tactical radius from 830 miles to 1,100 miles. Ultimately, fifty-one Tornados were rendered nuclear-capable by the time Second Call concluded in March 1954.[11]

Throughout this interval, Bill Crowley, North American technical representative, labored at Langley to facilitate the Back Breaker program. He recalled one memorable incident: "We did the first mockup loading in one of the hangars at Langley. We had the airplane jacked all the way up, and we rolled the bomb in, and at that time the cranes to lift it up were inadequate. The big hook that held the bomb was probably fourteen inches wide and about three or four feet long. We finally got it up and hooked and it was locked in — we thought — and suddenly there was a big bang and the next thing I knew I'm standing, looking over a squashed hulk. The bomb group officer was across from me and I can remember his face was white, and the sergeant next to him — his face was white — and I said, 'You guys better sleep this off!' You talk about sweat popping out — we knew there were 100 pounds of TNT in the front area of the missile."[12]

In practice, considerable fine tuning was necessary to make the B-45 and the Mark 5 fully compatible. The solution adopted also reflects the high degree of imagination and spirit of improvisation characterizing Tornado maintenance from its earliest days. "When we first got the mission at Langley, this was a major problem because the damn weapon wouldn't go into the bomb bay," Sergeant Terry Little reflected, "so we called NACA, which was the forerunner of NASA, and they brought their engineers over and they had a lot of great ideas. They could build a pit and put the weapon down there and tow the airplane over it and load it, or they were going to build a ramp and tow the aircraft up and straddle the weapon. Neither of these were economically or operationally feasible. And this is a true story: I had a little airman second in the armament shop with me, and we were looking at it one day and he says, 'Why don't you take the bomb bay door off?' And that was the answer. And we put quick disconnects on the bomb bay doors." As events proved, this would not be the final solution to bomb-loading a B-45.

Other changes were in the wings. TAC, formerly subordinated to the Continental Air Command, became operationally independent as of December 1, 1950. Around this time a handful of officers from the 47th Bomb Group had begun filtering through an intensive atomic weapons course held at the Sandia Laboratory, New Mexico. This practice was formalized through a special mission directive issued on December 27, 1950, and the cadre, drawn exclusively from the 84th Bomb Squadron, became responsible for "testing, devising new techniques, and establishing doctrine that would serve as a foundation for TAC's initial entry into the field of atomic employment." The promulgation of a tactical doctrine was viewed as critical for harmonizing military relationships between "the weapon, its associated equipment, and the delivery system." Not surprisingly, the squadron developed atomic tactics with a composite unit consisting of nine B-45s and seven F-84s, both of which were ultimately deployed in England with the 49th Air Division. In the course of these top secret activities, the 84th Squadron weathered the usual litany of shortages, including trained specialists, bombing ranges, low supply priority, and aircraft modifications that were seldom in place when needed. Still, during the second half of 1951, they managed to drop 639 practice bombs and inert "shapes," roughly half of which were photo scored.[13]

From their training activities, personnel of the 84th Bomb Squadron began forging outlines for Air Force tactical nuclear warfare. They gradually deduced that, as far as B-45s were concerned, the most survivable tactic was approaching and departing target areas in level flight at high speeds and altitudes. They computed that the circular errors of bomb drops between 5,500 and 7,500 feet were half of those which had been released from 25,000 feet, but minimum-altitude deliveries required prompt breakaway maneuvers to negate critical overpressures generated by the blast. This necessitated "a full 2g pull up into a climbing turn of about 3000 feet per minute while maintaining 2gs to a radial heading away from the bomb burst." Simultaneously, crew members were to protect themselves against intense thermal radiation unleashed by the weapon: "One second before burst time pilot and co-pilot should look down and close their eyes to prevent blindness and reduce the possibility of thermal radiation burning the skin behind the goggles; other personnel should cover their goggles with their arms; all personnel should take particular precaution to be certain that all bare skin is covered and that no direct exposed metal parts of the aircraft touch bare skin for at least one minute after the explosion." It was also suggested that the B-45s utilize high speed and high altitude as optimum defensive tactics during the approach to target, as well as available cloud cover when possible. The study concluded by recommending against formation take offs, fast join-ups, and close formation flying because of the potential danger of mid-air collisions.[14]

The actual approach-to-target tactics remained a subject of considerable technical wrangling. As situated, B-45s were outfitted with at least four distinct delivery systems to facilitate their mission. The most accurate system was Shoran (nicknamed "Ronnie"), which could be utilized in all weather conditions, but was restricted to the line-of-sight range of the two ground transponders. The onboard MSQ-1 radar system also proved functional, but was constrained by its dependency on ground controllers, who were themselves constricted to line-of-sight operations. Unlike Shoran, MSQ-1 required only one transmitter, but the target location had to be known and plotted by ground personnel in advance. The ubiquitous APQ-24 radar differed from the above-mentioned units in completely divesting itself of ground control; however, given the variability inherent in radar pictures, it was the least accurate. It was also overly complicated and subject to frequent breakdowns. Sergeant James Kirk, a radar technician with the 85th Bomb Squadron, neatly summarized the challenges facing this essential piece of equipment. "Looking back on it I realize this system had been built on the shoulders of the technology that had emerged in World War II," he noted, "The bugs had been worked out — they knew how to do it; how to get rate motors controlled to where you could keep cross hairs over the target and if you could do that you knew exactly how far you were from the target. Then it became a ballistics problem." Once all these gremlins had been resolved, the APQ-24 became the staple of B-45 bombing operations and a reasonably reliable delivery system.

Rounding up this quartet of delivery systems was the old Norden M-9B bombsight employing World War II-type optical sighting technology. It rated higher than the APQ-24 and between Shoran and MSQ-1 in terms of accuracy, but it was limited by darkness and cloud cover and proved of little use for target identification. A study recommended that all available bombing systems should be evaluated on a mission-by-mission basis and changed according to the dictates of accuracy and equipment. In December 1951, TAC headquarters officers had also formulated extensive plans for fighting the Soviets in Western Europe, and they compiled a list of 123 fixed targets throughout East Germany, Austria, Czechoslovakia, and Hungary. Their priority, in descending order, were airfields, troop concentrations, railheads, oil-storage depots, production facilities, and above-ground munition dumps. Such "retardation" missions had been previously designated to SAC bomber units flying slow and extremely vulnerable B-29s. The faster B-45s enjoyed much better prospect of surviving their missions, which were intended to slow, not stop, Soviet advances by disrupting rear-area, supply, and transportation activities.[15]

Not surprisingly, the officers ordered to undergo "Bomb Commander" instruction at Sandia Laboratories found it a most daunting regimen. "I went to Sandia out in New Mexico," Major Hubert M. Blair notes, "and went through the atomic bomb school and that was the most intensive training I have ever gone through in my life — 30 days. We got there and they showed us a spaghetti factory [blueprint] of the atomic bomb and they said 'When you leave here you'll be able to draw this schematic from memory'— I couldn't believe them. The most intensive course and greatest instructional group I ever worked under." Captain Edward J. Sanderson was similarly struck by security measures attending this endeavor: "My wife didn't even know where I was. We couldn't tell a damn thing about it. You went in that classroom in the morning and you came out in the evening and you couldn't take any papers in and you couldn't take any papers out. Everything had to be up here [points to head]." Perhaps the most eloquent protest was penned by Lieutenant (later major general) Daryl E. Tripp, when he wrote, "This course was almost a Gestapo operation similar to what was imposed on the 'Enola Gay' crews. Security would have watered the eyes of a Senate Select Intelligence Committee of today. We could take no notes. In fact, they went as far as to check the latrines to see if any of us were writing wiring diagrams, barometric pressures, or implosion details on toilet paper for the final exams." Security measures back at Langley were equally intense around the 84th Squadron hangar and parking area, especially in light of activities occurring there. "All entries and departures to and from the guarded area are positively controlled by armed guards and the use of a controlled identification badge," the unit history recorded.[16]

In addition to framing atomic tactics, the Tornado also figured prominently in the nuclear testing program itself. The first four B-45Cs, numbered 48–001 through 48–004, were billeted with the 4925th Test Group (Atomic) of the Air Force Special Weapons Center at Kirtland AFB, New Mexico, where they participated in classified operations. Not surprisingly, the Tornado favorably impressed the pilots assigned to fly them. "No approach drogue chute nor air brakes," Major John D. Hardison cryptically noted. "With power at idle, [it] glided like a sailplane."[17] The first series of tests were designated Operation "Buster/Jangle" whereby number 48-001 (call sign "Rosebud") dropped an experimental TX-7 warhead nicknamed Thor. Previously, a series of six inert drops were conducted on the Salton Sea Range, California, with circular errors averaging 285 feet from the target. On November 1, 1951, the B-45C participated in the last of the five-drop live series, designated "Shot Easy." It lifted off from Kirtland with the bomb in its belly, and made two dummy runs over the drop zone before releasing it from an altitude of 24,500 feet and an airspeed of 350 miles per hour. The resulting blast registered 31 kilotons, while the circular error registered only 200 feet from the target. Interestingly, 48–001 was the first B-45 to employ a "Norden nose" utilizing a Norden bombsight in conjunction with a remote Sperry autopilot. The ensuing mushroom cloud towered to a height of nine miles and was easily seen from Caliente, Nevada, 105 miles to the southwest, "as tall as a 2.3 inch toothpick held at arm's length."[18] The Tornado once again carved its name into aviation annals as the first jet bomber to detonate a nuclear weapon.

In the late spring of 1952, a second series of tests called Operation Tumbler/Snapper unfolded. On May 1, 1952, number 48–001, under the call sign "Cutthroat," participated in the fourth drop, or "Shot Dog," which again delivered a Mark 7 bomb. The device was released from 19,000 feet with the bomber cruising at 273 miles per hour, and exploded with a force of 19 kilotons near Yucca Lake, Nevada. During the bomb run, the Tornado lost all VHF communication with ground units and completed its mission by relying on high frequency radio. What made this live drop so unusual was the degree of military activity on the ground. After the explosion, several truckloads of Marines arrived near ground zero; however, high levels of radioactivity were encountered at 900 yards out, which necessitated a quick withdrawal.[19] The Mark 7 bombs in question were intended for F-84G carriages; nevertheless, B-45s were outfitted with shackles and other equipment to deliver those weapons if necessary.

Compared to more spectacular events occurring in New Mexico and Nevada, B-45 activities back at Langley remained far more routine and dogged by the usual flurry of technical problems and malfunctions. On July 7, number 47–034 suddenly spun in near Floyd's Knob, Indiana, killing one officer. Two crewmen, including aircraft

The mushroom cloud arising from Test Easy, Operation Buster, after being dropped by 48–001 (U.S. Department of Energy).

commander Captain Walter J. Hearn, escaped by parachute, but the fact their ejection seats were inoperative prompted authorities to ground all B-45s for immediate inspection. The following month Tornados flew simulated bomb runs against the Western Air Defense Force in California, and, it was noted, the "Defending fighters had very little success against the B-45 in interception missions." On September 22, 1950, Major George B. Thabault, Captain Raymond L. Fitzgerald, and Major Henry F. Butler also set a cross-country record by flying nonstop from March AFB, California, to Langley in only four hours and 6 minutes. "At the end we had to let down through a thunderstorm," Captain Fitzgerald related. "Instead of making a fast descent as we could, we had to pull it back so we wouldn't shake the airplane to pieces."

Tragically, Captain George T. Hollis was flying 47–028 on October 6, 1950, when it suddenly crashed near Suffolk, Virginia, killing the pilot and copilot. The accident triggered a massive recovery effort that waded through Dismal Swamp looking for survivors, and eight truckloads of debris were ultimately retrieved and sent back for analysis. "It just so happens that I was one of the ones they sent out on a bus," Sergeant William Bombkamp recalled. "They gave us a .45 and put us out into the country. I said, 'What's the .45 for?' and they said, 'That's in case of bears, or snakes, or if you find any part of the airplane, you can signal with three shots.'"[20] Authorities subsequently deduced that a compressor explosion in the number one engine weakened the nacelle area, which tore off and triggered in-flight disintegration of the entire aircraft. All B-45s were subsequently grounded, pending examination of a certain block of J47 engines thought susceptible to in-flight explosions. In this manner a further six Tornados were found to contain no less than nine defective engines, which were removed and replaced. It also dawned on authorities that construction activities near the airfield resulted in an unsafe amount of foreign debris on the runway. Said material could be potentially ingested by taxiing aircraft, thereby contributing to cracked engine blades and compressor explosions. The runways were immediately swept cleared of all such matter.[21]

On the 25th of October 1950, the 363rd Tactical Reconnaissance Group was ordered by headquarters to transfer all but nine of their Tornados to the Strategic Air Command at Barksdale AFB, some of which reverted to the Air Training Command. A month later all remaining B-45s were assigned to the 84th Bomb Squadron for atomic mission purposes. Still, because of the lack of viable light jet bomber aircraft within TAC, discussion also arose regarding a possible successor aircraft to the B-45 (either the Martin XB-51 or English Electric Canberra) in the near future, with many officials questioning when or even if the Tornado could ever fulfill its tactical mission.[22] The problem can be traced to an official lack of clarity regarding the aircraft's intended use — and this two years following its operational debut. In fact, until the adoption of the nuclear strike role, Air Force officials remained muddled over the B-45's precise role. The two choices under consideration were day bombardment or night intruder missions but, because both flight profiles required different equipment and training, no commitment was made towards either.[23] Thus the Air Force, having acquired and maintained several squadrons of Tornados at a cost to the taxpayers of several million dollars, had yet to assign them a formal military mission. This changed only with the adoption of Project Back Breaker.

The new year ushered in further downturns in B-45 activity at Langley. In light of the handful of Tornados still available, wing headquarter officers requested to be relieved from duties associated with Army air defense activities in the Washington, D.C., area.

Operations, meanwhile, remained plagued by subsystem failures, innumerable unsatisfactory inspection reports issued, unresolved technical compliances, and a general lack of
responsiveness from higher authorities. On January 11, 1951, group commander Colonel
Benjamin G. Willis outlined a list of ten pressing technical problems, which he forwarded
to TAC superiors. He delineated faulty alternator drive-pad bearings, a lack of parts for
Shoran navigation and ARW-9 automatic formation release equipment, along with other
small but persistent shortfalls which cumulatively prevented any semblance of routine
operations. "In view of the present critical world situation and the priority missions
assigned to this organization, it is urgently requested that every effort be made to expedite action on the above projects," he warned. "Without these modifications, this aircraft
cannot be considered combat ready."[24] To bomb wing officials entrusted with their deployment, it seemed unconscionable that the Air Force would allow the B-45 project to lan-
guish further through simple neglect. Other problems begged solutions as well. Two years
into its operational life, the Tornado still lacked a viable tail defense, despite repeated
complaint of authorities. Mr. Harold E. Dale, the North American Aviation B-45 project engineer, finally arrived at Langley to explore the problem. Talks initially revolved
around the Emerson A-1 fire control system, still under development, but no further
action resulted. A more serious problem was uncovered with the Tornado's bomb bay
doors. "High speed bombing capabilities by the B-45 aircraft assigned to this headquarters are seriously restricted by in flight vibration and flutter," Colonel Willis informed
superiors. "An aircraft upon which restrictions have been imposed cannot perform the
mission for which it is designed." He urged the immediate addition of bomb-bay door
bumpers, overlap strips, and revised electrical circuitry which had obviated similar problems in the B-45C and RB-45C aircraft. Maintenance efforts were further hampered by
the time consuming and hazardous practice of conveying B-45s in and out of hangars
that were simply too small for them. "On this [matter] no improvement is expected as
the whole matter appears to be a dead issue with the Air Installations section," the historian concluded.[25]

Fortunately, big changes were in store for Langley. On March 12, 1951, the stringent
"economy period" ended and the 47th Bomb Wing was happily reactivated as "the only
operational jet bomber unit in the United States Air Force." Colonel Willis F. Chapman,
who had shepherded B-45 operations since their inception in March 1949, made his welcome reappearance and briefly resumed his old perch. He remained in place until August
1, 1951, and was finally succeeded by Colonel Charles D. Jones. Chapman, more than any
other individual, was responsible for shaking innumerable bugs out of the B-45 program,
guiding it through a difficult gestation, and helping transform it into a viable weapons
system. The aircraft remained unperfected during his tenure and continually hamstrung
by lack of funding and spare parts, but he never received the credit he deserved for per-
severing over a two-year period marked by continual highs and lows.[26] "I thought he was
a good commander," Captain Edward J. Sanderson emoted. "I hated to see him leave."

The 84th and 85th Bombardment squadrons, meanwhile, were transferred back to
their parent unit, while a greatly reduced 363rd Tactical Reconnaissance Group was
shunted over to Shaw AFB, South Carolina. Moreover, a federalized Air National Guard
unit, the 115th Bomb Squadron, was attached to the Bomb Wing, bringing it up to full
strength. Over the next three months prospects brightened further as greater emphasis
on securing spare parts resulted in expanded operations. The biggest changeover from

Langley AFB, Virginia: A lineup of B-45As, colorfully arrayed in their new 47th Bomb Wing livery (National Archives).

this period was when the 85th Bomb Squadron finally phased out the last of its Douglas B-26 Invaders, accepted delivery of fifteen B-45s, and resumed all-jet operations. The unit historian quickly noted how morale throughout the 47th Bomb Wing giddily rebounded, undoubtedly "due to the welcome change to an all-jet, all-bomber unit, rather than the previous combination of jet bomber squadron, conventional bomber squadron, reconnaissance squadron and reconnaissance tech squadron, which had been the case under the 363rd Tactical Reconnaissance Group organization."[27] More time was necessary to winnow out all the bugs completely, but two years of heart-wrenching work began paying off.

The transition proved a happy one. Because the 84th Squadron remained preoccupied by atomic training, the bulk of training and flying activities reverted to the 85th Squadron, whose personnel were already B-45 proficient. By the end of June 1951, all of the B-26s had been replaced by jets. However, the Tornados now trickling into Langley had previously been cocooned while awaiting delivery, and they arrived in unserviceable shape. "The reason for their poor condition was evidently caused by an extended period of storage at the contractors from the date of manufacture in 1947 until actual delivery late in 1951," the historian wrote. Try as they might, the 47th Bomb Wing never got a break. Still, the 85th Squadron flight crews continued training with their Tornados while personnel from the 115th Squadron arrived at Barksdale AFB, Louisiana, to attend the B-45 Mobile Training Unit. Meanwhile, newly arrived aircraft lacked visual bombing equipment and were wholly dependent upon the APQ-24 radar for aiming purposes. When these units functioned poorly at high altitude, technicians determined that they required pressurization for the system modulator kits, parts for which had been ordered from the manufacturer back in May 1950. The requisite equipment fortunately materialized nearly a year later, the sets were modified accordingly, and bombing scores improved commensurately. Taxiing problems also arose after the jets began finding themselves competing for takeoff time with B-26s of the 4400th Combat Crew Training Group, which was also at Langley. It was essential that the jet bombers launch quickly to conserve fuel, so a system of staggered takeoff and landing times was adopted for both units. Sufficient Tornados were also on hand to allow three aircraft for a flyover of Clarksburg, West Virginia, during Armed Forces Day, May 20, 1951. Three additional B-45s were likewise dispatched to Shaw AFB, South Carolina, to participate in firepower demonstrations held at Fort Bragg.[28]

In August 1951, Langley-based B-45s of the newly invigorated 85th Bomb Squadron participated in Operation Southern Pine, a large-scale joint service maneuver. The aircraft completed sixty-five missions during the August 11–12 training phase, with only eight aborts due to weather or mechanical failure. During the ensuing operations phase, B-45s flew 211 sorties and completed 173 missions. Thirty-nine of these were aborted, but only sixteen resulted from mechanical failure. Throughout these proceedings, Tornados executed simulated attacks against "enemy" airfields, railroad bridges, and marshaling yards with considerable success. Their activity also revealed that the Initial Point (IP) utilized was usually too close to the intended targets. High speed turns were sometimes required to correct this anomaly, which often resulted in bombers overshooting their target areas. New directives were then issued: "Bomb runs should be at least four minutes duration or approximately 30 nautical miles." This long-axis bomb run gave Tornado navigator-bombardiers more time to line up on a target without stressful 60 degrees turns. Formations of three to eight B-45s were also employed in formation bombing behind number 47–087, which acted as the lead ship and employed MSQ-1 ground radar and the AN/APW-1 beacon. Results here were also judged satisfactory. In fact, the only problem encountered was spotty communications with Combat Operations due to unreliable teletype machines.[29]

Routine activities dominated the 47th Bomb Group's agenda for the balance of the year. Officers and enlisted personnel of the 84th Bomb Squadron remained preoccupied with their special training activities, while B-45s continued passing in and out of Norton AFB and Kirtland AFB for fitting and testing to meet Back Breaker requirements. The unit historian also commented that test drops using Shoran proved far more accurate than those attempted with the still balky APQ-24 radar system. A training regimen was subsequently enacted to perfect Shoran bombing runs from 15,000 feet. New personnel also joined the 47th Bomb Wing roster to flesh out its component squadrons. Captain Leonard Baer, newly assigned to the 85th Bomb Squadron in the fall of 1951, was delighted after checking out in B-45s, yet he was perplexed about the remaining bomber fleet: "I thought the B-45 was not only outstanding—I had 1,000 hours in B-50s and 2,500 hours in B-29s—and I could not understand *why on Earth* the government was wasting their money building B-50s, when they had a B-45 that was so much better."

Sergeant Mike Columbus, a mechanic with the same unit, also pensively recalled his first flight in the Tornado. "We were taking off and I was riding in the jump seat," he reflected, "And I thought I felt funny and I looked up — and I could see the ground from the canopy. And he did a roll — with me in it — that I remember! My stomach was ... [laughs] that was the biggest scare I ever had."

The rhythm of activity was interrupted only on November 16, when a parade was arranged at Langley. The 84th Squadron contributed several B-45s to a mass fly by: "Reviewing officers were very pleased with the maneuver." The 85th Squadron likewise busied itself with officers passing through their atomic paces at Sandia, while their aircraft returned to Norton for modifications. This left the unit with only four Tornados to conduct their many exercises. Worse, after a long, accident-free period, number 47–064 crashed on December 12, 1951, killing Captain Russell M. Gibbons, Lieutenant Russell E. Leggett, and Captain Melvin W. Knuth. They had departed on a routine navigation flight at 6:00 A.M., and climbed to 25,000 feet without incident. Soon after Gibbons, a veteran instructor pilot, radioed that number four engine fire warning light was illuminated, he shut both right-wing engines down and was proceeding back to base. The craft, however, flew erratically, missed its first landing approach, then circled around for another pass. A nearby Navy tugboat captain subsequently reported that 47–064 descended silently into the frigid waters of Chesapeake Bay. A week later the wreckage was salvaged, but no evidence of fire could be found in either engine. Accident analysts concluded that the B-45, flying with one wing tank full of fuel and the other almost empty, "skidded" while turning, which sloshed fuel away from the booster pumps and inadvertently flamed out engines 1 and 2.[30]

Surprising and entirely welcome news arrived on December 29, 1951, when the 47th Bomb Wing was alerted by Headquarters, TAC, that they were slated for overseas deployment commencing in April 1952 (see appendix). The pace of preparations intensified at every level to meet the upcoming deadline, four months hence. In January the wing received a second notice revising the readiness date to May 20. Alarmingly, at this late date the bulk of B-45s were still at Norton AFB, California, for Back Breaker modifications, so the 47th Bomb Wing was reduced to a combat readiness rate of only 6 percent. The aircraft were then receiving vital equipment, including the addition of chaff dispensers, nacelle-tank keel modifications for auxiliary fuel tanks, and installation of tail gun turrets. To obviate the group's low combat-readiness index, workloads at Norton were ordered redoubled and a seven-day work week was instituted to finish all conversion work no later than March 31, 1952. According to technical representative Harry Pollard, a 33-year veteran of North American Aviation, "We put nuclear capabilities in the aircraft and out they went. I worked seven days a week, 12 hours a day for three months. We were all dead but we made it." The accelerated scheduling worked and by April virtually all of the modified aircraft were back at Langely, where the wing's combat readiness index soared to 72 percent.

Another big change occurred on February 12, 1951, when Colonel David M. Jones replaced Colonel Charles D. Jones as wing commander.[31] "Davy" Jones was known as a cause celebre in Air Force circles owing to his service as Colonel Jimmy Doolittle's pathfinder during the spectacular Tokyo raid of April 18, 1942. As a commanding officer, Jones left his subordinates with differing but indelible impressions. "Davy Jones is a genuine American hero," Captain Raymond Fitzgerald exclaimed. "He's a leader." Major

James Story, however, waxed more circumspect when evaluating his old commander. "We called Davy the 'Black Dragon' because when he got mad you'd better just stay out of the way," Story cautioned. "Then he'd cool off and he'd just be ol' Davy Jones again." Captain Robert Schamber also seconded Story's trepidation by noting, "He was kind of an abrupt guy — he'd let you know right away if you were not doing something right." Such pronouncements simply rolled off Jones, a decorated combat veteran who had flown B-25 Mitchells in Asia and Italy, was captured, and later helped dig tunnels in Germany that allowed POWs to escape. Jones also took quite naturally to this newest North American product, the B-45. "Super," he declared, "very honest performer. Oh, I enjoyed it immensely."

Other activities for this period included thirty-six penetrations mounted against the Eastern Air Defense Command during these simulated attacks, again with predictable results. As Captain Don Orr explained, "Whenever they were running fighter intercepts on us with [F-] 84s or 80s, we could run away from them and turn inside of them — they couldn't stay with us." The Tornados were also sometimes tested against radar-equipped Lockheed F-94 Starfires, demonstrating that these all-weather interceptors could catch them only with afterburners ablaze. But to Sergeant Ray Fleshman, a newly arrived gunner with the 84th Bomb Squadron, these flight activities were anything but routine. He flew his first-ever mission over Harrisburg, Pennsylvania, at 40,000 feet and with F-94s in hot pursuit. "I didn't have a gray hair when I started that day," he reflected, "but when I came back they were starting. It's scary if you've never been up that high." The official report noted that "the high proportion of enemy passes from 5 to 7 o'clock following a stern chase indicates that tail gunners in B-45 aircraft had excellent opportunity for inflicting damage on attackers."[32]

Extreme front view of a Tornado highlights details of the bombardier's position and the excellent view afforded pilots by the tear-drop canopy (National Archives).

During the last two

Posterior shot of a B-45 illustrates the highly canted tailplanes and the tail gunner's bubble. Also note the auxiliary ferry tanks slung under each engine pod (National Archives).

weeks of March, Captain Warren T. Whitmire ventured to San Bernardino, along with 24 maintenance personnel, to expedite ground and flight testing before the Tornados were ferried back to Langley. On his return flight, Whitmire related a humorous incident: "I was once in Denver and got on the runway to go, and a guy pulled up in an F-80 behind me and he says to the tower, '80 on the runway, I'd like to follow *the cow* out onto the runway.' And I said, 'I'm *the cow* on the runway and you can go with me if you want to; line up.' 'Okay, I'll do that.' And I knew what was going to happen to him [laughter]. So I accelerated and pulled the nose up, pulled the flaps up and the gears up and left it down flat to accelerate and ran it right up to 475 miles per hour before I started to climb and did a chandelle on the way. So he says, 'My God, what do you have in that thing?' I said 'Four J47s. Goodbye.'" The B-45s continued humbling many a fighter-jock.

Still, back at Langley, the vexing problem of parking space refused to go away. In fact, the unit historian claimed, "Aircraft are parked so close together that, to taxi a B-45 out for take-off or back in upon return, has become a most exacting science." The issue was partially resolved by assigning specific parking areas for each squadron.[33] Other difficulties still persisted in simply moving the aircraft around. "Of course, we didn't have a tug with a friction clutch like we have now," recalled Captain Bruce Deakin, the 47th's service and supply officer, "Some of these [tug-driving] jockeys would let the clutch out and practically pull the nose gear out from under the airplane. So we had problems with ground handling equipment that was not developed completely."

The satisfactory performance of the wing was suddenly and painfully marred by a rash of fatal accidents. On March 21, 1952, number 47–075 crashed near Paducah, Texas, on a ferry flight from California; the crew of four was killed. According to eyewitnesses, "The plane skidded about 700 yards after it hit, and left a gash ten feet wide and four feet deep in the ground." Exactly a week later, on March 29, number 47–085 lifted off from Langley on a routine training flight, then suddenly dove into the Chesapeake Bay five minutes later.[34] On the 26th of May, only days before the bomb wing's scheduled embarkation, number 47–088 was also lost near Franklin, Virginia, incurring the death of Lieutenants Herbert O. Remington, Jerry O. Causely, and Anthony S. Butler. The aircraft had apparently experienced structural failure during violent maneuvers to avoid a midair collision with another aircraft.[35] Attention had also focused on the B-45's fuel-filter deicing system, for the 47th Bomb Wing had accumulated 15,000 hours in Tornados, in all types of foul weather, without having activated it once. Because this device contributed little to safe aircraft operations, group officials sought permission to remove it, eliminating 150 pounds of deadweight.[36]

Finally, after what seemed an eternity to those manning them, the Air Force decided to formally deploy B-45s to Europe as its first nuclear-strike aircraft commencing in June 1952. This forward-based bombardment mission was not in the scope of tasks for which the Tornado had been originally designed; nonetheless, this extended activity became the role for which the jet bomber is best known. It also proved to be the latest significant chapter in a lengthy operational career and the latest of many aviation firsts. The struggle to make B-45s a viable weapon system, and all its attendant sacrifices over the past three years, had been difficult, even exasperating, but not in vain. In the words of General John D. Stevenson, himself a prime mover behind TAC's new atomic capability, "We were able to do this, however, in a very short period of time, because a priority was established for the original two units, just below the striking forces of SAC. And with this high priority and some splendid personnel, we were able to move ahead on schedule."[37] So, after three years in the wilderness, the Tornado had finally found its aeronautical niche.

CHAPTER SIX

Flying Cartographers

"Our RB-45 Tornados are ready to zoom to any point in the world in a matter of hours."
— Colonel Everett W. Holstrom[1]

The history of RB-45C activity resumes at Barksdale AFB, Louisiana, where the 91st Strategic Reconnaissance Wing had undergone training since it was organized in the second half of 1949. Select flight and ground crews were continually rotating from Barksdale to Langley AFB for B-45 MTU familiarization prior to receiving their own Tornados. However, as the unit historian pointed out, "Due to the fact that there were no RB-45Cs available, training toward the Skilled ratings were delayed." On July 24, 1950, the first three RB-45Cs assigned to the 323rd Strategic Reconnaissance Squadron touched down at Barksdale from California — and were as quickly transferred to the Continental Air Command for the benefit of TAC crews! The nine officers and 22 enlisted men of Detachment A spent several weeks in photo reconnaissance training with the 323rd before departing for Korea.[2] The picture brightened considerably on August 26, 1950, when squadron commander Major Raymond T. Eakes, Captain W.L. Slagle, and Major Robert Recce touched down at Barksdale with number 48–016, SAC's first RB-45C. The new aircraft basked in its celebrity status as more than a dozen generals and colonels visited the air base to catch a glimpse and observe test hops. Spirits rose further on September 10, 1950, when a second Tornado arrived and the Strategic Air Command's first all-jet bomber squadron began forming in earnest. SAC had reached a critical transition point in terms of national security; however, since the long-awaited RB-47s would not be available for nearly three more years, General Curtis E. LeMay pushed Air Staff officials to outfit all three squadrons of the 91st Strategic Reconnaissance Wing with RB-45Cs. He argued that gaining realistic experience with multiengined jet aircraft was essential to the wartime mission of SAC. The idea was well-received, and LeMay's diary noted approvingly how "General Edwards was very enthusiastic over General LeMay's request for B-45s for reconnaissance work, stating that perhaps we could equip with them rather than with B-29s, thereby building up our reserve of jet-trained people."[3]

By October, the 323rd's inventory had expanded to a total of seven jets following the arrival of five more RB-45Cs. These aircraft were manned by select combat crews, who absorbed the rigors of classroom instruction on in-flight refueling and aerial photography techniques. Unit esprit de corps was further bolstered by the issuance of the new blue uniforms "that have been expected for so long." Consistent with SAC thoroughness, a comprehensive study of the RB-45C was initiated by Major Eakes, which praised the aircraft's performance while noting deficiencies in celestial navigation, excessive fuel consumption at low altitudes, extreme cockpit temperatures during ground operations, and abnormally long takeoff rolls in hot weather. The young pilots on the base were nevertheless thrilled by the Tornado's debut. "I was awestruck and about as cocky as you can get," Lieutenant Alvan Barrett declared. "Here's all these old guys running around in lumpy, World War II bombers — and we're going to go fly jets! Of course, the only people who had flown jets were fighter pilots — this was the first four-engine jet in the Air Force." Captain John Mackey shared in Barrett's youthful exuberance. "We were sort of like the forerunners of the jets and we were very proud that everybody else on the flight line was flying old-fashioned B-29s," he exclaimed, "and here we are at one end of the field as a special jet outfit!"

Overall, SAC officers were delighted by their pilot's gradual transition to jets. That stance was further confirmed when the Air Staff formally approved LeMay's original suggestion to equip the entire wing with Tornados, if only as a temporary expedient. "The use of B-45s is an interim measure," they reasoned. "The RB-47 is programmed for the 91st Strategic Reconnaissance Wing, but they are not available at this time." LeMay, who monitored events at Barksdale closely, was likewise pleased by the progress and professionalism of his men. "A memorandum received from the Director of Operations indicates that progress on the RB-45C aircraft has been very successful," his wrote in his diary. "There have been practically no maintenance problems; aircraft are in commission more than pilots are able to fly.... Pilots and crews are enthusiastic about the aircraft, volunteering for missions at any time of the day or night in order to build up their time on it."[4] Another significant page in the Tornado's operational history beckoned to be turned.

It is easy to fathom why SAC pilots took to the Tornado as enthusiastically as their TAC counterparts had done. "It was a fantastic airplane from a pilot's standpoint," Captain Hal Austin gushed. "I loved to fly the airplane ... because after I finished flying the B-45, I flew Boeing airplanes for the rest of my career — the B-47, the B-52, and KC-135. Well, when Boeing built an airplane, they built the thing for a guy about six foot six inches, with arms about four feet long because the throttle throw, as an example, from idle to 100 percent, took a real long arm to reach it. I don't care which airplane you're in — it's a Boeing airplane. Whereas the B-45, the total throw from idle in all four engines was maybe six inches.... The B-45 was a nice-flying airplane, it did everything with relatively fingertip control in comparison to a Boeing airplane, which you had to manhandle."[5] Captain William Kristen also spoke affectionately about the Tornado. "I'd do 500 miles per hour on the deck, start trimming the nose up, and start bringing the engines back, and at idle go to 20,000 feet," he declared. "It was a big fighter plane — if it had power controls instead of boost — it would have been *unbeatable*." Lieutenant Francis Martin concurred in these sentiments: "It was a fabulous airplane. It flew like a dream. It was just fun to fly, a good-looking airplane in my opinion, too ... one of the sharpest airplanes ever built."[6]

In time, SAC pilots gradually encountered one of the B-45s most endearing — and hair raising — qualities, its seeming reluctance to return to earth from high altitude. Sleek and bereft of drag, Tornados literally hung in the sky. According to Lieutenant Jay E. Spaulding, "Once it got into the air, it would keep climbing until the fuel ran out. Forty-five thousand feet was easy to reach and if I remember correctly we had one to about fifty-five thousand one time. The problem was at those altitudes it didn't want to come down. The fuel/air compensation for altitude actually ran the engines at or above cruising speed at those altitudes. It was without dive brakes and the only way to descend without exceeding Mach limits was to raise the nose until it almost stalled, drop the flaps and gear, and open the bomb bay doors. Let it mush down holding the nose high until you got low enough to clean it up and ride the Mach needle down." Spaulding was not alone in observing this peculiarity. "We fussed about the lack of braking from day one with the RB-45," Captain Austin insisted. "You couldn't get it out of the sky."[7]

Pilots also voiced off over another familiar complaint about the Tornado — the excruciating buildup of cockpit heat while grounded, a problem exacerbated by the blazing Louisiana sunshine. Air conditioning had been provided to crewmen but, despite the best engineering efforts, the forward section subjected crews to wide temperature variations. "In the summer it got pretty hot at Barksdale, and the crew-compartment temperature was unbearable," Captain Austin recalled. "Every time the maintenance men put a meat thermometer in there to measure the temperature, the thermometer would blow up. Our maintenance people installed brackets alongside the canopy so we could carry a shade. Even with a shade, it was still hot as Hell when we first got in. So it was our procedure to taxi out, push all four engines to 80 percent to cool down the cockpit, and finally the crew chief would take the shade off the cockpit."[8]

Curiously, when flying at high altitude, the situation was usually reversed. According to Captain Robert A. Schamber, "One problem they have with all multi-crew airplanes is that the pilot and co-pilot sat, in this case, under the canopy and were usually nice and warm, and the navigator, down in the nose, was always hollering for more heat. He didn't have an individual control down there. And this one guy down there kept stomping his feet and kept calling for more heat while, of course, the guys up in the sunshine were too hot as it was. The navigator smoked; he took off his mask and lit up a cigarette — and somehow the oxygen was flowing and lit his mask on fire. So he tore his helmet off and threw it on the floor there, and the pilot looked down and saw this thing burning, and the navigator looked back at him, put his hands over the fire — and rubbed them together!"[9]

By October the number of Tornados at Barksdale had risen to fourteen. Another milestone was also reached that month when the 323rd began pioneering the then delicate art of air-to-air refueling. On October 3, an RB-45C rendezvoused with a Boeing KB-29 tanker of the 91st Air Refueling Squadron some 50 miles southwest of Barksdale. The two aircraft machines made their refueling contact at 10,000 feet, transferred a load of fuel, and decoupled without incident. On October 26, 1950, a second test with an RB-45C and a Boeing KC-97A tanker from Eglin AFB was successfully concluded.[10] These flight tests demonstrated how well adapted Tornados were for aerial refueling, by being very responsive to throttle movements and stable as a rock. Captain Kristen recalled the ease of this procedure: "I would come up behind the tanker where the downwash would stop about fifty feet out. I would put more power on, add twenty degrees of flaps down, break through that and then follow the lights and the instructions from the boom operator. It got so that I knew the position and after that I could fly it in and stay in the green. This airplane was a snap — just pull it in, and take on 6,000 gallons of fuel in about ten minutes." Captain Austin concurred with this assessment: "The air-refueling receptacle was behind the canopy, so the airplane ended right up under the KB-29 tanker and didn't feel the prop wash as much as one did in the newer B-47, with its receptacle in front of the canopy." Lieutenant Spaulding managed to make light of the entire process. "The refueling receptacle was located directly behind the co-pilot's head," he jested. "You tended to hope the boom operator was not a golfer that might mistake your [white] helmet for a golf ball."[11]

The year closed out on a high note for the 91st Strategic Reconnaissance Wing. In November, the 322nd and 324th squadrons were designated all-jet organizations and the B-45 MTU detachment relocated from Langley AFB to Barksdale to facilitate personnel instruction. Systematized training procedures were drawn up for combat crews, with quarterly requirements in flying and photography to maintain their skill ratings.[12] By December the 323rd Squadron possessed 14 RB-45Cs and the 324th had six, while the 322nd operated six older B-45As for training purposes. As an indication of mounting crew proficiency, a large-scale aerial mapping project of Indianapolis, Indiana, was undertaken with satisfactory results. Nevertheless, old tactical problems reappeared when RB-45Cs were intercepted by F-84 Thunderjets that managed to slip in unseen from behind to make tail passes on the unsuspecting bomber. The continuing lack of proper tail defenses, so painfully apparent in Korean operations, reignited urgent calls for remedial action. "Since the mission of a reconnaissance aircraft is to return with photographic information for higher staff planners, the problem of protection other than speed and altitude should be considered," Major Eakes pointed out. "The crew of the RB-45C cannot see at all below the level of the horizontal stabilizer and has difficulty seeing between the 5 o'clock and 7 o'clock positions level since the rear ejection seat obstructs his vision to a greater extent than normally would be expected. This lack of visibility will allow enemy fighters to approach within firing range without detection unless a tail gunner is aboard or some type of radar is made available. This weakness would nullify any advantage in speed, climb rate, or maneuverability that the RB-45C might put to use in order to accomplish a successful mission."[13]

Before this long-standing deficiency could be addressed, big plans were being readied for the 91st Wing. On December 27, 1950, Headquarters, Second Air Force, issued orders to deploy four Tornados and four KB-29P tankers to the United Kingdom on January 10, 1951, for 30 days of operational training under the designation Project Mid-Winter. Because of the lack of jet facilities in the Azores, the RB-45Cs were designated to fly the northerly, "high flight" route over

Close-up of the "duck snout" nose section of the RB-45C (History Office, Air Force Flight Test Center).

Keflavik, Iceland, and Scotland towards RAF Manston, Kent. Significantly, Wright-Patterson AFB, Ohio, was chosen as the staging area to preserve fuel over the long northern route. In the event of tanker problems, the Tornados still possessed sufficient fuel to divert into Prestwick, Scotland, if necessary.[14] All of the squadron's personnel made hasty and excited preparations for the "big jump" to be made in January.

Tornado operations in the United Kingdom form a separate narrative, since the overwhelming bulk of 91st Strategic Reconnaissance Wing remained stateside. By January, the group mustered 22 RB-45Cs and 11 B-45As, and the winter months were passed honing photographic and in-flight proficiencies while operating out of Barksdale. Soon after, flying hours were severely curtailed by a lack of tires, which grounded nine of the RB-45Cs. This glaring shortage incurred the loss of 5,088 hours of flying time for the entire wing. Arrangements were finally made to ship fifty-one tires from various sources, and the problem subsided. Training was further compromised by a lack of D-1 Sextants for celestial navigation; only five were on hand instead of the "assigned" twenty-three. These recurring parts shortages — an old story as far as Tornados are concerned — were gradually overcome and the unit historian happily noted how "the RB-45 has proven attractive to command pilots."[15]

In February it was decided to commit the entire wing to flying as part of a series of Eastern Air Defense Forces area penetration exercises. This was the RB-45C's first maximum effort sponsored by SAC headquarters. On February 8, 1951, sixteen penetration missions were executed with varying results against targets along the eastern seaboard, including New London, Connecticut; Frederick, Maryland; Quonset Point, Rhode Island; and New York City. Due to various mechanical failures, most radar photography was judged "unacceptable," but the visual photography was rated as "fair to good." On February 21, 1951, a second series of missions staged over Kansas City and St. Louis, Missouri; Birmingham, Alabama; and Indianapolis, Indiana. Results were again disappointingly mixed, because "only one aircraft of nine dispatched performed the mission as briefed." Nonetheless, the wing commander, Colonel Joseph J. Preston, concluded that his crews were capable of executing the mission assigned, and the training it imparted was "very beneficial." Foremost among the lessons learned was the necessity of expending fuel as judiciously as possible until in-flight refueling became practicable. Navigator Captain Vance E. Heavilin recalled that, upon returning to Barksdale, the field was "socked in" by fog; consequently, the control tower directed his aircraft to land further east at Summit field, Louisiana. His Tornado was extremely low on fuel but the pilot complied with instructions. "As we were on final approach," Heavilin stated, "the tower called and said they 'wished to inform us that they didn't have any jet fuel on the station.' Dick Miller, our pilot, shot back, "Well, you don't have anything on us — *we don't have any up here, either!*"[16]

Until Tornado pilots learned how to better finesse their fuel consumption, crews sometimes ended up making unscheduled landings in unusual places. In June 1951 Lieutenant Oliver "Snapper" Nasby was executing a reconnaissance sortie from Shreveport to Omaha, Nebraska. He recalled the following:

> We encountered bad weather before air refueling — heavy rain, thunder, lightning and hail —
> which tore off the antennas for our radio, so we lost our means of navigating and contact. We
> flew out of the weather into a clear spot that showed a river and a town of some size, but we
> were better than 35,000 feet and decided that it must be Salina on the Missouri — as far as

the navigator could tell — but it was actually Quincy on the Mississippi. We dropped down, because we saw a field which looked like a mile-long county field to land on, and came back across town trying to read the name on an elevator or something. We came right up Main Street, half flaps, and so low that we had to raise one wing to keep from hitting the steeple on the Catholic Church!

We came straight on out, timed our downwind leg to the airport, waggled our wings, walked the rudder a bit, and they gave us a green light to land. We turned, came in, landed, but burned the brakes up stopping and smoked the nose tires — we were used to a two-mile runway and this is like 5,000 feet. They had to fly in power carts, tires, and brakes. We also borrowed a truck from somebody there and used it as a hard stand to get up on the airplane. And there was that *little doll* sitting there in a cab, and my buddy says, "We might be here a few days," and I think, "I hope so, I'm going to get acquainted." He says, "You'd better be careful or some farmer will put a pitchfork in you."

Nasby ultimately married the "little doll" he met in such an untimely — and unforgettable — manner.[17]

The Tornado chalked up another record when Captain John J. Mackey departed from Fort Worth and cruised the entire distance to Barksdale AFB in only fourteen minutes. "Dallas must be about 300 miles west of Shreveport," he reflected, "and we're just getting settled down when somebody said, 'Hey look, there's Cross Lake!' and I said, 'No, it can't be, we just left Dallas, that can't be Cross Lake.' So we tipped the airplane over and sure enough it was Cross Lake — in other words we had picked up a 300 mile per hour tail wind." Apparently, Mackey reached an estimated 886 miles per hour, "a figure which the Air Force officials modestly admitted was probably a record — at least for that type of plane."[18]

Unfortunately, aircraft 48–028 was destroyed on February 9, 1951, in an engine fire incident near Cherry Point, North Carolina. While cruising at 38,000 feet, Captain Jack G. Emerson heard a muffled explosion from his left nacelle, whereupon he shut down both engines and tripped the CO_2 extinguishers. Molten metal began dribbling from the nacelle as Emerson attempted an emergency landing. While descending, he lost control after the aileron boost failed, and he ordered his crew to jump as the airplane slipped into a flat spin. Captain J.E. O'Neal and Captain Roy L.K Jackman ejected successfully, but Emerson's seat only rose four inches, forcing him to vault over the side. The Tornado impacted near Plymouth and was completely destroyed. All three survivors escaped with only minor injuries. Subsequently, crash investigators found that an alternator-pad bearing failure had severed the hydraulic fuel line, igniting an unquenchable fire. All RB-45Cs were consequently grounded until all alternator drive shafts could be inspected and replaced as needed.[19]

By March, the three squadrons of the 91st Strategic Reconnaissance Wing boasted twenty RB-45Cs and ten B-45As in their inventories. That month also proved productive, with 983 hours flown, including twenty air refueling contacts accomplished. A minor accident with major implications occurred on number 48–062, when Sergeant Wayne M. Allen lit a cigarette in the tail gunner's compartment. It flared furiously in the highly oxygenated atmosphere, burning Wayne severely and forcing him to crawl painfully along the length of the bomber to the cockpit. The pilot aborted the mission and flew home, where the unlucky gunner was admitted to the hospital with 2nd and 3rd degree burns. Thereafter crew members were forbidden to smoke until oxygen levels had returned to normal levels. Disaster struck again on March 21, 1951, as number 47–041 was completing a courier mission from Tinker AFB, Oklahoma. Twenty miles out from Barksdale, Captain Melvin W. Kaiser radioed that he had an in-flight fire and was shutting down two engines. During his final approach, Kaiser suddenly aborted and applied power to the two remaining engines for another go around. The B-45 climbed , then stalled on its left wing and fell 2,000 feet to the ground, crashing just left of the runway. Kaiser, Lieutenant Floyd R. Herberling, and Captain Kenneth. E. Neville all perished. Hours later, the tragedy was compounded when the smoldering wreckage exploded while inspectors were combing through it, killing Sergeant William H. Shelton of the 301st Air Installations Squadron.[20]

April represented a downturn in wing activity, as all the RB-45s and B-45s were successively grounded to replace solenoid valves or any fuel boost pumps accumulating more than fifty hours in service. This time-consuming task was further compounded by the discovery of hydraulic leaks, broken lines, and other difficulties related to replacing pumps. Consequently, the number of training hours dipped below the previous month's level of activity — only 175 hours. Nevertheless, the squadrons collectively logged 708 hours of flying time while assisting the Army Corps of Engineers during flood control efforts along the Knife River in North Dakota. The first mission flown, on April 1, 1951, returned with footage from K-22, K-17C and K-38 cameras that was deemed "excellent." The only excitement during this period occurred on a test hop in number 48–024, on April 28. No sooner had Captain Frank W. Hayslip lifted off from Barksdale than his hydraulics system failed. "[Since] I had no hydraulic pressure," Hayslip recalled, "I called the tower and told them we couldn't get the gear down. Then all the experts got in the tower and told us what to do — none of them said *pray!* So we had to come in and crash land." Anxious moments ticked by as Hayslip circled the field to burn off fuel and then brought his Tornado in with its nose gear down and the mains retracted. On touchdown, 48–024 sparked, settled on its belly, and skidded 5,000 feet down the center of the runway, at which point the canopy was jettisoned for emergency egress. Fortunately no fires broke out and damage to the Tornado proved negligible. Colonel Lewis E. Lyle subsequently explained the accident to General LeMay, assuring him that pilot error was not a factor and that Hayslip did a superior job of landing his aircraft with a minimum of damage. LeMay, notorious for sacking any pilot who damaged *his* aircraft, let the incident pass without comment.[21]

On May 22 and 31, twelve RB-45Cs sortied to obtain radar-scope and visual photography of various targets as a SAC "capability test." Once again, various cities in the upper south and Midwest were targeted. Men and machines performed capably but "the overall success of the mission was considered only satisfactory because of the low quality of some of the initial-point-to-target runs of radar photography." However, a success rate of only 30 percent could not long escape General LeMay's attention — or ire — and it sparked a menacing missive to General T.H. Atkinson, commander of Barksdale AFB. "The unsatisfactory performance of this unit gives me concern," Lemay wrote. "I want you to find out what happened and what you can do to improve the capability of this wing. When you have determined this I want you and the 91st Wing Commander to come to my headquarters with appropriate members of your staffs to discuss this exercise."[22] Nothing like a little chat with the boss, so to speak although, to those so summoned, a visit to LeMay's lair must have been as inviting as the Spanish Inquisition.

Worse still, on May 7, 1951, the wing's busy routine was interrupted by disaster. That day, number 48–030 lifted off on a short training flight from Barksdale to Fort Worth and back. The aircraft had been performing its IP-to-target radar run at 20,000 feet when a suburb of Houston was suddenly showered with Tornado parts. Three crew members, Major Robert C. Reese, Major Jerome M. Rappaport, and Lieutenant Claude L Couk, were all killed in what initially appeared to have been an onboard explosion. Miraculously, pilot Lieutenant Robert L. Hempen was thrown from the plane in midair and survived. According to his accident report testimony, Hempen regained consciousness with the sensation of "being wrapped up inside a tumbling ball of debris and flames when a second explosion took place. This knocked the pilot unconscious for a few seconds and his next conscious thought was that he was away from the main wreckage." Hempen managed to open his chute and survived with only minor injuries. Crash investigators arrived the next day and began reassembling the remains of 48–030 at nearby Ellington AFB.[23] Colonel Lewis B. Lyle, now squadron commander of the 323rd, accompanied the team members and related what they had deduced: "We found one of the bomb bay doors and it had hit something. They had a big bomb bay tank that held something like 1,000 gallons of fuel so it would give us more range. The tank was held in by two stainless steel pins — the tank had dropped down for some reason, and when they reassembled it, instead of putting in stainless-steel bolts they put aluminum. As the airplane was flying along, the tank broke loose, hit the bomb bay doors, and one of the doors got knocked off and hit the tail section. All this happened in only a fraction of a second — and as the airplane turned at 600 knots, it exploded, just tore apart."[24]

In June 1951, some minor reorganization occurred within the 91st Strategic Reconnaissance Wing, which equally distributed thirty-seven Tornados among its three squadrons; hereafter each possessed seven RB-45Cs and five B-45As apiece. This reshuffling placed "B-45-A aircraft in each reconnaissance squadron, which can be used for transition, thereby reducing wear and tear on reconnaissance-equipped aircraft." The move was also done in preparation for enlarging Detachment I in the United Kingdom, now slated to receive a rotating force of seven RB-45Cs, five B-45As, and six KB-29s every ninety days. Despite these expansion efforts, the wing remained well behind commitments in celestial navigation training owing to the persistent shortages of D-1 periscope sextants. Additionally, because Tornados had been deemed an interim aircraft by SAC planners, Boeing RB-47s received first priority for such essential training equipment.[25]

Much of the summer of 1951 passed while preparing Detachment I to deploy overseas, beginning in August. From July 11 through the 17th, the wing also performed flight tests aimed at developing evasive tactics against jet interception. Detachment 2's experience in Korea clearly demonstrated how vulnerable RB-45Cs were to swept-wing fighters such as the MiG-15; mock battles against F-86s further highlighted this reality. A total of seven sorties, at altitudes from 2,000 to 30,000 feet, were staged against Sabrejets operating in pairs, which experienced few problems boxing in Tornados and making "shoot down" passes. Major Louis H. Carrington, the Detachment A veteran, noted, "When the fighters began their pass, a sharp turn was made into the closest pair of F-86s as steep and tight as maneuver stress limits permit. The fighters were definitely superior." Only at 40,000 feet and above did the RB-45 enjoy maneuvering advantages over swept-wing antagonists, with the most effective maneuver being a hard turn in the direction of the attack and scissoring with the attacking fighters if possible. "Although this evasion tactic will not be successful when used," officials noted, "it will make the fighter's job more

A good indication of the RB-45c's photographic capabilities are in this 1950 photograph of Los Angeles from ten miles up. Taken by noted test pilot Chuck Yeager (John Mott).

difficult, thereby giving the RB-45 a better chance of survival." The study concluded by reiterating calls for installing a tail defense or warning radar, and recommending the use of fighter escorts when flying against heavily defended targets.[26]

Between August 3 and August 8, 1951, the wing dispatched a large contingent of men and aircraft to the United Kingdom by stages, while the five Tornados already deployed there rotated home. The remaining RB-45Cs at Barksdale nonetheless accrued 300 hours of flight training, despite this major distraction. Significantly, that same month, a party of Royal Air Force personnel arrived at Barksdale for training in the RB-45C. Three flight crews, headed by squadron leader John Crampton, underwent 120 hours of flying and classroom seminars before transferring, with the rest of the 91st Strategic Reconnaissance Wing, to Lockbourne, AFB, Ohio.[27] This move occurred because Lockbourne was viewed as a better location for supporting sustained operations in Europe. The first Tornado to touch down at Lockbourne was 48–012, piloted by Major Louis H. Carrington and Colonel Joseph J. Preston, the wing commander. September also marked the one-year anniversary of the RB-45C Tornado with SAC, an overview of which was detailed in an "Analysis of Operational Problems" from wing headquarters. It noted how difficulties, mainly operational and training in nature, "stem from the fact that up-to-date operational data for this aircraft is generally non-existent." This condition was an outgrowth of the fact that the RB-45C's rapid deployment had outpaced testing programs at the Air Materiel Command. Nevertheless, the report concluded by noting that, "If highly qualified rated personnel are to be used in the B-45 program, it would seem that much valuable information for future jet operations can be gained from their experiences in this program. It is apparent that experience gained from the B-45 will be most valuable and adaptable to the B-47 program."[28]

The final months of the year proved to be productive ones at Lockbourne, although infinitely more arduous due to the onset of winter weather. In October the wing completed 1,012 hours — 400 more than the previous month — even though one-third of its aerial inventory was deployed abroad. The totals would have been even higher except for a concerted repair effort to eradicate fuel leaks in the RB-45Cs, which consumed 500 man hours. The only other activity of note was the continued presence of RAF personnel attached to the 91st. The fact that Colonel Preston reported to SAC headquarters in Omaha, Nebraska, and personally briefed General LeMay on their status suggests that this was somehow more than a routine exchange. It was subsequently decided to fly the British to Carswell AFB, Texas, where they could receive additional APQ-24 training on B-36s based there. Immediately afterwards the RAF teams returned to Lockbourne for the purpose of flying long-range mission profiles in RB-45Cs. All told, Crampton and his RAF personnel successfully weathered SAC's demanding reconnaissance routine, which culminated in their coveted status as a "combat crew."[29]

British personnel assigned to the elite 91st Strategic Reconnaissance Wing were invariably hand picked and accomplished fliers. Lieutenant Maury Seitz commented upon the excitement of flying with one such crewman following a rash of RB-45C crashes. "I believe most of these accidents occurred because of a flap retraction," he reflected. "I flew with Bill Blair — RAF — on a test flight where we proved it. He actually dived the airplane with flaps until a flap failed — and I saw the B-45 through eight consecutive rolls! I remember yelling out, 'Can I help? Can I help?' and he says, 'No, this bloody thing, its beautiful, let it ride. It's not hurting!' So we lost all our hydraulic fluid on that one ride — we came in and landed and we had to use emergency brakes. I'm up there shutting down the cockpit and not thinking of anything and Jim Deskin gets out and Bill gets out. And all of a sudden I look out the window and here's Jim Deskin jumping up about four feet up in the air waving, 'Get out of there! Get out of there, you stupid kid!' And I was shutting down all the stuff, leisurely walked out to the front door and went to go out the ladder, looked back — and the tire was burning under the fuel tank!"

Throughout November, training for the 322nd Strategic Reconnaissance Squadron accelerated in anticipation of its forthcoming sojourn to England. On November 21, 1951, the squadron began transferring men and aircraft overseas and, six days later, elements of the 324th Squadron began trickling back into Lockbourne. Among those departing Ohio at that time were squadron leader John Crampton and his RAF crews, who were now operationally attached to Detachment I at Sculthorpe. The wing also participated in a major simulated enemy penetration attack with the Eastern Air Defense Command to test the soundness of the air defense system. Five Tornados performed as aggressors, but two missions were scrubbed because of faulty radar and fuel shortages. "Radar malfunctions have in the past been a source of serious concern to this Headquarters," the historian noted. "This situation is further aggravated by the inability to perform in-flight maintenance on the RB-45C type aircraft." The only other noticeable problem was apprehension over the Tornado's lack of tail defenses. Colonel Preston noted that the new turret installed on B-45As was impractical, due to weight considerations. In addition, he suggested that RB-45Cs adapt the A-model's "fish bowl" canopy to provide a greater cone of vision for the gunner.[30]

The year closed with another major downturn in flying hours — only 532 in December — largely on account of worsening weather. Sergeant Richard Forsberg, an aircraft mechanic, recalled how winter conditions imposed severe hardships on his already overworked maintenance crews. "I can remember when we moved up to Lockbourne, there were no hangars, and how cold it was in the wintertime. They put tents out on the flight line with gas heaters, and we used to spend 24 hours a day out there, sometimes seven days a week. We didn't have hours of work assigned; for instance, when the airplane came back, we just stayed there and worked on it until it was fixed again. Sometimes they even brought food out to us!" Icy runways, low ceilings, and all-around poor visibility rendered flying extremely hazardous, so most of the RB-45Cs transferred to MacDill AFB, Florida, to continue training there.

For Tornados remaining at Lockbourne over the harsh Buckeye winter, conditions militated against man and machine, especially during the delicate procedure of starting the J47s. According to Sergeant Wayne L. McCann, 4211 Armament and Electronics Squadron, "It's *cold* in Ohio — twenty below zero, snow drifts five feet tall. To start one of them you had to use an auxiliary power unit, or APU, which had a four cylinder Lycoming aircraft engine in it, two 28 volt generators, and one 400 cycle alternator. Each engine required 200 amps of at least 28 volts. The power units had to be started in the hangar, hauled out to the aircraft, then plugged into the socket on the left side of the aircraft. When they were ready to start one, we would man fire extinguishers and stand slightly behind to the side of each nacelle and the J47 engines were notoriously hard to start. They had a bad aspiration system in them. What they did was start winding them up with the power unit, and when they got to a certain rpm, they would throw fuel into it, and they'd hit the spark plug to start. Well, they had what you called 'hot starts.' If we saw a puff of smoke come out the back we'd immediately shy away because that meant there was going to be a sheet of flame five or six feet long right afterwards. And five hot starts and you had to pull the engine — that was mandatory. It was an ordeal."[31]

The only notable accident for this period occurred on December 7, 1951, when a crew, flying number 48–043 without a navigator, departed Los Angeles for Barksdale AFB. They apparently got lost en route and could not make a radio-compass approach to their home base; instead they attempted touching down on a small airfield near Stroud, Oklahoma. The Tornado ran out of fuel, rolled off the 2,600-foot runway, and collapsed its nosewheel after hitting a dike. No injuries were sustained, but damage proved extensive and the aircraft was scrapped. It is not known if action was taken against the crewmen, but General LeMay scowled at the thought of losing valuable equipment to anything that even remotely resembled ineptitude. For this reason the loss, and the reasons behind it, were driven home for other pilots. "Proficient and safe flying require that a plan of action be ready and utilized in an emergency," a cautionary article declared. "This pilot had none, and as a result an aircraft was wrecked."[32]

Adverse weather at Lockbourne restricted flying to 640 hours throughout January 1952; consequently the flight crews assigned to MacDill AFB, Florida, continued training there amidst clearer skies. Yet, as number 48–036 returned to Lockbourne on January 3, its number one engine exploded while the plane was climbing to 6,000 feet. Lieutenant James H. McGrath, aircraft commander, shut down both engines on one side but his automatic and manual boost-pump cut-off switches both failed. Consequently, the Tornado began spiraling uncontrollably downwards and towards the densely populated Tampa area. At 3,000 feet McGrath ordered everybody out, whereupon the navigator and a passenger dove from the nose section. However, after the canopy refused to jettison, McGrath shut down engine number four, which supplied the boost system, then he and his copilot gradually wrestled their careening craft back under control. To avoid risking damage to the city, he swung low over Tampa Bay while still flying on one engine. McGrath then ejected his wing tip tanks, and managed to land safely at MacDill. He was subsequently lauded as "Pilot of the Month" for quick and effective action which saved his Tornado and countless lives on the ground. His success was somewhat muted after Major William F. Hughes, the navigator, parachuted into a lake and drowned before rescuers could reach him.[33]

The "all-seeing eye" of many RB-45Cs. This cyclopedian motif lends an air of surrealism to the craft (National Archives).

During February the wing flew 770 hours, even through only eleven RB-045Cs and six B-45As remained on station. This marginal upswing notwithstanding, operations remained impaired by parts shortages, through which an estimated 1,810 hours of flying time were lost. "Although this figure represents a noticeable decline from January's total," the historian noted, "it is still excessively high and tends to illustrate the seriousness of critical parts shortage on Lockbourne Air Force Base." Wing officials, to promote greater use of celestial navigation, also advised Headquarters, Second Air Force, that installation of astrodomes and D-1 sextants in RB-45Cs was still highly desirable.[34] March flying produced another slight increase, with 939 hours flown at Lockbourne. The biggest event that month was concluding Detachment I's activities in the United

Kingdom and a phased withdrawal of the 322nd Strategic Reconnaissance Squadron beginning on March 18, 1952. The last RB-45C reached Lockbourne on March 26, closing a highly successful episode in the history of the 91st Wing. A new unit, Detachment 3, comprised of American and RAF exchange crews from the 323rd Strategic Reconnaissance Squadron, subsequently rotated back to England on a 90-day TDY with little fanfare.[35]

April also witnessed another rise in flying, to 1,224 hours, despite terrible weather and severe flooding along the Missouri River. For this reason a handful of Tornados assumed mapping responsibilities to assist the Corps of Engineers and photographed waterways stretching from the Dakotas to St. Louis. Wing operations also tightened up requirements for pilots and observers, with renewed emphasis on training, especially pre-strike radar photography. Furthermore, authority finally arrived to address the Tornado's tail defenses and extensive testing began with a Bell M-7 turret mounted in number 48–021. However, this productive period was marred by two ground accidents. On April 19, 1952, number 47–047's right main wheel collapsed while taxiing. Ten days later, number 48–039 sustained damaged to its radome after being struck by a jeep.[36] This was followed by another downturn in operations following a nationwide strike in the petroleum industry. Fuel shortages resulted in postponement of a major mission destined to be held in conjunction with the Air Defense Command. The wing nonetheless logged 593 hours of flight time, with RB-45Cs completing several radar mapping proficiency missions as required by SAC's new proficiency regulations. Other flights were undertaken to test and determine the capability of A-5 photo flash cartridge ejectors during nighttime visual photography runs.[37]

The national fuel strike had finally abated by June, and operations soared back to previous levels, with 1,466 hours flown. These flights fulfilled quarterly training requirements for SAC combat crew ratings and completed final testing with the A-5 photo-flash cartridge ejector. Experiments were also undertaken by number 48–021 to ascertain characteristics of the Bell M-7 tail turret, including a trip to Wright-Patterson AFB for accurate weighing. Overall, firing tests held at the Savannah National Defense Gunnery Range were encouraging; the guns produced only a slight nosing down of the aircraft when fired down from a six o'clock position. A recommendation was also issued that "a relief tube be placed in tail gunner compartments. A can would get in the way and would be unhandy to use and store by the gunner."[38] The mid-summer months passed with the usual training routines until being interrupted by Operation Signpost, a major exercise along the northern border staged between Air Defense Command and the Royal Canadian Air Force (RCAF). Previously, the wing had engaged in public relations work by dispatching Tornados for flybys and static displays at Barksdale, Turner, MacDill, Fairchild, Castle, March, Rapid City, and Walker AFB, as part of the AFROTC summer encampment program. On July 27, 1952, General LeMay made a personal appearance at Lockbourne to observe simulated penetration missions. August produced additional flybys scheduled for the Detroit Airport, the American Legion Parade in New York City, and Columbus, Ohio, the latter honoring World War II aerial combat ace Don Gentile. The routine continued uninterrupted until September 19, 1952, when the 91st Wing received orders to dispatch four RB-45Cs (Detachment Four) on a 60-day TDY to England.[39]

On September 30, 1952, number 48–034 brushed closely with disaster during an in-flight refueling mission. As Major Francis H. Riggs was approaching a tanker craft over Centralia, Illinois, a loud thud was heard, followed by fire lights on engine numbers one and two. Riggs quickly shut the engines down, fired the CO_2 extinguishers, and watched in relief as temperatures plunged from nearly 1,000 degrees to zero. He coaxed his ailing craft back to home base, only to discover that his nose gear refused to extend. Riggs circled for another try while attempting to get his front wheel to lock. Meanwhile, he was hard-pressed to maintain 150 miles per hour on just two engines with his landing gear fully extended; nevertheless, he managed to bring the Tornado home safely. For quick reactions that saved his airplane and crew, Riggs received a written commendation from General LeMay. Subsequent investigations by the aircraft accident board concluded that without promptly triggering the fire extinguishers, his plane might have exploded in as little as twenty seconds.[40]

The winter of 1952 was another period of transition and tragedy. The number of RB-45Cs deployed at Lockbourne dwindled further after Detachment 4 departed for the United Kingdom on October 21, 1952. Meanwhile, the base hosted the annual SAC Reconnaissance and Navigation Competition, in which two RB-45Cs participated and finished third.[41] Even fewer Tornados were available that month, as several aircraft flew to San Bernardino Air Materiel Area to receive tail turrets. Disaster struck again on October 20, 1952, when number 47–052 rolled down the runway for what appeared to be a normal takeoff. After reaching 160 miles per hour the B-45A suddenly veered off the runway and raced down the shoulder for 3,000 feet until striking a pile of construction debris. The impact collapsed the nose gear, punctured the fuel tanks, and brought the damaged plane to a screeching halt. Before the Tornado could be abandoned, Captain Jack A. Trapp, Captain Floyd B. Wilhelm, Captain Orval V. Fraker, and Sergeant Roger B. Thompson all perished in a fiery conflagration.

Captain Jim Brownlow was standing nearby when 47–052 was incinerated, and he describes the horrific scene: "I was just sitting on the runway when it happened. I was out there in a jeep and saw the crew die in the airplane — they were still strapped in and couldn't get out. Huge fire — the nose gear collapsed underneath and punctured the bomb bay tank and it spilled under the airplane and the whole works went up in flames." Captain Robert A. Schamber also saw the shocking accident: "I think on take off a tire blew out, which would have been a routine matter, but they wandered off the right side of the runway and the nosewheel ran over a small pile of debris — the nosewheel tore off and that in turn ruptured the bomb-bay tanks and the thing was a blazing inferno just that quick. So there were about fifteen kids out there, I guess, who lost their Dads that morning — all four people on board had a lot of kids." Due to the advanced state of destruction, no cause was ever attached by the accident board; therefore the remaining Tornados were not grounded.[42]

Activities throughout November remained sharply curtailed because the bulk of the RB-45Cs remained at San Bernardino to obtain tail turrets. General LeMay arrived at Lockbourne unannounced to attend ceremonies honoring the winners of the reconnaissance and navigation competition previously held in October. Ongoing parts shortages continued vexing the thirteen Tornados still on station, with the unit historian noting that, "since the B-45 type aircraft is no longer in production, it is becoming more difficult to obtain parts for said aircraft." Still, in December Major Roy L. Strong was honored for becoming the first Air Force pilot to log over 1,000 hours in a B-45. On December 9, the wing aircraft also launched several aircraft for Operation Turkey Run against the

Eastern Air Defense Force, with successful reconnaissance missions over Boston. Three days later, aircraft belonging to Detachment 4 returned to Lockbourne, marking the last time SAC Tornados deployed to Europe. As an indication of future wing activities, plans were underway to begin phasing out the 323rd's RB-45Cs with brand-new RB-47s as of April 1953. For this reason SAC headquarters requested permission from Headquarters, Second Air Force, to transfer all of their Tornados to Norton AFB, California, for disposal.[43]

Ferry flights to Norton AFB throughout this period became increasingly routine, some of which required stopovers at Biggs AFB at El Paso, Texas, where the combination of high heat and short runways produced some memorable incidents. Lieutenant Grant Angelus recalled refueling there, where "like a damn fool — I didn't need a full load of fuel. When I took off on that short runway, with full bore on four of those damn J47s clicking away — I wasn't getting any airspeed since it was so damn hot! I finally just forced the plane off the ground at the end of the runway and got about 50 feet in the air, got the gear up, and I'll bet I went ten miles across that desert to get to 200 feet!" On another flight, Lieutenant Maury Seitz mentioned how they "ran off the end of the runway and fricasseed some rabbits; we just had to keep going — I swear we went a quarter of a mile just skipping from the tops of one sand dune to another."

Crewmen pose with the ground handling equipment necessary to start up and maintain the RB-45C (David Menard).

Return flights back to Lockbourne also occasioned their share of misadventures. Captain John Keema remembered one not-so-routine attempt to leave San Bernardino:

We taxied out, when suddenly we stopped and I asked, "What happened?" The tip tank had dropped off. When we went back, they sent some people over from the factory at North American, who put a new tip tank on; we went out again, then drove up and down the run-ways, putting on the brakes and trying to shake this thing off; however, it stayed on. We came back in, filed a flight plan, taxied out and — at almost the identical place — the tip tank fell off again! "*So what do you want us to do now?*" The factory people said they'd take the other tip tank off and fly it to the factory. So we flew the aircraft back to the factory and when we came in and we almost ran off the end of the runway, brakes screeching all the way, and blew both tires. The factory people came out and Captain Auburn asked, "*What do you want us to do with the airplane?*" They said, "*Get out of the airplane and leave it!*" So we did and they made us take a commercial airplane home. That was a funny deal.

The year ended on a tragic note with the loss of two more Tornados. On December 24, 1951, number 47–060 departed on a routine training exercise and was climbing to 5,000 feet fourteen miles out when it inexplicably rolled violently to the right. Major John E. Dougherty, the aircraft commander, described what happened next: "The nee-dle on the turn bank indicator was full over to the right and the altimeter was starting to unwind, going down through 5,000 feet. My next sensation was realizing that I was out in the open air, still with the seat strapped to me. I got away from the seat and opened my chute and the wreckage was coming down around me and I could see pieces all in flames." This harrowing experience proved especially memorable to his copilot, Captain Eugene F. Snyder, then experiencing his first flight in a B-45, which, in his words, "lasted a total of three minutes and ten seconds." He recalled that, "As we climbed out, we were leveling off a 5,000 feet, the aircraft commander had just started to make his call and there was this flash fire in the cockpit. We then proceeded straight ahead for just a few minutes when I noticed the airplane was banking to the right; at that point I started to reach up and help him level the airplane, but there was a big burst of flame off to the right, and the aircraft began cartwheeling around the sky. As it rolled inverted the first time, the canopy popped off and I assumed that the crew was expected to get out. I was very ardently attempting to do this, since it was all on fire, there was fire coming out of the pressurization duct right between my feet!" Fortunately both Dougherty and Snyder survived the crash, although Lieutenant John S. Brace, their navigator, did not. Harry F. Pollard, the North American technical representative, subsequently speculated that the cause of the crash was main spar failure outside of the number four wing tank. He also believed that this defect was complicit in at least four other B-45 crashes.[44]

Equally harrowing was the loss of number 48–039 over Pine Bluff, Arkansas, on Christmas Eve 1952. The aircraft had just completed an in-flight refueling when a fire suddenly erupted in the aft compartment. The aircraft commander, Captain Frank W. Hayslip, recalled his ordeal in detail:

We met a tanker over Louisiana and were refueling; while refueling the boom operator said "Breakaway!" As we backed off and the Boomer said, "Sir, you're on fire!" It was hard to breathe so I turned to look back and it looked like I'd been shot down, with fire pouring out of my tail end. I told my navigator, "Nick, get out!" As he opened the door on the side, it caused the crew compartment to rupture which brought all the fire back there up to and join us. We went through the Martin-Baker ejection seat routine but nothing happened because the canopy would not come off. So the "45" rolled over and started down. Soon everything was shaking, which caused the canopy to come off. I hung upside down until I released the seat belt.

Captain Thurber Hoyt, the copilot, likewise recounted his brush with eternity:

It was the night before Christmas and we had one more flight at Lockbourne. We had to refuel with a KC-97 and my pilot had some trouble refueling. We had several brute force disconnects, which ruptured the fuel manifold behind the copilot, where the navigation equipment was. It caused about 1,000 gallons of JP4 to spill into the compartments, which immediately caught fire. The boom operator told us we were on fire, so we made some sharp turns to verify that we were indeed burning, and then began looking for a base, but none near enough to make an emergency landing — so we elected to bail out. We attempted to fire our ejection seats, which didn't work, then we tried to get the canopy off, but that didn't work either, so we tried all the back up devices and, again, nothing worked. It was indeed time to get out, some way! As the smoke started making us unconscious, the plane turned upside down and started breaking apart. It kicked the canopy off (by this time we had unfastened our seatbelts). We then fell out into the cool night, pulled our ripcords, and fluttered down near Pine Bluff, Arkansas. We were in the hospital for a couple months recovering from our burns.

Fortunately, Hayslip, Hoyt, and their navigator eventually returned to active duty.[45]

The final year of Tornado operations at Lockbourne proved relatively uneventful.

An RB-45C couples with a KB-29 in mid-air. Tornadoes helped pioneer and perfect the art of in-flight aerial refueling that gave them the range necessary to conduct strategic reconnaissance (San Diego Air & Space Museum).

Total flight hours continued fluctuating month by month as the number of RB-45Cs dwindled. In January the total hours flown dipped to 704 largely because all B-45As were grounded following the crash of number 47–060 in December, while several RB45Cs lingered at San Bernardino to receive tail turrets. The bomber versions remained inoperative until their main spars were meticulously dye-checked for cracks. Additionally, owing to mounting unease over combustible, nylon flying suits, the suits were withdrawn "in view of the widespread near-hysteria regarding this item" and replaced by cotton. On the upside, a minor milestone was achieved in January when one of the wing's KB-29 passed the two-millionth gallon of fuel to an RB-45C piloted by Captain William J. Kristen.[46] February also proved routine, save for a near-accident experienced by number 47–055. On February 27, as Major Richard D. Christensen concluded a local test hop, he discovered that his landing gear was inoperable. Repeated lowering was attempted, but hydraulic fluid levels were inadequate for a "down and locked" indication. Consequently, the crew reverted to use of the manual override handle, which dropped the mains but failed to lock the nosewheel in place. Fortunately, North American technical representative Harry L. Pollard was in the control tower, and he advised Christensen to bleed jet fuel from the fuselage-tank sump drain and pour it directly into the emergency hydraulic reservoir. Navigator Major Cecil A. Hubbard then pumped the emergency landing-gear handle until the nose gear light indicated down and locked. Christensen consequently executed a hair-raising landing without brakes, flaps, or nosewheel steering; however, he kept the aircraft squarely on the runway, although rolling to within 25 feet of the fence. For his cogent advice Pollard received an official commendation, while Christensen was inducted into SAC's exclusive "Heads Up Flying Club"—the first B-45 pilot so admitted.[47]

A lineup of RB-45Cs of the 91st Strategic Reconnaissance Wing. The "Box I" tail insignia is prominently displayed (John Mott).

After restrictions on B-45As were lifted in March, wing hours flown again rose, to 1,469, despite the fact that three RB-45Cs were deployed to Korea and others remained at San Bernardino awaiting turrets. Six additional B-45As were deposited at Norton AFB in anticipation of being replaced by the eagerly expected RB-47s.[48] On April 25, 1953, the Tornados became increasingly irrelevant to wing operations once the first Stratojets began arriving at Lockbourne. By June the wing boasted twenty-seven of the sleek new RB-47s. SAC, meanwhile, which had agitated superiors to phase out all existing B-45s from its inventory, finally received permission to transfer them to the Tactical Air Command. Much to SAC's surprise, six qualified combat crews were also ordered to TAC. Headquarters, SAC, protested this move, declaring that this infringed on their ability to carry out the emergency war plan, particularly since the 322nd Strategic Reconnaissance Squadron was converting to RB-47s. Air Staff officials agreed and reduced the number of transferees to two flight crews and sixteen tail gunners. In May, the first six RB-45Cs were released to TAC after reconditioning. These six would be followed by an additional four each month in July, August, and September, with the final aircraft departing in November. Those Tornados, finally sporting tail turrets, were ultimately transferred to the 363rd Training Wing at Shaw AFB, South Carolina.

Another operational incident occurred on June 8, 1953, when an RB-45C piloted by Captain Howard S. Myers sustained an engine fire on takeoff at only 600 feet. He quickly shut down both engines on the left side, fired his extinguishers, dropped his wingtip tanks, and executed a safe landing. For quick thinking, Myers became only the second Tornado pilot nominated for SAC's "Heads Up Flying Club."[49]

By the summer of 1953, any lingering presence of Tornados at Lockbourne was becoming an afterthought; however, SAC's remaining seventeen RB-45Cs still scrambled on an emergency war plan profile mission in early July. Thirteen targets across the South and Midwest were scheduled for reconnaissance coverage. Although four aborts occurred due to radar malfunction, 60 percent of the radar coverage and 85 percent of the visual photography were judged successful. Concern was also evinced that, even after the 91st Wing had divested itself of Tornados, it still remained responsible for equipping and manning the four RB-45Cs still deployed with Detachment 2 at Yokota, Japan; SAC officials petitioned Air Staff planners to relieve them of this task. During August the transfer of the remaining B-45As to San Bernardino was completed, while four RB-45Cs were also deposited there. A month later only a solitary Tornado reposed at Lockbourne, exactly three years after it had become SAC's first multiengine jet aircraft. This holdout finally transferred to San Bernardino on October 4, 1953, closing an important chapter in the history of the wing — and opening another.[50]

In time, B-47 Stratojets became one of the best-known symbols of Cold War aviation, whereas the RB-45C slipped quietly from SAC's inventories and memory alike. Yet, to properly assess the B/RB-45's place in unit history, the 91st Squadron historian succinctly gauged its contributions to the Air Force's experience at handling large, complicated jets: "Perhaps what this aircraft will be most remembered for by people will be the inherent shortage of parts for it (subject aircraft went out of production in 1948), the fact that it was the first multi-jet type aircraft manufactured, was the first multi-jet to cross the Pacific non-stop, thereby establishing another record for this wing, that it was the first jet type assigned to the 91st Wing, that it was an excellent interim aircraft while the RB-47 was being developed and manufactured and will further be remembered as being the first multi-jet assigned to the Strategic Air Command for reconnaissance purposes."[51]

Experience gathered with RB-45Cs insured that SAC enjoyed a successful transition to the longer-ranged RB-47; meanwhile, some pilots still regarded the rakish newcomer with some ambivalence. In fact, many clung steadfastly and affectionately to their old Tornado. "Except for the range, I thought it was a better reconnaissance airplane than the RB-47," Captain John Keema insisted. "It was so much more maneuverable." Captain Angelus also stated, "We used to fly into these bases where nobody had ever seen them before. With no tip tanks and light in fuel, we'd just hold it on the ground and then climb out at a 45-degree angle and just dazzle them. It was just a good airplane." Perhaps Major Louis H. Carrington summarized the general attitude of many Tornado pilots most succinctly: "At the time I was picked to go to RB-47s, I did not like that assignment," he said with a grin. "I was a B-45 man. I didn't want to go."

CHAPTER SEVEN

NATO's Shield

"If there had been a war in Europe, in my opinion, the tactical weapons delivered by the 49th Air Division and SAC would have been absolutely decisive."
— Major General John D. Stevenson[1]

In the summer of 1952, United States nuclear deterrent strategy underwent a para-
digm shift in capability following creation and deployment of the new 49th Air Division. This organization, the handiwork of Brigadier General John D. Stevenson of the
Air Staff, U.S. Air Force, emerged as the Tactical Air Command's first atomic-dedicated
strike force.[2] As the moniker to acquire tactical nuclear weapons — Back Breaker — implies,
its sole function was to "break the back" of any Soviet thrust into Western Europe. To
this end, the 49th Air Division fielded the 47th Bomb Wing under Colonel David M.
Jones, equipped with thirty-one Tornado bombers in two squadrons, and the 20th Fighter
Bomber Wing of Colonel John A. Dunning, which operated eighty-six nuclear-capable
F-84G Thunderjets. B-45As of the 84th and 85th Bombardment squadrons also received
striking new unit liveries of red and yellow stripes, respectively, denoting their special
status as among TAC's finest. The division itself reported to the United States Air Force
in Europe (USAFE) under General Lauris Norstad, as part of the Third Air Force. In this
capacity, they supplanted SAC B-29 units slated to perform deep, all weather nuclear
interdiction raids, thereby confirming TAC's centrality to NATO's defense. As military
analyst Hanson W. Baldwin aptly summarized, "One of the first and most important elements of the defense of Western Europe must be a Retardation Air Force, or atomic air
force, equipped and trained to deliver tactical A-weapons against enemy airfields, supplies, communications, and troops." Thus situated, the 49th Air Division helped offset
the gross preponderance of Soviet ground forces in Central Europe, permitting smaller
numbers of American troops without endangering western security. Success here paved
the way for gradual deployment of thousands of tactical nuclear devices over the next two
decades, a singular reality deterring hostile moves by the Russian-dominated Warsaw Pact
until its demise in 1991.[3]

The 47th Bomb Wing had labored incessantly on their overseas deployment ever
since the alert was raised the previous December. The advance echelon of fifteen officers
and forty-eight airmen departed by troop carrier aircraft on May 2, 1952, arrived at
Sculthorpe two days later, and commenced preparations to receive the rest of the wing.
The main body sailed from Newport News, Virginia, onboard the troopship USS *General
Hahn* on May 21, 1952, and landed at Southampton, England, eight days later. Airman

Ray Fleshman protested the transit, noting, "The Army flew over, the Navy flew over, the Marines flew over, but the Air Force went by boat!" Concurrently, flight crews were rehearsing North Atlantic route navigation, survival techniques, and bail out procedures over water. The B-45s began sorting on June 6 when sixteen departed Langley, with eight scheduled to land at Goosebay, Labrador, while the remaining eight continued on to Keflavik. The following day another sixteen Tornados repeated this process, although the detachment at Iceland lingered several days owing to adverse weather. Still, the "Big Jump" was a memorable event for many crewmen. "We had yellow rubber survival suits which probably would have given us only a few minutes' protection in the North Atlantic," Lieutenant Ray Bowers reflected. "My first sight of our new base amid the green of the Norfolk farm country, looking down through my little window as our four ships buzzed the field, is unforgettable." Both squadrons finally reassembled at RAF Sculthorpe by June 12, 1952. To ensure a safe transit, this was also one of few missions where the jets carried large, 500-gallon fuel tanks under their engine nacelles. The 47th Wing's transfer was 30 days behind the Air Staff deadline but, considering the difficulties encountered and surmounted, it represented a considerable achievement. Their deployment is also a significant historical event, being the first-ever, mass Atlantic flyover by large, jet-powered aircraft and beating out B-47s of SAC's 306th Bomb Wing by a year. The fact that this complicated maneuver proceeded smoothly and without major mishap reflects the highest credit on both the planning and personnel involved.[4] Men and aircraft alike had performed superbly.

The airbase at Sculthorpe, Norfolk, East Anglia, was situated in northeastern England, sixty miles from London and only a few miles from the "Wash," or North Sea. Prior to that, its only significant claim was for being obliterated by the Black Plague during the Middle Ages. Aviation facilities first arose there in 1943, and Sculthorpe briefly hosted a Free French Squadron flying Douglas Boston IIIs (A-20 Havocs), then RAF 2 Group arrived with large numbers of superlative De Haviland Mosquitos. In 1944 use of the field passed over to the British 100th Group, which operated lend-lease Boeing B-17 Flying Fortress IIs outfitted for ECM missions. The immediate postwar period found Sculthorpe handed off to the Strategic Air Command, which enlarged its facilities to accommodate heavy bombers such as the B-29 and B-50. SAC, however, sought newer and larger venues, so Sculthorpe declined in significance and finally reverted to the Tactical Air Command as of May 1951.[5]

Unfortunately for the new tenants, the British Air Ministry tightly constrained what could or could not be done on government property. In fact, any kind of adjustments or repairs were restricted to local union or guilds — and then only after lengthy negotiations lasting several months. As the division historian bemoaned, "American airmen no longer had a free hand in making and improvising those things which were not on hand and could not be requisitioned. Men were told that no partitions could be moved, no electrical wiring, outlets and connections revamped, no painting etc. down in setting up the offices, shops and work areas." Morale shuddered under these impositions, but things improved once airmen readjusted to their new clime and focused upon their tasks.[6] Still, the Spartan arrangements at Sculthorpe were storied within the 47th Group. "I'll never forget when I got there on the 23rd of December, when it was dark and cold by the time we got from South Hampton to that BOQ," Captain Ted Crichton recalled, "and I said, 'This is where I'm going to be living for three years?' It wasn't a Quonset hut, but a cinder block type-structure with no installed heat. I used to wear fur-lined boots!" The gastronomic fare, never exactly enticing, also took a decided nosedive according to Sergeant Ed Byrne. "The food?" he snapped. "I recall a garbage truck pulling up to the mess hall one day, and a sergeant came out and said, 'Are you picking up or delivering?'"

The new base also posed certain operational hazards for B-45s not encountered in the States. According to Lieutenant Bill Sanders, "One of the peculiarities of Sculthorpe — it had an alkaline base under the runway and when it got wet, which was frequently, the stuff would soak up and come through as a scum on the runway. They called it soap scum, I think, and to touch down on that was like being on oil. And a number of them touched down and put on the brakes, and they'd be going down the runway sideways and slide off and get in the mud." This was a phenomenon first observed by RB-45s of the 91st Strategic Reconnaissance Wing deployed there in 1951 and now, with atomic bombers present and at risk, the airfield required immediate resurfacing.

No sooner had the 47th Bomb Wing settled into their new abode than they were put through their paces by Colonel Jones. They had hardly unpacked before several flybys were staged for secretary of the Air Force Thomas K. Finletter, Lieutenant General Lauris Norstad of USAFE, and Major General Francis H. Griswold, Third Air Force. On June 23, 1952, the wing next engaged in Exercise Buster to test combat effectiveness by launching missions against thirty-five targets over West Germany. Owing to various technical inadequacies, only twenty of the strikes were judged successful, which underscored the need to refine communication procedures between the 49th Air Division, USAFE headquarters, and the Third Air Force. The following July, B-45s participated in Exercise Judo, an intensive radar scope maneuver judged completely successful, followed by Exercise Midgen that August to test Shoran capabilities. Due to communication lapses with headquarters, none of the four Shoran beacons ("Ronnies") received advanced warning of H-Hour, so the exercise terminated in failure. In September Tornados and F-84s flew under the aegis of Operation Hi-Ball to test dispersal techniques to satellite fields, which were judged adequate. Lessons drawn from these initial maneuvers highlighted the need for better planning and coordination between various headquarters and their operational control rooms. The approach of winter also heralded the onset of dreadful weather conditions, and greater emphasis was placed on sharpening all

Colonel David M. Jones, who led the first overseas deployment of the 47th Bomb Wing to England in 1952 (National Archives).

aspects of GCA approaches.[7] Only after all these shortcomings had been addressed and remedied could the 49th Air Division rank as a combat ready unit.

Because the wartime mission of the 47th Bomb Wing involved accurately delivering atomic ordnance, flight crews were constantly drilled in so-called White Elephant Missions involving inert "shapes" which simulated the Mark 5 bomb. For want of suitable bombing facilities, this entailed dumping them in the ocean off Norfolk, far from the public eye. Captain Clyde Ream recalled the effect of releasing these heavily weighted items from his Tornado. "It was funny," he notes. "We were the only ones with the nuclear bomb there and had shapes filled with cement that we would drop up the Wash, the range in the North Sea. And when that thing left the airplane it automatically gained about 2,000 feet. It would just pop right up there." Nor were the missions without a degree of political peril to all involved. Lieutenant Daryle E. Tripp stated, "The principal checklist item of emphasis to watch very, very carefully the warning light indicating that the bomb release shackle was securely locked. That glued almost as many eyeballs to it as if it had been an engine fire warning light. Even an accidentally dropped dud 'shape' found in an English hayfield would have invited a feeding frenzy by the London tabloids."[8] Moreover, there should be no illusions as to the Tornado's wartime mission. Due to the inherent short range of tactical aircraft, and the distance to targets that they were assigned, most B-45s, assuming they survived swarms of MiGs and other Soviet air defenses, were simply not returning. After a successful bomb run, most crews would either try landing at the nearest NATO airfield or simply bail out over Warsaw Pact territory and continue their sojourn on foot.

A survey of attitudes reveals that the "one way" nature of B-45 missions wielded surprisingly little effect on the crews of the 47th Wing, despite grim implications for man and machine alike. Lieutenant Walt Collier asserted, "Return was only a cruel joke, since we had no way of getting through all of the radiation patterns that would have been displaced upon the dropping of atomic bombs or the nuclear devices that would have saturated Europe." Yet, most crewmen waxed fatalistic and simply shrugged off whatever fate befell them. "It's what you're getting paid for," Lieutenant Stephen Neile reasoned, "what you signed up to do. Bother you? Sure, it bothers you, but it's not anything you're going to dwell on. You just had to figure out how you're going to be able to accomplish it and still live." Perhaps Major Frank Riggs and his no-frills approach best encapsulates the dedication of the 47th Bomb Wing to their task: "Put your damn head down and go in there, get everything set and do the absolute best job you can — and if they get you in the meantime, that's tough. The job is to get the bomb on target." The 47th Wing knew its business well — and meant it.

Colonel Jones himself may have been relatively relaxed in matters respecting military protocol, but he brooked no foolishness from his high-spirited and youthful charges who, or so it seemed, always found new and better ways of trying his patience. A telling anecdote is related by Lieutenant Neile:

> When we would go and fly our missions out of Sculthorpe, we would come back and call the tower for permission for what we called a "compass check" down the runway. And that means you'd back off and come zipping down the runway at about 25 feet as *fast* as you can go, peel up out of that, then come in and land. Well, everyone was doing it, and Colonel Jones was having a staff meeting and chewing out his staff about something (this is what was told us by the people at the staff meeting at wing headquarters)—and the fellow that I had been co-pilot

with came back from his mission over Germany or the London bomb plot and then back home. And he called in and wanted a compass check down the runway; "Roger, you're clear"—so here he comes roaring down the runway, right by wing headquarters, and Davy Jones is up there lecturing people. It was so loud that he had to stop talking. Then he'd start getting on the people again. About that time I got back from flying a mission and the same thing—came roaring down the runway about four or five minutes later. And, again, he had to stop talking. He was obviously perturbed, but he didn't say anymore. About four or five minutes later our squadron commander at that time, Raymond Fitzgerald, came back from a mission—compass check down the runway—come roaring by. Davy Jones said, "*That's it! I want that pilot in my office in 10 minutes!*"—our squadron commander. Well, they sent a staff car right out, picked Fitzgerald out as soon as he hit the hard stand, and took him right to Jones's office. He stood up there and got his a__ chewed, and didn't say a word, just took it all because Jones obviously thought that the same airplane had made all three passes. Fitzgerald came back to the squadron and immediately called a pilot's meeting. He said, "As of *right now* we'll have no more compass checks down the runway!

Flying in England also mandated some readjustment by American pilots, previously spoiled by the accommodating weather of tidewater Virginia. Here a combination of fog, rain, low visibility, and even lower ceilings made every takeoff and landing an adventure. "The wonderful British weather was as advertised," Captain Donald Orr declared. "It was foggy and rainy and miserable, and you were always on GCA. I remember I took off one night and all you could see is one light ahead—you couldn't see the length of the airplane—and they were parked out there. Those who operated off the field during the day knew the field and could taxi around there all night in a fog because they knew where they were all the time, but the staff people who didn't do that would come out there and have to be guided in to the runway otherwise they'd get lost." Major Edward J. Sanderson also fondly recalled his run-ins with fabled British meteorology. "I remember one time I went down to Turkey for three days," he quipped, "and I came back, and the maid looks at me and she said 'Major Sanderson, you missed summer while you were gone—it was yesterday!'" Perhaps the most cogent observation—from a pilot's standpoint—was rendered by Lieutenant Don E. Feltus. "When you went there and started flying," he declared, "you were either an instrument pilot to begin with, or you became an instrument flier, or you went home in a pine box. There was no alternative, it was just that simple. I wasn't an instrument pilot when I got there, but I was very shortly thereafter."

Relations with nearby British units, while cordial and professional, did have a certain edge—after all, it was *their* island. Lieutenant Nick Hannibal, quartered at Swanton Morely, lived next door to a neighbor whom he reviled as "Banfield the Bastard" for the following incident. Banfield, who worked at a nearby RAF radio operator's school, learned that the 47th Wing's Tornados had been grounded due to extremely foggy conditions. The Britisher unhesitatingly cranked up his ancient Avro Anson and mockingly buzzed Sculthorpe several times without careening into anything. According to Hannibal, "The second time around he dropped a package out of the airplane consisting of a pair of British boots stuffed with Royal Air Force recruiting literature—addressed to me. It said, 'Join a flying organization!' It was a fantastic trick. Well, the ambulances were running around, the fire trucks were running around, and he finally left. After they got the package, I was called up to see Davy Jones. '*What the Hell is going on? What's this all about?*' I told him he was my next door neighbor, he knows we're grounded, and he's just pulling a trick. I mean it was *pea soup*—how he found the tower, I'll never know. I tried to get Colonel Jones to give me permission to run a mission over Swanton Morely and drop some toilet paper on them and he said, '*No — too risky, politically.*'" Sergeant Wayne L. McCann also enjoyed a memorable RAF encounter at Sculthorpe. "I had the pants scared off me one time by a Canberra that came down below the 500-foot level — and it was at the *50-foot* level. I was standing in the doorway, and the Canberra had a unique sound that you couldn't miss. From where I was I could look *down* over the aircraft, and this Canberra came up, over, and down — right across me! We were right in his cross hairs and if he had guns going he could have wiped us out." Naturally, the Yanks took all this good-natured joshing in stride — all the while hoping for a chance to return the hijinks in kind.

Tornado crews labored diligently all summer to increase unit proficiency and operational stamina. Not unexpectedly, more efforts were required to simply wring the bugs out of existing procedures and techniques. In October the 47th Bomb Wing staged Exercise Final Check to gauge B-45s utilizing their APN-3 (Shoran) equipment. A series of tests demonstrated that the aircraft received usable navigation pulses from 25,000 feet and at ranges of 200 miles from the broadcasting station, although reception varied between aircraft. More disturbing and potentially harmful was the shortage of JP4 at Sculthorpe, which forced B-45s to use 100 octane gasoline. No degradation of performance resulted, but there was always the risk of catastrophic explosions while handling or loading such volatile fluid. Experiments were run to see how well Tornados operated while burning British AVTUR (jet fuel) as a substitute for JP4 in the United Kingdom. Initially results proved satisfactory, but the Air Proving Ground at Eglin AFB, Florida, continued running additional tests in the interest of safety. Other issues arose over the limitations imposed on flights carrying nuclear training "shapes," which were summarily restricted to English air space. Wing headquarters protested: "This greatly restricts the amount of training that can be accomplished on these missions, and permission was sought from Third Air Force to carry the weapons while exercising over the Continent." The onset of winter conditions also triggered implementation of weather minimums for B-45s: 500 feet and ½ mile during the day, 500 feet and one mile at night. This took some readjustment, even among veteran pilots. According to Captain Robert Ashby, "One thing about the B-45 is that it was such a stable airplane, which is very good over in England because you're making instrument approaches just about every approach you make. In America you report what is unusual, tomorrow we might have some clouds or rain or something like that. In England they said we might have some scattered bright periods, so *that* was unusual." Consequently, the base weather station was ordered to broadcast more frequently and relay potentially dangerous conditions within three minutes of pilot inquiry.[9]

Not surprisingly, for maintenance crews braving the vicissitudes of an English winter, working on B-45s outdoors made a difficult task even more arduous. According to Sergeant Leonard Satterly, a gun mechanic with the 85th Squadron, "It was cold on the flight line. I can remember trying to replace a booster motor underneath the B-45 on the flight line in the winter — and I could not melt the solder. I could not get the *goddamn soldering iron* hot enough to solder the wire together!" Sergeant John B. Wiltshire found himself in a similar predicament. "I froze to death working on the flight line," he said, "You had to take your hands out of your pockets and you couldn't work with gloves." To many Yanks, Albion was seldom more perfidious than in winter.

The first six months of the B-45s in England proved constructive and accident-free, so USAFE scheduled them to fly in a major winter maneuver. However, on December 14, 1952, number 47–070 suddenly shed both wings over Germany, killing the copilot and a passenger. Sergeant Dale Hamilton, the tail gunner, related his role in the mishap that happened shortly after take off: "All of a sudden I was pinned up against the top of the turret bubble and then pushed straight down onto the little seat I'm sitting on, and I look out to the right and the horizontal stabilizer is bent up. I saw something fly by which must have been the wing, then I felt the G forces. Almost immediately, Major Grovert came on the horn and said, 'We've lost our wing! We lost our wing! Everybody bail! Hamilton, get out!'" The gunner managed to work his way out of the gunner's compartment, but his shroud line tangled on his feet and he tumbled downward in a partially opened chute. Fortunately, he crashed into a tree at an angle, his chute snared a branch, and he survived, shaken but intact. "So for starting off doing everything wrong, *the man* was with me all the way," Hamilton reasoned.

Major Warren T. Whitmire, the wing's leading engineering officer, was called in to investigate the recent crash, resolution of which required some artful detective work. By now several B-45s had been lost on account of structural failure, only this time *both* wings had been shed. Whitmire had suspicions as to what the culprit was and he pursued the matter relentlessly. "There wasn't anything we could do except to search for the wings and we found them pretty close, one of the right and one on the left, so we brought them back to Sculthorpe and we put them in a hangar. Myself, and the people doing the investigation, started looking at them and did not know what had happened. We were held up in our investigation waiting for people from the Safety Office in California, and a representative from North American Aviation. We felt that we had found something that had been killing all the pilots and so we stood down. They came in and they spent three or four days looking and talking, and they concluded that the airplane had 'over G-ed' on the climb. I was with Grovert all the time and they were about to convince him, 'Well, maybe I did,' when I said, 'Bob, you don't you be influenced by what these people say. You know a 'G' from 'ten Gs,' and you know you were in a climb.' But that's the way he left it, and left and went back to London to go home. In the meantime, I found out where the spars had been cut into by a drill when the airplane was manufactured. Both front and back spars had been almost cut in two, and so we started looking at other airplanes and, sure enough, they were all that way. We called them back from London, and they came in and decided that it was not 'over Gs,' it was fatigue."

All Tornados were immediately grounded pending a complete investigation and, as the wing historian lamented, "The effect of this action on our combat readiness is serious and necessary inspection of aircraft is being performed as outlined in message from Headquarters AMC." The B-45s consequently failed to partake of Operation Red-Flag the following month, a major test of aircraft dispersal tactics in a simulated emergency.[10] Furthermore, any mishap in this sensitive unit, no matter how trivial, harbored unsavory consequences for the commanding officer. "If you had an accident, you were down in London at the front office," Colonel Jones declared. "*You didn't like that*— that was not good. I went down there on a couple of stupid things." In consequence of Grovert's crash and Whitmire's revelations, the B-45s stood idle well into the new year as main wing spars underwent time consuming dye checks for cracks. Then, in a technical innovation, steel plates (locally dubbed "morale patches") were attached on aircraft wings to strengthen them. This modification apparently rectified wing shedding problems, but the 47th Bomb Wing performed little in the way of training until the process was completed. Their prolonged absence from the Air Force order of battle engendered consternation at security-minded NATO headquarters and prompted General Norstad, head of Third Air Force, to offer assurances. "The very temporary nature of this grounding is emphasized in the minds of the people here by the fact that the 49th Air Division has participated fully and effectively in several exercises during the past eight months," he wrote. "[General] Ridgway fully understands that the grounding of the B-45's is a safety precaution, that they would operate with full effectiveness in the event of an emergency."[11]

As this problem sorted itself out, the Tactical Air Command began fretting over the necessity of maintaining high training and proficiency levels throughout the 47th Bomb Wing. They also requested the Air Staff to transfer another eight Tornados and strengthen the squadrons already deployed in England. This demand for additional craft granted new impetus to the "Second Call" program, already underway at the San Bernardino Air Materiel Area, and TAC established new priorities for refurbishing and reconditioning B-45s wherever they could be rounded up. This new order sidelined all B-45 aircraft assigned to towing service until they could be atomic-armed and ready for deployment. Efforts were also underway to equip the 115th Squadron with B-45s in anticipation of their deployment to Europe. TAC officials were subsequently informed that the four Tornados still available had been previously outfitted with Norden M-9C optical bombsights and could not accept APQ-24 radar sets without extensive modification. Manufacturing four new noses would prove both time consuming (12–14 months) and costly, so headquarters decided to exchange them with four B-45A-1s presently employed as towing aircraft. This process required only two weeks and the B-45s in question could then be brought up to Back Breaker standards quickly. At this time USAFE also established a vigorous program to begin an inspection/repair as necessary (IRAN) program for Tornados in the United Kingdom. This mandated all B-45s to be ferried across the Atlantic to Norton AFB, California, on a regular basis, another duty that would have to be assumed by already overtaxed flight crews.[12]

Despite infrequent flying, there was no lack of harrowing activity around Sculthorpe. In late January 1953, the region was beset by gale force winds that inundated low-lying areas of Kent, Essex, Suffolk, Norfolk, and Lincolnshire counties. Literally thousands of families were made homeless by the flood, including personnel from the 47th Bomb Wing residing in the area; seventeen Americans and fifteen British died. One individual, Airman Reis Leming, of the 67th Air Rescue Squadron based at Sculthorpe, personally succored twenty-seven civilians from impending death and received the King George Medal, Britain's highest civilian award. Afterwards, army cooks from the 39th Anti-Aircraft Battalion pitched in to victual the survivors for several days, until they could be safely relocated. Such heroic efforts by Third Air Force personnel did much to cement relations with the nearby populace, who remained favorably disposed towards the Americans, whatever their controversial mission seemed to be. During this storm, gale force winds, measured at 85 knots, had also rattled the aircraft parked at Sculthorpe and four men were assigned to each B-45 to check on them every half-hour. The fact that the Tornados were pointed into the wind with inert 500 pound bombs hanging from their noses to prevent rearing is a good indication of the storm's strength. The only other incident of note occurred on March 9, 1953, when a B-45 tail gunner badly burned himself in a flash fire at high altitude. Thereafter the accident board recommended that smoking be prohibited altogether while airborne in a highly oxygenated environment.[13]

By spring, repairs on the B-45s, totaling 300 man hours per plane, were completed and the wing historian wistfully hoped that "all the 'bugs' have now been ironed out." Another illusion. No sooner had grounding restrictions been lifted in April 1953 than three consecutive J47 engine compressor explosions forced an immediate reimposition. An exasperated Colonel Jones had little recourse but to ground the entire fleet and order all one hundred and twenty-four engines in the entire group removed and inspected for defects. No less than fifty-seven J47s had to be replaced in time for the 47th Bomb Wing to participate in Operation Prophecy, an upcoming and major NATO maneuver. This feat proved a tall order, but maintenance crews of the 47th Wing responded with aplomb, eliciting amazing results. "To the ordinary laymen, this may not seem astounding," the wing historian beamed, "but when one considered the man hours involved in such a project, plus the fact that only five days were available in which to perform this task, the aspect changed to one of unbelief." The repaired Tornados were now available for flying in Prophecy, the first of many Operational Readiness Tests (ORT) inflicted on the 49th Air Division. This intricate maneuver required crews to fly, disperse, and bomb targets from airfields as far away as Norway and Italy. Sortie rates proved more than adequate but, despite Herculean efforts, the B-45s and F-84s barely scored a 50 percent effectiveness rating. More work and practice was needed, especially in securing bombing ranges capable of accurately grading radar bombing runs.[14] Unscheduled, emergency scrambles also highlighted some operational deficiencies. "We had exercises to get every airplane off the ground in fifteen minutes in case of someone flying something nearby," Lieutenant Leonard Baer reflected. "We had several embarrassing cases where pilots took planes off the ground with instruments disconnected."

At some point in these festivities, Colonel Jones performed his most celebrated act as head of the 47th Bomb Wing, which he recalled as follows:

> I remember one time we were at Frankfurt, and we had about 18 or 20 airplanes there, and we were supposed to attack England. The idea was to take off from Frankfurt and go in trail and then at the point of time we would all make a left turn and we'd approach England line abreast, 18 or 20 airplanes.... We get into the air and we were an hour off, as we cleverly figured out after. *"What the Hell do we do?"* We yakked amongst ourselves in the air. "Okay, what we'll do on my signal, everybody execute a right turn and fly for half an hour and make a 180, come back, and then we're all set." Now you can imagine, we knew damn well we got close to, if not over, Russian territory or East Germany. And I imagine that we caused them a little consternation in some of the control centers because all of a sudden here are eighteen B-45s heading east and we flew for half an hour that way [laughter]. Of course, by that time we were in a no-way-in formation. Nobody saw anybody, no one could see anybody. Everybody ran low of juice. Half our planes landed all over England. Didn't hurt anybody, but sure as Hell confused the defenses, I guarantee, including ourselves.[15]

Navigator Robert Davis also fondly recalled Jones' celebrated foray, particularly the return leg:

> We finally turned around and let down as we got near the coast to about 5,000 feet so that we'd be below their radar. We picked up our speed as we got over the water and we were down to about 500 feet, although it was not very good because we were flying through scud. We wound up flying about 50 feet, bumpier than Hell, and went whipping across a small

freighter — and they said we flew right across their deck! It must have been scary for them because they probably never saw us. If they were looking the other direction, coming out of the scud, they'd heard almost like a boom! and then turned around, and we'd be going back into the scud on the other side. So we got over to the coast, pulled up to 15,000 feet, hit our targets, and then landed. No one was intercepted, it was impossible for the RAF to dive down through clouds and level off to within 50 feet — that's not conducive to long life! So nobody picked us up.

Summer arrived and the 47th Bomb Wing remained subject to its usual and steady regimen of aerial exercises. Operation Daddy's Girl was planned as an all-weather capability test using Shoran facilities but, of 155 missions flown, only 55 percent managed to contact ground beacons. Better luck was achieved with Operations Moose Jaw and Sample Copy to gauge night loading proficiency and striking radar targets respectively, both achieving success rates of 81 percent. The intense training was paying dividends. Joint intercept/gunnery missions against RAF Gloster Meteors and Royal Navy Hawker Sea Hawks from West Raynham were also arranged and executed. Once again, the agile Tornados had little problem dispensing with their adversaries. "Numerous times fighters would make a pass at us and due to the maneuverability of the B-45 I would outmaneu-

Fine in-flight study of a pair of B-45As. Note the auxiliary ferry tanks under each engine pod. Tornados were attractive machines from virtually any angle (John Mott).

A gaggle of B-45As flying in tight formation. This was a relatively rare sight in British skies as Tornados constantly flew and trained individual strike profiles (San Diego Air & Space Museum).

ver them and end up on their tail," exulted Captain Robert Ashby, "because I would pull up into a steep climb and turn into them, they went sliding out and I would throw it over on the other wing and drop down behind them ... we could easily outmaneuver any of the fighters at altitude." Still, the close proximity of devil-may-care RAF fighters to Sculthorpe led to some interesting midair encounters. As Captain Dick Hardin recalled, "They had Meteors at West Raynham and when you came down in the soup it wasn't at all unusual to hit jet wash — we didn't see anybody. And if you're on GCA final in a pattern, coming down on a beacon and suddenly hit jet wash, it's disconcerting as Hell. And we blamed it on the blokes and called them up to fuss at them, and they'd say, 'No sweat, Yank, you know the odds are 500 to one!'"

Another pressing problem, the lack of suitable bombing sites, was somewhat alleviated after the Americans gained access to the Luce Bay Bombing Range. The site functioned well until August 28, 1953, when a live bomb aimed by Captain Alfred Hosher sank the target ship, necessitating its closure for three months. December 20, 1953, also heralded the arrival of the 422nd Bombardment Squadron, which had deployed to Sculthorpe without combat ready crews. Consequently, trained personnel were gleaned from the 84th and 85th squadrons to build up its strength. This composite unit then served as the nucleus of the reconstituted 86th Bombardment Squadron, a constituent unit of the 47th Bomb Wing that had been deactivated in 1949. "What they decided to do is that they took a third of each and assigned them to us with a third of ours," Lieutenant Alan McLaren beamed. "Well, we kept our best and we made them give us their best, so obviously we were the best squadron!" Like the other squadrons, Tornados of the 86th received their own flashy livery, this time in blue. The wing also suffered an additional loss on October 8, 1953, when number 47–037, flown by Major Louis B. Panther, Lieutenant Craig E. Crowley, and Lieutenant Robert J. Ford, crashed outside Norton AFB, California, during an IRAN acceptance flight; there were no survivors.[16]

In the course of a rather busy and productive year, B-45s demonstrated their tactical utility by landing and operating from diverse fields in Morocco, Italy, Malta, Germany, Greece, Belgium, Scotland, England, Denmark, Norway, Canada, Iceland, and the Azores. And, while pursing their deterrent mission, they had become a common sight in the skies of Europe — and a reassuring one. To this end the 47th Bomb Wing also conducted public relations missions during Battle of Britain celebrations and arranged static displays at RAF stations where "thousands of British civilians inspected the B-45 Tornado." On a lesser note, number 47–059 became the first B-45A to fly continuously for 1,000 hours without mishap and, as if to underscore his faith in the taxpayers' investment, California congressman Chester E. Holifield boarded one for a well-publicized test hop on August 25, 1953. The 49th Air Division, in its first year of service, posted impressive gains in proficiency and solidified NATO's nuclear deterrent. The unit historian, however, quickly pointed out that "our road toward being the premier air division of the USAF has not been easy.... To have many of these troublesome items brought to our Commander's attention by that diabolical instrument of effectiveness — the Operational Readiness Test — was more than shocking, it was brutal."[17]

The new year began inauspiciously for the 49th Air Division, as its top secret cover was blown by an article appearing in the *New York Times* on January 22, 1954, which accurately assessed its classified role. "It underwent special training at the Sandia atomic training center in New Mexico before arriving here in May 1952," the essay read, then it went on to describe B-45 operations out of Eleusia, Greece, on Russia's vulnerable southern flank. This revelation prompted Brigadier General Stevenson to request that his unit be downgraded to "unclassified" and unnecessary restrictions on his operational planning eliminated.[18] While headquarters pondered his request, the 47th Bomb Wing resumed intensive training activities that spring. Foremost among these was Operation Big Chance, May 1–3, 1954, a complicated endeavor that closely approximated one of the dreaded Operational Readiness Tests. The 84th Squadron Historian noted how "the organization lived in tents, messed from a field kitchen, and flew under some of the worst weather conditions imaginable." B-45s nonetheless executed 70 missions with a 74 percent success rate, while the maneuver was regarded as "the most successful ever placed into execution by this Division."[19]

The wing was enlarged through formal reactivation of the 86th Bombardment Squadron on March 23, 1954, and its crews began circulating through the two senior formations to gain experience. The 84th Squadron also received a distinguished exchange visitor from the RAF, Squadron Leader Gordon D. Cremer, who had first acquainted himself with B-45s at Barksdale in 1949. Cremer and his crew completed nine additional hours of flying before rotating back to their unit. Sergeant James Kirk, a radar technician, also occasionally flew training missions with RAF crews while riding in the tail gunner's compartment. "Listening to them over the intercom was something like out of a World War II movie," he blustered. "You could tell they were British."

The only accident during this period happened in January, when number 47–050 touched down under icy conditions at Wethersfield, ran off the runway, and sank axle-deep in the mud. Two days of work were needed to extract it from the morass. The following month, during Operation Magnaflux, another Tornado was slightly damaged when a nose panel blew out at high altitude.[20]

The balance of 1954 was spent on additional exercises to further hone operational techniques and crew readiness. Among them was Operation Dividend, a major test of United Kingdom defenses held in conjunction with the Royal Air Force, and Operation Nice Try, an extensive series of "Ronnie" simulated strikes which earned a 74 percent rating.[21] The biggest news at Sculthorpe, however, occurred on September 20, 1954, when General Stevenson's request to declassify the 49th Air Division's atomic mission was approved. He now felt at liberty to speak freely about his unit to the British public — who responded with either mild interest or complete indifference. "Our mission previously has been highly classified," Stevenson conceded on December 6, "but now I am permitted to tell you that the 49th Air Division is the main supplier of NATO's atomic potential." Greater publicity was achieved that December when newspaperman Anthony Brown became the first British civilian to receive a guided tour of American facilities and Tornados at Sculthorpe. "These men in olive drab fatigues or blue uniforms fly, equip, and maintain aircraft which can carry bomb units capable of more destructive power than all the aircraft based in the U.K. during World War II," he wrote. " I went to the operations centre. Here the edict is 'Be ready for massive retaliation.'"[22] If there had been any prior doubts, the harsh reality of Cold War deterrence had come home to roost.

The year 1955 ushered in even greater changes and transitions for the 47th Bomb Wing. These began with the usual spate of grueling exercises like Operation Fogbound to test communication systems, followed by Cart Blanche a full-blown NATO atomic scenario. This maneuver required B-45s and F-84s to deploy to outlying bases and launch simulated strikes against "aggressor" forces on the Continent. Men and machines bore up well under duress, although in April landing gear failures on numbers 47–092 and 47–061 forced the grounding of all Tornados until their trunnions were inspected or replaced. An even bigger headache was the continual attrition of trained personnel through rotation back to the Zone of the Interior and their subsequent replacement by inexperienced flight and ground crews. This placed undue hardships on the three squadrons to simultaneously maintain high levels of training, maintenance, and operations. A more dramatic change was the departure of Colonel David M. Jones on June 16, 1955, and his replacement by Colonel Joseph R. Holzapple. Like Willis F. Chapman, Jones became indelibly associated with the B-45 Tornado and his steely resolve proved the underpinning for its success abroad. In three and a half years of grueling activity, he guided the 47th Bomb Wing throughout a seminal phase of its operational history, rendering it a viable factor within NATO's military equation. Jones waxed philosophical about working with the wing, and stressed the importance of dispersing assets for at least seven days in a crisis situation. "I believe that after this period if we have only been partially successful, we will then have ample time to gear ourselves to sustained operation," he wrote. "If we have not been successful, it won't make any difference anyhow."[23]

As it had previously, the Third Air Force placed continuing emphasis on good relations with the British public, and on Armed Forces Day, May 1, 1955, static displays of warplanes were made available at no less than twenty-two bases throughout England. As a further sop to interservice cooperation and mutual respect, plans arose to display RAF machines next to their American counterparts for the first time. In the words of marshal of the Royal Air Force Sir William Dickson, "It will be a splendid opportunity to demonstrate further the close working relationship between our two services." For its part, the 47th Wing allowed a British journalist to fly in a B-45 for only the second time and, once again, the eight-year-old bomber continued winning kudos from impressionable passengers. From his vantage point in the back seat, aviation writer C.M. Lambert conceded, "The B-45 is a puzzling aircraft, and my impressions are all colored by the feeling that it ought to be more difficult than it is.... Yet the B-45 is delightful to fly, steady, light and responsive, and completely straightforward. It can be driven on the ground almost like a car and flown like a much lighter aircraft; it woffles over the hedge at only 130 m.p.h. and is quite happy on a 2,000-yd runway." Still, by this date in their operational history, B-45s were getting somewhat long in the tooth and plans were afoot for a replacement aircraft. Headquarters, Third Air Force, had originally hoped to provide sleek new Douglas B-66 Destroyers once they became available, but a decision arose to supplant them with Boeing B-47Es instead. This transition never came to pass and three years of deliberations elapsed before the tactical torch finally passed over to the Destroyer as originally planned.[24]

Improved Soviet capability for delivering tactical nuclear weapons of their own was also a growing concern by this time, and the Air Force began dispersing its assets across England to render them less vulnerable. Accordingly, the 86th Bombardment Squadron departed RAF Sculthorpe on September 15, 1955, and temporarily berthed at RAF Alconbury in Huntingdonshire, 70 miles distant. The junior squadron had performed admirably in its assigned duties, a fact attributable to the presence of Major Frank Riggs, formerly of the 91st Strategic Reconnaissance Wing, as operations officer. According to Lieutenant Alan McLaren, "Everybody who sees him figures he's a little guy — he stands about five-foot eight, but to me the guy is seven-foot eight because he was a Helluva leader, a Helluva ops officer. He alluded to the fact that if we weren't exactly sure of dropping that bomb on the way in, that we could fly thirty miles, turn around, come back and get it on the way out. If we weren't sure about it that time to go back and try again — and if we weren't sure that time to keep on going and you'd better damn well not come back to the base because *he's going to kill you*— I can remember that particular briefing pretty well!" And, like its parent unit, the 86th Bombardment Squadron enjoyed soaring morale and esprit de corps. Canadian expatriate Sergeant Glenn Ludlow spoke for many when he said, "It was the tightest thing I'd ever run across, and I mean we really were — we felt like it was an 'us against the world' sort of thing. This became very strong when the 86th went all by itself down to Alconbury to open up the base down there. Frank Riggs, who eventually became commander, maintained that 'we were the 86th Bomb *Wing*, because we did everything our way.'"

When it came to operational independence, Major Riggs was not exaggerating. Consider the 86th Squadron's innovative solution to winter conditions at Alconbury. According to Riggs, "I don't know who got the bright idea, but somebody said, 'Let's take those airplanes out there and melt that ice off the runway.' That's what they did! They'd take an airplane out and let it sit for a little, just at idle, and that draft from the tail pipes would eventually make a little open spot. So then you'd get down on the open spot and set your brakes, then pour it on full-bore, and all this ice would come flying off all over the place. So you'd clear off this 500 feet, then you'd clear off this 500 feet. The you'd go down the middle, come in at the right speed, crank that thing down, hold her nose up, and let it fall down by itself, gently ease the brakes until you had 500 feet to really bind the brakes if you had to. Never had anybody go off the end, and it worked like a charm!"

The rest of the year passed in a deluge of continuing exercises like Operations Pogo Possum and Panther Paw to sharpen crew proficiencies with Shoran and APQ-24 bombing before the annual ORT was unleashed upon the wing. Operation Brown Cow, another grueling maximum effort, began on August 24 and ground on through September 2, 1955. It maximized the now-standard routine of dispersing aircraft to satellite fields, then staging mock atomic runs against targets in London or Frankfurt, Germany. By month's end Tornados also sortied as part of Exercise Beware against Royal Air Force defenses, which now utilized superlative Hawker Hunter jet fighters. These swept-winged dervishes were a quantum jump in performance over the straight-winged Meteors and Vampires they replaced. Lieutenant Alan MacLaren recalled one mock engagement that illustrated the Tornado's advancing age. "We got jumped over the Continent by two F-100s and two Hawker Hunters at about 39,000 feet," he noted, "As they made their fighter break on us, Bob Ryan, coordinating with the tail gunner, waited until just as they were getting into their firing position. Bob then racked the airplane up and turned into them, and they didn't have the wing area we had and, of course, when they tried it they'd stall out and go spiraling down. So we got rid of the first two F-100s, and then the next guy comes

A B-45 captured in flight over the finely manicured English countryside (David Menard).

in with a Hawker Hunter and he had speed brakes — which are also on the F-100s, but they weren't smart enough to use. The guy in the Hunter popped them and he ate us up!"

Results were good for the fall and the only deviation from the norm occurred October 14–16 when engines on numbers 47–059 and 47–091 exploded within two days of each other, necessitating another mass grounding. All aircraft were dutifully inspected before passing back into service three days later. Another spate of misfortune struck in December when numbers 47–043 and 48–023 both suffered collapsed gears while landing and taxiing, respectively. Equally notable was an incident occurring on December 2, 1955, when Lieutenant William Sanders accidently ejected himself from a stationary T-33 trainer — fortunately while the canopy was open; his injuries were not extensive and he resumed active duty within days. All told, the year proved a productive one, yet maintenance efforts still lagged owing to the continuing influx of inexperienced replacements from the ZI.[25]

Ongoing IRAN flights back to San Bernardino also continued at regular intervals and were basically uneventful, but sometimes they highlighted the Air Force's own ignorance about the B-45s. Lieutenant Neile, returning from California, failed a low altitude compass check and landed unannounced at Randolph AFB, Texas, for repairs. "There were two 'Follow Me' jeeps at the end of the runway waiting for me," he reflected. "What the Hell is this? Nobody's around and I know where I'm supposed to park. They brought me right up in front of base operations, all these people in blue suits lined up on a ramp next to them, with a *red carpet* out. We opened the hatch and this guy jumps in and starts shaking my hand — I said 'What's going on?' 'We want to congratulate you!' I thought, '*Jesus, what have I done now?*' and I asked, 'For what?' 'For delivering our first *B-57* here!' They didn't even know what a B-45 was — none of them. I thought my wings were gone right then, turned out they were so embarrassed they didn't want to say anything!"

The continuing evolution of the 49th Air Division concluded in the spring of 1956 when authorities amalgamated its administrative functions within Headquarters, Third Air Force. Previously, the division operated under the guidance of the Third Air Force in peacetime only; in the event of war, it reported directly to the Supreme Allied Commander, Europe (SACEUR). Through this new arrangement Headquarters, Third Air Force, wielded greater control over combat operations and day-to-day functions, promoting greater economy and efficiency. The 49th Air Division finally disbanded on July 1, 1956, although activities within the 47th Bomb Wing were scarcely affected. In light of the ongoing Suez and Hungarian crises, Colonel Holzapple increased emphasis on training to cut down reaction time during alerts. This proved no mean feat for, due to perpetual housing shortages at Sculthorpe, the majority of wing personnel were widely dispersed throughout Norfolk county, sometimes at distances of thirty-five miles. A new scheme was instituted which divided the county up into regions, each with its own alert warden. Each region, in turn, was subdivided into groups headed by group leaders, who were responsible for notifying at least four households when an alert was sounded. In this manner it became possible to get 90 percent of off-base personnel to their respective stations in only ninety minutes, as opposed to three hours.[26]

For B-45 personnel, Hozapple also upped the ante in terms of combat readiness and reduced reaction time, which he now measured "from the time the alert is called to the time that the bomber loaded its DOD weapon, taxis into number one position on the runway, runs up at 100% and releases its brakes." He began running a series of simulated alerts, usually between 3:30 and 5:30 A.M., to shave off as much time as possible. Continuing practice resulted in bomb loading time dipping from three hours to an hour-and-a-half. This emphasis on alacrity paralleled realization that Soviet IL-28 bombers stationed in East Germany could strike English airbases in as little as ninety minutes. The division historian said that "more practice is needed before the combat wings are in a position to state with confidence that they cannot be caught on the ground even under the worse conditions of surprise attack." Another important innovation, unique to B-45s, also evolved about this time. Previously, loading the Mark 5 bomb was a laborious, time consuming process involving removal of the left bomb bay door, then hand-cranking it into position, all of which took 46 minutes. Captain Oliver T. Knapp, 85th Squadron, then suggested tipping the Tornados back on their tail skid so that the weapons dolly could maneuver directly under the aircraft at a considerable savings of time.[27] Sergeant John Butts also recalled the general's renewed emphasis on speed. "We had atomic capability and when the whistle blew we had so many minutes to get a loaded airplane out to the runway, he explained. "That caused a lot of people to go in a lot of different directions — and they called it the Holzapple Shuffle." Sergeant George Watson, by contrast, proffers a more baleful reflection. "I had the world's biggest alarm bell right outside of my room, and it would shake the wall when they rang it," he shuddered, "and that would ring any time."

In light of the increasingly tense world situation, the various alerts and drills assumed a gravity they heretofore had lacked. Many false alarms ensued, but to the flight crews destined to fly the missions their realism could be startling. Lieutenant Donald E. Feltus recalled attending a raucous squadron party at the officer's club late one Friday night: "A bunch of wing weenies from London were there and we were getting along real good, everybody was as happy as could be — then that bloody bell rang just before midnight!" Feltus describes how inebriated flight crews made arrangements to hurriedly get their wives home before staggering back to the base for a quick change of attire. "Well, the officers were pretty happy when we got down to Ops and called in — and then they started calling targets down! Well, maybe we ought to get out of our party clothes and into our war-flying clothes and look like it anyway." The crewmen lumbered out, preflighted their aircraft, called the tower, and received taxi instructions. Feltus continues: "The wing weenies were there and they knew what kind of shape we were in —'they wouldn't let us launch as drunk as we were'— we all thought. And that poor tail gunner sitting back there all by himself, sober as a judge, and knowing what shape the three folks up front are in. Sure enough, the B-45s taxi to the end of the runway and called; the tower responded 'Roger, you're clear for take off.' *Oh, no! They can't be doing this! They can't be serious!* And this was probably one-thirty in the morning. So anyway, we jumped off and, someway or the other, we got around it and got back."

The new loading bomb techniques proved convenient for handling Mark 5 bombs, but certain hazards remained. As Sergeant George Watson recalled, "We got about halfway up and the cable on the right hoist broke and the bomb started to drop and, because of its weight, it immediately snapped a cable on the other hoist. Fortunately, it landed perfectly in the cradle, there wasn't a mark on the bomb. We found this out later —*I wasn't about to look then.* I hit the ground running, yelling and screaming 'Run! Run!' We went maybe 50–60 yards into a depression and hid there figuring we were going to be really

safe if that ever blew." Sergeant Glenn H. Wines, 4th Tactical Depot Squadron, also proffered some interesting facts about nuclear security at Alconbury, especially for keeping
the warheads secure from a hypothetical Soviet commando raid: "We had a plan to blow
them up, if we had to. This one igloo had 30 bombs in it, each one had 3,000 pounds
of high explosives, so you are going to get a big band. On two of these we placed a 40-
pound shaped charge, prepositioned onto the weapon with a wooden stand to give it the
proper stand off. Then we ran a cable up to what they called the 'Hell Box'—push it and
they all go. The plutonium capsules had to be destroyed separately. All this was never
done, fortunately—but if it came to that we knew how to do it!"

The only incident marring an otherwise fine performance by the 47th Bomb Wing
during this period occurred on January 30, 1956, when B-45 number 47–059, returning from a mission in Germany, crashed on final approach to Lakenheath outside of Brandon, Suffolk. It was snowing and pitch black at the time, and Sergeant John Butts, the
tail gunner, recounted what happened next: "A few seconds after an exchange between
the aircraft commander and the GCA operator, the AOB came on the intercom in a
pretty high pitched voice and said, 'Watch the altitude, George!' At that particular moment
I noticed a bunch of sparks and stuff flying from the front of the airplane going past my
head on both sides and later determined that we were hitting the tips of trees and were
ingesting tree limbs. I just blacked out and I came to sitting, believe it or not, in an upright
position in the tail. The tail of the aircraft broke off and went in another direction with
me inside." Three crew members died or were fatally injured, but Sergeant Butts survived.[28]

Another Tornado, number 47–092, struck a low bank and slammed into a field near
Rudham, Norfolk, on July 12, 1956, killing the AOB. Within days the stricken craft was
dismantled, loaded onto a flatbed truck, and hauled over to the base 47th Field Maintenance Squadron at Sculthorpe. Approximately 1,290 man hours later, by using parts cannibalized from the wrecked 47-072, this B-45 was restored to operating condition, on
December 15, 1956. It was an impressive effort considering how aircraft this heavily damaged were usually taken, at great expense, to the nearest depot for repairs. Squadron maintenance received official commendation for a job well done.[29]

It was not until the spring of 1957 that Headquarters, Third Air Force, finally dis-
carded their notion of equipping the 47th Bomb Wing with B-47Es and recommitted
the unit to receiving B-66s. Further confusion arose as to exactly what kind of nuclear
device would be carried by the Destroyer. Headquarters originally intended to utilize the
Mark 6 bomb but, upon further reflection, concluded that this combination "was not
compatible with the mission of the 47th Bombardment Wing. The Wing bases its requirement on the operational fact that it must launch its strike aircraft within the time of tactical warning and not strategic warning. For the United Kingdom this tactical warning
is on the order of 1½ hours. The loading time alone for the B-66B/Mk 6 was around two
hours with a great deal of ground handling equipment which had to be in place at that
start." It was decided to retain the Mark 5 bomb and ground handling equipment carried by B-45s to keep arming time down to a minimum.[30] Operationally, the 47th Wing
continued having problems connected to the influx of new, untrained personnel, especially in terms of navigator-bombardiers. This occurred because the wing was the sole
operator of nuclear capable B-45As, all of which were European-based, so "the task of
training aircrews is entirely done within the wing." This operational lapse might have

infringed on operations elsewhere, but 47th Bomb Wing personnel were habituated towards success — whatever their situation. Newcomers were thoroughly grilled and relentlessly, irrespective of their station or standing. This ingrained doggedness and professionalism culminated in February 1957 when the 47th won the first-ever USAFE Tactical Proficiency Award for the period 1 July to 31 December 1956.[31] Such plaudits are convincing testimony that the B–45-equipped 47th Bomb Wing was probably the best overall combat unit within the Tactical Air Command. Moreover, it acquired and maintained an operational excellence equaling or exceeding many of its SAC contemporaries.

This year the biggest change on the ground came for the 86th Bombardment Squadron. After fifteen months of flying from substandard conditions at RAF Molesworth, the transfer to rebuilt accommodations at RAF Alconbury finally transpired. Yet, despite the change of venue, operating conditions remained problematic. Captain Ted Crichton recalled what happened while attempting to land at Alconbury one night: "We let down and did that procedure of flying over the RAF station and picking up the required track, started the time, and let down to 700 feet. When the time ran out I was still looking at clouds underneath me and I looked at the fuel and we had none to go anywhere. I remember the ejection procedure went through my head very vividly." Fortunately, Crichton managed to find a break in the clouds and touched down safely: "Halfway down the runway I was into the fog again — we were lucky that night." And, if operational conditions

A lineup of B-45 As at an undisclosed tarmac, probably Langley AFB. Note that most of the tail guns have been removed in this shot (National Archives).

at Sculthorpe were sometimes less than accommodating, at Alconbury they were worse. "It was just a muddy mess," Captain Sylvester O'Brien declared, "just like World War II." Gunner Sergeant William V. Menkevich also disparaged his new abode, and described it unsentimentally. "One word: mud," he noted, "Walking across the street to the shower and latrines in the middle of winter was rather interesting. Yes, it was brutal at the onset but things improved."

B-45s at Alconbury also shared the sky with British jets operating from nearby RAF Whitton, which, once bad weather was thrown into the mix, lent an air of excitement to routine matters like flying. "In 1957 air traffic control in England was, at best, rather scratchy," Captain Cletus Dold reflected. "You got out of low altitude and you got into high altitude and it was kind of, 'Well, you're on your own, don't hit anybody.' And sometimes the British weather was solid up to 38–40,000 feet. Let me put it this way: myself and a Canberra — I think we exchanged paint jobs one day! We were that close to each other in the clouds. It was so close you didn't have time to be scared, it just went whoosh! I didn't get scared until I thought about it." Tornado operations were also hobbled by some ongoing, if unrelated, accidents. Two B-45s, numbers 47–045 and 47–050, were lost in fires or crashes at IRAN facilities in California. Then, on May 17, 1957, number 47–055 departed Alconbury, made an emergency landing near Shepherd's Grove, England, and ran off the runway before collapsing its nose gear. On June 3, 1957, number 47–071 also went down near Saxlingham, Norfolk. The crew, consisting of Captain William J. Royle, Lieutenant Edwin L. Philip, Lieutenant Edward G. Newyear, and Sergeant Kenneth A. Seaborn, all parachuted to safety, although they landed in the Wash and were rescued by an English lifeboat.[32]

By fall, wing headquarters advanced preparations to drop all remaining B-45s from its inventory and phase in the newer B-66s. The 84th Bombardment Squadron accordingly transferred all sixteen of its Tornados to the 85th and 86th squadrons, while the majority of its flight and maintenance personnel attended conversion classes at Eglin AFB, Florida. Shoran training also terminated at Sculthorpe, as Destroyers were not equipped for that mission. Still, many pilots remained unimpressed by the sleek newcomer and remained loyal to their Tornados. "The B-66 was obviously faster," Lieutenant Neile remarked," but it wasn't as high and it wasn't as capable. There's never been a bomber that the Air Force ever had that could take off with a full fuel load and a full bomb load, climb straight to 40,000 feet and *then* start a cruise climb from there. No other bird could ever do that." Years later the issue of whether the B-66 was actually an improvement remained a contentious issue in the minds of many. "That has been discussed in reunions if whether the B-66 brought any more to the table that the B-45," Sergeant Butts reflected, "and the general answer is no."

Despite the ongoing conversion process, the 47th Wing dutifully maintained its Emergency War Plan (EWP) capabilities, another point of pride. "To the best of our knowledge," the wing historian boasted, "this is the first time that any tactical organization has converted aircraft while maintaining complete wartime responsibilities." Around this time the director of Logistics Plans, Third Air Force, finally decreed the Tornado's fate: all were declared obsolete and destined "for fire fighting training of personnel at USAFE stations within the European theater of operations."[33] It was a sorry ending for a useful airplane. Finally, in the course of routine operations, another serious mishap occurred on September 20, 1957, when 84th Squadron commander Major Torino V. Di

Salvo took number 47–083 on a training flight from Sculthorpe, caught fire shortly after takeoff, then crashed near RAF West Raynham. Di Salvo, Lieutenant Gustave E. Budruweit, and Lieutenant Floyd E. Martin all perished in the crash.[34]

The waning days of B-45s in Europe proved anticlimactic throughout the spring and summer of 1958. Commencing on January 18 of that year, increasing numbers of B-66s arrived at Sculthorpe while the ranks of Tornados dwindled commensurately. The 86th Bombardment Squadron began exchanging aircraft in March 1958, while the 85th, which postponed converting until July, dispensed with them the following September. Beforehand, several Tornados concluded a final, five-day maneuver to Ben Guerir Air Base in Morocco in March, operating with a minimum of spare parts to test self-support measures in combat, and the ingenuity of service crews.[35] Afterwards, training flights grew less and less frequent. The only aberration to this otherwise uneventful transition occurred on June 13, 1958 — Friday the thirteenth — in one of the most bizarre episodes associated with the B-45. Apparently Airman Second Class Vernon L Morgan, a married twenty-one-year-old Indiana native, had entered into an illicit tryst with a local sixteen-year old girl. When the affair ended at the behest of her parents, Morgan inexplicably jumped into number 47–046 at Alconbury, fired up the engines, and took off. He apparently lost control of the jet three minutes later, spun in near Wood Walton, Peterborough, cartwheeled across the ground, and blocked the main Edinburgh-London rail line. Morgan died instantly, but a bigger disaster was narrowly averted after an approaching train successfully braked before striking the wreckage.[36] This is the last recorded crash of a B-45 and also its last fatality.

Within months of deactivation all Tornados, stalwarts of the 47th Bomb Wing since 1949, were deposited at various airdromes across Europe, burned up in fire drills, and largely forgotten. It is hardly ironic that, even as scrap metal, B-45s still served a useful purpose to an Air Force that scarcely appreciated them. Its six-year tenure at Sculthorpe may have been unheralded at the time, but it was nonetheless highly successful and constitutes an important chapter of American nuclear deterrence at a dangerous period of Cold War history. Naturally, their departure was tinged with some sadness from the men who flew and fixed them. "She's a good airplane," Sergeant Marvin C. Indorf, who had labored on Tornados since 1950, admitted. "They've got all the bugs worked out of her now, and she's very serviceable. It's sort of a shame to lose her after all the work we've put into her."[37] Indorf touched a raw nerve and undoubtedly spoke for many.

The historical obscurity surrounding the 47th Bomb Wing, one of the Tactical Air Command's crack organizations, remains as unwarranted as it is unfathomable. Yet, the wing's efficacy is no mystery to the men who helped secured it. "I am of the opinion that the 47th Bomb Wing did one Hell of a job that needed to be done," opined Captain Edward J. Sanderson. "It was a thorn in the side of Russia, we had atomic capability, we had combat-ready trained crews. And I think we fulfilled that mission." Captain Nick Hannibal concurred fully in his assessment of the wing. "It was the best unit. I've never, before or since, seen so much esprit de corps as in that unit. We knew we had a mission and everybody was dedicated to go the whole route. It was the most wonderful unit I ever served in, bar none." Equally glaring is the lack of official recognition towards the role that Tornados played in Cold War. This is much less a quaint omission than a gaping wound to many B-45 veterans, especially considering the voluminous literature on the period. But memory of the aircraft dies hard among them, if at all. "When I was in it, I thought it was the grandest thing in the world," Lieutenant (later general) Howard M. Fish confessed. Lieutenant (later general) Ted Crichton concurred wholeheartedly: "I spent 36 years in the service and I flew for 30 years, solid. It still stands out as one of the best airplanes I ever flew. It had many, many fine features, in addition to being very smooth and quiet." It falls upon Ed Philips to conclude this chapter on a note of indignant pride that any ex-Tornado hand would recognize. "The thing that bothers me is that it was never given any credit for much of anything. You look through the history books and what do you find? The B-47, grand and glorious![38]

CHAPTER EIGHT

Distant War, Perilous Vigil

"The B-45 is doing a great job over there. I'd like to see them doing the bombing in Korea instead of the B-29s; I know our losses would be a lot lower."

— Major James Jabara[1]

In May 1951 a new chapter unfolded in the history of Detachment 2, once the first team of trained SAC pilots from the 324th Strategic Reconnaissance Squadron arrived at Yokota AB to relieve the original TAC complement. The detachment leader was Captain Stacey D. Naftel, seconded by Lieutenant James H. McGrath, and accompanied by their respective crews. Naftel, a combat veteran of world War II, was favorably impressed by the Tornado. "I liked it better than the B-25. It was quieter; both of the aircraft were extremely reliable in my opinion. I flew the A-26 as an instructor for a period of six months and I compared the B-45 very much to the A-26. Very maneuverable. I never did, but you could roll the aircraft." After being checked out in the combat mission area by Captain Louis H. Carrington, Naftel and McGrath conducted eight routine reconnaissance missions over North Korea without incident.[2]

Events picked up dramatically that June once General Curtis E. LeMay began agitating for RB-45C radar photography coverage of Manchuria and the Chinese mainland. Overflights of Soviet territory were still prohibited at the time, but the SAC staff nonetheless assembled an extensive list of potential targets in the event that war in Asia spilled over. Securing permission for such activity, however, threatened to intrude on SAC's closely guarded autonomy. The existing mechanism for overflights required permission from commander-in-chief General Matthew Ridgway, on a mission-by-mission basis. Colonel Winton R. Close, a SAC officer temporarily assigned to FEAF, was displeased by this chain of command respecting authorization. "At the present time these missions are directed by the Director of Intelligence, FEAF," he noted. "In other words, Intelligence chooses the target and dispatches the B-45 to get the pictures and, incidently, throws in as much airfield reconnaissance on the mission as possible. This allows Intelligence considerable leeway and leaves us open to being short-changed on occasion."[3] Since documentation on the topic is scarce, the exact channels of authority behind these clandestine endeavors cannot be discerned with accuracy. Nevertheless, such highly classified top secret RB-45C flights *did* take place.

Captain Naftel's first known overflight occurred at Lop Nor, site of China's atomic energy program, and involved extensive Central Intelligence Agency planning beforehand. "I was briefed on that by the CIA," he reflected. "I was real concerned because they came and were going over this thing, laying out maps on our dining room in our Quonset hut in Yokota, and our maid or house gal was running back and forth. I just felt real uncomfortable and I finally told the guy, 'We can't talk about this here — I need to go down to Tokyo, where we can have security and get this thing laid out the way we want,' because I didn't know a CIA identification from zilch." When Naftel, accompanied by copilot Lieutenant Edward Kendrex and navigator Captain Robert R. Dusenberry, took off on June 5, 1951, they were closely shadowed by an electronic intelligence (ELINT) aircraft. Their flight, considering the vast distances covered, was apparently also one of the earliest combat missions to utilize aerial refueling. Yet, because this practice remained shrouded in secrecy, it is not alluded to in any surviving documents.

This particular RB-45C mission proved anything but uneventful. "It was planned, as were all our night special missions, to take advantage of full darkness," Naftel reflected. "As I recall, the target area was in central China, close to the Yichang area. This was shaping up to be a long, hairy mission. Some thirty minutes after penetrating Chinese airspace south of Shanghai, we received orders to abort, turn around, and get back out. The reason was that the sky was filled with contrails. We could see this at sunset dead ahead and assumed correctly that they were MiG fighters. The electronic intelligence aircraft, or whatever it was monitoring our mission, reported that there was no way we were going to get through Communist Chinese air defense that night. It was just getting dark, but heading west we could easily see the heavy concentration of contrails heading to intercept us, and we were most happy to turn around and high tail it out of there!"[4] Back at Yokota the crew was debriefed by Sergeant Stadille, head of the 91st Squadron's interrogation team, who apprised him of a mysterious event. "The crew reported seeing lights following them and we sent it in as a UFO. That was kind of strange because these guys indicated that these lights were following them all the while they were on their mission, on the return part."[5] Other than some head scratching in high places, nothing came of this aberration.

The remainder of Detachment 2's activities were otherwise routine. On June 1, 1951, Bomber Command placed "MiG Alley" off-limits to all unescorted reconnaissance flights because Fifth Air Force refused to provide F-86 fighter escorts. The latter usually preferred using available RF-80s for bomb damage assessment, which were better at evading MiGs on their own. Consequently, the bulk of nine combat sorties flown were concentrated south and east of Pyongyang, safely out of harm's way. Rain and extensive cloud cover also militated against good photographic results. Three aborts were reported, two caused by engine failure, and one due to a radar malfunction; nevertheless, high levels of maintenance prevailed. "The airmen have done a highly commendable job without exception," Naftel observed in his biweekly report, "The men should be praised for their earnest effort, their untiring devotion to duty and their ingenious methods of keeping our aircraft flying against many obstacles."[6]

In July, Headquarters, SAC, continued pressing their case for continuing radar coverage of potential targets on the Chinese mainland. The propitious date of July 4, 1951, was therefore selected for Captain Naftel's second deep penetration mission, across 500 miles of hostile airspace to a military area in the Harbin region. "About halfway up that line of flight, while cruising at an altitude of about 34,000 to 35,000 feet near the city of Fushun, the copilot and I noticed what appeared to be Roman candles exploding off our right wing," he remembered:

I banked the aircraft sharply to check the ground, thinking this must be some hellishly high anti-aircraft fire. There was nothing but blackness below us, so as the Roman candles kept popping off our right wing I asked Kendrex to turn his seat around to see if there was anything back there. What seemed like a fraction of a second later, I heard Ed exclaim, *"My God, Stace, there are about seven aircraft back there in echelon. They've all got their navigation lights on!"* Of course, we were blackened out. They were in echelon to the right and appeared to be firing in turn until each expended their ammunition, and dropped off to the left wing to be replaced in line. This went on for some time, while we went through a series of corkscrew maneuvers, varying heading and altitude, trying to shake them and spoil any lock-on ability they might have at that altitude. We were riding the RB-45's "red line" and whenever I felt the aircraft start to shudder due to our high speed, I would ease off or pull up some. The corkscrewing and altitude changes varied the airspeed from 20 to 30 knots. The navigator, Bob Dudenberry, called me on the interphone, urged me to give it the gun, and I replied, 'Bob, the engines are on the limits now.' Anyway, this attack and our evasive maneuvers lasted for about 29 minutes.

The MiG fighters we encountered had no problem staying right with us, but they probably ran low on fuel because they were expending a lot more fuel than they normally would trying to get us lined up in their sights. According to the information I was given, this was the first time that our intelligence sources determined that the Communist Chinese had the capability for night airborne interception, and our side picked up a lot of electronic intelligence from that mission. Our "Roman candles" were probably 20mm tracer or exploding shells. I do not know whether they had proximity fuses in them or not. We did not get into that, but the only fireworks that we saw *that* Fourth of July were provided by the enemy![7]

Naftel gingerly nursed his RB-45C back home towards Yokota, grateful to be intact. However, one more ordeal await his tired crew:

We called for a ground control approach assist on landing as the ceiling was down to 300 to 500 feet. Everything was fine until we lined up on the final approach and the operator started giving me reciprocal headings for the final approach. After the night flight we just had, it was almost too much. I aborted the approach and called for the senior supervisor to take over. We pulled up and onto the downwind leg. Fuel at this point was critical. Brigadier General James E. Briggs, commanding the Far East Air Forces Bomber Command, and Maj. Henry J. Walsh, the operations officer of the 91st Strategic Reconnaissance Squadron, were on the flight line to meet us and take us to the debriefing. Maj. Walsh commented, "Stacy, when you pulled up, I watched the clouds, expecting to see three parachutes any minute. What a relief it was to see you break out of the clouds on the final!" We landed with less than 300 gallons of fuel at chock point — about enough to fill the fuel lines.[8]

While operations to obtain radar photography proceeded smoothly, SAC and FEAF continued their turf war over competing priorities. "We had some difficulty getting FEAF to process this work rapidly," SAC Colonel John B. Henry complained. "It required several visits to the Reconnaissance Section in FEAF headquarters in order to get these photos as soon as we did. There is a little 'dragging of the feet' in this section because one colonel there is unhappy of having lost operational control of the 91st Reconnaissance Squadron to us. I don't think it is serious, and I an sure we can work it out all right."[9] Interagency diplomacy remained sparse at the highest levels and occasioned fierce bickering, but RB-45C operations were not duly affected.

In July, Detachment 2 completed seventeen regular combat sorties over North Korea, despite terrible weather. The mission flown by newly promoted Captain James H. McGrath on July 15, 1951, also involved the first *recorded* instance of in-flight refueling with a flying boom-equipped aerial tanker executed under combat conditions. The ren-

The impressive photographic suite of the RB-45C made it an indispensable reconnaissance asset throughout the Korean War (Getty Images).

dezvous had to be made visually after electrical failures onboard the tanker and 2,750 gallons of JP1 fuel were successfully transferred. The successful action was duly noted by FEAF headquarters, and a complimentary report was issued to General LeMay on McGrath's behalf.[10] However, Sergeant Stadille, of the 91st Squadron intelligence section, was subsequently shocked by Japanese knowledge of these supposedly covert activities: "One thing I saw in the *Tokyo Times,* or whatever the name of the paper is, is the refueling of a B-45. I couldn't believe it because Colonel [Thomas] Coleman and I both knew that was supposed to be secret. There, on the *front page,* was a picture of it! And I said 'What in the Hell is *this?*' I just could not believe it at the time." The Air Force's highly secret aerial refueling program was apparently sensational enough for front-page copy.

On August 6, 1951, a new Detachment 2 commander, Captain Robert D. Christensen, arrived at Yokota with two replacement crews. Naftel, however, had another daunting flight to perform before returning to the Zone of the Interior. By this time, prohibitions against overflying Soviet territory had been relaxed somewhat, for his target was the strategic Russian port of Vladivostok. The mission was flown on or about 8 or 10 August, 1951. Naftel wrote about it: "The weather forecast called for a low overcast ceiling of about 1,200 to 1,500 feet and we let down below the overcast to about 800 feet, our airspeed at approximately 440 knots, with all visual cameras on. That included the nose camera, a forward oblique, three trimetrogons, and a K-17 vertical. All cameras were going when we broke out of the over cast. Flying the length of the harbor, we sure caught the attention of a lot of deckhands on Soviet warships and freighters anchored there. They were really scrambling as we completed our run and pulled back up into the overcast. We were soon in the clear at about 16,000 feet and on our way back to Yokota. We detected no enemy fire during the run." What made this flight unusual was the presence of Jim G. Lucas, staff writer for Scripps-Howard newspapers — reputedly the first civilian to ride a jet bomber into combat. Lucas dutifully reported what he saw, although he was deliberately misled into believing that their objective was Pyongyang, not Vladivostok. The reporter squirmed upon being informed that Communist radar was tracking their course, for the crew had previously warned him of the possibility of antiaircraft fire. "Captain Naftel cut in on the interphone. His voice was meant to be soothing. 'They can shoot this high,'" Lucas wrote, "'but seldom do we get flak at this altitude.' That's reassuring, of course, but it seemed wise to check our instructions again, just in case. For instance, you don't jump from a jet bomber, you're thrown out-shot out as a matter of fact, buckled to your seat." Within days Naftel, McGrath, and their respective crews returned to Barksdale AFB in Louisiana. For sterling airmanship and skill in planning and executing plans under fire, Naftel became the first Tornado pilot awarded the Silver Star.[11]

Shortly after this one, another top-secret mission was flown by newly arrived Lieutenant Robert L. Hempen. On August 25, 1951, he departed from Yokota in the morning, refueled en route, and winged his way over Shanghai, China. Hempen completed two runs over the city, cameras and radar rolling, then departed without incident. However, his return flight was complicated by monsoon conditions, which forced him down at Haneda Airport, Japan. The RB-45C sat out the storm for several hours until the weather abated and then completed its mission.[12] Hempen's navigator, Captain Vance E. Heavilin, later commented on that night's activities: "I do not recall the target because I did not record it. I was not supposed to record anything because of the classification. It was flown at night — very uneventful — just strictly radar photography which I took full-scope pictures and sector bomb-run pictures of the target. I know that when I finished the mission I was going back to the room for a crew rest and I was called and told I was to be at the film lab at 1:30 or so in the afternoon to meet with someone who wanted to look at the film with me. It turned out to be a brigadier general!"

While this incoming classified information proved useful for fleshing out American target dossiers, there remained the problem of distributing the spoils among competing branches within the Air Force. Continued infighting between SAC and FEAF authorities generated hard feelings at the highest levels. "By now you should have all the scope photography on the three RB-45 missions which have been run for the Strategic Air Command so far," General Robert H. Terrill declared. "It has been most difficult worming this photography out of FEAF. My difficulty seems to be that although I initiate the mission as SAC X-RAY and execute the mission as Bomber Command, I have no control over the film after it leaves the airplane and goes to the 548th Reconnaissance Technical Squadron."[13] This squabble reflects conflicting command priorities: SAC was overwhelmingly concerned with obtaining intelligence for a possible expanded war with Russia and China, whereas FEAF remained engrossed in waging the one at hand. Had a full-scale conflict ensued in Asia, relations between SAC and FEAF would have ruptured wide open. LeMay, as head of SAC, insisted that operational control of all SAC units then on loan to FEAF (B-29s, RB-29s, and RB-45s) immediately revert back to him for strategic operations against the Soviet Union. FEAF, however, insisted on retaining these assets to keep tabs on the Chinese in and around Korea. "I have done everything I can to keep from stepping on anyone's toes in my second responsibility as Deputy Commanding General, SAC XRAY," Terrill observed, "however, I managed to get myself in a kettle of hot water with General Weyland as a result of my recommendation to you not to consider the diversionary crews as part of the FEAF strike force."[14] Months passed before the issue could be cordially resolved.

Bickering also ensued between Bomber Command's Generals Otto P. Weyland and LeMay over exactly how many RB-45s should be assigned to the Pacific theater. On August 15, 1951, Weyland telexed SAC headquarters citing the inadequacies of RB-29s for reconnaissance purposes and requested additional Tornados. "In the event of an all out war we must have readily available intelligence info on China and Manchuria mainland, and on northern Russian-held island," he insisted. "We have an urgent need for addl RB-45 capability for above reasons." One week later LeMay fired a telex back to Weyland, outlining his own predicament. The 91st Strategic Reconnaissance Wing at Barksdale presently operated only 24 Tornados; of these, seven were on duty in England while the remaining seventeen remained sidelined by parts shortages or factory visits for being fitted with tail turrets. Hence, only six RB-45Cs were presently in service stateside and not expendable. "In event of emergency the RB dash four five constitutes our only means of obtaining BDA photography when weather prevents high alt coverage by RB dash three six," LeMay tersely declared. "In view of above conditions I feel that one addl RB dash four five and crew is the extent to which we can augment the det now in FEAF."[15] Furthermore, in light of ongoing incursions into Soviet airspace, LeMay also objected to the manner in which his Tornados were dispatched. "The RB-45, without a tail gun installation, should not, in my opinion, be committed to deep penetrations within Russia during hours of daylight. Steps are being taken by AMC and North American to install a rear gun turret in the RB-45. Until these aircraft are so equipped, however, and pending the arrival of the RB-47, our lack of an aircraft capable of obtaining bomb damage photography from low levels will remain one of our most serious deficiencies."[16] Squabbling over the RB-45Cs continued for several more months into the war.

While SAC and FEAF sparred over use and control of Tornados, Detachment 2 flights under Captain Christensen carried on as usual. Operational levels for the month of August had been severely curtailed by bad weather; consequently, only seven combat missions were mounted. On the maintenance side, numbers 48–013 and 48–014 started running ragged after almost a year of continuous service and a major overhaul was overdue. Still, with no replacement aircraft available, the solution adopted was to stagger inspections, to keep a minimum of one airplane in commission available for active duty. Other problems required greater effort. When a fuel leak was discovered in 48–014, the entire right wing had to be removed for repairs. Concurrently, once the APQ-24 radar set in 48–013 started emitting images described as "weak and milky," it was stripped and repaired, another painstaking process. Captain Christensen was nonetheless pleased by the performance of his men in their first month of duty; however, he told superiors it was "strongly recommended that only the highest qualified air and ground crews be sent. Due to the limited amount of flying time available, it is not practicable to attempt to conduct any training of aircrews."[17]

Despite this emphasis on maintenance, the two war-weary Tornados were growing prone to system failures that nearly curtailed flying for the entire month of September. During this hiatus, number 48–013 underwent a 400-hour inspection that grounded it for two weeks, while 48–014 also sat sidelined for five days to rectify various mechanical ailments. Efforts were further complicated because new repair crews arriving from the ZI were unaware of the ad hoc procedures pioneered at Yokota. Consequently, only two classified sorties could be mounted that month. On September 21, 1951, Captain Hempen left Yokota in 48–014 and made continuous film and radar runs over Hang-Chou, China. As usual, enemy resistance was nil. "I can only recall a couple of times that we encountered MiGs and both times we were fairly close to the coast," Captain Heavilin declared. "We just started heading out over the water and put the nose down and got all the speed we could and they didn't seem to follow us over the water." One week later, newly repaired 48–013 was launched in bad weather for Amoy, China, apparently piloted by Christensen himself. He endured marginal flying conditions en route to target, became disoriented, and touched down at Formosa (Taiwan) for refueling. He then resumed operations and arrived over Amoy, only to find it masked by thick clouds. Completing his radar run, Christensen departed without incident, refueled at Okinawa, and finally landed at Yokota. The previous mechanical problems with the radar sets had apparently been corrected, for

© *Hank Caruso 2001*

"Speedy Photo Service"

North American Aviation's four-jet B-45 Tornado was the first contender to fly in the U.S. Air Force's quest for its first generation of jet bombers. Although designed as a bomber, its most noteworthy service accomplishments are associated with reconnaissance and intelligence gathering (in plain talk, spy) missions. The RB-45C reconnaissance version shown in this Aerocature™ was first used in combat during the Korean War.

"Speedy Photo Service": Artist Hank Caruso's apt caricature of the RB-45C in action over North Korea (Hank Caruso).

the results were judged "excellent." Word was also received that a third RB-45C had been dispatched from the ZI on September 20, and would make its appearance shortly.[18]

The ordeal of Captain Floyd E. Wilhelm in number 48–016 is noteworthy because of the mechanical glitches he surmounted en route. Wilhelm departed Barksdale on September 20, 1951, for Travis AFB, where a rudder boost motor failed and required replacement. The next day he flew onto Hickham Field, Hawaii, and left five days later for Midway. One hour out Wilhelm discovered that his bomb bay tanks would not feed and he returned to Hickham. There a new shutoff valve motor was flown in from Midway, where the spare-parts loaded C-54 had already been dispatched, and them item was conveyed to him by a scheduled air/sea rescue flight. Wilhelm took to the air again on September 26 and made a memorable touchdown at Midway. "There were thousands of birds in the area and the plane seemed to attract them," he observed. "It is estimated that the aircraft struck between fifty to sixty of them upon landing and landing roll." Number 48–016 resumed its sojourn that afternoon, arriving at Wake Island the following day.

Two days later Wilhelm sortied again, but adverse headwinds prevented him from flying directly to Tokyo. He therefore steered for Guam and landed safely. "When we left Wake Island we sat on the end of their runway at take-off power for a while to stabilize power," Lieutenant Alvan Barrett recalled. "The tower was raising Hell because we were blowing great chunks of their over-run into the ocean." After coasting into Andersen AB, Guam, Wilhelm refueled and departed on September 29, only to suffer an engine failure during takeoff. He consequently ate up all but 500 feet of the runway before his Tornado staggered aloft, then as quickly turned around and landed again. A replacement J47 engine was immediately ordered from Hawaii, which arrived by air on October 3. Wilhelm installed and test flew the new engine before departing the following day, and finally reached Yokota on October 4, 1951. There he discovered his APQ-24 radar set was inoperable and his aircraft was also scheduled for an intermediate inspection. Test flights on October 12 and 13 revealed that various engine O-ring seals had failed, along with the no. 1 fuel regulator. Rather than subject the ailing aircraft to combat missions, FEAF sidelined it to serve as a guinea pig for testing a new tail turret installation.[19]

Flight crews had long wearied of waiting for tail turrets, tail radar, or some kind of defensive mechanism, so they improvised if only to convince MiGs that there was at least *something* there to give them pause. "We had no guns," Lieutenant Calvin Pace declared. "Somebody said, 'Let's fool 'em' and they took some water pipe like you have in your house, and stuck one straight out and another at 45 degrees down and punched it out the tail cone. Then they improved on that; somebody got two .50 caliber machine guns to put in there and they looped the ammo. It was my experience that if you got four rounds out of those guns, you did a good job. I used to fire them when we coasted out of Korea. I'd turn them on and shoot them to let them know we were there."

The arrival of number 48–016 signaled a revival of RB-45C activity at Yokota. FEAF headquarters, which had previously restricted RB-45 flying to classified missions, now backtracked and ordered them to resume reconnaissance flights over North Korea. A total of thirteen sorties were completed by all three aircraft, the only mishap occurring on October 21, when an engine compressor on number 48–014 exploded. Detachment 2 continued posting a high mechanical readiness for the entire month but, due to camera parts shortages, it proved impossible to keep all three RB-45s in commission at once. Only one classified mission was logged in October and thereafter Headquarters, FEAF, dictated that "Due to the necessity of perfect weather over the scheduled Top Secret Targets, which cannot be attempted a second time, these missions must only be flown under ideal conditions." Apparently weather conditions were fine on October 9, 1951, when newly promoted Captain Hempen sortied north on Project 51, entailing a peek at southern Sakhalin Island in the Kuriles. He made his ingress at an altitude of only 18,000 feet, ideal for bomber-hungry MiGs, but no opposition materialized. Captain Heavilin subsequently noted, "There was always anticipation over what might happen but we knew we weren't going to find any more or anything any different than we were finding in Korea. We were probably flying against the same people." Project 51 concluded without incident, which served to heighten appreciation of the detachment and its work. "'Your RB-45s are the most important aircraft in this theater,' is an oft-repeated phrase here," Captain Christensen trumpeted. "From the great concern shown over their maintenance status shown by everyone including the Commanding General of FEAF and by the nature of the missions assigned, I am convinced that the above phrase is true."[20]

Accompanying Captain Wilhelm on his many missions was Lieutenant Barrett, an attentive observer. He recalled a typical mission profile — and some inexplicable radio traffic that cropped up while he was flying.

> You take off at Yokota, 9 o'clock in the morning, you've got to get out to the combat zone — it takes about an hour to get there. As we got into the combat zone you had F-86s, F-84s, British Meteors, Navy Panthers, AD-1s, shooting at each other or the North Koreans. And we'd get there about 10:30 or 11 o'clock and you can hear all this radio activity — radar directing people to intercept, the T-6s with their spotter rockets painting artillery pieces so that the fighters could come in and shoot them — all this is going on real hot and heavy. And we're setting up to do mapping of Pyongyang and then the crescendo drops down to almost zero. And we're up there flying these lines mapping with the Trimetrogon — probably had all the cameras running. So, about 12 o'clock it dawned on me that those SOB's *had gone to lunch,* because an hour later the crescendo builds up again, and here comes all these directions and voices, guys checking in, guys looking to intercept MiGs, etc. It was like listening to a radio show! I went on maybe fifteen missions and noticed this phenomena several times.

While at Yokota, Wilhelm and Barrett apparently flew several classified missions for which no official records were kept. "Every now and then we have what we call a 'Joint Chiefs of Staff' mission, and we knew we were going close to 'somewhere else,'" Barrett reflected. "On these Joint Chiefs of Staff missions with the RB-45, we'd come back and we'd have what we called a 'mission whiskey.' That's where they debriefed you and put a bottle of whiskey on the table and said it was courtesy of the Joint Chiefs."

November marked another milestone in the Tornado's operational history; it had been flying continuous combat missions without interruption for a year. However, the latest downturn in Detachment 2's activities occurred towards the end of October when only eight combat missions were mounted. For once the cause for this lull was not mechanical, but rather MiGs. On November 9, 1951, Captain Wilhelm was completing a routine photo mission over Haeju, North Korea, when he was unexpectedly boxed-in by a large flight of hostiles. No details of the encounter survive; however, he escaped intact without incurring damage. "We were knowledgeable that the Soviet fighters could surely get us if they got close," Lieutenant Barrett said. "But we were pretty high, too, we were doing this work between 38 and 43,000 feet." However, their close call carried unintended consequences at FEAF headquarters, for the MiGs were apparently now willing to operate further from Andong than previously; the RB-45Cs were again restricted from flying in or near "Mig Alley." Adding insult to injury, Tornado crews also found themselves performing mapping missions about the Japanese mainland. Wilhelm bristled at the thought of being handmaiden to RB-29s at Yokota and curtly stated as much in his biweekly report. "Due to the increased range and activity of the MiG-15, FEAF Bomber Command has shown reluctance in using the RB-45 over North Korea," he protested, "There seems to be no further classified missions scheduled for this Detachment, and I believe the time has come to return the three (3) aircraft to the Zone of the Interior."[21] The captain could well afford such cavalier posturing, for two replacement crews were already headed to Yokota as his 90-day TDY drew to a close.

Wilhelm's successor as detachment commander was Captain Robert A. "Curly" Schamber, who arrived on December 13, 1951, with another crew under Captain Robert E. Carlson. A minor problem arose beforehand when his ground crews arrived without priority stamped on their routing orders, and they were detained at Camp Stoneman for processing as regular replacements. Schamber's debut still proved momentous, for Detachment 2's overall flight activity rose again to fourteen combat missions. This was despite the fact that the exclusionary zone for RB-45Cs over North Korea had been enlarged from the previous month. Nine mapping missions of Japan were also accomplished. Then Headquarters, Air Materiel Command, made life interesting for already harried repair crews by declaring mandatory intermediate inspections at 50-, 100-, and 150-hour intervals, with major inspections scheduled at 200 hours. The biggest headache these uncovered was another fuel leak in 48–014, necessitating removal of the left wing for repairs. The detachment was further notified that they would soon be outfitted for carrying and testing photo flash bombs. "This requires a shield for the rear bomb bay tank, which we do not have in this theater," Schamber advised superiors. "Request three of these shields be sent to this detachment as soon as possible."[22] As usual in such matters, the reaction from headquarters was glacial.

The RB-45 crews resumed flying their usual combat sorties, including one near Haeju, where Captain Wilhelm had been jumped the previous November. Schamber revisited the area on December 27, 1951, but broke off immediately after observing contrails on an intercept course. "These aircraft proved to be Meteors, but by the time positive recognition was possible, our distance from the target precluded turning to it," he explained.[23] For navigator Lieutenant Francis Martin, the bulk of combat flying proved relatively mundane and uneventful. "Most of our day-to-day grunt work was in support of the ground troops. They needed coverage of what the bridges were like and bases and supply depots and all that stuff. Whatever they asked for usually involved a straight run, which we took in because of the cameras we had were fabulous and could photograph anything."

The new year dawned inauspiciously, with the RB-45s still operating under tightly imposed restrictions. Consequently, most flying that occurred was connected with the ongoing Japan-mapping project. Captain Schamber prepared his men to undertake night flash photography testing as soon M-120 flash bombs and bomb bay shields arrived. This project necessitated removing the front bomb bay bladder tank to accommodate the bomb, with commensurate reductions in range for missions planned below 30,000 feet. A bigger headache for Schamber proved to be "friend or foe" (FOF) identification, applicable whenever unknown contrails vectored towards a Tornado. "Unless immediate evasive action is taken by the aircraft commander at the time the contrails are first seen," he noted, "the crew is guaranteed several uncomfortable minutes pending identification, and possibly several more afterward."[24] Schamber opined that the installation of tail turrets would improve the situation, but action on this essential measure remained stalled. So, in light of poor weather and the FEAF clampdown, no combat sortie could be mounted until January 24, 1952; this endeavor proved ineffectual due to cloud cover blanketing the target area. Another mission lifted off on the following day, only to be intercepted by "seven swept-wing jet fighters presumed to be MiGs." FEAF headquarters subsequently scrubbed RB-45 missions, pending an investigation; flying did not resume until the end of the month. However, one top secret mission successfully concluded on January 31, 1952; its target remains unknown.[25]

Detachment 2 operations improved slightly by February, but results worsened due to uncooperative weather. Of twenty-nine combat missions planned, sixteen were scrubbed on account of rain, while only two aborted because of mechanical failure. Only six of eleven combat sorties mounted were judged satisfactory. Schamber, meanwhile, struggled to equip his Tornados for night flash photography. The conspicuous lack of M-120 flash bombs also necessitated substituting regular 500-pounders for APQ-24 calibration testing at night. Two test flights were flown with number 48–014, which had bomb racks and other equipment installed in place of the forward bomb bay tank. These endeavors were sidelined by recurring mechanical and electrical malfunctions, particularly after wind blasts tore off the pressurization exhaust duct from the rear bulkhead. All told, January and February were frustrating and nonproductive for reconnaissance activity outside of Japan mapping projects. This situation, and the FEAF restrictions that brought it about, did not sit well back at Lockbourne AFB, new home of Headquarters, 91st Strategic Reconnaissance Wing. In fact, wing leaders began pressing for the return of Detachment 2 aircraft since "all existing combat commitments for the RB-45 have been cancelled."[26] They most likely felt that the 91st Wing, with detachments in both Japan and England, was overstretched in terms of aircraft, personnel, and spare parts. SAC's vaunted capacity for conducting reconnaissance in wartime was also falling under public scrutiny once it was learned that MiG-15s "recently chased an RB-45 for 150 miles, continually making passes at it." In light of Soviet jets casually toying with American jet bombers, aviation writers began questioning SAC's ability to effectively deliver atomic bombs with slower flying B-50s and B-36s.[27] Still, Tornado crewmen generally found the specter of enemy opposition somewhat less daunting. "The F-86 boys always enjoyed our flying," Lieutenant Calvin Pace said with a grin, "because that sucked the MiGs out!"

On March 3, 1952, a new detachment commander, Captain Thomas Broughton, arrived at Yokota with his replacement crews. His appearance coincided with a FEAF request to resume daylight reconnaissance around the lower edges of "MiG Alley" for acquiring better BDA photography. A total of 33 missions were launched at various points around North Korea without Soviet or Chinese interference; however, Broughton, in consultation with FEAF officials, temporarily suspended the practice. "It has been proven beyond any reasonable doubt that the RB-45 is not capable of making successful daylight penetrations deep into enemy territory," the squadron historian wrote. "Only very good luck on the part of RB-45 crews and very poor gunnery on the part of MiG pilots has prevented the loss of all the RB-45s in this theater."[28] Henceforth, Broughton placed renewed emphasis on nighttime photography for his Tornados. This practice, however, remained hampered by a perpetual lack of proper equipment, including essential site bomb bay shields and M-120 flash bombs, in sufficient quantity. A minor milestone was nonetheless reached when number 48–013 logged an unprecedented 107 hours and 10 minutes that month without mechanical failure, a new record for the RB-45C. Thanks were officially accorded to Sergeant Victor Ayers and his ground crew for a fine performance. Meanwhile, Schamber, still on hand as acting commander, managed to take his various problems in stride. He noted: "The B-45 maintenance in the states was not really as good as what we had. A lot of that credit goes to our good people for that; we always had aircraft in commission and we flew over 100 hours on one of them in one month — which was unheard of." Navigator Lieutenant Martin, then completing his first tour with Detachment 2, echoed Chamber's respect for the repair crews. "They had all kind of trouble getting parts. They were very inventive though, and they managed to keep us flying — good maintenance crews, really outstanding guys."

The only other significant activity for Detachment 2 during this interval was Mission No. 265, executed on March 18, 1952, by 48–013 to Vladivostok while an RB-50 ferret aircraft lumbered behind to monitor Soviet radar signals. "One time we flew a mission out of Yokota and we went up northward to the Russian border, then we turned south and paralleled the border, and they had an RB-29 down below getting radar electronic intelligence," Schamber said. "Our purpose was to just stir up the Russians and have them turn on their radar and see what happened. And we did have a couple of fighters come up and parallel our flight but there was no hostile action." Aerial opposition never materialized, so the Tornado completed its orbit and returned to Yokota unimpeded.[29]

At Yokota AB, racy nose art remained something of a tradition on bomber and reconnaissance aircraft, despite SAC regulations to the contrary (David Menard).

April saw the long-awaited trial runs with night flash photography finally transpire. Bomb bay tank shields finally arrived at Yokota and they were installed in number 48–014, which then completed three missions with M-120 flash bombs. Results proved mixed; the first mission on April 21 was entirely successful with excellent results. However, the second effort ended in failure due to the high reflections from low-lying haze. Then the third mission suffered poor results when nearby mountains obscured radar returns while pinpointing the target run. Most important, crews discovered that the RB-45C shuddered heavily with bomb bay doors open at 290 miles per hour, and the vibrations were "so severe that the radar scope and flight and engine instruments become unreadable." Further night photography was suspended so the detachment could attend to other duties. A total of fourteen combat missions were completed over North Korea, although with mixed results attributed to incessant rain.[30] Ultimately, Detachment 2 finally abandoned its attempt to utilize nighttime flash bomb techniques. "We are pretty well convinced that the targets of prime importance in this theater simply are too difficult to find with radar to permit consistent success in night photo flash operations," Broughton explained. "It is just another case of the whole attempt over here to employ a strategic Air Force in a tactical war."[31]

May proved another uneventful month, with 21 missions flown, equally divided between combat reconnaissance and Japan mapping. One change of note was placing Detachment 2 under direct control of the 91st Strategic Reconnaissance Squadron's operations officer to promote better cooperation with the host unit. Flight and ground crews performed well, but Detachment 2's aircraft were becoming frayed from incessant use, parts shortages, and recurring spates of cannibalization. "During the past week we have experienced a series of aircraft malfunctions that have almost stopped us cold," Broughton complained to Colonel Lewis E. Lyle. "[48-] 8013 is our present parts supply and now stands short one bomb bay tank, one main inverter, and one aileron boost control valve, all taken off to keep the other two aircraft flying.... Naturally, there is a limit to this cannibalization, and today I gave instructions to bring it to a halt." He also pleaded with superiors at Lockbourne AFB to begin rotating Detachment 2's overworked aircraft back from Yokota, because the three RB-45Cs present had compiled 59 technical order compliances (TOC) and required modifications that could not be made in theater.[32]

June proved a lackluster period for the Tornados, with only two combat sorties flown, while seven test hops were required to iron out persistent mechanical problems. Significantly, the dangers of flying overworked aircraft were underscored when disaster struck on June 6, 1952. A crew consisting of Captain Joseph L. Schaffer, Lieutenant Calvin Pace, and Lieutenant James W. Deskin had just taken off in number 48–016 when number three engine suddenly exploded. This was Pace's sixth flight in a craft appropriately dubbed "The Widow Maker," and he relates what happened next:

> We had just got off the ground and yanked the gear up and then the flaps, then *whump!* I looked to the right and I could see a hole a little bigger than your head out there, and the fire light came on. Obviously there was a compressor failure and it started smoking. There was a little fire there—a magnesium fire—and as I recall there was molten metal flying back—and there was a fuel tank back there with just a little aluminum over it!
>
> I heard Joe call the tower—I remember he used some obscenities said "It's a goddamn Mayday!" After hearing Joe declare an emergency, I reached down and got my ejection seat, you pull the left lever and then the right one—one of them would take the canopy, except it didn't work in my case. Then there's a big lever over here on the side, you squeeze the handle and pull it all the way down and that takes the canopy off—that didn't work either. I couldn't get that damn thing down. So anyhow Joe pulled up his ejection seat handle and when he did, that blew off the canopy. Meanwhile, Jim [the navigator] is down there trying to get out in his seat—when he pulled his little cord his seat rotated about 45 degrees, the spoiler came

out on the side of the door and then the door is supposed to fall off.

So I pulled my ejection seat, I pulled the trigger then *thirrrp*! It popped up about a half inch or something, so I undid my seat belt and was trying to get down, the only problem was I had my chute on, and had a Hell of a time. I always tell a story that I think I was so scared that I peed my pants and that lubricated me — I slid out [laughter].

I finally got down in the aisle way to crawl up to the front door and here's the navigator, leaning back in his seat, kicking the door with all his strength. The door did not come off. I said, 'Wait a minute Jim' and I reached up and grabbed the door handle, pushed hard, and it took off. I was amazed because the spoiler was out. By God something worked! Anyway Jim fell back. He wasn't waiting for me, he was just off balance, but as he left, as he stuck his head out he was still plugged in. I tried reaching to knock off all these cords and hoses off him. But it didn't bother him, he still got out fast. I didn't want to jump on Jim — I estimate he was only 60 feet away as we were going down — but I stuck my head out the door it just sucked me out.

I remembered, "Got to pull that ripcord" and I looked down and, S——, there's no rip-cord! Apparently I had popped it on my escape. Anyhow, the last thing I recall was that I had both hands grabbing for that D-ring and apparently the chute opened about that time, and when it did it hit me in the mouth and knocked out several teeth. I came to at about 100 feet, I guess, right over the rifle range — there was a couple of B-29 crews down there qualifying. They had an ambulance and everything right there. So I landed and they came over and exclaimed, "Oh, God!" I thought what the Hell was with them — then I got a mirror out and I looked kinda bloody! The people on the ground said it was less than ten seconds from the time that they saw my chute before the airplane hit.[33]

The crippled aircraft crashed and exploded, completely destroyed. The remaining two Tornados were grounded pending a full investigation and finally released for flight on June 11, 1952. Problems subsequently arose when number 48–014 began inexplicably losing power during takeoffs, rolling 17 percent farther than the computed ground runs had indicated. Extensive ground checks by North American field representatives uncovered that three of the four tailpipe temperature gauges needed calibrating or the engines would never develop full thrust. The repairs were made and the aircraft returned to duty. Additional problems developed with the all-important APQ-24 radar system, after it was discovered that new replacement parts would not function correctly with the jury-rigged systems devised by the detachment.[34]

A complete turnover of crews and aircraft occurred in July when the creaky numbers 48–013 and 48–014 finally rotated back to the ZI. The new detachment commander, Captain John J. Mackey, arrived at Yokota on July 15, 1952, while Captains Shaffer and Broughton returned to Lockbourne. Mackey, despite the sensitive nature of his assignment, was never overly awed by it. "Theoretically I was detachment commander," he said, "but, of course, two airplanes don't make a Hell of a big detachment." During his tenure nine combat sorties were mounted over North Korea without incident. RB-45C pilot Captain J. F. Patterson was also assigned to attend planning sessions for a classified mission at FEAF headquarters in downtown Tokyo. "The intelligence received at this briefing was so "hot" that Captain Patterson and crew were restricted from flying combat missions over Korea," Mackey reported.[35] However, Tornados wracked up another aviation first on July 29, 1952, when number 48–042 departed Elmendorf AFB, Alaska, accompanied by two KB-29 tankers. The RB-45C was piloted by none other than Major Louis H. Carrington, who had served with Detachment A two years earlier. He was seconded by copilot Captain Wallace D. Yancey and navigator Major Frederic W. Shook. Air Force

Major Louis Carrington (left) and his crew Major Fredrick W. Shook and Captain Wallace D. Yance, performed a Mackay Trophy-winning transpacific flight from Alaska to Yokota, Japan (John Mott).

officials had previously chosen to send them along the northern Pacific route because it was 2,500 miles shorter than the mid–Pacific crossing (via Hawaii), and also afforded better navigation facilities. Carrington's was also the first nonstop jet crossing from Alaska to Japan, which he accomplished in 13 hours and 47 minutes in bad weather and icy conditions. The flight itself proved uneventful, save for problems with the hydraulic system. "We knew we had lost fluid in our hydraulic system," Carrington reflected. "We had the type of system that you could make it inert, you just turn it off, and you'd have no pressure at all. Anyway, we started saving up *all liquids*— every kind we could collect to pour into that reservoir, and the gear came down and we landed [laughter]." For his efforts Carrington and his all–Texas crew received the prestigious MacKay Trophy for 1952.[36]

Accompanying Carrington on his record flight was number 48–027, flown by Captain William J. Kristen, with copilot Lieutenant Oliver Nasby and navigator Lieutenant Joseph Giraudo. Unlike Carrington, Kristen had launched into a freezing headwind and was forced to return to Elmendorf. He finally completed his transpacific flight on August 2, 1952, after three inflight refuelings, and covered 6,700 miles in 17 hours and 9 minutes before reaching Misawa AB on Hokkaido. Beforehand, Kristen had been meticulous in his technical preparations: "I had permission from my squadron commander, and with a North American tech rep, to heat up my engine to 690 at 97 percent rather than 690 at 100 percent, and we put wheatstone bridges on them, and made sure that all the gauges in the cockpit were accurate and working correctly. We also flew on EGT rather than on tachometer settings. This adjustment took ten minutes off my time to climb to 30,000 feet; it also increased the true airspeed to 400 knots while flying at 87 percent RPM. And it increased the range of the aircraft by about 300 nautical miles, which is a good feeling when crossing the Pacific."[37]

Meanwhile, FEAF Bomber Command officers initiated a study as to how best utilize the RB-45C in their overall reconnaissance scheme. By now daylight B-29 bomber raids and RB-29 photography missions were driven from the sky by MiGs, while prestrike and poststrike photo reconnaissance data suffered accordingly. The final document acknowledged that RB-45s remained the only viable means of conducting daylight missions in the proximity of MiG Alley. Nevertheless, the aircraft "is particularly vulnerable to flak and automatic weapons. Even the slightest rip tear, or battle damage affects the operational characteristics. High speed fragility is not exceptional in jet aircraft but the RB-45 is probably equal or more so in susceptibility to flutter disintegration of structure." The study concluded by stating that improved GCI control to alert Tornados of enemy activity represented the best way of preserving them during unescorted missions.[38]

Daylight missions over North Korea still remained perilous for RB-45Cs, as evidenced by the experience of Bill Kristen, "Snapper" Nasby, and Joe Giraudo. "Our targets were on the east coast of Korea, they were below Wonsan, and I was going southbound on the target," Kristen recalled. "We were at 18,000 feet, and Joe and I worked as a team. I would slide the aircraft sideways so he could keep his photo view finder on [the target] and tell me how far to the side we were. 'Kris, we're about 1,000 feet too far to the side and I don't think you can correct it.' 'Okay, I'm turning around going north.' As I did that Navy GCI called four unidentified bogeys over Kowan. I asked Snap where Kowan was and he said 'We're right over it'—and he was an ex-gunner and could focus on infinity, not like you and me on the newspaper. 'You see anything?' 'Nah, I don't see a thing.' 'Okay, keep your eyes out.' Well, he did. We turned south and were lined up perfectly. Then I looked out—and there were four MiGs coming up on the right side of my airplane—head on—and when I looked in the cockpit I could see the stitching of his parachute harness, the hump on his mask, and the hump on his helmet. I bent to port to go out to sea and at the same time yelled 'Camera runaway!' I believe we got the first pictures of the MiG-17—they were in *Time* magazine the next week. These MiGs didn't have a single mark on the fuselage or wings, not one black number or anything. When we beat out to sea they followed and were blinking their flash lights. We had two fifties in the tail, one firing straight back with a lot of tracer rounds, and one firing down at a thirty-degree angle, but I never had time to get to them before they broke off. The MiGs had fixed sights for low speed aircraft—they couldn't have hit us if they wanted to."[39]

The halcyon days of July bled into August with a new tally of eighteen RB-45C combat missions. All were over North Korea, although a handful aborted due to in-flight technical difficulties. Mackey had hoped for "one combat mission a day" with the high maintenance levels available, but he was overly optimistic. Replacement aircraft number 48–042 needed extensive sheet metal repairs around its engine nacelles, so "veteran" 48–014 remained in theater as a precaution. However, as if in protest, this war-weary aircraft experienced four consecutive aborts due to various malfunctions, none of which proved serious. Then number 48–027, which had arrived in excellent condition, suffered a ruptured hydraulic reservoir during a test hop on August 8. As it landed on a wet runway, the pilot employed full emergency brakes before veering off the runway centerline and finally rolling to a stop. Fluid also seeped into the aft camera compartment, rendering the lens useless until it was thoroughly cleaned. On the bright side, a poststrike mission over the Hoechang Ore Processing Plant on August 6, 1952, provided photography so clear and informative that Mackey, copilot Captain Hugh B. MacCauley, and navigator Captain Paul F. Boehm all received written commendations from General Wiley D. Ganey.[40]

Increasing use of searchlights by North Koreans and Chinese also began intruding upon previously safe night flights. Their efficiency at detecting and tracking the high-flying Tornados became an area of consternation for FEAF officials. During one nocturnal foray, Captain Kristen recalled how "We flew the Baker Line from the Yalu down, pinpointing flak and searchlights. Most of the flak was dirty orange, which wasn't HE (high explosive). Finally, when we got beyond Ping-pong (Pyongyang) we noticed that the searchlights were a little more accurate. We were in one, but we cast no shadow so they didn't see us. But there this radar gun began nipping at me. We knew there were radar guns at Ping-pong, so we headed into the jet stream. The 38th Parallel and jet stream are synonymous almost year-round, right across Tokyo and out to Midway. I just kept going out to sea, I had the airplane shuddering on the mach, 38,000. I changed altitude, usually up, and as soon as I could I would go up for more. I finally got out of range and then they let go."[41] Countermeasures were subsequently explored at Yokota to neutralize this latest threat.

Detachment 2 labored hard throughout autumn to keep all aircraft aloft, and the crews bettered the previous month's record with a September total of 19 combat missions. Once again, veteran 48–014 proved the biggest headache, with a thrown forward nose gear bearing on one flight and a radar system breakdown on another. Repairs were intricate but ultimately successful. Number 48–042 also remained grounded pending the arrival of factory blueprints needed to repair its engine nacelles properly. Captain Mackey nonetheless hoped that the aircraft would be certified as operational no later than mid–October.[42] Still, the following month turned out even better for the detachment, which mounted twenty-one missions, including three classified flights. Mackey himself conducted one foray along the China coast after taking refueling in Korea. "When I flew over, it was like Sunday morning. Everything was quiet, calm, their MiGs were lined up wing tip to wing tip, and nobody scrambled anything. In fact, I often wondered if they ever knew we came because we had come over … because I had flown about ten feet off the water before we got within their radar coverage, and just before we got to the target, we swooped up to 10–20,000 feet, took pictures, and then dove back down to just over the water. I was thinking that they didn't even know that they had their picture taken." Around this time Captain Kristen also squeezed in a secret flight north to Vladivostok. "Tom Broughton had done it before with a K-38 camera, and we flew by about eleven miles off the coast at 20–25,000 feet. I had my sights on and my K-30 camera picked up everything on 9 × 18 film. As we were getting ready to line up, the CGI radar up there began calling 'Butterfly! Butterfly! Butterfly!' which meant *abort*. I went as far as I could, taking some obliques, but they had Russian aircraft stacked every 5,000 feet, clear across the sea to the Kuriles Islands — with our aircraft flying formation *alongside* them. I aborted that one. They were letting me know that they could intercept me. They certainly could have because *they were there!*"

Maintenance schedules increased after the return of number 48–042 from the repair shops, while 48–027 and 48–014 — the old stalwart — endured their intermediate inspections. Problems proved relatively minor; however, on the return leg of the October 24, 1952, mission, after 48–027 touched down at K-13 airfield (Suwon) to refuel, the Tornado's weight caused the landing ramp to collapse around the right main gear. Little damage was sustained by the aircraft, which flew home unimpeded. Then, after 48–042 was repaired, it received the first tail gun and radar installation system for tests at Yokota. Mackey reported, "This aircraft is now in excellent condition and should stand up very well."[43] He also spoke highly of his ground crews and their incessant labors. "Before we'd take off they'd give you a kind of maintenance log, a log listing a number of things that were wrong with the airplane — not enough to keep you from flying it — but just enough, like one of the compasses might be out. Then you figure, 'Well, I have the other compass, I don't need the second back up.' Still they would take great pride occasionally coming to you and showing you a log that had nothing on it. I had the feeling that they were thinking, 'These are my pilots and I want to get them back!'"

On November 13, 1952, a new detachment commander, Captain Howard S. "Sam" Myers, appeared with two flight crews and additional ground support personnel. Once Mackey and the others rotated back to Lockbourne, Myers wasted no time acquainting himself with his charge. He was impressed by the quality of maintenance encountered but, because the weather proved abysmal over the next two weeks, Myers estimated, "We lost over thirty two hours of flying time." Consequently, the detachment conducted only fifteen combat sorties, including two top secret missions. The November 21, 1951, mission, flown by Captain Myers himself, skirted Sakhalin using a side-looking, 100-inch focal length camera installed in the bomb bay. "We could fly at twenty-five thousand feet over water and shoot into the Soviet Union and get great pictures of their airfields," he marveled. "It worked real well for photographing Sakhalin Island. We used our powerful bomb-bay camera for high-altitude photography and the nose camera for low-altitude work."[44] No resistance or opposition materialized during the flight and he returned safely to Misawa. On 28 November 1952, the detachment was required to drop a T2 paraflare bomb on a training bomb range in Japan. That test was accomplished while flying at 25,000 feet and at 470 miles per hour; results were judged excellent and no further drops were scheduled. As the month concluded, Myers grew concerned about the defenselessness of RB-45Cs and nudged his superiors into action. "The tactical desirability of having turret equipped aircraft in this theater cannot be overlooked," he wrote. "Therefore, if these aircraft are available in the immediate future, I recommend that they be ferried to this detachment without delay."[45]

The year ended on an upbeat note with Detachment 2 accomplishing twenty-one combat mission totaling 81 hours of flying time — the highest output for the entire year. Of these flights, only one was classified: on December 17, 1952, Myers shepherded number 48–027 out of K-13 airfield, swung west towards Chingtao, China, then headed back along the coast to Suwon. This flight involved both visual and radar photography and concluded without enemy interference, but Myers noted how "we flew against a tremendous headwind of around 125 knots. I had to crank the RB-45C about 30 or 40 degrees to stay on the target's path." As the year concluded, the captain happily declared that "The RB-45 is fully justified in this theater if for no other reason than accomplishing FEAF's highly classified type of photographic missions."[46]

The New Year began with high-level discussions in Washington, D.C., and FEAF Headquarters, Tokyo, over the need to expand the latter's long-range reconnaissance capabilities. By now the specific limitations of the RB-45C under combat conditions were well-appreciated, and talks centered upon introducing Boeing's new RB-47 to Korea after it deployed later in the year. Predictably, General LeMay objected to any diversion of strategic assets from SAC and made no secret of his displeasure to the chief of staff, General Hoyt S. Vandenberg. "I strongly recommend against replacing RB-45 acft in FEAF with RB-47s at this time," he argued. "Exposure of the RB-47 type acft to combat would give the enemy valuable info on its performance and defensive capabilities. Further compromise would result if an acft were lost over unfriendly territory. If such info were gained by the USSR, it would enable them to plan a more effective defense against the SAC atomic force than is now possible." Air Staff officials subsequently decided to add two additional RB-45Cs to Yokota rather than risk LeMay's valuable jets in a war that was already winding down.[47] At this time, the venerable 48–014 also rotated back to Lockbourne, leaving only two Tornados in theater.

Meanwhile, Detachment 2's operations continued apace. During January the unit completed nineteen combat sorties, totaling nearly 82 hours of air time. No top secret missions were flown, but Captain Myers orchestrated a major experiment using searchlights and fighter interceptor aircraft. An unpainted RB-45 was easily tracked at night by powerful searchlights, even without the assistance of contrails. An F-94 Starfire on loan from the 41st Air Division also encountered few difficulties spotting the high-flying jet, once caught in searchlight beams or illuminated by a full moon. Captain Myers noted, "Much to our chagrin, it was determined that relatively inexperienced ground crew searchlight operators were able to track our high flying RB-45C clipping along at 460 knots plus ground speed from about ten miles out. They would simply sweep the sky, lock on a contrail, follow it to where it began, and there was the B-45, shining and glistening against the blackened sky." Conversely, a plodding, all-black RB-29 proved impossible to detect by searchlights at any altitude. The study concluded by stating that "only RB-45 aircraft that have black undercoating and a black tail section [should] be used in night operations against targets defended by searchlights and fighters."[48]

February brought another downturn in missions and hours flown due to inclement weather, and the fact that one RB-45 was sent to northern Japan to await a special mission while the other sat in a hangar awaiting its black laquer overcoat. Only ten missions were flown that month, of which two were designated "Top Secret." On February 19 and 28, the all-black number 48–027 slipped out of Yokota for target-run bomb-scope pictures of airfields in Manchuria and Tennei, China. No resistance was encountered and Myers reported that the greatest danger he faced came from the U.S. Navy: "We were cruising along at thirty-five thousand feet heading for the sea of Japan, when by chance I overheard a flight of two navy F9F Panthers calling their carrier, which was sitting right in front of us. The lead navy pilot was saying that they had spotted an IL-28 bomber heading for the carrier and they were going in for the attack. Luckily, I happened to be on their frequency when I heard the radio call. My adrenaline level rose instantaneously, and for a moment I felt like the bull's eye at a rifle range. I immediately called to let them know I was friendly. The shipboard radar had seen us coming from the north, assumed we were hostile, and launched the Panthers. The F9Fs finally got the word and broke off their attack, but not before making a pass at us close enough to rock the aircraft with their jet wash." Myers subsequently held discussions with FEAF officials regarding their increased emphasis on nighttime radar photography. Considering the complications and risks involved, he strongly recommended that "future photo navigators assigned to this detachment be extremely well qualified in [AP]Q-24 operation, and that no 'greenhorns' be considered for this duty."[49]

March witnessed the arrival of a new and final wartime detachment commander, Captain Charles J. Adams. On March 2, 1953, he and Captain F.J. Chiocchi guided numbers 48–021 and 48–025 from Lockbourne AFB, Ohio, on the first leg of their ferry mission to Travis AFB, California. Two days later they departed California for Hickham Field, Hawaii, refueling in flight. En route, 48–021 broke the tanker's boom nozzle in it receptacle, but the airplane and crew arrived safely. A few days later the two craft departed for Kwajalein, but 48–021 missed a rendezvous with its tanker and returned to Hawaii while its stablemate continued on to Yokota, touching down on March 9. Adams, flying 48–021, departed Hichkam a second time on March 8 and landed at Kwajelien, where he waited two days for temperatures to cool owing to the island's short runway. He departed on the 10th despite radio failures and bad weather en route, finally landing at Haneda, Japan. These RB-45Cs finally rendezvoused at Yokota on March 11, 1953. Significantly, these were the first Tornados arriving in Japan with fully functioning tail turrets.[50]

Routine operations continued at Yokota, resulting in forty-one hours of combat flying and ten sorties. On March 13, 1953, number 48–027 departed the base, refueled at K-13, and continued onto Kaesong, North Korea, for oblique coverage of the target area. Meanwhile, number 48–021 received its black overcoat and successfully completed a final series of tests against search lights. The Tornados were also retrofitted with a safety warning device in the gunner's compartment, which triggered a light in the copilot's position whenever the crewman slumped down due to hypoxia, or fell unconscious due to anoxia. Meanwhile, Captain Myers departed for the ZI on March 19, 1953, taking with him the racy, all-black 48–027. "Upon landing at Lockbourne, via Guam, Johnson Island, Hickham, Travis, and finally to home port, the bird was an absolute mess," he recalled. "Seems that 90% of the outer black paint had peeled off due to the salt air across of the Pacific. This left only the yellow zinc chromide undercoating remaining. We arrived with 10% black and 90% yellow, with a peek of bright aluminum."[51]

These home-bound aircraft were replaced by numbers 48–033 and 48–035, which flew from Lockbourne AFB on April 8, 1953, under the command of Captain Louis L. Pfeffer. Bad weather delayed their departure from Travis AFB until April 12, and number 48–033 successfully refueled and landed at Hickham Field, Hawaii. However, 48–035 lost two generators in midair, aborted, and hobbled back to Travis. The pilots departed the following day and again proceeded to Hawaii. High headwinds detained both RB-45s there until April 16, when they proceeded onto Kwajalein. The Tornados finally arrived at Yokota on April 20, 1953. Captain Adams observed, "It was ironic that they were within a very few minutes of having exactly the same time to go for a second intermediate inspection as 8021 and 8025." The need to conduct four inspections at the same time resulted in additional work for the hard-pressed maintenance crews, but no serious problems surfaced.[52]

The presence of four RB-45s at Yokota facilitated an upswing in activity for April, resulting in 87 hours flown and twenty-one missions completed, including two nighttime leaflet drops over North Korea. These drops offered Communist pilots $100,000 to deliver a MiG-15 to UN lines. Three top secret missions were also flown; two by Captain Adams on April 12 and April 18, which covered Chinese airfields throughout

While not perfect, the RB-45C performed yeoman work throughout the Korean War by continuously darting in and out of restricted regions where propellor-driven RB-29s and RB-50s faced certain annihilation at the hands of MiG-15s (San Diego Air & Space Museum).

Manchuria. On his first sortie Adams lost pressurization and VHF radio contact while coasting into enemy airspace. Worse, "All crew members encountered slight cases of aeroembolis and severe gas pains due to the length of time at altitude." His second mission over Mukden proved more routine, although tense moments arose once Adams was bracketed by radar-controlled searchlights over the city. Another mission, piloted by Captain Chiocchi on April 16, took in the airfields at Yingk'ok and An-shan, Manchuria, where some minor flak bursts were observed while Chiocchi was returning, near the Yalu River.[53]

One of the most intriguing overflights of the entire war transpired on April 13–14, 1953, although precious little is known of it. Sergeant Vernon Scott was a member of the top secret U.S. Air Force Security Service (USAFSS), an arm of the National Security Agency (NSA); Scott made several flights on the RB-45C as a radio traffic/crypto analyst. Having completed a crash course in Russian at the Army Language School in Monterey, California, Scott flew in the aisle behind the navigator while operating a radio receiver and a wire recorder. His purpose was to monitor and record Red Air Force radio chatter, usually while orbiting off the coastline near Vladivostok. This mission, however, was out of the ordinary. According to Scott:

> We were making a trip in an RB-45 into deep China and Russia. It would be at least 17 hours' flight time. This was quite well-planned since it would be approaching the extreme range of the aircraft. We were loaded with fuel and were carrying as much as the 45 could hold, with special tanks installed for long flights. The flight was to be to the area of Lake Baikal and the city of Irkutsk and Ulan Ude. All went well and the flight was scheduled at an extreme altitude of above 45,000 feet. We were well covered by their radar sites, but there were some places that could not cover us due to the sparsely populated areas we were flying over. If we were picked up on their radar, they were tracking us quite accurately. This we

knew due to our interception of their radio broadcasts to their central control. There were
areas that we would go out of their range and not hear from another tracking station for
15–30 minutes. This meant that there was no radar that could cover the area and was unattended. This indicated areas that were not covered by them and would be good entry spaces
if need be.

We headed home by a different route, things were rather quiet and no threats of hostile
intervention. As we approached friendly territory, I tuned my Hamlund SP600 radio to Radio
Moscow. They were always good for classical music. Just as I tuned in they were just starting
Ravel's "Death of a Princess" (*Pavane pour une infante defunte*). Now anytime I hear that
piece it brings back the memory of that flight. A few shivers down my spine and even a tear
or two. As far as I know that was the only flight ever made into that area. It was a good flight
and we received a lot of info from it.[54]

If true, Scott's mission into southern Siberia constitutes one of the deepest Tornado
penetrations into Soviet airspace and equals, in daring, the better-known RAF overflights.
As with so many of the RB-45C's clandestine ventures, documentation for this intriguing matter is utterly lacking. Its connection to events in Korea also seems tenuous, and
was most likely undertaken to discover potential gaps along the vast Russian radar net in
the event of future hostilities. The intrusion also marked a high point in Scott's career,
for the remainder of his missions proved relatively uneventful. "Some of them were pretty
quiet and peaceful," he recalled, "and other times we would encounter Russian MiGs.
Sometimes they would just come along and fly with us and watch us, and a couple of
times they did act a little strange, so our pilot just said' That's it!' — and we knew he was
turning around to go home because of the way he turned. He didn't waste any time!"

Operations continued at the same high levels into late spring, with Detachment 2
executing eighteen combat sorties and flying 77 hours. The additional weight of the tail
turrets, however, resulted in new restrictions while operating from Yokota's 8,000 foot
runway; takeoff temperatures hotter than 80 degrees Fahrenheit were deemed unsafe. On
warmer days, the fuel load was lightened commensurately to ensure safe departures. Missions for the month included another special nighttime leaflet-dropping sortie and two
top secret flights. On May 11, 1953, Captain Adams guided number 48–033 along on a
course that covered Taushan, Feng Cheng, and Tapao airfields; he noticed that "Outside
temperature was minus 70 degrees, causing some frosting of the canopy." Searchlights
and flak arced about in the distance over Andong, but the mission ended without incident. On May 11, 1953, Captain Chiocchi photographed Andong and Tatung airfields at
night; he lost the use of two generators in the process and landed at K-13 Airfield to make
repairs.[55] In June Monsoon conditions grounded Detachment 2 for twenty-one of thirty
flying days, with a telling reduction in hours flown. Eleven combat sorties were mounted,
representing a total of 46 hours of flying, but intense overcast limited the effectiveness
of all but two flights. Adams also received word that his detachment's tour was being
extended an additional 90 days. "The flight crews were, to say the least, disappointed,"
he reported.[56]

By July, the anticipated armistice led to a near-cessation of combat activity for
Detachment 2, which completed only twenty-six hours in seven combat missions over
North Korea. Most flying hours logged were spent in pilot proficiency training, air defense
penetrations against fighter aircraft, and radar-scope photo practice. Prior to the end of
hostilities on July 27, 1953, aircraft numbers 48–021 and 48–033 were also outfitted with

electronic countermeasure (ECM) suites, although no missions of this nature were performed. An inflight engine explosion on July 17 that destroyed both engines in number 48–033's right nacelle provided the only excitement. Captain Adams managed to land safely, after which the aircraft was grounded pending an engine change and repairs to the nacelle. Detachment 2's tour of duty ended on an anticlimactic note. "Morale has been high," Captain Adams observed, "but the extension of the Detachment, together with the signing of the Armistice, has made us all wonder what our mission will be for the remainder of our tour."[57]

The Korean War drew to a close, ending one of the earliest and most concerted episodes of Cold War reconnaissance by the U.S., but clandestine activities by RB-45Cs in the Far East were far from over. Their unheralded jaunts across the skies of North Korea, Manchuria, China, and the Soviet Union constitute a high point in the aircraft's operational history. The crews and machines rendered yeoman service in spite of MiGs, horrendous weather, and endemic part shortages — a Herculean and highly productive effort. Regardless of this performance, Air Force leadership regarded the RB-45C's presence circumspectly and their final verdict was couched in reservations. According to FEAF's official report, "The RB-45 did not achieve appreciably better results against opposition than did the RB-29. The RB-45 was evaluated early in the war by Fifth Air Force [officers] for suitability as a tactical reconnaissance aircraft. The conclusion was that it was too vulnerable to both air opposition and to ground fire to be suitable. As used by the 91st Strategic Reconnaissance Squadron, the aircraft was less concerned by ground fire. However, air opposition presented a sufficient problem to survival."[58] It was a somber reminder of the inherent limitations straight-wing jets faced when pitted against swept-wing opponents. Yet, in Detachment 2's capable hands, Tornados transcended these shortcomings and contributed significantly to theater reconnaissance at the strategic level, swooping in and out of areas where propeller-driven aircraft faced certain annihilation. Success here also signaled the rebirth of American strategic reconnaissance, which had languished since the end of World War II and now became a standard fixture of Cold War intelligence gathering. None of this could have been achieved without the RB-45Cs at Yokota.[59] For nearly three years they compiled a distinguished, if unheralded, litany of achievements, but more difficult work lay ahead. In the words of FEAF commander General Otto P. Weyland, "I think the most significant job those RB-45s did was after the Armistice in Korea."[60]

CHAPTER NINE

Cordial Collusion

"We are proposing to send three crews to Barksdale Air Force Base about the
end of the month in order that they may be converted to the B.45 under
arrangements which have been made by General LeMay."
— Air Chief Marshal Sir Ralph A. Cochrane[1]

It is seldom appreciated that before B-45As began their celebrated tour at RAF
Sculthorpe with the 47th Bomb Wing, RB-45Cs of the 91st Strategic Reconnaissance
Wing had been greasing tarmacs there for over a year. In fact, Tornados were the first,
four-engine jet aircraft to routinely ply European airways, another historic first. Their
presence is easy to comprehend: global tensions arising from the Korean conflict rever-
berated throughout the West and American leaders, distracted by events in Asia, feared
that a Soviet lunge towards Europe was inevitable. For NATO war planners to contain
and counter such aggression, they required updated cartographical and geographical information about their constituent members. This information could then be used to produce Target Complex Charts and Target Complex Mosaics, stretching from the East
German border to Switzerland, for possible wartime use. The only reconnaissance aircraft capable of acquiring such valuable information quickly was the RB-45C, thus Project Mid Winter arose in December 1950. Here, the 91st Wing would assemble and deploy
Detachment I in England to perform routine training and unit rotation, while also gathering the desired photographic intelligence. A special photographic processing and development office was also established by the British at West Drayton for the express purpose
of processing and disseminating this information. As events unfolded, these outwardly
routine Tornado operations cloaked one of the most daring covert operations of the Cold
War.

The initial deployment occurred on January 10, 1951, when Colonel William J. Meng
led a flight of four RB-45Cs, 323rd Strategic Reconnaissance Squadron, and four KB-
29 tankers from Barksdale AFB on a 30-day TDY abroad. These aircraft threaded their
way across the Atlantic via Goose Bay, Labrador, and Keflavik, Iceland, then RAF
Manston, Kent, the first home to Tornados in England. If anything, their arrival spurred
snide commentary from at least one nativist aviation writer. "As a matter of interest, the
flight of the B-45s was the first crossing of the Atlantic by a large jet aircraft, although
it was not flown non-stop," he assured readers. "Perhaps the Canberra will by now have
led the way in that respect."[2] Detachment I went immediately to work, despite the usual
gripes about lack of spare parts and inadequate refueling equipment. In their first month

of operations, the RB-45Cs accumulated a total of 106 hours in the air and transferred 2,575 gallon of fuel. The period closed uneventfully, but the wing historian cautioned that the detachment's TDY would probably extend to 90 days in February, and a change of stations also seemed probable.[3] The following month Tornado activity declined to only 100 hours, principally because all aircraft were grounded on February 14 to replace alternator shaft bearing assemblies. This kept all aircraft idle for two weeks, and operations did not resume until the 28th. Still, the interval was put to good use by transferring operations from Manston to RAF Sculthorpe, Norfolk, where better accommodations awaited. Wing headquarters also announced that, commencing in March, they would enact a continuous rotation plan to keep aircraft and crews cycling through Detachment 1 on a regular, three-month basis.[4] Meanwhile, actual operational control of RB-45Cs reverted to Seventh Air Division Headquarters, Strategic Air Command, at South Ruislip. Big plans, as yet unclear, seemed in the offing.

Captain Gerald Ramsey, who accompanied one of the earliest sorties to England, related this anecdote regarding his stopover at Goose Bay. "When we were ready to leave, my navigator and I worked up a flight plan, and we weren't going to use air refueling. But we figured we could make Sculthorpe at a high cruise setting and set a trans-Atlantic record. And there would be a KB there to launch in case we didn't make it. So we had to request permission from SAC headquarters to make this try and, as I remember, the telegram came back, *'When I want records made, I'll let you know–LEMAY.'* I guess he didn't want North American aircraft to mess up the B-47 contract!" Captain C.N. "Jack" Rice also reflected on the slipshod nature of early operations in England. "We didn't stay at Manston very long and then we moved to Sculthorpe, and most of our mapping was out of Sculthorpe," he stated, "but at that time the British did not really have an air control system. The only thing we were briefed on was not to fly over London. We'd take off and not even file a flight plan with the tower; we'd just tell them we were going 'Round Robin' for six hours or whatever and off we'd go!"

March witnessed arrival of the first replacement crews and airplanes at Sculthorpe. However, RB-45C activity remained curtailed for want of alternator shaft bearings and new SAC regulations requiring that 50 percent of available aircraft remain grounded, in commission and combat ready, at all times. So the Tornados, if they flew at all, only racked up 77 hours in the air while burning through 28,840 gallons of fuel in various exercises. The biggest obstacle to smoother operations turned out to be the lack of adequate refueling equipment. Two 2,000 gallon trucks were present at Sculthorpe; but these were insufficient for detachment purposes; hence a 4,000 gallon unit was requested from headquarters. The remainder of the month passed flying celestial navigation missions and Meng, in his semimonthly report, advocated a nonstop RB-45C flight from Sculthorpe back to Barksdale for practicing long-distance navigation and refueling.[5] By April the situation showed little improvement and the Tornados accomplished only 22 hours of flying due to shortages of booster pumps and solenoid shutoff valves that, again grounded them for most of the month. Nevertheless, two long-range tactical missions were successfully concluded; these lasted sixteen hours and consumed 7,800 gallons of fuel, further demonstrating the detachment's capacity for extended operations. Plans were also afoot to enlarge the detachment in England by adding three more Tornados and one tanker by month's end.[6]

Detachment 1 was accordingly augmented by the arrival of numbers 48–011, 48–020,

A massed flyby of RB-45Cs over RAF Sculthorpe; B-45As of the 47th Bomb Wing are arrayed along the bottom of the photo (John Mott).

and 48–027, which flew from Barksdale AFB on May 2, 1951, to Wright-Patterson, Ohio, then on to Goose Bay. All three aircraft then experienced radio difficulties on the final leg of the journey, forcing them to haul back to Goose for repairs. These Tornados, commanded by Major Eugene Broemmelsiek, landed safely at Sculthorpe on May 8, after covering 2,135 miles in only five hours and forty-five minutes; Broemmelsiek was nominated for the MacKay Trophy in January 1952. His presence in England had the more immediate effect of increasing flight time for RB-45Cs to 190 hours and 23,100 gallons of fuel transferred. Maintenance problems had also abated somewhat, thanks to the arrival of vital parts and other materiel from Barksdale, that had been shipped on April 13 and 19. Detachment I was girding itself for expanded operations when a teletype arrived from Headquarters, Seventh Air Division, declaring that bomb bay fuel tanks could no longer be serviced, except in the event of an emergency. This was most likely because of continuing shortages of that essential item; but the wing historian duly noted, "This restriction has eliminated the possibility of flying profile type missions within this detachment."[7]

Once ensconced at Sculthorpe, American airmen could not help but get intimately acquainted with the notorious British weather. Colonel Lewis B. Lyle remembers the time he touched down during a huge thunderstorm and a 200-foot ceiling. "The crosswind on that runway was sixty knots," he stated. "I had to keep enough power on so that I'd have enough control to keep the airplane from veering into all those planes parked on the ramp. So I ran out of runway — fortunately all I did was hit the mud and it stopped. That was *interesting*." Less fortunate was the fate of 48–026, which ended up sliding down a rain-slicked runway on May 15, 1951. "We took off and lost two engines, and we were in a rainstorm, and they told us to come back," Lieutenant Maury Seitz recalled. "The runways over there were built out of soapstone and we hydroplaned for over 7,000 feet, and went off the runway at over 100 miles per hour. The airplane stopped — I didn't — my seat broke loose and I got a back injury out of it. The airplane was totaled. The investigating officer told us that was the first recorded accident attributed to hydroplaning." Seitz also noted — with some trepidation — that twenty-four hours later General LeMay arrived at Sculthorpe to *personally* grill 48–026's crew about their recent mishap. He left satisfied that it was, in fact, an accident and not pilot error, which could have ended their careers.

June heralded the appearance of a new detachment commander, Lieutenant Colonel Marion C. ("Hack") Mixon, an officer who figured centrally in subsequent events. That month he reported that RB-45Cs flew 193 hours, up significantly from May and due largely to another influx of much-awaited spare parts. A period of extended flying ensued, with a total of 52,258 gallons transferred by tankers. Detachment I also commenced running missions coordinated by higher headquarters, including prestrike, bomb damage assessment, map charting, and Sonne strips, radar photography and mosaic runs — in sum, a full reconnaissance regimen. The only persistent problem remained refueling abilities on the ground and Mixon reiterated pleas for a 4,000 gallon truck. He also noted that once camera heaters were shut while refueling, condensation collected around the shutter and lenses, damaging them. The biggest event came in the form of operational orders for Detachment I, issued by the Seventh Air Division and submitted to Headquarters, SAC, for approval. "We were given the project of drawing up the entire plan, so if it is accepted by SAC and not suitable to us it is our own fault," Mixon wrote. Rotation plans were also altered to include the transfer of seven RB-45Cs, five B-45As, and six KB-29s, with attendant personnel, every ninety days.[8]

Mid-summer found the detachment heavily engaged in executing its new operations order, which ran entirely through August. Accordingly, RB-45Cs performed 253 hours of flight time and accepted 70,990 gallons of fuel from the KB-29s. Tornados were also entrusted with radar and visual coverage of 72 targets on the Continent, of which forty-nine were successfully overflown by July 14. Their routine was interrupted briefly that week when three bombers and accompanying tankers winged down to Casablanca, Morocco, in celebration of Bastille Day. Mixon also found time to conduct several VIP tours of Sculthorpe for the editors of the *New York Herald*, the governor of Maryland, and the presidents of TWA and Fairchild Aviation — all of whom marveled over the rakish RB-45s. Public relations, however, were not without a degree of peril. Sergeant Merle Sollars recalled what happened as a Tornado was being readied to fly a major general. "I believe that the copilot gave up his seat to that general at that time, and he was going to ride in the walkway. Regardless, they started the engines up and blew two engines with him in the airplane. We just lost the engines and shut the airplane down. Actually, the guy hardly knew what happened because there was no big explosion or anything — we just threw compressor blades all over Hell." Operational levels dipped somewhat towards the end of the month when Tornados became scheduled for regular maintenance, but these rebounded quickly. "I'm not having to push the boys too much as the pilots as well as the ground crews are eager to get the ships into the air," Mixon proudly noted. He also announced that nine RAF exchange officers were temporarily appended to the detachment on its journey back to Barksdale that August.[9]

Late summer brought Lieutenant Colonel John A. Des Portes to Sculthorpe as the new Detachment I commander. On August 1, 1951, seven RB-45Cs and five B-45As of the 324th Strategic Reconnaissance Squadron and six tankers from the 91st Air Refueling Squadron departed Barksdale in relays, headed for England. Tragically, the operation suffered a loss on August 4 as Captain Rodger Elliot was landing number 48–032 at Goose Bay, Labrador, on instruments. Heavy rain severely reduced visibility, but the pilot followed GCA guidance dutifully until his aircraft suddenly vanished from the radar scopes. Apparently, Elliot's craft had careened headlong into a hillside five miles from the runway; this feature appeared as 500 feet high on the letdown chart but, in actuality, towered up to 850 feet. The entire crew perished along with their Tornado, but the loss was made up by retaining number 48–020 at Sculthorpe.[10]

All detachment planes were in place as of August 10, while the previous occupants safely relocated back to Louisiana. Once settled, Des Portes oversaw implementation of the new SAC Operational Order Number 18–51, requiring radar and visual coverage of no less than 287 targets in Germany, France, Belgium, the Netherlands, and Italy. The first mission sortied on the 13th, and by month's end the Tornados had accumulated 360 hours of flying time. No less than 76,030 gallons of fuel had been transferred in flight, with one RB-45C setting an unofficial endurance record by remaining aloft twelve hours. Four B-45As were also detached for joint aggressor maneuvers, in concert with F-84Es of the Twelfth Fighter Escort Wing, to Oslo, Norway. A subsequent SAC directive, 51AM-10, required mosaic coverage of fourteen cities along the Rhine River, ranging from Strasbourg to Wesel. Radar scope results were judged 87 percent acceptable, but bad weather played havoc with trimetrogon and split-level photography, which consequently received ratings of 45 percent. All told, the detachment fulfilled a demanding schedule with acceptable results. "My people are pretty well settled and we're trying to salvage what started out to be a Hell of a month," De Portes conceded. "Morale is good, including my own."[11]

September found the RB-45Cs still deeply immersed in their SAC operational directive. A total of 210 flying hours was reached, which entailed the transference of 92,690 gallons of fuel from the tankers, a new record. This was burned off obtaining the radar photography of the fourteen cities along the Rhine River from Wesel to Lorrach. Visual photography proved somewhat less productive, with acceptance rates of 74 percent owing to the seepage of hydraulic fluid or jet fuel over the camera ports in certain craft. Concurrently, the nominally spare-parts stricken B-45As were impressed to fly weather-related missions to assist the reconnaissance craft; they also flew as bomber bait for the 12th Fighter Escort Wing. So the Tornados were flying again, and flying regularly. "That was really a moral victory," Des Portes beamed, "and proves that it can be done in spite of a 24 percent AOCP factor and general excessive maintenance." The only interference from Headquarters, Seventh Air Division, were orders to avoid Sculthorpe during inclement weather, as rainfall upped accident rates. Tornados were now obliged to use alternate fields at Lakenheath or Rhein Main until their home base could be resurfaced at some later date.[12]

October was another productive period, with 228 hours flown and 77,880 gallons transferred. Photographic results over the Continent were again highly successful for radar coverage, but the percentage of visual records dipped again to 58 percent. This resulted from mounting problems with the K-38 and O-15 cameras, which experienced sheared pins and other problems requiring intensive repairs. Worse, on October 20, 1951, Lieutenant Robert H. Ahlborn was guiding number 48–040 on its final approach to Sculthorpe when he suddenly saw a flash and heard explosions from his right nacelle. He promptly shut down both engines and landed safely on the remaining two. Accident investigators attributed the mishap to a large seagull being ingested by the number four engine, resulting in a compressor explosion. Colonel Joseph J. Preston, reporting the mishap to General LeMay, suggested the addition of air intake screens as, "Birds and sea gulls are numerous in the Sculthorpe area and, as this accident shows, represent a hazard to high speed, jet type aircraft."[13]

The onset of winter posed certain operational problems to Detachment I after Sculthorpe endured severe storms for several days. These conditions led to commensurate drops in operations, with only 128 hours flown and 31,400 gallons transferred. Photo missions, when they could be sortied, also shifted away from Germany and were directed towards Spain, Italy, and the Balearic Islands. Sculthorpe was also visited by the 91st Wing inspector, who reported the aircraft in good shape, then ordered greater emphasis on camera maintenance and repairs. He further noted the local hangar queens, 47–047 and 47–060, which sported forty-five discrepancies apiece, were to be restored to flying condition.

During this period, Detachment I underwent a periodic turnover as members of the 322nd Strategic Reconnaissance Squadron under Lieutenant Colonel Hal C. Connor arrived on November 21, 1951, while Des Portes rotated back with his 324th Squadron to Lockbourne. The newcomers were accompanied by a thoroughly trained RAF detachment of three crews under Flight Commander John Crampton, who remained on the unit roster until further notice.[14] The year closed on a downside note, once again attributed to spare part shortages. These proved so pressing that Detachment I mechanics began cannibalizing B-45As to keep the recce birds airborne. Consequently, only 181 hours were flown and 23,875 gallons of fuel transferred. By dint of hard work, Tornados still executed forty-nine sorties for their continental mission, despite the fact that only three of seven RB-45Cs were serviceable. The aircraft flown also had to land at airfields other than Sculthorpe for, lacking booster pumps, they could not utilize all the fuel remaining in their tanks. Lieutenant Colonel Connor nevertheless marveled at the tenacity and ingenuity of his crews, even under a workload increase of 400 percent. He also commented favorably when a KB-29 pilot assisted an RAF Vampire fighter, almost out of fuel and in solid overcast, in landing at Sculthorpe. The entire detachment really stiffened — then gave a collective sigh of relief— in the wake of an unannounced inspection by the head of SAC himself. "Gen. LeMay has come and gone," Connor was relieved to report, "and we've heard no repercussions as a result of the visit."[15]

The new year began with an upswing in Tornado activity despite bad weather and continuing parts shortages. The detachment managed to accrue 236 hours aloft, execute eighty-eight reconnaissance sorties, and accept 39,800 gallons of fuel. All seven RB-45Cs were utilized at this time, although the majority of them flew in ANFE (aircraft not fully equipped) condition. As the wing historian observed, "This situation is a tendency of Crew Chiefs, fighting to maintain their aircraft in commission rather than be AOCP for

Lieutenant Colonel Marion "Hack" Mixon (left) and Squadron Leader John Crampton pose in front of their RAF-painted RB-45Cs. Judging from the grins, the two are clearly up to something! (John Mott).

months, to minimize the severity of improper operating parts, such as sticking tail pipe temperature gauges, intermittently operating fuel booster pumps, and other items of a critical nature." Parts shortages of B-45s had become nothing short of legendary at this point, but Connor could still point to the performance of his men. "Considering the miserable weather we've had for maintenance, scheduled flight cancellations due to weather and ice on the runways, we did remarkably well during January," he beamed. The following month also proved productive, with Tornados posting 268 hours in flight and consuming 70,590 gallons of fuel. Fortunately, Connor's plight finally stirred some action back at wing headquarters, and on February 26, 1952, Detachment I hosted Colonel Joseph P. Preston, wing commander, and Colonel William J. Meng, director of materiel. After viewing operations firsthand over a period of ten days, they ordered increased emphasis on parts procurement and also authorized retention of twenty-five technicians from the divisional depot at Burtonwood to allay personnel shortages. As to widespread cannibalization, nothing was said — and for good reason. "If cannibalization had not been practiced no aircraft would be in commission," the historian candidly admitted. "With the cooperation of higher headquarters continuously hammering at AMC for parts, the AOCP list has been shortened."[16]

March 1952 closed out another successful chapter in the history of the 91st Strategic Reconnaissance Wing. Detachment I, having operated continuously in England since January 1951, finally rotated home for good. Its tenure abroad, although taxed by technical difficulties, proved highly successful from a reconnaissance standpoint and provided allied war planners with updated cartographic information for defending NATO territory against Soviet attack. It also reconfirmed the viability of RB-45Cs as reconnaissance platforms, especially in the hands of superbly trained SAC flight crews. Having fulfilled his monthly quota of flying, Lieutenant Colonel Connor prepared to return men and machines back to Lockbourne AFB in relays, commencing on March 20. Two days previously, the detachment sustained its second major accident when number 47–043 exhibited a loud noise in flight, followed by severe vibrations and a violent 30 degree bank to the left. Pilot Captain Henry J. Rodgers deduced that the bomb bay doors had somehow opened but, upon checking visually, he saw that the left main landing gear had lowered and cut the hydraulic line. Radioing an emergency, Rodgers nursed his Tornado down through the overcast and successfully touched down without flaps. His aircraft veered off the runway, blew a tire, and nearly ground-looped before sliding to a halt. All aircraft consequently endured inspections of their landing gear and door up-locks. An even bigger mishap occurred on March 26, as RB-45Cs transferred back to the Zone of the Interior. Captain John S. Leak took number 48–020 on his final approach to Goose Bay when he inadvertently struck a fifteen-foot high snow bank situated 100 feet from the runway's end. The aircraft tore its left main gear, while the right main and nose gear collapsed, and the plane skidded 1,600 feet down the runway. The crew survived uninjured, but 48–020 was declared unsalvageable. No action was taken against Leak by SAC headquarters once accident inspectors deduced that "the pilot's depth perception was probably made faulty due to lack of shadow detail caused by overcast and the time of day."[17]

Captain C.N. Rice, Leak's copilot, vividly recalls the accident in detail:

> When we got into Goose Bay, they cleared us for a landing and I checked everything out and it looked just fine. I then looked at the pilot and said, 'Jack, pull it up a little bit.' So we came back and he got it pretty well on the glide slope. I was tightening up my harness and I looked back out and shouted, 'I've got it!' as I grabbed the wheel and hauled it back — just in time to keep us from going in nose first. They had cleared the runway, and right at the end they left a six foot wall, a bank. Jack was looking right through that bank at the runway — and that's what we hit. We knocked off the nose gear, knocked off the main gear, and the airplane went off the runway. I'm shutting off everything in back and steering the rudder with my feet, got it back on the runway and came to a stop.

Lieutenant Earl Huggins had just touched down in the aircraft ahead of 48–020, and commented on the landing conditions he found there: "Because of the snowfall in Labrador during the winter time, the snow plows would clear the runway and blow the snow high on each side and to the ends of the runway," he reflected. "Consequently it was almost like landing in a tunnel and there was also what was called 'white out' where everything looked the same and altered depth perception."[18]

Concurrently with Detachment I's withdrawal, a new reconnaissance unit, Detachment 3, began arriving in relays at Sculthorpe to replace it. Unknown at the time, their presence coincided with one of the most critically important episodes in the Tornado's history, an event shrouded by the utmost secrecy for nearly forty years. It also marked the return of Lieutenant Colonel "Hack" Mixon as detachment commander. Four RB-

45s of the 323rd Strategic Reconnaissance Squadron and five KB-29s departed Lockbourne on March 19, 1952, and flew to Sculthorpe, although number 48–019 was temporarily detained at Goose Bay pending an engine change. In the course of this, Major Charles S. Graham, piloting 48–042, reached England in only four hours and fifty-six minutes, an unofficial speed record. Immediately after arriving, Headquarters, Seventh Air Division, directed that control of the detachment's aircraft be transferred to the Royal Air Force as of April 5, 1952. Ostensibly, the British were to test highly "modified" APQ-24 radars in concert with their Photo Reconnaissance Unit at RAF Upwood and also evaluate various profile missions. Consistent with SAC's iron protocol, no questions were asked.

To all appearances, Detachment 3 operations appeared entirely routine, and American air crews completed ten sorties in the final week of March, logging sixty-seven flight hours and transferring 15,360 gallons of gasoline.[19] The following month, however, produced some unusual activity at Sculthorpe. The three Air Force RB-45C crews present were inexplicably flown back to the Zone of the Interior, at which point their mounts passed to an RAF Special Duties Flight under Squadron Commander John Crampton. This unit consisted of three flight crews who had previously qualified on Tornados while at Lockbourne. More striking, all four RB-45Cs were stripped of American insignia and repainted with RAF roundels on the wings and fuselage. Subsequent operations were jointly jostled between Seventh Air Division headquarters and RAF Bomber Command as Crampton's crews put their Tornados through their paces. Detachment 3 maintained its facade of routine operations with a number of profile missions and two maximum efforts staged on April 12 and April 17. These flights amounted to twenty-four hours of flight time whereby 17,200 gallons of fuel were transferred by tanker. All told, Crampton and company executed forty-one sorties in their RB-45Cs, receiving a grand total of 65,805 gallons via aerial refueling. Furthermore, all radar film taken was dispatched by courier to Seventh Air Division headquarters, and then to RAF Bomber Command, for further evaluation. The well-trained and professional RAF crews executed their tasks capably and higher headquarters felt pleased to pronounce their endeavors, such as they were, a complete success.[20]

On May 5, 1952, the four Tornados in RAF employ were quietly transferred back to the United State Air Force. Detachment 3's sojourn then concluded its 90-day TDY and returned to the United States with little fanfare. Lieutenant Colonel Mixon was pleased by the performance of all concerned, a fact reflected in his final mission report. In fact, he noted only one contentious item in a survey of British civilian attitudes; one irate individual felt that the U.S. Air Force should decamp the United Kingdom immediately because "American servicemen were disrupting the moral standards of the young feminine populace."[21] It all seemed innocuous enough, especially considering the long association RAF personnel had enjoyed with the Tornado. None could have realized that Detachment 3 activities masked one of the most daring overflights of the entire Cold War.

The United States had conducted clandestine reconnaissance of the Soviet Union since the end of World War II under the aegis of the Peacetime Airborne Reconnaissance Program (PARPRO) and for good reason. It appeared — commencing with the 1948 Berlin blockade, the coup in Czechoslovakia that same year, and detonation of Russia's first A-bomb in 1949 — that Soviet dictator Joseph Stalin was beginning to flex his muscles abroad. Western leaders worried that mounting belligerence was but a prelude to overt confrontation, possibly even World War III, yet relevant military intelligence necessary to wage it successfully was grossly lacking. Ongoing PARPRO activities had been restricted to the borders of Russia and its allies and their peripheral nature imposed severe restrictions which created an intelligence gathering problem. If the United States were to fight the Russians, the first wave of American retribution would necessarily arrive by strategic air power. In this context, accurate geographical and topographical information for assembling viable target folder information and mission planning was essential. In other words, Strategic Air Command bombers had to know what they were striking — to say nothing of how to get there — before ever leaving the ground. Given the hermetically sealed nature of Soviet society, such information could not be easily discerned through spies or defense attaches at embassies. As Colonel Charles P. Hollstein cogently assessed, "Our potential enemy, smug behind the Iron Curtain, rules an empire which, insofar as geographic and military intelligence is concerned, may well be called the Dark Continent." High altitude reconnaissance was, by default, the West's only viable method of obtaining the target information necessary to insure the credibility of American nuclear deterrence, or, failing that, massive retaliation.[22]

The precise process and timetable through which the United States commenced regular reconnaissance overflights has never been pinpointed historically. The earliest date mentioned in any study is May 5, 1950, when spiraling global tensions, and the concomitant threat of war, induced President Harry S. Truman to authorize clandestine missions over Soviet territory on a broader scale.[23] To that end, RB-45Cs were involved in Northeast Asia, with minor incursions along Russia's eastern coastline and occasional sorties through Manchurian airspace. However, securing information relative to Soviet bomber forces stationed closer to Western Europe entailed overflying the Russian heartland — a dangerous and dicey proposition at best. Truman, therefore, turned to a little help from his friends. In December 1950, British Prime Minister Clement Atlee, worried that the Americans might introduce nuclear weapons into the Korean conflict, paid the president an official state visit. His appearance could have hardly been reassuring to the Americans. Atlee, an earnest man of good intentions, was apparently naive in his prior dealings with the Soviets and, in 1947, he arranged for the transfer of advanced Rolls-Royce *Nene* jet engines to Russia, over strenuous American protests. Such technological treason facilitated development of the MiG-15 fighter, which accounted for hundreds of American airmen in Korea. As Stalin himself aptly remarked of the incident, "What fool will sell us his secret?"[24]

Yet, Communist aggression in Asia provided a dose of *realpolitik* that even the idealistic Atlee could absorb. The prime minister secured from Truman a pledge to refrain from using nuclear weapons against the Chinese; and Truman, in turn, prevailed upon Atlee to facilitate joint reconnaissance missions over their potential adversary. This was done strictly on the basis of forestalling any possible surprise attack against Western Europe or the United States. Again, details of the agreement lay sequestered in secrecy and only the rough outline can be reconstructed with any accuracy. The two leaders decided that, at some time in the near-distant future, the United States would "loan" some RB-45Cs to the Royal Air Force, to be manned and flown by British crews. This was an essential precondition for the entire endeavor; the RAF would not receive its first Canberra PR.9 jets until 1953 and, in fact, they were still dependent upon World War II-vintage Spitfires and Mosquitos for high-altitude reconnaissance. The allies further concurred that any information derived from overflights would be jointly shared between SAC and RAF Bomber Command, the latter then pursuing its own atomic deterrent, V-Force. In the event of a shootdown, the United States could point to British insignia on the aircraft and disclaim any knowledge of this potentially war-making event. Both sides also reasoned that British crews caught violating Soviet airspace would be far less provocative in any case. The allies hoped to acquire a veneer of legitimacy for what historian Walter J. Boyne dismisses as "a ludicrously simple and completely transparent cover story."[25] The vagaries of national security and the exigencies of strategic reconnaissance, made for strange bedfellows, or so it seemed.

Back in London, Atlee authorized the Air Ministry to put the joint reconnaissance venture in motion, and planning for what ultimately emerged as Operation Ju Jitsu began in earnest. Air Chief Marshall Ralph Cochrane next entrusted selection of relevant personnel to Squadron Leader Micky H.B. Martin, a survivor of No. 617 Squadron, the celebrated "Dambusters." Martin, in turn, chose six exceptional pilots and three navigators to form a "Special Duty Flight" to execute the mission. Central to these proceedings was John Crampton, the six-foot, six-inch head of No. 97 Squadron (*Lincoln*). In July 1951 Crampton found himself ordered by the commander-in-chief of Bomber Command to report immediately to headquarters. "I was to assume command of a Special Duty Flight in conditions of utmost secrecy," he recalled. "The flight would be equipped with the North American RB-45C four-jet strategic reconnaissance aircraft, and the crews concerned would proceed almost immediately to the United States to begin training in the aircraft." Crampton, flattered by this attention, didn't think much of his assignment initially; but neither he, nor any of the personnel selected for this jarring jaunt, had the faintest inkling of what lay in store for them.[26]

Events also progressed on the American side, although the dire secrecy surrounding the project nearly compromised it. In addition to President Truman, only Generals Curtis E. LeMay, Hoyt S. Vandenberg (Air Force Chief of Staff), Nathaniel F. Twining (Vandenberg's successor), and Thomas D. White were apprised. Problems unexpectedly arose when Major General Roger M. Ramey, USAF director of operations, began questioning why superiors were lending four Tornados to the British when they were in such short supply stateside and while others were already deployed at Sculthorpe! Ultimately, Ramey was let on in the secret to secure his quiet compliance. In May 1951, the ubiquitous Lieutenant Colonel Marion C. "Hack" Mixon, 323rd Strategic Reconnaissance Squadron, was appointed liaison officer to the Special Duty Flight and flown to Sculthorpe, England, to commiserate with his British counterparts. He then returned to Barksdale with Crampton and company in tow on August 3, 1951, at which point training on B-45As commenced. A month later the British transferred to Lockbourne AFB for familiarization with the RB-45C. All hands took readily to the craft, although one pilot "pranged" his Tornado during a hard nighttime landing. "The dramatic result of this," Crampton notes, "was that Lockbourne's Base Commander, myself, and the pilot concerned were flown to Omaha, HQ of Strategic Air Command, there to be interviewed by General LeMay, who did not like people who broke his aircraft and left us in no doubt of the fact." After an unforgettable close encounter with LeMay at full throttle, a replacement RAF pilot was found and training resumed. Once the nuances of flying and refueling RB-45Cs were mastered, Crampton's command returned to Sculthorpe in December 1951, although still technically attached to the 323rd Strategic Reconnaissance Squadron stationed there.[27]

The project thus far appeared on track, but problems relating to political willpower nearly scuttled it. Prime Minister Atlee had pledged his cooperation for the overflight endeavor in December 1950. Yet, eight months later, Air Chief Marshall Cochrane candidly admitted, "We have not yet obtained the political agreement which will be necessary if the full project is to be undertaken." Atlee's waffling might have, in fact, jeopardized the entire operation, for no clandestine mission could be launched from British soil without the government's consent. This recalcitrance did not go unnoticed at the highest levels of Air Force leadership, and LeMay anxiously noted in his diary how "the matter now stands that Prime Minister had disapproved the project and it will be discontinued for the time." Fortunately for Western security, British voters ended Atlee's temporizing by ejecting the Labour Party from power and returning a Conservative government in October 1950. This signaled the comeback of a redoubtable American ally to 10 Downing Street and Sir Winston Churchill, every inch the veritable "British bulldog," enthusiastically embraced the means and objectives of Operation Ju Jitsu. Churchill unflinchingly granted authorization for the mission whenever it was deemed ready to execute. In fact, the prime minister evinced a most bullish enthusiasm for the entire matter. "Operation JIU JITSU will be done by us if the Americans cannot be persuaded to do it," he tersely instructed his secretary of state for Air. "I am to be informed at least a week before it happens."[28] The British lion never roared louder, nor more nobly.

Crampton and his crews returned to Sculthorpe as ordered and resumed flying and training with members of the 323rd throughout the spring of 1952. Relations were cordial and professional as always, but the commander waxed uncomfortable over his singular inability to explain their presence there: "We still had no idea what was planned for us. There was much speculation, mostly centred on comparative trials of the Boeing flying-boom in-flight refueling method against the probe and drogue favored by the RAF. It was a tense time for us and our hosts because nine RAF crews flying with an elite USAF squadron raised eyebrows, which none of us were able to lower." Everything became chillingly apparent once Crampton and his navigator, Lieutenant Rex Sanders, were suddenly summoned to High Wycombe near London for what they anticipated to be a routine briefing. The revelation stunned the airmen and seldom in RAF history was there a requirement for stiff upper lips to be stiffer. "This was the moment of truth and I confess to some apprehension when the charts were unrolled to show three separate tracks from Sculthorpe to the Baltic States, the Moscow area, and Central Southern Russia." Flight sergeant and copilot Robert Anstee, a veteran of fifty bombing missions over Germany and a usually unflappable sort, proved equally aghast when informed: "I thought at that time "Oh my God, what have they let us in for? Why? Why us? Why did we get lumbered with it?" Crampton finally briefed his crews about their upcoming mission and problems erupted when one pilot "washed his hands of the whole affair and returned to his parent unit where I feared he might entertain his chums to this extraordinary tale." Fortunately, no leak occurred, a B-45-capable RAF replacement was readily found, and the exceptional undertaking continued on schedule.[29]

The tempo of events accelerated that April when the four RB-45Cs were formally transferred to the British, who then flew them to RAF West Raynham. There, in Crampton's words, "a hangar was cleared and several gallons of paint stripper were put to use by a number of very mystified airmen." The aircraft emerged divested of all U.S. insignia and resplendently bedecked in RAF livery. Once back at Sculthorpe, Crampton and his teams prepared for an essential dry run by flying down the Berlin air corridor and back to gauge the reaction of Soviet air defenses. They departed on the evening of March 21, 1951, without incident and, as a precaution, the vaunted British Y-services remained attentively attuned to Russian radio traffic. Whatever technical intelligence they gathered that evening was deemed insufficient to deter the project, so the green light finally arrived on April 17, 1952. That evening three RAF-manned and decorated Tornados lifted off from Sculthorpe on what appeared to be another routine training flight. Operation Ju Jitsu, spawned of strategic necessity, was now a perilous reality.[30]

The first phase of the mission required the RB-45Cs to rendezvous in three separate refueling tracks over the North Sea, Denmark, and central Germany, with a like number of KB-29s. Lieutenant Maury Seitz, recently transferred to tankers, indelibly recalls events of that memorable day. "I was on top of a hangar and there was a whole bunch of stuff going on down below, and they taxied out a B-45 with British markings," he noted. "That night we took of and flew a six hour mission and there was radio silence from the very beginning — there was no tower clearance, we were given lights and after that we were airborne. We had a profile and ended up north of Denmark, and it was just at dusk and a B-45 shows up in British markings and we were the standby tanker. He came up, took on his fuel, turned off his lights, waggled his wings, and headed east."

The mission plan called for three distinct tracks: the northern-most leg would swing through the Baltic states, the center flight would investigate the Moscow region, and the most distant leg covered targets down through the Ukraine. Crampton, as flight leader, naturally opted to handle the longest and most perilous route. Radio silence remained absolute throughout the flight — even during refueling — with only an OMG (Oh My

Lieutenant Maury Seitz snapped this photo of an RAF-painted RB-45C as it left the hanger at Sculthorpe. A group of American officers is in the foreground (Maury Seitz).

God) frequency available for dire emergencies. Fully gassed, the three Tornados streaked through byzantine darkness at 35,000 feet without encountering opposition and unaware that Soviet radars had detected their approach and interceptors were scrambled to engage them. The latter proved impossible since MiGs lacked airborne radar, whereupon the Russian fighter command ordered its pilots to ram the intruders, if possible. Fortunately, visual contact proved impossible in the inky blackness. All three British crews glided along the starry Russian night, dutifully radar scoped their objectives, then swung west for home. The ten-and-a-half hour excursion proved remarkably uneventful, save for a final refueling en route to landing. Crampton touched down at Sculthorpe as planned, but a second aircraft under Flight Lieutenant Bill Blair greased onto RAF Manston on account of low overcast. Meanwhile, Flight Lieutenant Gordon Cremer's fuel filters inexplicably iced up and he lingered at Copenhagen for several hours before landing at Prestwick, Scotland. Considering the dangerous variables in play, not the least of which were disastrous consequences for the prime minister had a Tornado been bagged, the flight was a splendid example of interservice cooperation. Neither age nor infirmity had diminished Churchill's justly celebrated verve and, for the United States and Great Britain, their "special relationship" was never more manifest.[31]

This endeavor — and the superlative manner in which it performed — constitutes the Tornado's finest hour. For the first time Allied war planners had secured reliable radar photography from the literal belly of the beast, and could begin fleshing out SAC target folders in the event of hostilities. Nobody appreciated this more than the Soviet high command, livid over its inability to halt, or even infringe upon, what ground radar undoubtedly painted as a leisurely stroll through Russian air space. A committee, which included Stalin's feared security minister, Lavernty P. Beria, was urgently formed to investigate such glaring lapses in the Motherland's security. Consequently, several air defense leaders were demoted or sacked, the hierarchy overhauled, and the Russians grimly resolved not to let such an episode happen again. Crampton and company, meanwhile, received Air Force Crosses and were flown back to Omaha, "where I again met General LeMay under much happier circumstances. He was gracious in all his compliments." The towering officer had one more surprise in store for him; once home Crampton discovered his transfer to No 101 Squadron at Binbrook, then flying the RAF's first Canberras, as commander. "A bit like landing the Spring Double!" he declared.[32] The entire matter was then officially "forgotten" without further comment.

No sooner had the British RB-45Cs alighted than their radar photography film was removed and sent by special courier to the RAF processing lab in West Drayton. The officer chosen for that assignment was the young tanker officer Lieutenant Seitz, whose experience reads worthy of a James Bond novel:

> There was an RAF facility there. Also high security. And I was supposed to go to building F. In the fog and condition of disrepair and other things, the bottom of Building E had weathered and I thought it said F, and so I went into the wrong building. When I walked in I was confronted by armed guards with weapons drawn, and I was told that I was not where I was supposed to be. Then an officer came out and I identified myself, and we exchanged information to the point that he realized who I was and that I was there legitimately. The interesting thing is that I think orders were issued after I was a caught, shall we say. I think they were issued to cover my tail.

Building E was just a top secret photographic intelligence building devoted entirely to photo interpretation of high altitude radar pictures. They had developed new techniques that allowed them to make models in three dimensions from radar. And from what they told me, they were used to build the models that were used in the radar trainers, bombardier trainers, back in the United States at SAC. I have actually seen one with the three dimensional models, and my information from the British was that this was how they made the models. So that when bomber aircrews went in they weren't going in flat. They were able to know where obstructions were, where the high buildings were, where the smokestacks were, and all that stuff.[33]

Things returned to as normal as they could be at Sculthorpe, if only for the time being. Detachment 3, its mission fulfilled, simply flew back to Lockbourne the following May for disbandment. Activities perked up again that fall when orders arrived for the 91st Wing to dispatch four more RB-45Cs, drawn from all three squadrons, and a requisite number of tankers back to Great Britain. This new unit, Detachment 4, coalesced on October 17, 1952, once more under the aegis of Lieutenant Colonel Mixon. The Tornados and KB-29s departed on October 21, taking separate routes to England, with RB-45Cs destined for Sculthorpe and tankers headed for Lakenheath. The flight proved uneventful, but the jets remained at Goose Bay for four days awaiting better weather. One aircraft, 48–029, developed a fuel leak and did not arrive at Sculthorpe until Novem-

This assortment of stiff upper lips constituted the Royal Air Force Special Duty Flight, October-November 1952. The easy smiles belie the direness of their mission (John Mott).

ber 3, 1952. There the detachment was greeted by another complement of nine RAF exchange pilots, again headed by Squadron Commander Crampton, and a familiar ritual was set in motion. Mixon formally turned the Tornados over to the British, which were then stripped of USAF markings and retouched with RAF roundels. As before, the Americans flight crews were suddenly dismissed and sent back to the Zone of the Interior. The British, meanwhile, underwent a period of rigorous reorientation in the airplanes with Korean veteran Captain Stacey Naftel serving as instructor pilot.[34] According to Mixon, "The RAF crews were a little rusty at first and it took several sets of tires, two booms, and a slipway door to get them back into shape." Flight Lieutenant Cremer did his part to complicate matters by taxiing number 48–036 into a parked C-47 at night, wrecking a wingtip tank.[35]

On the issue of tip tanks, Lieutenant Earl Huggins, the squadron supply officer, recalled one unforgettable incident from this period:

One of the RAF crews had a cabin fire and the pilot, in the process of trying to "dump" cabin pressure, inadvertently dumped the right tip tank in the North Sea. I got to Base Supply to attempt to draw a tip tank, I was advised that they did not have such a thing and it would have to be ordered from the states. Not accepting this answer as a fact, I went nosing around in the supply storage yard and discovered this large crate which contained an RB tip tank. Upon returning to the supply storage yard, I was advised that it couldn't be a tip tank because there was no inventory card for it, therefore it didn't exist and could not be issued. You would have to know supply personnel in that era to really appreciate the stupidity of this. After pushing the issue as far as I dared, I went to the Motor Pool and procured a truck and a crane. I stole ("procure" was the word you used when you got caught) that damn tip tank and we installed it on the aircraft. Needless to say I was in a peck of trouble and Col. Mixon just laughed, wouldn't help me, and later told me that he wanted to see how a lieutenant would handle such a problem.[36]

Relations with the 47th Bomb Wing at the other end of the field remained cordial, and Mixon openly shared the pooled resources of B-45As stationed there. Over the next two months Detachment 4 conducted fifty-three sorties with their RAF guests, including the usual regimen of test flights, radar calibrations, and profile type missions. Such activities consumed 179 hours of flying time along with 54,300 gallons of fuel transferred by tanker. Furthermore, all radar film developed was dispatched to RAF Upwood for evaluation, whereby no written evaluation was issued. Still, there was nothing overtly suspicious about Detachment 4's activities until the Bomber Command summoned a special meeting for Crampton's flight, the date for which remains unknown. Training then wound down, and the RB-45Cs were transferred back to the Americans on December 8, 1952. The jets subsequently streaked home ten days later without ceremony, arriving safely. "Snow was blowing at Lockbourne when we arrived," Mixon noted. "There were some surprised looks by the ground crews when we taxied in, resplendent in the colors of the Royal Air Force." Raised eyebrows notwithstanding, little became of the issue and it quickly subsided.[37]

The reader has probably deduced that Detachment 4 intended to cover another British overflight. Apparently, intelligence gathered by Crampton's first mission in April had wended its way through SAC and Air Staff headquarters, which felt that additional information was necessary. Word then circulated through the appropriate channels for the Royal Air Force to have another go at it, and Special Duties Flight was reassembled sunder

Flight Leader Crampton. "We flew hard through November and, by the beginning of December, when we were trained to a concert pitch, the show was suddenly cancelled and we were ordered back to our units," he recalled. "Among the rumors floating around was the belief that the political risk at that time was too great. If any one of us had gone down in Russia the balloon might have gone up."[38] This abrupt denouement halted RB-45C overflights of Russia for the time being, but by no means ended them. Shady work remained in store at Sculthorpe two years hence, but by then the Tornados would be under entirely new management.[39]

CHAPTER TEN

Russia Redux

"So in March 1954 it was back to Sculthorpe, 'Hak' Mixon, the big stretched Cadillacs, American flying clothing and the American language, plus the raised eyebrows."

— Squadron Leader John Crampton[1]

It will be recalled that the Strategic Air Command phased out its RB-45Cs in the fall of 1953, replacing them with RB-47s. This left the remaining twenty-two Tornados looking for a home and their plight soon came to the attention of Lieutenant Colonel Ralph D. Steakley of Tactical Air Command reconnaissance. After some discussion, he prevailed upon superiors to transfer the entire lot to TAC, then shackled with propellor-driven B-26 Invaders for photographic work. On June 5, 1953, word came down to accomplish exactly that, although delivery dates would be staggered as the aircraft passed through the San Bernadino Air Materiel Area for reconditioning and the addition of new Bell M-7 tail turrets. Headquarters, U.S. Air Force, thereupon ordered reactivation of the 19th Tactical Reconnaissance Squadron (Night Photo Jet) at Shaw AFB, South Carolina, to employ the RB-45Cs. This unit first arose in July 1942 as the 19th Tactical Mapping Squadron, which saw only limited combat operations in World War II before being disbanded in June 1949. For administrative purposes, the new 19th Squadron was to be attached to the 363rd Tactical Reconnaissance Wing, which enjoyed concurrent experience with B-45As. The new formation had an assigned strength of twelve RB-45Cs and one spare, although these joined the roster in driblets as they completed their overhaul at Norton AFB.[2]

The officer selected to head up the 19th Squadron, like most individuals associated with the B-45 Tornado, proved himself an exceptional military leader. Major John B. Anderson, born in Bridgeport, Ohio, in 1921, saw service in World War II and performed 150 flights during the Berlin airlift (1948–1949). Unlike more flamboyant contemporaries, Anderson was a somewhat reticent, low-key individual who nonetheless enjoyed a reputation for efficiency. Moreover, he was extremely popular with the men and officers of his command. Lieutenant James Wold described his superior this way: "Major John B. Anderson — 'Major Andy' — as we all know him — was a quiet, unassuming man. You immediately respected him and he had an aura of command about him. He enjoyed the fierce loyalty of everyone in the squadron. He was the kind of man you just wanted to do what was right for him, you didn't want to embarrass him." According to Captain Ray Schrecengost, "He had a different kind of tack when it came to managing a squadron than a lot of people, he certainly was not hard ass like a lot of people seemed to be." Captain Jack Yoder also concurred in this favorable assessment of the CO: "He was one of the greatest commanders I've ever had. He wasn't very forceful when it came to something that really perhaps should have been more forceful, but he had a way about him of getting the job done."[3]

So the final unit operating Tornados, like those before it, was capably led and it quickly emerged as a crack outfit. Part of this can be ascribed to the 19th Squadron's rather unique genesis. It was formally reconstituted on July 20, 1953, but the only aircraft available was a Lockheed T-33 trainer and this only arrived the following October. In fact, the first of the RB-45Cs would not depart San Bernadino for Shaw AFB until December 12, 1953, seven months hence. This anomaly might have unduly embarrassed any other combat unit, but Major Anderson began corralling squadron members way in advance and trained them for roles other than flying. "Lack of aircraft during this formative period had one beneficial aspect," the squadron historian noted. "It enabled supervisory personnel to organize their sections completely and to outline training programs in detail prior to completion of crew assignments and assignment of aircraft." Anderson also enjoyed the rare luxury of personally selecting pilots and other key personnel. "We had a year to

The quiet and unassuming Major John B. Anderson was one of the most effective reconnaissance officers in the Tactical Air Command (John Mott).

get ready to go, so the base commander told me I could pick out anybody I wanted on the base for the squadron," he stated, "so I got some real good people." Among them were several former SAC combat crews from the 91st Strategic Reconnaissance Squadron who effected transfers rather than transition to RB-47s. According to Lieutenant Oliver "Snapper" Nasby, "When the B-47s came out they flew our squadron commander on one of the first ones to land at Lockbourne, and we were all entitled to switch over or stay with the B-45 and go to Tactical Air Command. A bunch of us stuck with the B-45 — we didn't want any part of the B-47. It looked like a duck — it didn't look like any fun at all to fly." Others pilots, like Captain Robert "Curly" Schamber, evinced less altruism for joining than simply to stay fly Tornados: "I volunteered — I was happy to get out of SAC!" From the onset, the 19th TAC possessed high morale and soaring esprit de corps, a fact reflected in its subsequent operational excellence.[4]

In November 1953, the 19th Tactical Reconnaissance Squadron received orders that it would ship out the following April and join the 47th Bomb Wing already at Sculthorpe. The commander in chief, USAFE, felt that there was no better unit to assist B-45 bombers in their atomic mission than a reconnaissance squadron composed of similar aircraft.[5] Ironically, the squadron still lacked Tornados, so crews departed for Lockbourne to train with the 91st Strategic Reconnaissance Wing, gaining practical experience beforehand. Once they began arriving, the RB-45Cs indelibly impressed young officers enjoying their first brush with jet aviation. "Absolutely fantastic," Lieutenant Wilbur Stevens insisted. "Its ability to take off, carry a good payload and accelerate right up to 40,000 feet in no time at all, was just absolutely fantastic."

The squadron remained engrossed by Operation Pack Up for several months until moving day arrived. The RB-45Cs continued arriving in spurts throughout the winter, and the honor of pranging the first Tornado went to none other than Major Andy himself, on December 23, 1953. "We had just gotten the airplanes from San Bernadino," Anderson recalled, "and flew the first one we got. My operations officer was checking me out and I was in the back seat. We flew around for a couple of hours and I got ready to land — and the gear wouldn't come down so we had to belly it in at Charleston, South Carolina." The ensuing damage totaled $12,000, so the following February Anderson ordered the aircraft flown by stages back to Norton AFB for repairs. This, according to Lieutenant Hugh McKay, was one the B-45's more memorable flights. "Half the fuel we couldn't get, the landing gear was bolted down, the bomb bay doors were wired closed, half the radars didn't work, and when we took off we had less than two hours flying time, so we zig-zagged across the United States because we had to find airfields that had strong enough runways for the B-45. I think the most flying we did in a single day was for an hour and a half, and only fifty miles or so." The Tornado arrived safely, was repaired, and returned in time for the big jump later that spring.

Meanwhile, RB-45Cs of the 19th TAC were spruced up in a distinctive livery consisting of blue stripes and conspicuous blue wingtip tanks, adorned by three white stars. Lieutenant Stephen J. Nicoloff was completely taken in by the adornments. "Seeing the tip tanks there made it look a little extra special, rather than just the 'A' models," he emoted, "and then the blue stripe with the white stars were very impressive to a young fellow." Marvelously bedecked, the 19th Squadron began relocating on May 5, 1954, when Major Anderson led a formation of six RB-45Cs from Shaw to Sculthorpe. Captain Dick Hardin distinctly recalled his first day in England:

> We decided to impress the 47th Bomb Wing by flying non-stop from Goose Bay to Sculthorpe, which we could do because we had those big old 1,200 gallon tip tanks and the bomb bay bladder tanks. There wasn't anything particularly great about it, and I landed there late in the afternoon. I was the first airplane from the 19th to land at Sculthorpe and Colonel Jones, the wing commander, climbed up behind me as we were shutting down our engines. I didn't know who he was, he was in coveralls, and the first comment he says to me was, "*Welcome to Sculthorpe and where in Hell is your survival suit?*" which we were supposed to wear crossing the Atlantic. Mine was in the rear of the airplane, and I was tired and said, "*It's in the back end of this airplane, where in Hell do you think it is?*" He looked at me kind of funny and said, "I agree with you, I don't blame you." And when I found out who he was I thought, "Oh, God!"—he let me off the hook for that one.[6]

Concurrently, the remainder of the squadron tramped aboard the troop transport USS *General Patch* for a wave-tossed journey to Portsmouth. For many ground personnel, their sojourn onboard this pitching, rolling vessel was the most trying ordeal they had ever known. "It was the worst experience of my life," Airman Edwin Carrington insisted." I have never been as sick in my life as I was on board that ship. I can remember passing out of the dining hall, and I started to go down the stairway and just leaned over the rail—and lost every meal I had for the last five years!"[7] The 19th Tactical Reconnaissance Squadron quickly sorted itself out at Sculthorpe on May 11, 1954, eager and ready for orders. Meanwhile, four aircrews remained behind at Shaw to ferry the last remaining RB-45Cs as they arrived from San Bernadino.

Shortly before the 19th's debut in England, their Tornados were to figure prominently in the final RAF interlude. The hijinks commenced in March 1953 when Lieutenant Colonel Marion C. Mixon, then serving with an RB-47 detachment in Nouasseur, Morocco, was summoned to Strategic Air Command headquarters. "Once I got to Offut, LeMay told me to go down to Shaw AFB in South Carolina; pick up four RB-45s; take them to Wright-Patterson AFB in Dayton, Ohio, for modifications to their radars, and then fly them over to Sculthorpe," he said. Accordingly, Mixon landed at Shaw as ordered and absconded with 48–031, 48–035, 48–037, and 48–040, all flown by Tactical Air Command personnel.[8] The aircraft lingered at Dayton for a month, where their radars were fine-tuned by British technicians and rendered highly accurate. The Tornados were then conducted by Mixon to Sculthorpe, at which point the locus of events reverts back to Squadron Leader John Crampton.

Since cancellation of the proposed second overflight in the winter of 1952, Crampton completed an uneventful assignment with No. 101 Squadron (Canberra), and in July 1953 he transferred to the operations section of HQ 1 Group at Bawtry. Ten months later he reported back to Bomber Command, High Wycombe, and was informed that his Special Duty Flight was being re-formed once again. Another classified mission was in the offing and they felt it appropriate to tender it to him first. The towering officer was flattered and he unflinchingly accepted, insisting, "I had begun to view the entire project as mine and would have been most upset if the job had been offered to anyone else."[9] For those accustomed to such monkey business, old times seemed close at hand once more.

Crampton dutifully reassembled his crews, including several new members, and was carefully briefed about the new mission profile. As before, three separate legs would be flown, nearly duplicating the flight paths of the first sortie. Crampton, again unflinchingly, selected the longest and most dangerous route, towards Kiev, and he was warned about being tracked by Soviet radar and possibly shadowed by high-flying Russian interceptors. However, authorities assured him that his assigned altitude of 39,000 feet would most certainly shield him from any flak—he simply would be too high. Accordingly, on the night of April 28, 1954, the three Tornados, again sporting RAF colors, roared off from Sculthorpe and steered for their initial rendezvous points. After taking on fuel, they doused their lights and winged eastward towards their objectives. The first two aircraft, covering the northern and central parts of the Soviet Union, supposedly roused some fighter opposition, but nonetheless photographed all their objectives and returned intact. Crampton, meanwhile, cruised towards his final target at Kapustin Yar, a suspected missile base in distant southern Russia.

The RB-45C coasted placidly along while its highly modified APQ-24 performed splendidly; navigator Lieutenant Rex Sanders reported capturing some very fine images. Gazing ahead, Crampton suddenly perceived a series of flashes, similar to an electrical storm, erupting distinctly below him. Sanders then cut in and requested that the plane's course and speed be maintained on the final approach to Kiev, which was done. Everything, at least on the surface, was normal. "My reverie was rudely interrupted by the sudden heart-stopping appearance of exploding golden anti-aircraft fire," Crampton stated. "There was no doubt about it; it was very well predicted flak — dead ahead and at the same height as we were. My reaction was instinctive — throttles wide open and haul the aeroplane round on its starboard wing until the gyro compass pointed west." Apparently, the Russians had massed several hundred antiaircraft guns in a wide belt directly under the Tornado's flight path, then let loose with a single salvo. This seemingly primitive technique nearly worked, save for some sloppy calculations. In Crampton's words, "The early attempts had ALL misjudged our height — and, thank God, the Kiev defenses had misjudged our speed; they had chucked up everything a few hundred yards ahead of us." The RB-45C winged its way home at top speed, buffeting mildly, and the pilot prepared for a final in-flight refueling over Germany. The tanker failed to connect and Crampton, fearing possible damage to his refueling port, set down at Furstenfeldbruck for the night. His RB-45C returned to Sculthorpe on the morrow where it joined the remaining two Tornados awaiting him.[10]

As previously, this RAF overflight secured valuable target folder information for the U.S. and Royal air forces, even though the main objective at Kapustin Yar was missed. Furthermore, Soviet flak calculations may have been off target, but they were disturbingly too close for comfort. Their proximity intimated that the mission had been compromised by a Soviet mole working within British military intelligence. Years later the Central Intelligence Agency concluded that Kim Philby, the notorious Cambridge turncoat, had tipped Soviet defenses off in advance by providing precise speed and altitude figures. The ploy nearly succeeded. Fortunately, the most disruptive effect of the entire mission was in alarming Danish defenses once they tracked an unknown aircraft over Copenhagen. The Danes scrambled several Gloster Meteor NF.11s (radar-equipped night fighters) to intercept the mysterious trespasser, whereupon they were summarily ordered back to base. NATO authorities were thus spared the embarrassing predicament of explaining why Danish-manned British fighters had intercepted a British-crewed American bomber returning from Russia in their airspace.[11] This concluded the last known episode of RB-45Cs flying under British auspices.

Shortly after the last RAF overflight, elements of the 19th Tactical Reconnaissance Squadron began trickling into Sculthorpe, whereupon wing headquarters issued their first mission directive. Henceforth, the unit would assist the 49th Air Division with visual and radar photographic reconnaissance of scheduled and contingency targets, as requested by the parent unit, along with routine bomb damage assessments. Moreover, in wartime the 19th Squadron would be precluded from any "combat visual photography" out of the need to conserve RB-45C aircraft from anticipated losses. Operations would, by necessity, be restricted to nighttime radar surveillance, for replacement aircraft were not available and the 19th Squadron possessed the only radar technology capable of supporting 47th Bomb Wing operations.[12] Major Anderson had prepared his men well for their intended role and on May 20, only six days after deploying abroad, his RB-45Cs began operations.

On June 19 and June 28, the unit was bolstered by three additional Tornados from San Bernadino, where only one remained behind. The biggest obstacle encountered was

A newly refurbished RB-45C of the 19th Tactical Reconnaissance Squadron, looking resplendent in its new color scheme (David Menard).

the lack of adequate squadron photo facilities, essential for handling radar work, so wing laboratories were utilized until the shortfall could be rectified. Moreover, few maintenance problems arose and the aircraft, newly refurbished, were in flying excellent condition. The 19th Squadron readily adjusted to its new clime and literally hit the ground running. In the words of Airman David Whittaker, "If this were a practice alert they would actually stop the aircraft on the perry strip just opposite the photo lab, and the camera repairmen would go out, remove the film, and walk right to the lab. Within minutes we would have it in the darkroom."[13]

This latest crop of Tornado pilots was not above some good-natured ribbing. Lieutenant Oliver "Snapper" Nasby was on a mission down to North Africa and noted, "We had this little discussion with the F-86 guys there in Tripoli, who knew they could run us into the ground and I told them, 'You guys can't even get close — when we leave here you can't even shoot me down — can't *even simulate* it.' Boy, they took that bet, and not one of them could. We flew so low there was water spray on the airplane — we were right on the deck. They didn't dare make a pass, they'd be dead!" Yet, the crewmen no sooner commenced operations than they began lodging rather pointed — and entirely too familiar — complaints. "The most memorable thing to me was the fact we were flying out of England, where the weather was typically crappy," Captain Ray Schrecengost observed, "and we never let that bother us at all. We would take off with ridiculous weather and come back with ridiculous weather. And if we couldn't get back, then we'd go to our alternate to land — we never let the weather screw around with us. I remember taking off in absolute zero/zero at night in Frankfurt, Germany, where we had to have the alert crew lead us out to the end of the runway because we couldn't see well enough to taxi." Ground crews found British meteorology equally vexing. "The weather was atrocious," Airman Carrington insisted. "I never saw a country where it rained so much. I think you walked around with web feet after a while. It was awful."[14]

Webbed feet notwithstanding, the 19th Squadron quickly established itself as among the 49th Air Division's best units and a model of teamwork and efficiency. Anderson's men performed well in a number of Third Air Force exercises, including Operation Carte Blanche, and executed their missions competently. The squadron photo lab performed so well that it ultimately absorbed the entire radar output of the 47th Bomb Wing without major problems. The engineering department also received kudos when number 48–035 flew consecutively for 108 hours without repairs or mishap, a record for this Tornado variant. The squadron's biggest test happened in August 1955 when it participated in Operation Brown Cow, another top NATO maneuver. For three days the squadron labored around the clock under simulated wartime conditions, weathering a spate of radar malfunctions. Yet, in the words of Brigadier General James F. Whisenand, 49th Air Division commander, they "bounced back like true champions." The remainder of the year was spent photographing Third Air Force bases in England and Germany, again to the complete satisfaction of superiors. More important, none of these crash-prone aircraft were lost to an accident, convincing proof that the Tornados had finally been tamed. In sum, Anderson's unit enjoyed a productive first year in England, averaging abort rates of only 7 percent in several hundred missions. As the squadron historian proudly quipped, "They are now ready to take their place among the military powers of the United States Air Force."[15]

An important part of the squadron's folklore occurred in the wake of one these intense aerial maneuvers. Men and machines of the entire 47th Bomb Wing were spent and enjoying a well deserved rest, until Major Anderson suddenly alerted all hands one Thursday and declared that he wanted every plane in the air for a base flyby on Friday. What followed was a triumph for the maintenance chiefs and their crews. "Everybody grumbled," Sergeant Russell Stover said, "but they slept on benches and everything else. It was something that was in your heart when you went outside, knowing that you're the only squadron on the whole damn base that had every airplane — three T-33s and twelve others — all in the air at the same time!" Sergeant Robert Wehr evinced similar feelings and motives. "I think we more or less wanted to show off because it happened right after one of the maneuvers, where we flew day and night, and when we got back to Sculthorpe we were one of few squadrons that could fly any of our planes." Airman Carrington also beamed with pride when recalling the event. "We went and fired up all the birds, put them in the air, and we flew over every squadron on the base and, boy, the old man got called up to wing headquarters and he said, 'How else can you prove we're the best outfit on the base?'"

Still, unscheduled gaffes do happen, even among the best of units, and the 19th TAC managed to commit their share. Captain Hardin recalled what happened at the end of another long and seemingly routine mission. "The weather was good, it was getting late, and we could see the runway lights, so instead of going through the let down procedure we said, 'The heck with this, we'll go land'— although it was not Sculthorpe! We landed at Marham, which was about 20–30 miles south of Sculthorpe. We were lined up perfectly and everything looked fine and we were still talking to the Sculthorpe tower and they couldn't see us. We were then taxing around the perimeter track — which looked a little funny in the dark — and finally a jeep pulled up and two RAF officers got out and said, 'Hey, mate, I think you're a little bit lost. We'll take you back to the end of the runway,' and I followed the jeep back and we took off and went home. I hoped we'd sneak back in without anybody knowing about it, but during the briefing the next morning either Jack [Yoder] or Burt [Grigsby] said, 'Now Captain Hardin is going to get up and tell us about what happened last night.' We had people in the tower at the time. It was one of the most embarrassing moments in my life!"

Major Anderson's excellent handling of squadron affairs, and the confidence it inspired among superiors, undoubtedly influenced what transpired next. The two previous RAF overflights, while useful, apparently failed to meet every expectation as hoped. Officials in the Air Staff decided to tempt fate once again by having Tornados bound across the Iron Curtain once more, although this time manned by *American* crews. Documents pertaining to the flight are nonexistent, so who precisely who ordered the overflight and when cannot be discerned. Naturally, such a high profile mission was kept a closely guarded secret, even from the flight crews, until the last possible moment. One day Major Anderson was called into operations for a routine briefing, and the plan was announced to him: a deep penetration mission that basically mimicked what the RAF crews had done previously, although stopping short of Soviet territory. It consisted of three simultaneous penetrations, north, center, and south, covering targets in the vicinity of Berlin, Budapest, and northern Yugoslavia. Anderson subsequently revealed the mission to three select flight crews. According to Lieutenant Wilbur Stevens, "We showed up for what we thought was a normal mission just before dusk, and Major Andy came in, and he had these folders and things. He said we had to make a decision at that particular time whether we'd fly it or not. We were told some of the basic nature of what the mission would be like and that there was always the possibility that we could be shot down and if so we were captured, and if we were captured then, of course, they would do everything possible to get us out."[16] As Major Anderson explained, "They also told us that if we were caught we didn't need expect to come back very soon. They'd probably hold us for a while."

On the evening of March 29, 1955, Anderson led three RB-45Cs from Sculthorpe towards a rendezvous with tanker aircraft over the mainland. Aircraft lights were then doused as the Tornados turned eastward towards Warsaw Pact territory. The northernmost aircraft was piloted by Captain Robert A. Schambers, who headed towards East Berlin. "About the time we got to the Russian zone border and made a hard turn to head towards Berlin the radar went out, and I recall hearing the navigator down there cursing and hitting the magnetron trying to get it going again. It came back on to a degree but wasn't very successful. They got some information, I understand, but it didn't work nearly as good as it could have. On that mission we had turrets and a tailgunner and some sort of aircraft did climb up and try to intercept us, but there were no shots fired and no overt action — I guess they just couldn't get close enough." In the backseat his copilot, Lieutenant Stevens, was increasingly apprehensive over a potentially hostile greeting. "The only thing I remember as unusual about that flight is that I kept starring at Mars all the time because it might be the light of an aircraft or something. We never saw anything and later on, after we got back, we learned that they had scrambled aircraft for us and a couple of generals lost their jobs over this because of their inability to have adequate defensive systems and shooting us down."

Major Anderson himself selected to fly the deepest ingress of the mission to Hungary. "I went into Budapest and did a cloverleaf, and I could see fighters below me coming up, so I expended my fuel climbing to get away from them," he reflected. "I guess I was probably over Budapest around midnight and I could see them circling around looking for me, but they were 5,000 feet or so below me. When I got back into Germany I was so low on fuel that I couldn't reach England, so I landed at Furstenfeldbruck and spent the night. I'm sure the photographs ended up in someone's target folder somewhere." As Lieutenant Francis Martin, Anderson's navigator, noted, "Upon landing we were met at the airplane by Intelligence personnel, who took the radar film and every scrap of paper or map we had in our bags."[17]

The final leg, flown by Captain Bert Grigsby, reached Yugoslavia and returned without incident. It was not until the aircraft had returned that some subterfuge had been afoot at the squadron level, prior to take off. Captain Hardin was incensed: "My crew flew without me! I had gone up to London on a pass for the weekend on leave, and when I came back I went down to the squadron ops. My first indication that something had happened was Grigsby in a flight suit looking a little ragged, and my navigator was there in a flight suit looking a little ragged, so they'd been flying — when you put two and two together.... Grigsby asked me to take him home after the mission and on the way all I could think of was 'Son of a b____!'" Like Hardin, Captain Schrecengost angrily remonstrated over somebody commandeering *his* airplane on a top secret mission. "It pissed us off, to be very frank, because we were both flight commanders in the squadron, and to be left out of the deal like that sort of ticked us off." In light of their leisurely dash into restricted airspace, all twelve squadron members involved received the Distinguished Flying Cross in a base ceremony. Lieutenant Stevens, how-

Major John Anderson "Major Andy" (left), receiving his Distinguished Flying Cross for the RB-45Cs' final penetration of Warsaw Pact airspace. The other men are unidentified (John Mott).

ever, downplayed the entire matter. "Absolutely routine," he shrugged, "nothing to receive a DFC for."

Anderson's 1955 overflight constitutes a high point in the history of the 19th Tactical Reconnaissance Squadron, and over the next three years their operations were business as usual. The biggest change occurred on December 1, 1956, when it was detached from the 47th Bomb Wing and reassigned to the 66th Tactical Reconnaissance Wing, Twelfth Air Force, based at Sembach, Germany. However, Anderson's squadron remained at Sculthorpe as a tenant organization, their mission and equipment intact.[18] The following spring, headquarters alerted the squadron that they were slated to receive the first Douglas RB-66s shortly, and crews began filtering through Destroyer training units back in the Zone of the Interior. By 1957 the 19th TAC had completed its third year of accident free flying, a fact attributed to scrupulous safety standards enforced by all ranks. A minor record was also set when number 48–027 accumulated 1,849 flying hours on its airframe without a major mishap. Another ship, 48–035, flew 108 hours in a single month without repairs. Yet, a big transformation proved in the offing. On February 1, 1957, the first RB-66 touched down at Sculthope and was gradually joined by others in the ensuing weeks. Meanwhile, the squadron's remaining RB-45Cs were concentrated in "A Flight" to make room for the newcomers.[19] As more Destroyers arrived, the Tornados accumulated less flying time, down to 29 hours that June, and by summer conversion efforts were complete. All remaining RB-45Cs were unceremoniously surrendered to the 47th Bomb Wing for use in fire drills. Not surprisingly, many pilots viewed the successor aircraft with suspicion and sorely missed their old friends. "I never felt comfortable in the B-66 like I was in the B-45," Lieutenant Nasby emoted. "It was like a Hertz rental." Lieutenant Martin was in complete agreement: "It was a cool airplane. I liked the B-45."[20] Another page in the Tornado's long ledger had turned.

Half a world away, the least-known or appreciated episode in RB-45C clandestine activities continued running its course. Four Tornados remained stationed at Yokota AB, Japan, as part of Detachment 2, 91st Strategic Reconnaissance Wing, and Major Charles J. Adams continued as unit commander. Immediately after the Korean War ended on July 27, 1953, numbers 48–021 and 48–033, were lacquered black and outfitted with electronic countermeasure equipment (ECM). This move was indicative of the shift from photographic overflights to signal collection intelligence under the aegis of Headquarters, Far Eastern Air Forces (FEAF). Provisions were accordingly made to carry a Russian-speaking linguist, attached to the Air Force Security Service (USAFSS), just forward of the bomb bay, where his equipment was stored. In flight, he sat upon a large dinghy facing rearwards and operated a radio receiver and a wire recorder. The two other Tornados, 48–025 and 48–038, retained their silver paint scheme and mounted special, side-looking K-30 cameras. These specialized devices utilized a 100-inch focal point and were used exclusively for peripheral, or side-looking, photography.[21]

Security service personnel, while military, answered directly to the National Security Agency (NSA), which was run by civilians. Their flights were sometimes undertaken in concert with RB-29s or RB-50s from the same unit, which performed ELINT activities while the RB-45Cs completed their orbits. In practice, security service personnel were strictly ordered not to discuss missions or any other activities with flight crews on the ground, or even in the air, even under the most dire circumstances. The NSA meant business. "They always told you to avoid talking to anybody or mentioning anything that you did," Sergeant Nick Toyeas recalled. "Say the secret word and split *20 years* between you!" According to Lieutenant Earl Huggins, "These radio/COMINT people would just turn up for the flight. They weren't friendly. They wore a flying suit with no insignia." Moreover, the secrecy accorded them made for interesting inflight exchanges, especially when MiGs were involved. "Sometimes we had to remind him that he was in the aircraft along with us and if we were shot down he was coming along," Huggins stated. "Anyway, when he would decide that they were getting close, he would alert the pilot and we would make a 180 degree turn and *run* like Hell!"[22]

Sergeant Toyeas, a radio intercept translator, describes what for him was a typical eavesdropping foray: "It was a four-hour mission. It would take us maybe an hour and a half to get across to the orbit section and we'd circle there — it was pretty close to Vladivostok. We'd fly around about two hours and then we'd spend another hour and a half flying back. So we would just linger and stay 50 miles off the coast. I would sit there and if I hear the Soviet commander ordering planes up, I would listen as to what altitude they were sending them up to. If they were above us I would notify the pilot with hand signals." Yet, for flight crews called upon to perform signal collecting missions, the experience could prove anything but routine. Lieutenant Robert Gould, an RB-45C copilot, will never forget one memorable night flight:

> At one point during our orbits, the SS crew member said to Lt. Col. Kaufman, "Sir, I suggest we leave." Col. Kaufmann, being efficient, said, "We'll finish this orbit and then we'll be on our way home." It wasn't long, seconds perhaps, that we noticed a light moving across the sky followed by a burst of light or explosion. Our first thought was that it was a shooting star, but what we saw went beneath our airplane. We thought that was strange. Suddenly, there was a loud roar overhead and we saw the glowing tailpipe of a fighter jet arcing away from us. He had just missed hitting us by just a few feet. Now it all added up. The shooting star was probably a rocket fired at us by the fighter that passed over head. I doubt that he ever saw us visually as we were flying a black airplane on a black night with no lights. Needless to say, we headed back to Yokota on the double at our max speed of Mach .86.[23]

Despite the recent armistice, and all the usual precautions, there would be no lack of excitement during many of these nocturnal excursions. Nor was the mere act of taking off any less memorable to Sergeant John P. Corryn, an electrician with the security service: "I think that anyone who flew out of Yokota on an RB-45 would remember trying to get off the ground. We had 10,000 feet of runway with 2,000 feet of overrun at each end; with a full fuel load, we would start at the fence at one end and still be on the ground when we hit the overrun 12,000 feet later. I never knew how much air we put between us and the crash barrier at lift off— not much!"[24] Some complaints never change.

Detachment 2 stood down in the wake of the Korean armistice and did not resume flying until August, when it executed three "special reconnaissance flights and a radar calibration mission." Due to the sensitive nature of these activities, their destinations are not revealed in the squadron history books.[25] The unit's usually high morale also soured after their tour of duty was extended by several months, and questions arose as to whether or not the detachment was going to be disbanded. FEAF, eager to retain their valuable intelligence gathering capability, protested the move to SAC headquarters and, on August 31, 1953, word arrived that Detachment 2 would resume normal operations. However, roughly half the Tornado's flying time would be dedicated intruder missions in support of the Japan Air Defense Force. With improved vectoring techniques, F-86s found the bombers relatively easy prey, a far cry from the early days of the Korean War. "Boy, did we clobber them this past month," their historian chortled. "Ten intercepts were attempted against the B-45s which 'snuck' into our area, and ten times the B-45s bit the dust!"[26]

With the resumption of regular activity that fall, RB-45Cs were again at the forefront of Cold War reconnaissance around China, North Korea, and the Soviet Union's eastern periphery. On September 10, 1953, Major Edward L. Krum arrived to serve as Detachment 2's final commander. Unfortunately, Krum's enlisted personnel, having endured an arduous flight from the mainland, were lodged in tents just as hurricane "Tess" decided to pay its respects. The historian noted that, "it rained over 13 inches with continuous drizzle coming down for days, and all the tents leaked like sieves." Once the weather cleared and the airmen had wrung themselves out, the Tornados completed nineteen sorties for a total of 62 hours. Of these, only three were highly classified FEAF-directed missions, and the rest were channeled into training, testing, and intruder flights. Krum also dealt with an officer board dispatched from Headquarters, FEAF, to sound the possibility of taking control of the detachment and its RB-45C operations. Were this to happen, it was inferred that Detachment 2 would by default assume responsibility for training all FEAF ground and flight crews assigned to them.[27]

In October the detachment witnessed a marked upsurge in overall activities, with RB-45Cs accounting for 101 hours in flying time through thirty-three sorties. Of these, eighteen were special FEAF missions, with no less than seven ECM flights performed by numbers 48–021 and 48–033. However, Krum complained about the glaring lack of replacement canopies in the theater, cracks in which could ground an aircraft for up to sixty days until spares arrived. Krum proved more sanguine over the progress of Project Phase Out, the training of FEAF personnel to fly and fix Tornados. These men had been culled from various Fifth Air Force formations and placed in an entirely new, top secret outfit, the 6091st Reconnaissance Flight. As the unit historian explained, "Since the missions are highly classified, security is a very important part of operations, and regular security meetings are held once every two weeks."[28]

The hazardous nature of aerial espionage, even by such adept practitioners as Detachment 2, should not be understated. The Soviets were alert and capable of defending their air space with deadly force, but the behavior of individual MiG pilots could hardly be described as predictable. "The first time we went up to Sakhalin Island, we couldn't see a thing," Captain Rice reflected. "It was completely socked in. So we're going back to Yokota and the tail gunner calls out and says, 'We've got somebody coming in on our tail.' I said, 'Can you tell what it is?' He said, 'No,' and began loading our tail guns, every other round was tracer ammunition. I said, 'Give him a couple bursts.' So he fired and it looked like there was solid fire coming out of that gun!' We always carried a camera with a 100-inch lens, and this guy came up along side. It was a MiG and we took his picture, and he waved at us and off he went!"

Detachment 2's flights may have been for the most part routine and uneventful, but in-flight mechanical failures were potentially more hazardous than MiGs. One such incident happened on a flight to Vladivostok flown by Captain Grant Angelus:

> Our routine was to burn the tip tanks, because you can always drop these in case you need maneuverability and speed. Then you'd switch to the bomb bay tanks. Well, we had a lot of fuel — an hour in each tip tank — and we headed out and switched to the bomb bay, and I really didn't notice what was going on. But as we headed out to Russia and over the China

An all-black RB-45C of the 6091st Flight during a refueling stop at Kimpo, South Korea. The tail displays incorrect numbers to disguise the fact it is a spyplane (Richard S. Hain).

Sea, I noticed that I kept pushing forward trim all the time—finally I couldn't push it anymore. I looked down and I had full forward nose down trim on the damn airplane, so I knew we had a problem. What was happening is there was a leak in the forward tank in the bomb bay, and a shut off valve between them in case you had to work on one. Thanks to those people who worked on the damn thing, it wasn't feeding. So the longer we flew, the worse our CG [center of gravity] became—it kept moving backwards! I aborted right there, once I figured out what was going on, and we never got to Russia that time. I headed back home, and I'm a long way out because I burned off my tips, so we let down and were now really burning fuel. By that time I've got full trim in and I had to keep the airspeed high so the nose did not pitch up.

They lost us on GCA on the first pass, and I really started screaming at them, "I've got a dangerous problem here, if you can't get me in on this move we've got to go!" I also had the guy in the aisle who spoke Russian who wanted to go crawl back in the bomb bay and cut the tank open with a knife, which would have worked but might have blown the aircraft up, too. So I said if we don't get in on this one pass we'll try that, and if we can't do it then we'll bail out. We went by again, this time they got us on the localizer, but I had full forward on the wheel, all my trim was full forward, and I've got to keep it at 180 knots so it won't pitch up. I still managed to stick it on the runway, cut the power—and blew all four tires.

I came to a stop at the end of the runway and Jack Rice, our maintenance officer, told me "Don't release the brakes. We'll come out and tow you in." So they jacked it up and put the tires on, and the airport was closed for a while. I was lucky to get out. Jack came back and put his hand on the front of the airplane, pushed on it, and tipped it right over on its tail— that's how bad the CG was. I'll never forget *that* one!

Fall found the detachment as fully engaged as ever, although November marked both an end and a beginning for the Tornados. Detachment 2 managed to compile forty-six sorties that month, including six classified missions for FEAF. The balance of missions that month were expended as part of Project Phase Out, whereby FEAF personnel underwent the exacting training regimen for which SAC was renowned. Major Krum, for his part, continued juggling operational matters with the usual spare parts shortages. Consequently, because the two silver Tornados enjoyed a higher priority this particular month than their all-black, ECM stablemates, number 48–021 was cannibalized for parts to keep them aloft. Detachment 2 finally ceased to exist as of November 29, 1953, and the bulk of its personnel were rounded up and shipped back to the United States for reassignment on RB-47s. Exempted from this transfer were fourteen highly skilled electronic and photo technicians who remained behind at Yokota to assist the newly formed 6091st Reconnaissance Flight. On December 1, 1953, this unit was formally activated under Lieutenant Colonel Leonard Kaufmann, who also accepted the four Tornados previously operated by SAC. In composing his final entry on the subject, the wing historian brooked no sentiment in declaring that the Strategic Air Command had finally "got out of the operations end of the RB-45 business once and for all." Yet the efficacy of Detachment 2, created by SAC in March 1951, is irrevocable: they had plied perilous skies for over two years and completed dozens of highly classified missions. Their achievements during the Korean War and the immediate postwar period grant the RB-45C a conspicuous perch in the panoply of Cold War aircraft.[29]

F-86 pilot Lieutenant Bertram E. Beecroft, who flamed a MiG-15 off north Korea in 1954 (Bert Beecroft).

FEAF was initially hard-pressed to scrape together enough qualified Tornado pilots once the SAC crews departed — the reverse situation of Detachment A in 1950. Captain Gere Ramsey, a veteran of RB-45C operations at Sculthorpe, was flying with a troop carrier squadron in Japan when headquarters offered to billet him with the new unit. He unhesitatingly accepted. Major Jim Brownlow, another former Tornado jock, was on a 90-day TDY in B-47s when he was likewise contacted. " I got orders one day from the USAF headquarters, all the way to England, to transfer me to Japan," he noted. "I was one of few B-45 pilots that they could get their hands on and that was still available to be shipped over." Once at Yokota, Brownlow gained appointment as the operations officer. The 6091st Reconnaissance Flight remains the most enigmatic unit to operate B-45s simply because, due to its classified nature, few records survive or can be easily accessed. Its chain of command is also a good indication of just how many chefs were stirring the soup: Far East Air Forces, Japan Air Defense Force, Bomber Command, 91st Strategic Reconnaissance Squadron, and, finally, flight operations itself. For administrative and logistical purposes it was attached to the 6161st Air Base Wing. This muddled scheme was slightly simplified on June 13, 1954, after Bomber Command was disbanded.[30]

The 6091st Flight, finally activated, resumed the clandestine work of their predecessor. In December five special missions were performed by RB-45Cs, although one aircraft aborted due to an engine fire. Of this total only one, a classified signal intelligence mission executed on December 9, 1953, by all-black 48–033, is recorded with its flight coordinates in detail. Training missions also continued apace, suggesting that flight crews were still honing the proficiencies necessary for this spy business.[31] The unit was brought up to speed by the new year, and in January 1954 it accomplished twenty-two special flights of various kinds, of which nineteen were listed as "combat missions." No less than twelve of these entailed secret photography runs; one RB-45C aborted due to radar malfunction.

Captain Gere Ramsey (center) hoists his tail gunner, Noel Carrigan, after the latter damaged a MiG-15 off North Korea in 1955. The other crew members are First Lieutenant Ramon Richardson and First Lieutenant Hubert Thornber (positions in photograph unidentified) (John Mott).

What the unit history fails to mention is that on January 22, 1954, one of the Tornados had a close brush with disaster. It was not unusual for RB-45Cs operating over the Yellow Sea to fly from Yokota, land at Kimpo in South Korea, and then stage from there after refueling. Several flights of F-86Fs would usually accompany the Tornado for its protection. On this occasion, Lieutenant Bertram E. Beecroft, 335th Fighter Squadron, provided top cover by commanding "D Flight" from 35,000 feet:

About 45 minutes into the flight we noticed about 15 or more MiG-15s, well above us and east over the land. The first radio silence was broken by someone who called "bandits at 3 o'clock high." That was for the B-45, as all the F-86 pilots had seen and were watching the MiGs. Our mission was to protect the B-45 and there was no intention of engaging the

MiGs. One of the MiGs suddenly left the others and started down through our formation, going straight to the B-45. I immediately fell in behind him and about the time I had him locked in my gunsight he began firing. Just before he fired, Colonel [Robert] Dixon called the B-45 to "break left," which he did. The MiG fired three 20mm cannon shots at the B-45, but his shots went behind him. I said "Keep breaking, he is shooting at you." Colonel Dixon said, "Get that Son of a B — —." I responded with "D Lead locked on," and began firing as he broke right and up off the B-45. From the time the MiG came down until I was firing at him was only 20 or 30 seconds.

Since I had been diving to stay with him, I was able to close as he started his climb out to the east. As soon as he was breaking away from the B-45, I started firing bursts at him. I could tell I was hitting him as first fuel and then smoke started coming from his plane. Then he started some evasive maneuvers, which I could easily stay with. He even did a barrel roll, which I thought was kind of silly, and I rolled right with him, firing and hitting him more. I saw more smoke and fuel streaming from the MiG and then my guns jammed; he slowed down and I pulled clear not to collide with him. I told my wingman, who was calling me "clear" the whole time, that my guns had jammed and I had lost sight of him. The wingman replied that the MiG-15 pilot had bailed out. Colonel Dixon then instructed the entire flight to return to K-14.

Beecroft's victim crashed off Sokto Island, 45 miles north of the Thirty-Eighth Parallel. This was the first Communist aircraft downed since the Korean armistice had been signed, and it sparked a flurry of diplomatic protests from the Soviet Bloc. General Maxwell Taylor, commanding the Eighth Army in South Korea, nonetheless felt impelled to "send congratulations" to the Air Force for their deed.[32]

Bad weather in February greatly impeded operations by the 6091st Flight, and that month only four RB-45C operations were staged: three ECM flights by number 48–033 and one photo mission. One of these sorties was scrubbed owning to a fire in its number three engine.[33] Conditions improved by March, so the Tornados accounted for eleven special missions and one top secret photo mission, in addition to numerous training flights. These were mostly conducted by ECM-laden numbers 48–025 and 48–033, which remained active in the Sea of Japan off Vladivostok and Sakhalin.[34] April proved another busy period, with the flight performing twelve ECM missions, two of which aborted due to malfunctions, and one cryptically "by order of higher headquarters." Mission R-451, executed on April 6, 1954, was of note, as it departed Yokota, landed at Kimpo (K-14) to refuel, awaited the Fifth Air Force's daily patrol, then orbited for three hours at 35,000 feet over the China Sea, listening in. Four weeks later, on the 29th, this same flight profile was repeated without incident.[35] May saw more of the same, with six special ECM flights accomplished. Mission No. R-644, completed by 48–033 on May 11, 1954, was unusual in that it coasted out of K-14 and orbited several hours in the vicinity of the Shantung Peninsula, China. The 6091st Flight also braced itself for some administrative hardships once Bomber Command was disbanded on June 18, 1954, with an anticipated loss of personnel, operational and materiel support. Bigger changes were also scheduled for September, when the flight experienced final conversion from an "assigned SAC" unit at Yokota to a FEAF-controlled one.[36]

Summer's onset saw no slackening of activities at Yokota, despite the scheduled changes. The RB-45Cs completed eleven special missions, including two K-30 photo and nine ECM flights, all without incident. Vladivostok remained an object of interest and had Tornados orbiting offshore on six occasions.[37] July proved more of the same, with eleven ECM missions completed without incident. Once again, the radio net around Vladivostok was scrutinized by no less than eight flights. August proved likewise routine, operationally, with one photo mission and six ECM flights accomplished. Vladivostok again became the locus of this activity; no unusual occurrences were reported.[38] Dick Hain, an onboard crypto-linguist, recited details about many of these proceedings: "I recall that our missions were flown at 35,000 feet and that we were on oxygen for most of the flight. We flirted with the 12-mile international boundary and I remember looking at Vladivostok at night and seeing searchlights on the horizon. Reminded me of an IGA store's grand opening. We often encountered Soviet interceptors but, due to my particular skill as a Russian linguist, we always managed to avoid them. Because I was the only person on board with a Top Secret Crypto clearance, I had control of such things as on course maneuvers and could alter altitude, etc., without explaining the reason to the crew."[39]

At this point, the 6091st Reconnaissance Flight was deleted from the 91st Strategic Reconnaissance Squadron and administratively transferred to FEAF.[40] It consequently disappears from the historical record and its activities are unknown save for one well-publicized incident. On February 5, 1955, an RB-45C streaked across the Yellow Sea to within 10 miles of the North Korean coastline, accompanied by twelve F-86s from the 335th Fighter Interceptor Squadron. At a point roughly 40 miles west of Pyongyang, and still over international waters, the Americans were unexpectedly challenged by a flight of eight MiG-15s. Such aggressive posturing was easy to understand: throughout the winter of 1954/1955 Red China was threatening to invade the islands of Matsu and Quemoy, off the mainland coast, and the United States was carefully monitoring any buildups of Communist airpower. Apparently, a Tornado was dispatched towards Manchuria for that reason — and MiGs were waiting for it 10 miles off the North Korean coast, roughly 40 miles west of Pyongyang.

That afternoon, as Captain Ramsey winged his way towards North Korea in number 48–021, he was closely followed by vigilant Sabrejets. Captain Ramsey recalled the incident:

> My crew was selected to go to K-14, brief, fly a mission in the Yellow Sea with F-86F escorts, 4th Fighter Wing, and perform a subject mission with a 100" camera, and a subject mission along the DMZ. We were briefed, Captain Williams was the flight leader, commanding. I was fully configured, I had tip tanks, which we normally left on, and the only thing other than a normal briefing was when Major General Roger Ramey, who was a flamboyant character, walked in and asked who was in command. Captain Williams approached him and he said, "If anybody cross-sights these boys, go to Moscow if you have to and shoot them down!"
>
> We took off and the flight was uneventful, clear blue all over North Korea and we got out to sea, headed roughly north into Port Arthur, and we counted fifty contrails over Manchuria. We were a little antsy, so we turned well short of the coastline and flew south. I didn't see much because I was working through a "ring sight" and the first thing I learned was when the tail gunner said, "There's a MiG!" and started firing. The guns weren't too good and they only averaged a burst and-a-half before the pumps gave out, and we didn't even test them because we didn't want to waste that one and-a-half. Everything got mixed up, we continued to maintain our distance. My copilot returned to picking out targets ahead for me. We finished our mission and the F-86s were doing what the general told them. We didn't see any MiG-15s. There were eight MiGs probably above 50,000 and I was at 30,000, two F-86s at 34, two at 38 and two at 42. They did not drop their wing tanks until after the engagement started. We recovered and my wife was threatening to miscarry, so I talked to Colonel Alexander about keeping it quiet and he came back and told me it was too big to keep quiet. The next day my other mission was scrubbed and I was told to return home.[41]

A different perspective is proffered by Lieutenant Charles Stonestreet, 4th Fighter Wing. He found escorting RB-45Cs wearisome because the bomber cruised along at speeds slower than Mach .82, forcing the Sabrejets "to weave continuously to maintain position." Events unfolded in a flash: "My Shark flight was in a shallow turn to the right in our weave and was just about to cross directly behind the RB-45 when someone shouted 'Hey! There are MiGs up here!' The North Koreans suddenly executed a single diving pass at the Tornado then hightailed it for home with Sabrejets in pursuit." The ensuing dustup saw the first Communist craft flamed by Lieutenant Charles D. Salmon. According to Salmon, "I saw their tracers streaking past our plane. They were firing from too far away. They dove past my flight and attacked the bomber. I rolled over on my back, slipped down to the left, and rolled out on the tail of one of them. I fired five or six bursts and he started to smoke. He burst into flame and slipped off towards the sea." A second MiG fell to the guns of flight commander Captain George F. Williams, although, to accomplish this, Williams and his wingman pursued their quarry over Pyongyang before finally downing it.[42] The MiGs, thoroughly chastised, made no further attempts to interfere, so Ramsey's RB-45C completed its mission unscathed.

Later that evening the fighter jocks threw a raucous celebration at the officers club. Stonestreet said, "The guys were really on an emotional high and partied and told war stories until the wee hours of the morning! The RB-45 crew, enlisted men included, partied with us."[43] Ramsey also recalled the festivities that evening: "I got to meet General Partridge, a fine gentleman. My crew was Hubert Thornber, my copilot, Ramon K. Richardson, my navigator, and Airman 3rd Class [Noel] Carrigan, who slept in the officer's club because we couldn't have him with the rest of the people due to the type of missions we were flying. We had a real good party that night, they got those two airplanes. The fighter wing commander made me go get my airman out of the Airman's Club and bring him to the Officer's Club. They went out and poured us 'general-sized' whiskies and my tailgunner, who was a nineteen-year old and didn't drink much bourbon, started calling all the generals 'colonel.' He finally told one of them, 'I never saw so much goddamn brass in my life, sir.'"

Unit insignia of the highly classified 6091st Flight at Yokota AB, Japan (John Mott).

The RB-45Cs days at Yokota were numbered once Martin RB-57s and North American RF-100s began arriving, and a new formation, the 6021st Reconnaissance Squadron, 6007th Reconnaissance Group (Composite), was organized. Sometime in the fall of 1956, the four veteran Tornados still on station were flown back to San Bernadino for final interment and a rendezvous with the welder's torch. Their departure concludes one of the murkiest episodes of Cold War intelligence gathering, and but does not diminish the central role that RB-45Cs played in it. Many of the pilots at Yokota subsequently transitioned to newer and more capable machines, but Captain Ramsey, at least, remained unassailably attached to his Tornado. "I didn't want to fly jets to begin with," he insisted, "and to me it was, next to my wife, my *best girl friend*." Captain Angelus was, by contrast, decidedly less sentimental. "We just left the B-45s over there," he laughed. "They're probably all cigarette lighters by now!"

CHAPTER ELEVEN

On Final

"You love a lot of things if you live around them, but there isn't a woman and there isn't a horse, not before nor any after, that is as lovely as a great airplane, and men who love them are faithful to them even though they leave them for others."

— Ernest Hemingway[1]

Any military aircraft accruing a decade-long service history is bound for co-option into niches far removed from its original intent. The B-45 was no exception, and its activities here proved wide-ranging, indeed. Some of these assignments bordered on superfluous, while others underscored the overall utility this design always exuded, particularly in advancing newer technologies.

One of the more quixotic uses envisioned for the Tornado was that of testing them on regularly scheduled airline routes. By 1950 it became embarrassingly apparent that the British had stolen a march on the United States by rushing ahead with development of their ill-fated DeHaviland Comet. This was a futuristic, four-engine machine with a penchant for inexplicable crashes and, although the cause for the mishaps was later identified as metal fatigue, it took much time and many lives to rectify. Meanwhile, a movement was afoot within the American government to coax the commercial sector into developing similar aircraft (which materialized as the magnificent Boeing 707 in 1957) and begin testing preliminary air routes and schedules beforehand. The progenitor of the scheme, secretary of commerce Charles Sawyer, had broached the issue with Air Force officials as to the availability of B-45s as early as January 1950. The Air Force, however, was less than enthusiastic about the project, owing to the unreliability of J47 jet engines then in use. "The airplanes have been grounded eighteen times since October 1948," Major General Donald L. Putt warned. "Based on the above facts, my opinion is that the B-45 is not ready for scheduled operation and that the USAF today does not have a jet bomber whose operation, through commercial scheduling, can materially contribute to the advancement and solution of problems associated with jet airline operations."[2] Such dismal figures could scarcely have been encouraging, but Sawyer nonetheless testified before the Senate Interstate and Foreign Commerce Committee about testing jet bombers over airline routes at government expense. The project he advocated involved hauling cargo on scheduled, city-to-city routes for a year. Yet, seeing how B-45s were never utilized in this role, Air Force reticence must have factored into their nonusage.[3]

In a lighter vein, the Tornado enjoyed a distinct, if fleeting, career in the Hollywood film industry. Howard Hughes, eccentric billionaire and aviation avatar, was a national celebrity and enjoyed considerable pull with both the government and Air Force officials. Therefore, when he requested using one of their new, expensive, and still unpredictable B-45s for his new RKO film *Jet Pilot* in 1949, the response was predictably affirmative. Moreover, the entrance door on this craft was to be modified by mounting a 12 × 14 inch glass so that a 35mm camera could film aerial sequences while aloft. Hughes would under-write the cost of modifications and also pay out per diem expenses to crew members as needed. An even greater indication of Hughes' influence is that he also obtained access to a Northrop F-89 Scorpion, a Bell F-59 Airacomet, and the McDonnell XF-45 Gob-lin parasite fighter, replete with its own B-29 mother ship. (Only the F-89 was filmed.)[4] Curiously, *Jet Pilot* was withheld from distribution until 1957, and it completely bombed with critics and audiences alike.

On at least three occasions, the Air Force also tried elevating the Tornado's public profile by entering bombers in various national competitions. The first attempt was on September 2, 1949, when Major George B. Thabault left Barksdale, Louisiana, for a run in the famous Cleveland Air Races. Unfortunately, he only got as far as Selfridge AFB, Michigan, when his Tornado was sidelined by mechanical problems and consequently failed to participate.[5] B-45s enjoyed substantially better luck two years later when three were entered in the Bendix Air Race from Muroc, California, to Wayne-Major Airport, Detroit, a distance of 1,925 miles. Because no race had been scheduled during the pre-

A B-45 piloted by Captain Bernard "Bull" Watts lifts off from Edwards AFB during the all-jet 1951 Bendix Air Race to Detroit Michigan (John Mott).

vious year, it was decided to hold an all-jet event in 1951 to showcase the military's latest aircraft. This was also the first time that bomber aircraft of any kind competed in the
Bendix.

The Tornados under Lieutenant Colonel Thabault, Captain Bernard "Bull" Watts,
and Major Leo M. Dykes all roared off the dry lake bed that Saturday, August 19, 1951,
and raced eastward, hoping for an elusive tail wind that could boost their airspeeds to
800 miles per hour. The bombers competed against a handful of F-86E Sabrejets and F-
84E Thunderjets for the prize. The odds appeared stacked against the swept-wing fighters
initially as the Tornados and Thunderjets flew nonstop, whereas the F-86s refueled twice
on the ground. The bombers streaked eastward seeking to humiliate their smaller rivals,
but glory was not to be theirs. Colonel Keith K. Compton, a senior F-86E test pilot at
Muroc, won the dash with a record speed of 553.761 miles per hour and a time of three
hours, 27 minutes and 56 seconds. An F-84 finished second, while Thabault's B-45 placed
third at 532.637 miles per hour and three hours, 36 minutes, and 11.2 seconds. As con-
solation, Thabault's flight constituted a speed record for the B-45, while Watts finished
fifth and Dyke came in seventh. The proceedings were viewed by an estimated 200,000
people in Detroit, who lingered about to inspect the military review assembled on their
behalf. Compton subsequently attributed victory to his maintenance and refueling crews,
noting. "They had to be good because the F-84s and B-45s were going nine miles for
each minute I was on the ground."[6]

In addition to military service, B-45s were occasionally lent (in legal parlance,
"bailed") to various civilian agencies for research purposes. Once such instance was the
National Advisory Committee for Aeronautics (NACA–a precursor to NASA), which
acquired a J35-powered Tornado, number 47–021, on October 1, 1948. This aircraft
received the NACA designation No. 121 and, over the next four years, it was continually
modified with flight-test equipment. Number 47–021 had completed 40 flights, totaling
59 hours in the air, when it roared aloft from Langley AFB on August 15, 1952, with
noted test pilot Herbert Henry Hoover at the controls. Hoover (no relation to the former president) was something of a legend in test flight circles. He originally flew survey
aircraft for Standard Oil during the 1930s before joining NACA in December 1940. Skilled
and fearless, he survived several close brushes with disaster and went on to become head
of flight operations at the Langley Memorial Laboratory in Hampton, Virginia. In this
capacity Hoover transferred to Muroc AFB in time to participate in the Bell XS-1 testing program along with other aviation celebrities like Chuck Yeager. On March 10, 1948,
Hoover flew the XS-1 to a speed of 703 miles per hour, becoming the first civilian and
only the second person to break the sound barrier. For his efforts at Muroc and elsewhere,
he received the Octave Chanute Award in 1948 and the prestigious Air Medal the following year.[7]

This day Hoover, accompanied by copilot John A. Harper, departed Langley in
47–021 to test various research instruments. Their flight profile required Hoover and
Harper to test B-45 "push down-pull up" maneuver by coming out of shallow, high-speed
dives at 10,000 feet and 450 miles per hour. The first attempt proved flawless, but did
not result in any negative g-values. Hoover then turned the craft around, entered a shallow dive for the second time, and had begun pulling up when disaster struck. According
to Harper, "At this point, the airplane pitched up very suddenly and acceleration of
approximately 8g or 10g resulted. My control column was back against the back stop and

shaking violently; the whole airplane was shaking violently. Following the abrupt pull-up, the
airplane did one or two snap rolls
and then settled down into a steep
dive. At this time I looked out the
right side and observed that the
starboard wing was gone from the
nacelle out and that the wing stub
was burning." For several anxious
moments Harper fumbled with the
canopy ejections system before it
finally worked. He managed to
eject safely and landed with only a
few minor bruises after the jet
impacted near Burrowsville, Virginia, and exploded. Hoover,
unfortunately, was killed while
ejecting after he apparently struck
some debris in mid-air; his body
was found near the wreckage with
his parachute unopened. Investigators subsequently deduced that the
B-45 suffered main spar failure
outboard of the engines, whereupon wing panels struck the horizontal stabilizers, shearing them
off.[8]

The distinguished civilian test pilot Herbert H.
Hoover, who was killed in a B-45 accident in August
1952 (Dryden Flight Research Center).

Four additional B-45s were also bailed to the Northrop Corporation for testing purposes associated with their pioneering but ill-fated Snark project, an early cruise missile.
Testing the system usually involved guiding the missile in flight while it was electronically tethered to a pacing JB-45. This process entailed launching the Snark from a rocket-
powered sled up to a proper altitude. Northrop test pilot Rex Hardy recalled one hazardous
encounter: "On an early trial one of the large rockets on the sled broke free and shot into
the air. It just missed the B-45, which was 4,000 feet above the ground, and those of us
watching from a nearby point (listening to the radio) heard the B-45 pilot, Fred Belcher,
shout, 'Holy Cheerist! What was that?' He later said that the rocket had passed very close
in front of the plane. The sled/Snark combination slithered sideways off the track and
considerable damage was done."[9] Equally significant, from a technological perspective,
was the missile's highly complex internal guidance system, which was partially capable of
navigating by star sighting. This futuristic device was plugged into the company's Tornados and flown over great distances to gauge its accuracy. "We were using the B-45 as
a higher and faster test bed for the Snark guidance system after we did all we could with
the B-29," Hardy noted. "The idea was to take off from Los Angeles airport and fly to,
in the case of the B-45, to [*sic*] Shreveport at night. A good many of those missions didn't
work out. We were flying directly controlled by the navigation system, which was hooked

into the airplane's autopilot, from Los Angeles to Shreveport. The pilot didn't really do much but take off with the airplane and hook the autopilot up."

It is estimated that between 1953 and 1958, the B-45s bailed to Northrop logged 196 guidance test flights lasting 450 hours. The first fully automated test flight of the Mark I system, completed without pilot interference, occurred on April 15, 1955, and was completely successful: the B-45 departed Los Angeles and landed at Tyndall AFB, Florida, several hours later, with "a terminal accuracy of within one-half mile." Yet even this surprisingly efficient internal navigation system could not save the Snark. By the time it became viable in 1961, it had already been surpassed by newer, faster intercontinental ballistic missiles (ICBMs) and it was unceremoniously scrapped.[10]

One of the most prolonged and unheralded activities of the Tornado during its operational life was its work as a tow target aircraft. In another historic first, it was the first jet bomber so utilized. Air Force planners realized that new jet fighters needed fast targets that approximated enemy aircraft if air-to-air gunnery training were to prove realistic. In September 1949, Headquarters, Twelfth Air Force, alerted the 1st Tow Target Squadron at Biggs AFB, Texas, that deliveries of J35-powered B-45A-1 jet aircraft could be expected shortly, although these remained at Barksdale AFB until squadron personnel were sufficiently versed in maintenance and operational procedures.[11] The first Tornados arrived the following spring and tests commenced by towing MK-22 target sleeves until the streamlined Aero X-27A high-speed tow targets became available. Not unexpectedly, old problems of maintenance difficulties arose, particularly as J35 engine liners had to be inspected or removed following only 50 hours of service. Consequently, three months of operations resulted in only 235 hours of air time for Tornados, as opposed to 1,531 for Douglas B-26s on station. Nonetheless, B-45s remained a standard fixture at Biggs for several years, and squadron authorities established a systematic training program to render pilots proficient as soon as possible.[12]

As the months ground on, part shortages and other mechanical problems reduced B-45 flying time to 122 hours with a daily in-commission status of 28 percent by July. Incessant problems with J35 engine liners remained the biggest obstacle, and B-45 work crews were broken up into two flights for closer supervision of maintenance. By this time seven Tornados were on station, but their employment as target aircraft remained problematic simply because the 45-foot long Mk-22 target sleeves would "oscillate prohibitively at high speeds. There is no question that only when high speed targets are made available will the B-45 be useful in towing missions."[13] For the year's final quarter Tornados registered a slight increase in operational use, 151 hours of flight time, but still only a one tenth of what the B-26s flew. Squadron authorities believed that future utilization of B-45 aircraft hinged upon the acquisition of tow targets that were better suited for high speed. Until that eventuality, the Tornados would be utilized for acquiring firsthand experience in jet engine maintenance.[14]

Despite systemic problems in early phases of B-45 towing operations, the aircraft invariably impressed pilots called upon to fly it. "It was a lot more like a fighter than it was a bomber," Captain Jack L. Drain recalled. "There was no doubt about it and it had good controls. It was a well-built airplane, you felt comfortable in it from the standpoint of sturdiness. It was a hardy airplane and didn't seem to be very fragile." Conditions endemic to Biggs, namely high desert heat and short runways, also insured that every takeoff was an adventure. "That was a kind of nip and tuck take off roll out there," Major

Everett G. Walker notes. "There were times when we could compute our take off roll and the roll itself would consume the whole runway. After one of our guys knocked the fence down we decided to always use the long runway." Lieutenant Cletus Dold seconded this observation: "On an 85-degree day, the take off run on a B-45 with the J35s was the length of the runway — there wasn't any to spare! And, if we went on that temperature, the runway was beneath our wheels as we retracted them."

The first year at Biggs proved hardly auspicious, but statistics improved as greater experience was acquired. For the first quarter, B-45s compiled only 226 hours aloft with an in-commission rate of 55 percent. Part of the drop was due to the fact that numbers 47–004 and 47–019 were sent to San Bernadino for an overhaul and modifications. The second quarter registered a further decline to 138 hours, but this gradually increased to 281 hours that fall, an operational rate of 71 percent. The year closed out with the final three months accounting for 206 hours in the air and in-commission rates of 69 percent–still not perfect but improving.[15] The following year evinced similar results, with increased hours flown and higher rates of maintenance. At this point the Army sought using the B-45s for radar ground tracking projects; the planes were to be flown at high speed and high altitude to simulate Russian jet bombers. The 1st Tow Target Squadron complied, but this placed additional work on ground crews to keep the "in commission status" as high as possible. Experiments with the much anticipated Aero A-1 (X-27A) tow target also proved dismal and, of fourteen flights, the majority either disintegrated in flight or were damaged after landing under tow. Squadron leaders also began pressing for higher thrust J35-A29 engines to replace the existing variants in use. This modification would ameliorate pressing and dangerous problems associated with lengthy takeoff rolls and "the future necessity of these aircraft outweighs the expense of the installation." The only other change for that year was transferring two B-45s (now designated TB-45As) to the 2nd Tow Target Squadron in Delaware.[16]

Safety precautions were prevalent in target towing throughout this period, but no pilot savors the prospects of being shot at on a daily basis. "I was a little leery of the F-86s," Captain Walker reflected. "We towed a radar target for them in the B-45 at 30,000 feet out at Yuma. At first we had some problems with their radar walking up the cable — the pilot couldn't see that happening. I was worried that they were getting behind that damn thing and firing rockets." Worse, as in any live fire practice, there was a certain element of danger to every flight. Captain Drain recalls one time when an F-89 Scorpion pilot unwittingly disabled his own radio — then secured a target lock on the Tornado. "He had his mike button depressed — we could hear him breathing, but we couldn't talk to tell him. And there was a chase plane pilot also trying to tell him that he was locked on *us* and *not* the target! He fired *all* his rockets at us — they went around us and not one rocket even scraped the aircraft. We were screaming at him on the radio trying to tell him, *Don't fire! Don't fire! You have the tow ship!'* but he never heard a word. We figured they'd take care of him when they got him back." Fortunately, no one was ever injured during these live fire drills and the squadron compiled a respectable safety record in their TB-45s — in spite of fighter pilots.[17] Lieutenant Dold admitted, "To me it was an extremely safe operation and, although it looked hairy as Hell, it's safe."

The Tornado's performance as tow target aircraft improved somewhat over the next five years, principally through adoption of equipment better suited for the task. Previously, they employed somewhat primitive arrangements for target towing, which were dangerous and ill suited for high speed flight. According to Captain Drain, "They installed a huge reel in the bomb bay of the B-45 and we had about 7,000 feet of armored, steel cable that we used to drag what they called a 'radar reflective target' that they could locate on their radar screen and they would fire the pods of rockets from F-89s and from the bottoms of F-94s." The chutes, unfortunately, proved unstable at high speeds and fluctuated widely as pilots drew their bead. A new system was developed that allowed the tail gunner to operate and control the tow reel, which was reeled into the bomb bay, fitted with new targets, and redeployed in flight. Tornados, however, were still prohibitively expensive to operate and maintain, so squadron leaders began pining for modified Martin B-57 Canberras when they became available.[18] These smaller, lighter aircraft promised better performance on a more cost-effective basis. Stringent requirements for jet pilot ratings were also introduced, which were impractical to attain for an outfit reduced to flying only four TB-45s. Therefore, in January 1955 an appeal went out for the assignment of Lockheed T-33 jet trainers to the squadron on a permanent basis to maintain pilot proficiency. On a lighter note, a TB-45 was lent to Warner Brothers as a camera ship for filming *The McConnell Story* (1954) and the squadron commander was formally thanked by studio officials.[19]

The period 1955–1957 were twilight years for TB-45s with the 1st Tow Target Squadron at Biggs. The most noted event during this interval was conversion of all aircraft to J47 engines by North American officials at Yuma County Airport. An even bigger change proved to be the adoption of a so-called "Dart target" mounted directly into the tail gunner position and operated from there. Sergeant Lloyd Miller did the initial engineering drawing for the device and it was constructed at the base machine shop. According to him the original system, "was kind of dangerous because, as they'd open the bomb bay, you didn't know where the target was going to go. And that's why we designed the mount in the tail gunner compartment so that when they dropped it would fall behind the airplane." Test runs flown by Captain Charles V. Dunn in July 1956 were promising. "I was very satisfied with the overall results," he wrote, "and I know that the capabilities of the B-45 will be greatly increased by use of the Dart target." By this time, however, increasing numbers of B-57s were on hand to perform the same chores and the Tornados began falling by the wayside. The end came in September 1957 when the four remaining aircraft were declared surplus and placed in storage to await their final disposition.[20] Their seven-year tenure at Biggs and Yuma as tow craft had proved earnest, if unspectacular.

The 2nd, 3rd, and 4th Tow Target Squadrons also utilized TB-45 aircraft throughout this period, if to a lesser extent. The 2nd was based at Newcastle County Airport, Delaware, while the 3rd operated from Sewart AFB, Smyrna, Tennessee. Operational histories for these two units are spotty, but it appears that they owned one or two Tornados apiece, flown chiefly in concert with army ground-tracking maneuvers. The 4th Tow Target Squadron, however, flew from George AFB, Victorville, California, and possessed four TB-45s. No real surprises were encountered, save for the usual supply parts headaches and labor intensive inspections to keep them operational. Number 47–003 is the only known Tornado assigned to this unit and it was flown in by Major Gus Weiser, the squadron commander. The biggest departure from routine operations came in the fall of 1952, when B-45s conducted extensive tests with additional Aero A-27-A glider type targets at nearby Edwards AFB. The prototypes were extensively modified by "beefing up" the wings and fuselage, hence they proved less prone to disintegration in flight than the ones tested by the 1st Tow Target Squadron at Yuma. Ten successful sorties were executed, then the planes disappear from the historical record. In 1954 an evaluation of TB-45s as tow type aircraft found them expensive to operate and difficult to maintain under existing circumstances, while the standard practice of dropping banner type targets out of the bomb bay and into the slip stream was likewise hazardous and unpredictable. The report also anticipated the day when B-57s, capable of performing similar tasks with fewer personnel and less expense, were available. The historical record of B-45 towing activity ceases at that point.[21]

Rounding off this litany of odd jobs is possibly the most significant, that of flying engine test beds. The Tornado's capacious bomb bay and prodigious lifting abilities made it ideal for the task, and it served longer in this capacity than any other, civilian or military. One of the earliest applications happened when the Air Materiel Command authorized bailment of a B-45C (redesignated as EB-45C) to General Electric for continued testing on the J47 engine. In June 1950, number 48–010 arrived at the Schenectady Flight Test Center, New York, where GE had operated a fleet of research aircraft since 1946. There it was regularly flown by Eugene M. Beatty, an American Airlines pilot. The Tornado flew there for two years before returning to the Air Force in March 1952, but it fulfilled all its assignments satisfactorily.[22] In fact, the biggest obstacle was the relatively short runway that all aircraft based at Schenectady operated from. Roger Story, a longtime jet engine operator with GE, reflected upon the dangerous potential involved: "You've got to go back and talk about how marginal some of those operations were at the time, because the B-45 had nothing but brakes as far as deceleration on the runway was concerned. No drag chute, no speed brakes, and we operated off a runway that was about 5,000 feet. You had to be right on — in other words, you had to put the thing down early on the runway and you had to get on the brakes immediately thereafter. And if there were any poor runway conditions you went somewhere else, really."[23]

The closest event to an accident at GE occurred in March 1951 when a B-45 window panel blew out at 36,000 feet and explosive decompression ripped Beattie's oxygen mask off, rendering him unconscious. The copilot managed to gain control of the aircraft and lower it to 18,000 feet, at which point Beattie revived. "Persons undergoing this condition have abnormal reactions," flight engineer Al Liptak wrote to NACA. "During the next few seconds, the copilot and engineer fought with pilot to regain control of the airplane. As a result, an almost vertical pullout ensued, inducing high 'g' loads on the aircraft."[24] Fortunately, Beattie was able to bring the aircraft home and land safely.

In time the GE Tornado was joined by a stablemate, number 48–009, which arrived in the fall of 1951. This aircraft had previously been modified by North American to accept the very large and experimental J53 engine in its bomb bay but, when that project was cancelled, the craft was fitted with a fifth J47–17 engine for reheat testing. In this configuration, the engine remained retracted into the fuselage until needed; it was then lowered in flight and started. The navigator's compartment had also been heavily transformed into a test operator's station with over 100 engine monitors and recorders. In the spring of 1953 fire gutted a B-29 aircraft intended for testing the new J73 engine, and it was quickly grafted into 48–009's bomb bay. In May 1955 this Tornado was subsequently fitted for the very large J79 engine which, when fully retracted, still protruded halfway through the bomb bay doors. Yet the testing proved entirely successful. Hard working

48–009 was finally returned to the Air Force in the spring of 1957, and presumably junked somewhere.[25] On a minor note, the Air Force also lent a B-45 to participate in services commemorating construction of the first American jet engine at the GE plant in Lynn, Massachusetts, in 1942. On May 12, 1955, elaborate ceremonies were held at the factory, climaxed by the unveiling of a monument of native fieldstone covered by a shroud. At exactly 3:30 p.m., a Tornado, cruising at 25,000 feet, swept over the factory and signaled to a remote controlled motor that slowly lowered the canvass covering, which "was whisked off electronically."[26]

The scene now switches to the Pratt and Whitney plant in New Haven, Connecticut, which acquired their first B-45 in 1956. The machine in question was JRB-45C number 48–017, the only Tornado in the entire production run fitted with speed brakes. This aircraft also carried a new J75 axial flow jet engine in the bomb bay, which was intended for such stellar craft as the Republic F-105 Thunderchief and the Convair F-102 Delta Dagger.[27] As before, the podded engine fit snugly into the Tornado's belly until needed and lowered. Not surprisingly, George Gordon, the P&W engineering test pilot, loved flying the JRB-45C. "It was a neat airplane to fly," he beamed. "Positive control, honest — it had the same speed and range as a Tee-bird." His fellow flight test pilot, Frank Bastidas, was equally delighted by it, although he added a technical caveat. "The only thing I could compare it to was the B-47, and I thought it was a lot livelier than the B-47," Bastidas stated, "a lot more responsive. I would say accelerated better. The only problem I ever had with it was the GE engines, you had to come to half power and sit there and wait about 30 seconds until the engines caught up, because if you didn't one of them would come up to power while the other three were still at idle and all of a sudden the airplane was flying sideways! That really got exciting on a touch and go landing."

Number 48–017 labored long and faithfully at Pratt & Whitney, and was not retired from service until 1972. This made it the longest utilized B-45 of the entire fleet, a total of twenty-four years without serious mishap. Fate still arranged plenty of memorable incidents in the skies over Connecticut, however. "The most exciting thing I had was a complete hydraulic failure," Gordon emoted. "There as an emergency hand pump with a separate reservoir to raise the engine if you couldn't do that. I landed the thing on the runway, put the brakes on and, because there was no hydraulic pressure and the nose gear dampener wasn't working, when the nose came down it started to shimmy like crazy–I thought the whole airplane was coming apart. We were throwing pieces of the nose gear out, the landing light was tossed out and there were big clouds of smoke. We thought the airplane was on fire so we just bailed out on the runway." The Tornado escaped with little serious damage and on June 22, 1972, Gordon and Bastidas conducted the last-known B-45 flight — to Offut, Nebraska, site of the new SAC Museum. This last hurrah had all the ingredients for a fitting display of aerial prowess. According to Gordon, "The only thing we did was ask for a high speed pass coming into Offut — well, a low pass — so we *made it* at high speed [laughter]. But, anyway, we came across the runway at pretty much all we could get it to go, and I pulled the nose up and was really on the verge of rolling it — and I started to and I chickened out. It would look pretty embarrassing to auger in on the last flight. But the temptation was there. We were sorry to see it go. It was a fine airplane to fly — it put out lots of black smoke!"

Two other companies, Westinghouse and Allison, were also known to have employed

The B-45A bailed to the Westinghouse Corporation as an engine test bed was painted Navy blue. This is the only Tornado to wear such coloration (Wright State University Special Collection).

B-45s as engine test beds, but documentation is lacking. This is unfortunate since several aircraft were procured by the U.S. Navy as JB-45As. Photographs exist of number 47–049, adorned in high-gloss navy blue finish as it tugged a J40 engine in its belly over the TEMCO-Dallas Plant in Texas. Other pictures denote that a J35-powered Tornado, number 48–009, operated out of the Naval Air Development Unit (NADU) based at South Weymouth, Massachusetts, during 1958.[28] There it would have been helped develop high-speed radar tracking technology (Project Lincoln) in concert with a host of other navy aircraft — including a couple of blimps. The only surviving example of Navy-employed B-45s is number 47–008, a J35-powered version that alternately served with the 47th Bomb Wing at Barksdale AFB, Louisiana, the Air Materiel Center at Norton AFB, California, and the Northrop Corporation, which retained its services until March 1959. Shortly thereafter it was transferred to the Navy, which employed it as a drone controlling aerial platform at China Lake Naval Weapons Center, California. Afterwards, 47–008 remained in storage for many years, until May 1980, before being reclaimed as a historical relic by the Air Force and shipped to Castle AFB, California, for display purposes. It resides there to this day. The only other employer of B-45s, Allison, was bought out in the 1970s by Rolls Royce of England, which absconded with all records highlighting company usage.[29]

Towards the end of the decade the handful of EB and JB-45s still flying were rounded up and delivered to Davis-Monthan AFB in Tucson, Arizona, for berthing in the famous "bone yard" — and a final rendezvous with the scrapper. What followed, in one instance, was indicative of the Air Force's short-term memory loss regarding the decade-old aircraft. Around March 1959, Northrop pilot Clarence Edmonds delivered one of the last remaining drone-directing aircraft from Florida to Davis-Monthan AFB, Arizona — then an active SAC base — and what began as a routine flight was enlivened by unintended consequences. "It was pouring rain, which was very unusual at Davis-Monthan," he noted. "At the time we filed a flight plan the Cold War was at its peak. SAC was in a panic and they established rigid procedures, and you had to be identified by flight plan. And the worse thing that could happen to you is that they lost your flight plan while you're airborne and they declared you Russian. Well, our flight plan for some reason had not got to Davis-Monthan. So I came on in and landed in the pouring rain and I knew that if I shut the engines off I couldn't get them restarted. And here comes all of them — you'd think it was an infantry division; vehicles, guns, everything on earth surrounded the airplane. They looked at it and they had never seen one and thought it was a Russian bomber. They finally decided to give up, so we taxied the damn thing over to the storage area and got rid of it — but it was an experience!" Our far-ranging sojourn, having taken the reader from Inglewood and Barksdale, Langley and Lockbourne, Yokota and Sculthorpe, and thence to Manchuria and Russia, now taxies to its finale beneath the glaring Tucson sun.

In a very real sense, the B-45 Tornado was aviation's first *stealth* bomber. It remains largely invisible to the historical community despite numerous records set, highly significant Cold War duties fulfilled, and enjoying, in every conceivable sense, a productive career spanning a decade. Yet, the handful of published accounts extant proffer less

A B-45A mounting the Allison J71 engine on a hydraulic lift (Rolls Royce Heritage Trust, Allison Branch).

Number 47–008 photographed at China Lake, California, in the late 1950s. This aircraft ended up on display at Castle AFB in 47th Bomb Wing colors, although it scarcely served with that unit (G. Verver Collection, Naval Air Warfare Center Weapons Division).

On June 22, 1972, George Gordon (left) and Frank Bastidas flew the final RB-45C mission from Connecticut to Offut AFB, Nebraska. The aircraft is currently on display at the SAC Museum (George Gordon).

history and more a blurry outline of events — good reading, perhaps, but lacking the substance and empirical evidence necessary to render a historical verdict. This is an enduring and inexplicable lapse that the author cannot explain, much less account for — although laboring two decades trying. But one indomitable issue continues to mystify inquiry and convention: the B-45, while overlooked, still elicits fierce loyalty from the wizened warriors who flew and fixed them. I find it no less intriguing that a half century's passage has little diminished their enthusiasm for either the airplane or the memories it engendered. Members of the 47th Bomb Wing, the 91st Strategic Reconnaissance Wing, and the 19th Tactical Reconnaissance Squadron still congregate in yearly, if thinning, reunions to shake hands, renew old acquaintances, and foment tales reflecting the strength and fire of youth. They also invariably revel in their affection for this shady chimera, the Tornado. To them, the B-45 very much remains a badge of pride — and a source of pain, for few aircraft or organizations performed so diligently throughout the Cold War with such scant recognition from posterity. Save for the three remaining examples on display, the Tornado and its crewmen have been reduced to mere footnotes in history's ledger. An exasperated Lieutenant Earl Huggins spoke for many when he declared, "Throughout the remainder of my Air Force career I was always amazed at how few people had ever heard of the RB-45C, let alone actually seen one. I always carried a photo it my wallet to prove that such an aircraft actually existed!"[30] This glaring and inexplicable omission, as unwarranted as it is hurtful, begs rectification.

The B-45 Tornado was in many respects an aerial anomaly, both cutting edge and anachronistic upon its debut. It is best construed as transitional technology that paved the way for other venues and higher vistas. Neither millstone nor talisman, the B-45 proved itself another nimble North American product, and markedly superior to the propellor-driven aircraft it replaced. In the late 1940s, jet bombers represented a problematic variable at best, expensive to construct and decidedly dicey to operate — yet the Air Force invariably assigned the Tornado important roles for which it was not originally intended. In all these capacities it proved more capable than brilliant, yet fulfilled critical niches in strategic reconnaissance and nuclear strike until better machines arrived. Therefore, neither the aircraft nor its many undertakings can be casually dismissed as marginal or insignificant. Nor should more mundane but equally essential endeavors such as

Respect at last: the plaque commemorating the B-45 Tornado on the gounds of the U.S. Air Force Museum, Dayton, Ohio (Raymond J. Witt).

target towing or engine testing be discounted. No less important are the crew members, flight and ground alike, whose pioneering efforts, and oftentimes painful experiences, bequeathed to the Air Force valuable knowledge from which its operational procedures benefited. In short, experience gained with the Tornado tutored an entire generation of jet bomber personnel and provided a much-needed catalyst for inevitable Air Force modernization. Its legacy is quite clear, according to Sergeant Terry Little: "The B-45 served an important role as a modern attack bomber, but its real efficacy was in providing the Air Force with experience with jet technology. They made a lot of mistakes, but the learning curve came down, and safety procedures were established based on the mistakes that were made previously. It made jet aviation safer." The present writer could not agree more.

Suffice it to say that the B-45 Tornado contributed indelibly to America's Cold War reputation and earned its rightful place among aviation's famous aircraft. It certainly basks in its unimpeachable status of being America's first jet bomber. The machine fulfilled its mission. The crews performed their duty. Together they amassed an enviable record that should be recognized. May plaudits due be rendered before both are forgotten and cloaked from memory by the corroding mists of time. As Howard "Sam" Myers succinctly mused, "There'll never be another true 'Tornado.'"[31]

Appendix: SAC Versus
TAC Bombing Competition

or

How a TAC B-45 Unit Was Selected for the Cold War
Deployment to England Over a SAC B-29 Unit.
Alfred E. Hoshor, Lt. Col., USAF Retired.

In early 1951, Headquarters, USAF, determined that the Air Force needed a light
bomber wing to be stationed in England as a deterrent to the Soviet Union during the
Cold War years. To be effective, the bomb wing selected would have to stand alerts and
be capable of deploying Special Weapons (i.e., atom bombs) if required. A SAC B-29
wing was tentatively selected for this deployment.

In June 1951, I was a new arrival at Langley AFB, Virginia, and was assigned to the
85th Bombardment Squadron, 47th Bombardment Wing. The wing, then equipped with
B-26 aircraft, was waiting to convert over to the North American B-45 jet bomber. My
first ride in this newly assigned aircraft occurred on July 10, 1951. I was assigned as the
AOB (Aerial Observer, Bombardier) on John R. Stoner's air crew, and we were beginning a very intensive training program designed to reach Combat Readiness status as
quickly as possible. In this respect, we were scheduled to fly almost daily, from Monday
through Saturday. Included in our training were practice bombing runs on targets, using
a SAC Radar Bomb Site (RBS) in Richmond, Virginia, with a ground-controlled scoring team to compute the simulated bomb's impact point. We made all the bomb runs
using our APQ-24 radar system. The SAC ground team would use aircrew inputs such
as altitudes, time of fall, and bomb release signals, and their radar track of the aircraft
path to plot the simulated impact point. The ground team would then relay this information to the aircrew and the wing as a "circular error" score from the target for each
run. A typical target was the corner of some building that had previously been surveyed.
This system was very accurate, and Squadron Operations maintained a record of all those
figures as part of each aircrew's training. All drops were made at our normal flight altitudes, between 35,000 and 40,000 feet, and 380 to 400 knots airspeed.

The 47th Bomb Wing staff learned of the Air Force decision to deploy a B-29 Wing,
and they felt that the B-45 jet bomber, with its higher flying altitude and faster airspeed,
would be a much better deterrent than the B-29s. Both aircraft used the same type bombing system and both could drop the same type weapons. However, the wing staff felt that
the stable platform of the B-45 in flight permitted more accurate bombing than the B-

213

29. The wing commander approved the decision and a message was submitted to HQ, USAF, requesting that they reconsider the type of aircraft to deploy, and to select the TAC 47th Bomb Wing for the mission, rather than the SAC unit. At that time, both SAC and TAC wings were in training and neither had yet obtained Operational Readiness status.

The request caused considerable message traffic between the TAC, SAC, and USAF. The SAC response was that they felt that they were further along in their training and should be the unit deployed. Finally, a decision was made by HQ, USAF, that the two wings in question should conduct a bombing competition. SAC was willing, as they ran and controlled all the Radar Bomb Scoring Sites, used the same APQ-24 bombing equipment, and their aircrews were more experienced in the use of SAC Radar Bomb Sites (RBS), plus they had the advantage of their B-29s flying slower and at lower altitudes than the B-45s. TAC was willing, as they thought they had the best aircraft and crews. USAF was willing, as it solved the selection problem and produced a result they could all agree to.

Certain ground rules had to be worked out and agreed to in advance. Essentially, these rules were that each wing would pick ten aircrews; each aircrew would make two simulated bomb runs at each of two RBS sites. Scope photography would be accomplished on all bomb runs. One run had to be made using an offset aiming point of the crew's discretion, and on the other run the crew had to make the run using the direct radar aiming point of the target. Aircraft would fly at optimum altitudes and airspeeds. No aircrew could fly over these sites prior to the competition. If radar photos of the target area were desired, the wing could send a nonparticipating aircrew over the sites to take photos, for study purposes; however, this aircrew could not participate in the competition. The two sites selected were Birmingham, Alabama, and Oklahoma City, Oklahoma. Normal Combat Information folders would be compiled and issued to each participating aircrew. Both TAC and SAC observers would be stationed on the ground at the RBS sites during the competition.

The ground rules appeared to be fair, although they favored SAC due to the following:

(A) The optimum altitudes of the aircraft, i.e., 20,000 to 24,000 ft. for the SAC B-29s versus 35,000 to 40,000 for the TAC B-45s,
(B) The optimum airspeed of the SAC B-29s was 200 to 230 knots, while that of the TAC B-45s was 380 to 400 knots,
(C) SAC operated the RBS sites and their aircrews were already aware of how to utilize them, whereas RBS bombing was something new to TAC aircrews at this time.

Upon receipt of the above listed ground rules, the 47th Bomb Wing concentrated on getting ten aircrews combat ready ASAP. As it turned out, our aircrew, assigned to the 85th Bombardment Squadron, was the 10th aircrew within the wing to attain Combat Readiness status, and we were selected to participate. In preparation for the competition, we were issued Combat Target folders for the two RBS sites, which we were to study. The folder contained maps of the two sites and radar photography of the areas which a nonparticipating aircrew had taken. We were allowed to fly practice bomb runs on Richmond RBS site to obtain additional experience in their use.

When the big day arrived, then Colonel David M. Jones, 47th Bomb Wing Commander, gave the selected crews a pep talk, which included the fact that he would personally provide the TAC aircrew who received the lowest score (i.e., Lowest Circular Error) total for all bomb runs with a bottle of champagne for each of the four aircrew members.

The B-45 assigned to our aircrew, along with the APQ-24, checked out fine, and we took off for our first two runs at Birmingham, Alabama. Both runs were made in accordance with our ground rules. As we departed the area, I informed John Stoner, the pilot, that both runs looked great, and we waited for receipt of the radio report for our scores. Unknown to us, we were one of the first B-45 aircraft to make a run on this site, and the ground scoring team were still using the B-29 scoring speed stick which, with the difference in airspeeds, made the drop appear as a gross error, which was given to us by the ground team. Needless to say we were very disappointed in the score. The error was soon discovered and the wing notified of the actual correct score; however, we didn't learn of it until we landed back at Langley. One score was a shack (zero circular error) and the other less than two hundred feet. Needless to say, the welcome back and the two phenomenal scores were almost overwhelming.

On our second mission (to Oklahoma), John Stoner was concerned because the plane we had flown in on the Birmingham flight was out of commission, and we were assigned another aircraft. We were both reluctant to fly such an important mission in a different aircraft, so we checked everything very carefully. Everything checked out fine, and I was no longer concerned. However, to satisfy John and assure myself that the radar was indeed working fine, I asked John to call Richmond RBS site, and see if we could make a practice bomb run. Everything was cleared and I made a bomb run on what I considered one of the easier targets. The score we received was great, so John and I were both satisfied with the change in aircraft.

Upon arrival at the Oklahoma RBS site, we made our two runs. The offset aiming point was very clear and not a problem (providing the compass was accurate). The second run was more of a problem as it was difficult picking out the exact aiming point due to excessive ground clutter. I knew I was close, but was not certain I was properly synchronized on the aiming point. After completing two runs, and before we received the actual scores, the TAC representative at the RBS site radioed to us that we should return to Langley and drink that champagne. Our total for the four runs in the competition turned out to be "502 and 112 feet circular error." The nearest score for any other TAC crew for the four runs was "900 feet" by AOB Jerry Walden, which is a phenomenal score. Other scores were good; yes, our aircrew won and drank the champagne.

As a result of this competition, the 47th Bombardment was selected to prepare for deployment to Sculthorpe RAF Station, England, in June 1952. This gave the wing plenty of time to become fully combat ready. Stoner's aircrew, with me as AOB, flew over to England as part of the flight element. I never did learn what the SAC aircrew scores were; however I understand they were significantly higher.

SAC, due to our low bombing scores, requested permission to send inspectors to Langley to verify the B-45 equipment. The inspectors came, and everything checked out fine. Later, individuals from SAC arrived and talked to both air and ground crews and Target Intelligence in an attempt to find out how the B-45 crew could bomb so accurately. They spent considerable time with the target Intelligence Section, and apparently took back some data that could help them in preparing their target folders.

Before departure for Sculthorpe, our aircrew and one other were picked to test the B-45 aircraft wiring and bombing system by dropping two special weapons (without the core) off the coast of Florida at Eglin AFB. The two drops were made using an air burst, and everything worked fine.

The B-45 bombing with the APQ-24 radar system was later proved to be extremely accurate. Shortly after arrival at Sculthorpe, permission was received to use Luce Bay bombing range, off the West Coast of England. Our crew and one other from the 85th B.S. were selected to make four bomb runs each on the target barge, using practice bombs. A request was submitted to the RAF requesting what offset aiming point to use to avoid hitting the barge. The response was "none" as the RAF had been using this same target for many years with no problem. The bomb impacts were scored from observers on the shore by visual means. All bomb drops were made from an altitude above 36,000 feet and 380 knots. The impacts of all bombs dropped received scores varying from 50 to 250 feet. However, upon return to Sculthorpe a message had been received that the range had closed. They had to locate a replacement barge. Six or eight months later a message arrived saying that the range was open again, but to have our aircrews use a one mile due south offset for our bombs. I wonder *WHY*?

Chapter Notes

Chapter One

1. Alden R. Crawford to L.C. Craigie, 23 April 1948, Hoyt S. Vandenberg Papers, Box 32, Manuscript Division, Library of Congress.

2. I.B. Holley, "Jet Lag in the Army Air Corps," in *Military Planning in the Twentieth Century*, ed. Harry R. Borowski (Washington, D.C.: Office of Air Force History, 1986), 123, 129–130.

3. Defensive Armament and Fighter Escort for Bombardment Type Aircraft, 27 May 1946, Case History for the B-45 Airplane, Vol. 1, Headquarters, Air Force Air Materiel Command, Wright-Patterson AFB.

4. Marcelle S. Knaack, *Post World War II Bombers, 1945–1973* (Washington, D.C.: Office of Air Force History, 1988), 61–63; Michael E. Brown, *Flying Blind: The Politics of the U.S. Strategic Bomber Program* (Ithaca, NY: Cornell University Press, 1992), 68–78; Bruce K. Holloway, "High Sub-Sonic Speed for Air Warfare," *Air University Quarterly Review* 1 (Fall 1947): 52.

5. Bill Gunston, "North American Tornado," *Aeroplane Monthly* 10 (December 1982), 633. These sentiments were echoed by Chief Engineer Harold E. Dale, who stated, "We followed the standard North American engineering practice that renders our craft relatively simple to construct. By that I mean we early consider the ship from a production man's viewpoint: will it be relatively simple in tooling, production and field service?" ("A Product of Teamwork," *Western Flying* 30 [October 1950], 44).

6. Robert Jackson, *Combat Aircraft Prototypes Since 1945* (Shrewsbury, England: Airlife, 1985), 16. Jackson goes on to state that this same design conservatism prevailed during creation of Britain's first V-Bomber, the Vicker's Valiant, whose career was cut short by main spar cracks.

7. Engineer Tally, Progress Report, 18 January 1946, page 3, Case History of the B-45 Airplane, Vol. 1, Headquarters, Air Force Air Materiel Command, Wright-Patterson AFB; "A Product of Teamwork," *Western Flying* 30 (October 1950): 44. This intragroup diplomacy proved more difficult than its sounds. According to George Gehrkens, "We had fights between the hydraulic group and the landing gear group. I would help sort it out."

8. Case History of B-45 Procurement, Record Group 341, Headquarters, U.S. Air Force, Deputy Chief of Staff, Special Project File, Box 222, National Archives.

9. Lt. Col. Robert E. Greer to the Commanding General, 18 July 1946, Record Group 341, Headquarters, U.S. Air Force, Deputy Chief of Staff, Special Project File, Box 222, National Archives. The late General (then colonel) Byron K. Boettcher, deputy chief Bomber Project officer, concurred with this estimation by telling this author they had "looked at the jet bombers we had in the X stage and we decided that the B-45 was the most practical, less complicated aircraft to put into production. We figured it was a straight forward airplane with jet engines."

10. Robert L. Trimble, "New Age Bombers," *Air Progress Aviation Review* 6 (Winter 1982), 38–39; Norm L. Avery, *North American Aircraft*, 2 vols. (Santa Ana, CA: Narkiewicz/Thompson, 1998), vol. 1, 155–156. "Another obstacle encountered in building a high-speed bomber was that of keeping its frontal area to an absolute minimum. The wing presented a king-sized headache to engineers attempting to house both the fuel and landing gear in a relatively thin wing" ("Tornado," *Skyline* 7, no. 2 [July 1949], 18).

11. "A Product of Teamwork," *Western Flying* 30 (October 1950), 44.

12. Robert L. Trimble, "New Age Bombers," *Air Progress Aviation Review* 6, no. 3 (Winter 1982): 38; Bill Gunston and Peter Gilchrist, *Jet Bombers from the Messerschmitt Me 262 to the Stealth B 2* (London: Osprey Aerospace, 1992), 25–27.

13. "Jet Bomber Cockpit," *Flight* 56 (13 October 1949): 498. According to Captain Howard S, "Sam" Myers, "The instrument panel was installed at a slight angle and sort of wrapped around the pilot. Everything was easy to reach and activate. Good visibility in all directions was provided by an ample plexiglass canopy" ("We Flew Tornados," in *Spyplanes: Air Classics Special Edition* 2 [1988]: 31).

14. Gunston, "North American Tornado," 634–635; Avery, *North American Aircraft*, Vol. 1, 156–157; "The North American B-45: Description and Brief History," 6, Case History of the B-45 Aircraft, Vol. 1, Headquarters, Air Materiel Command, Wright-Patterson AFB. Sgt. Claude Riddell, 84th Bomb Squadron and one of the earliest Air Force technicians assigned to the jet bomber program, was rankled by certain aspects of the XB-45: "The first thing I didn't like about it was that I didn't see any guns on it. And I commented that there ought to be a gun turret on this plane. At least some civilians down there said 'We don't need a gun, it outruns anything that flies' And I said, 'Would you be surprised if one happens to pull up alongside and he's got the guns and you don't?' And he said, 'Sergeant, what makes you think like that?' I said, 'Well, I've been caught with my pants down out there before and it doesn't feel good.'"

15. The craft's debut was somewhat marred when the Bendix Corporation failed to provide the specially designed tires in a timely fashion. But Kindelberger did not suffer delays gladly, so "a pair of XB-35 wheels were borrowed from the Northrop Aircraft Company and, by use of special bushings, North American was able to roll the airplane out of the factory on these wheels" (Progress Report, 27 September 1946, Case History of the B-45 Airplane, Vol. 1, Headquarters, Air Force Air Materiel Command, Wright-Patterson AFB). Tire shortages plagued the program until the cusp of

the XB-45's initial flight; these tires were essential on Muroc's dry lake bed. One anxious technician observed that "With the present equipment on hand, it is pointed out that if a tire should blow out on the first XB-45 airplane while it is out on the lake, the airplane can not even be towed to the hanger until a spare tire arrives" (Progress Report, 23 January 1947, Case History of the B-45 Airplane, Vol. 1).

16. "Recording Test Data on the North American B-45," *Aviation Week* 47, no. 6 (11 August 1947), 24–25. "New methods of structural testing were introduced in the course of development. Structural loads were measured in flight by tiny wire strain gauges installed at 147 points in the XB-45. Readings were recorded on three oscillographs installed in the airplane. Plans for these tests were thoroughly worked out in advance; as a result it was possible for the AAF to cancel the static test article originally ordered under the XB-45 contract" ("The North American B-45: Description and Brief History," 5–6, Case History of the B-45 Airplane, Vol. 1, Headquarters, Air Materiel Command, Wright-Patterson AFB).

17. North American Aviation Press Release, 14 April 1947, B-45 File, National Air and Space Museum Library, Smithsonian Institution. Other prototype details are in "XB-45 Completes First Test Flight," *U.S. Air Services* 32 (April 1947): 16; "North American Grooms XB-45 Jet Bomber," *Aviation* 46, no. 5 (May 1947): 71; "North American Jet Bomber Flies at Muroc," *Aviation News* 7, no. 12 (March 24, 1947): 9; and "XB-45," *Interavia* 11, no. 4 (April 1947): 14–16.

18. North American Press Release, 14 April 1947, B-45 File, National Air and Space Museum, Smithsonian Institution. According to Paul Brewer, "The most marked impression was when we got airborne and when the gear doors came all the way up the silence was deafening. We could talk back and forth in the cockpit without mikes, it was that quiet." One anonymous reporter present during these festivities reported that "American aircraft manufacturers were jubilant over these results here last night. They have so long been hearing of British superiority in the jet field that they took particular satisfaction in grouping a number of General Electric jets ... to obtain thrusts not yet reported from any other country in a single aircraft" ("U.S. Builds Fleet of Jet Bombers," *New York Times*, 15 April 1947, 1).

19. Robert L. Trimble, "The L.A. Tornados," *Air Classics* 10, no. 11 (November 1974): 31.

20. Trimble, "New Age Bombers," 40. As Paul Brewer subsequently recounted, "Landing that baby was a real problem under those conditions. I had to use every bit of strength I could muster to wrestle the wheel on an emergency approach, while Krebs operated the elevator and rudder pedals. You couldn't land the plane from the rear seat because of visibility limitation, and it was almost funny the way Krebs and I were almost fighting each other on elevator control" (quoted in Warren Bodie, "Breaching the Walls of Fortress Europe," *Air Power* 3 [September 1973]: 44).

21. "Flight Test, Incident, and Accident Data on Selected Multi-Engined Bombers," 147–149, Headquarters, Air Materiel Command, Wright-Patterson AFB. Paul Brewer knew Cardenas well: "Bob Cardenas was a very enthusiastic pilot, as I recall. In fact ... we had trouble getting him to come down whenever he got his hands on the XB-45. Many times he would go for just one more test point and then would scrape in with dry tanks. It was not all unusual for the ground crews to have to go out with a tug to bring the airplane in" (quoted from Bodie, "Breaching the Walls of Fortress Europe," 44).

22. Albert Boyd (1906–1976). For a figure of his stature, no full-length biographical treatment exists. All information presented herein is gleaned from the Website of the Air Force Flight Test Center, Edwards AFB, www.edwards.af.mil/history.

23. Chuck Yeager, another test-flight notable, left this graphic description of his boss: "He was six feet, two inches, lanky and balding, with thick dark eyebrows, and a thick hard jaw. Think of the toughest person you've ever known, then multiply by ten, and you're close to the kind of guy that the old man was. His bark was never worse than his bite: he'd tear your ass off if you screwed up. Everybody respected him, but was scared to death of him. He looked mean and he was.... Whenever I got out of line, he swatted me down. I've got the scars to show it. Outside of Glennis [Yeager's wife] he became the most important person I've ever known. He completely changed my life in ways I never could imagine" (Chuck Yeager and Leo Janos, *Yeager: An Autobiography* [New York: Bantam], 1985, 89–90).

24. "Major General Albert Boyd," www.edwards.af.mil/history. When Captain Glen E. Edwards was killed testing the Northrop YB-49 on 8 June 1948, Boyd proved instrumental in having Muroc renamed Edwards Air Force Base in January 1950.

25. Penn Leary, ed., *Test Flying at Old Wright Field by the "Wright Stuff" Pilots and Engineers* (Omaha, NB: Westchester House, 1991), 20. Shortly after the crack-up, the testing division at Wright Patterson contacted his superiors in Washington, D.C., explaining that "A B-45 aircraft is required as a replacement for the XB-45 aircraft, serial number 45–59479, which was damaged beyond economical repair 28 1949 during an emergency landing terminating a functional test flight" (Telex dated 4 August 1949, Record Group 341, Headquarters, U.S. Air Force, Deputy Chief of Staff, Materiel, Production Engineering Division, Box 11, National Archives).

26. E-mail from Dave Menard to author, 21 September 2007. He continues: "AFOG in those days had a mission of showing the taxpayers some of what they were paying for by hauling full size a/c around on flat beds, fuselages also on flat beds, and setting them up at country fairs, air shows, etc. No malls in those days!"

27. "Flight Test, Incident, and Accident Data on Selected Multi-Engine Bombers," 160–163, Headquarters, Air Force Material Command, Wright-Patterson AFB.

28. "AAF Developing 500 MPH Multi-Jet Bomber Fleet," *Aviation News* 7, no. 15 (14 April 1947): 7. The increasing research and development costs for new aircraft led to new levels of cooperation between science, industry, and the military, hence, "Even more significant than the technical progress of the program is the pattern it set for a coordinated military-research-manufacturing development program." Another enthusiastic reporter trumpeted that four aircraft manufacturers, "in cooperation with Wright Field and the National Advisory Committee for Aeronautics are putting the new planes into test flight within twenty eight months of drawing the plans. This compares with as much as six years taken to develop the combat planes which finished the late war" ("U.S. Builds Fleet of Jet Bombers," *New York Times*, 15 April 1947, 51).

29. Bill Gunston and Peter Gilchrist, *Jet Bombers*, 15–17; Richard K. Schrader, "Douglas XB-43," *Air Classics* 25 (July 1989): 14–20, 32, 37.

30. Jackson, *Combat Aircraft Prototypes*, 28–29; Knaack, *Post World War II Bombers*, 522–526; Joe Mizrahi, "The Last Great Bomber Fly Off," *Wings* 29 (June 1999): 41–46.

31. Walt Boyne, "Convair's Needle-Nosed Orphan," *Airpower* 6 (September 1976): 66. The craft exerted no less a grip on Major Robert L. Cardenas, who recalled it fondly: "The XB-46 was a dream bird. Slender, beautiful design, and that was the first airplane that gave us technical data on what we could expect if we had something like the B-1 flying low level because the fuselage was so long and slender that it 'twanged.' The XB-46 told the engineers, 'Hey, you've got to do something about this.'"

32. Jackson, *Combat Aircraft Prototypes*, 30; Knaack, *Post*

World War II Bombers, 528–534; Mizrahi, "Great Bomber Fly Off," 46–53.

33. John R. Breihan, Stan Piet, and Roger S. Mason, *Martin Aircraft, 1909–1960* (Santa Ana, CA: Narkiewicz/Thompson, 1995), 156–158; Bill Gunston, "Martin's Six Jet Bomber," *Aeroplane Monthly* 10 (August 1982): 432–436.

34. Brown, *Flying Blind*, 85–86; Jan Tegler, *B-47 Stratojet: Boeing's Brilliant Bomber* (New York: McGraw Hill, 2000), 1–9.

35. Brown, *Flying Blind*, 83; Tegler, *B-47 Stratojet*, 11–19. The Air Force position on the B-45 was appreciably unsentimental and straightforward: "It was expected that considerable information relative to the operational techniques and procedures of jet bomber operations would be gained from the actual use of these aircraft in tactical units. In addition to technical and procedural knowledge gained in this manner, it was felt quite certain that the thorough testing by a tactical unit would reveal many discrepancies in the first jet bombers which could be corrected in future production" (Case History of B-45 Procurement, Record Group 341 Headquarters, U.S. Air Force, Deputy Chief of Staff, Special Project File, Box 222, National Archives).

Chapter Two

1. "North American XB-45," *Air Force Magazine* 30, no. 6 (June 1947): 44.

2. Linda McFarland, *Cold War Strategist: Stuart Symington and the Search for National Security* (Westport, CT: Praeger, 2001), 24, 31.

3. Quoted in Herman S. Wolk, "The First Five of the First 50," *Air Force* 80 (September 1997): 54. Officially, the Air Force defended the shift toward strategic weaponry so as to "achieve a more effective 'Air Force in being' with minimum delay" ("Air Funds Diverted to Heavy Bombers; 239 Craft Cancelled," *New York Times*, 12 January 1949, 1, 15). As early as the summer of 1948, future tactical considerations weighed heavily upon Air Force leadership regarding their purchase of additional B-45s, whose operational usefulness had yet to be determined: "The composition of the 70 Group Program calls for five light bombardment groups. To plan procurement for the equipping of all, of the major portion, of these groups with a single aircraft, such as the B-45, would commit the Air Force to the use of such an aircraft for several years and prevent the unit testing and possible acceptance of a more desirable jet bomber" (Memorandum for General Vandenberg: B-45 Procurement Program, 7 July 1948, History of the B-45 Aircraft, Record Group 341, Headquarters, U.S. Air Force, Deputy Chief of Staff, Special Projects File, Box 222). Also, "Curtailment of B-45 production would be satisfactory in the opinion of this Division because of the fact that in all probability there exists only a requirement for two (2) groups of B-45s. Therefore, elimination of the B-45s would make money available for other uses" (Procurement of the B-49 Airplane, 28 June 1948, Case History of the B-45 Airplane, Vol. 1, Headquarters, Air Materiel Command, Wright-Patterson AFB).

4. Robert F. Futrell, *Ideas, Concepts, Doctrine: Basic Thinking in the United States Air Force, 1907–1960*, 2 vols. (Maxwell AFB, AL: Air University Press, 1989), vol. 1, 244. Rising potential for nuclear hostilities with the Soviet Union was a guiding principle throughout this decision: "In view of the importance of the atomic offensive, the Board decided, that if the state of the art permitted, means must be found to deliver the atomic stockpile under the most adverse conditions foreseeable, which were the loss of advanced bases and unexpected failure of the refueling technique. The Board was cognizant of the steadily improving performance of the B-36 and the engineering studies which indicated the feasibility of obtaining greater combat speeds and atti-

tude," (Memorandum for Mr. Forrestal, 25 February 1949, James Forrestal File, Dwight D. Eisenhower Papers, 1916–1952, Box 42, Dwight D. Eisenhower Library).

5. Memorandum for Mr. Forrestal, James Forrestal File, Dwight D. Eisenhower Papers, 1916–1952, Box 42, Dwight D. Eisenhower Library; "Air Funds Diverted to Heavy Bombers; 239 Craft Cancelled" (*New York Times*, 12 January 1949, 1, 15). Air Force Chief of Staff General Hoyt S. Vandenberg, if not outright contesting the cutback, obliquely questioned its wisdom: "As you know, the last suggestion to you was that we might cut off at the 139th article. We find, however, that the 1948 Supplemental, which has for an additional 51, have all been certified to both by the Bureau and the President. The operations people feel … that we have about as much justification for two groups as one. It is our intention, if you approve, to make the cut-off at the 190th article.… If you agree to leave it to Mr. [Arthur S.] Barrows and myself, we intend to continue with the 51 contained in the Supplemental, but we need an immediate go ahead or stop" (Hoyt S. Vandenberg to W. Stuart Symington, 14 July 1948, Hoyt S. Vandenberg Papers, Box 32, 1948 File, Manuscript Division, Library of Congress).

6. "Lay-off Ordered on Coast," *New York Times*, 12 January 1949, 15.

7. Investigation of the B-36 Program, 81st Congress, 1st Session (1949), vol. 28, 339.

8. The North American B-45: Description and Brief History, 8, Case History of the B-45 Airplane, Vol. 1, Headquarters, Air Materiel Command, Wright-Patterson AFB; Marcelle S. Knaack, *Encyclopedia of U.S. Air Force Aircraft and Missile Systems*, vol. 2: *Post World War II Bombers, 1945–1973* (Washington, D.C.: Office of Air Force History, 1988), 69–70; Bill Gunston and Peter Gilchrist, *Jet Bombers from the Messerschmitt 262 to the Stealth B-2* (London: Osprey Aerospace, 1993), 26; Norm C. Avery, *North American Aircraft*, 2 vols. (Santa Ana, CA: Narkiewicz/Thompson, 1998), vol. 1, 159.

9. "Tornado," *Skyline* 7, no. 2 (July 1949): 18. Leo Hunt, an NAA technician assigned to Muroc, said, "The first B-45s they took up, none of the instruments worked—the instruments hung. And the guys had to hit on them because the engines were so smooth—so they had to put a little electric motor with a vibration to fix them. One of the biggest complaints was they didn't know how much fuel they had!"

10. Ibid., 18. "To increase the B-45's rate of descent for convenience in landing, extra drag is created by leaving open the main gear doors as well as lowering single-slotted wing flaps. When the wheels are lowered, these doors remain open until the wheels make contact with the runway. On takeoff they remain closed until the gear-up signal is given, thus creating a minimum of drag when it is not desired" (History of the North American B-45: Description and Brief History, 4, Case History of the B-45 Aircraft, Vol. 1, Headquarters, Air Materiel Command, Wright-Patterson AFB).

11. Teletype dated 27 December 1949, Record Group 341, Head Quarters, U.S. Air Force, Deputy Chief of Staff, Materiel, Production Engineering Division, Box, 11, National Archives. According to Warren Bodie, NAA service engineer, "They had dozens of B-45s stacked along the field—pickled, they didn't have the money to operate them."

12. Jet Bomber Operations, Project AU-4740, Air Force Historical Research Agency, Maxwell AFB. Colonel Peterson hoped to avoid saddling jet bomber units with special ground handling devices, but appeared resigned to their utilization: "Perhaps the only answer will be to design new equipment with which to 'top off' the tanks before take off, or to tow the aircraft to take off position, or to attach 'taxi-tanks' and drop them before take off."

13. Knaack, *Post World War II Bombers*, 71–72.

14. "Air Force Reveals Two Fast Bombers," *New York Times*, 28 September 1948, 54.

15. "Potential Capabilities of the B-45 as an All-Weather Fighter," November 1949. Air Force Historical Research Agency, Maxwell AFB, 14. The only negative commentary uncovered came from General Muir S. Fairchild discussing the various merits of night fighters then under development: "The limited number of 197 and some undesirable characteristics preclude the use of the B-45 as a night fighter" (Muir S. Fairchild to Ennis C. Whitehead, 3 August 1948, Muir S. Fairchild Papers, Box 1, Manuscript Division, Library of Congress).

16. H.A. Shepard to the Chief of Staff, undated, Record Group 341, Headquarters, U.S. Air Force, Deputy Chief of Staff for Development, Director of Development, Box 36, National Archives.

17. "Tactical Capabilities, B-45A Airplane, Interceptor Configuration" [24 May 1950], Record Group 341, Headquarters, U.S. Air Force, Deputy Chief of Staff, Materiel, Production Engineering Division, Box 11, National Archives.

18. Raymond D. Sampson, "An Evaluation of the B-45 for Tactical Air Operations in Comparison with the A-26," Air Force Historical Research Agency, Maxwell AFB. See also Comparative Evaluation of Tactical Air Support Aircraft, 15 September 1949 (AD223678), Defense Technical Information Center (DTIC), Ft. Belvoir. There is little need to disparage the proclivities of the B-26 Invader. It undertook yeoman work throughout the Korean War as a hardhitting tactical bomber and night intruder and later performed useful work in Vietnam.

19. "Evaluation of the Feasibility of Employing B-45 Type Aircraft For Ground Attack Operations," Tactical Air Command History, 1 January–31 December 1949, Vol. 2, 15, Air Force Historical Research Agency, Maxwell AFB. The report itself is dated 1 May 1950, and apparently appended to the document afterwards. Page 17 unequivocally states, "In as much as air-to-ground rocketry requires high maneuverability, it is evident that the employment of airplanes stressed to 3.67g would jeopardize the safety of aircrews and equipment. In effect, B-45 utility in ground attack operations is questionable in view of the operational limitations imposed by a stress factor that is considered to be insufficient for maneuvers required in such operations."

20. Ibid., 18. The concept of the B-45 as a ground support craft died hard. As late as 8 September 1950, Colonel Jo K. Warner of AMC submitted a study to General K. B. Wolfe for the purpose of utilizing 32 B-45A jets still in storage for use as a low-level attack bomber and close ground support airplane in Korea. In it he made the usual recommendations of adding speed brakes, eight forward firing .50 caliber machine guns, and provisions for 24 5" HVAR rockets, while still acknowledging that "Beef up of the airplanes to increase the structural limitations is not feasible because of the engineering and manufacturing problems involved" (Jo K. Warner to K.B. Wolfe, 8 September 1950, Record Group 341, Headquarters, U.S. Air Force, Deputy Chief of Staff, Materiel, Box 11, National Archives).

21. Joseph T. McNarney to Arthur S. Barrows, 16 July 1948, Case History of the B-45 Airplane, Vol. 2, Headquarters, Air Materiel Command, Wright-Patterson AFB.

22. Robert L. Trimble, "The L.A. Tornados," Air Classics 10 (November 1974): 64; George A. Larson, "America's First Four Engine Jet Bomber," Friends Journal 24, no. 2 (Summer 2001): 39; Joseph T. McNarney to Arthur S. Barrows, 16 July 1948, Case History of the B-45 Airplane, Vol. 2, Headquarters, Air Materiel Command, Wright-Patterson AFB. While the B-45C was still in the developmental stage, the Air Materiel Command waxed enthusiastic over proposed range increases since "It further permits the B-45 to carry the 22,000 pound bomb [at] 850 miles radius, or approximately the same distance the B-24 and B-17 carried a 4,000 bomb during World War II and at twice the average operating speed" (B-45 1948 Fiscal Year Procurement,

27 June 1947, Record Group 341, Headquarters, U.S. Air Force, Deputy Chief of Staff for Development, Directorate of Development, Box 36, National Archives).

23. N.T. Perkins to Earl Partridge, 28 June 1948, History of the B-45 Aircraft, Record Group 341, Headquarters, U.S. Air Force, Deputy Chief of Staff, Special Project File, Box 222, National Archives.

24. Knaack, Post World War II Bombers, 87. Regarding tip tanks, mechanic Leo Hunt recalled their preliminary installation: "We installed them for a test flight to the Edwards drop area. The release was made, however, the tanks would not drop or leave. The tanks had their own lift and the wing tip was in a socket. They were loose and continued to fly along so the pilot had to zigzag to make them leave. We later installed wing rudders set at an angle to pull the tanks away" (communication in possession of the author, undated). The huge tanks also awed NAA service engineer Warren Bodie upon viewing them for the first time at Long Beach airport: "When I saw the 1,200 gallon tanks on the wingtips I thought 'Wow!' I don't know any other plane in the world that can do this. Just think of the weight at six pounds per gallon!"

25. R.B. Landry to Carl Spaatz, 30 January 1948, Carl Spaatz Papers, Box 28. A SAC study noted, after decrying the obsolescence of aging RB-29s then in service, that "The RB-45, a jet powered aircraft, is unarmed and must depend upon its greater speed to evade the enemy. The RB-45 has a limited range, but it is capable of low-level flying, which makes possible reconnaissance where the target might otherwise be obscured by low overcast. Another decided advantage of the RB-50 and the RB-45 is the fact that they can both be refueled in flight" (Study C Reconnaissance Activities, June–July 1950, Curtis E. LeMay Papers, Box B196: Both Manuscript Division, Library of Congress).

26. Preliminary Design Specification Directive for RB-45A Photo-Reconnaissance Airplane Modification, 30 July 1948, Case History of the B-45 Airplane, Vol. 2 Headquarters, Air Materiel Command, Wright Patterson AFB.

27. "Eyes of the Air Force," Flying 48 (May 1951): 168; Andrew Hamilton, "SAC's 'Seeing Eye Jets,'" Skyways 2, no. 6 (June 1952): 12; "The New Look with the RB-45C, Latest Air Force Photo Airplane," Skyline 8, no. 3 (August 1950): 10–11. Speaking of the Sonne camera, "The S-7A is specifically designed for low altitude reconnaissance, at which it is far superior to any other camera in which the film is stopped for each exposure. To illustrate this, not too long ago an S-7A was mounted in a jet airplane which photographed another jet airplane traveling in the opposite direction. The planes were about 1,000 feet apart and the speed of each airplane was about 500 mph, which made the difference in speed between the camera and its target about 1,000 mph. The resulting picture clearly defined the details of the photographed airplane" (Photo Reconnaissance with the RB-45C, Air Intelligence Digest, Second Air Force, January 1951, 3, Air Force Historical Research Center, Maxwell AFB).

28. One of the B-45's earliest, unofficial records happened sometime in the spring of 1950: "In a routine test flight an RB-45C made a series of photographs over Los Angeles at an altitude of approximately eight miles, the highest photos ever taken from an airplane" (The Aircraft Yearbook for 1950, Washington, D.C.: Lincoln Press, 1950, 105). The pilot of that flight was apparently none other than Captain Chuck Yeager, by that time having gained notoriety for breaking the speed of sound in 1947. Captain Francis Riggs, who accompanied Yeager to test and certify various camera equipment, noted, "He was just like satin on the controls." Leo Hunt, a NAA mechanic assigned to the B-45, also met Yeager and left a memorable impression: "He wasn't as tall as I thought he should be, but a real nice guy."

29. Hamilton, "Seeing Eye Jets," 52; Knaack, Post World War II Bombers, 88–89; John W. Sheehan, "North Ameri-

can B-45 ... The USAF's Tornado," *Air International* 35 (November 1988), 244–245. According to one source, "On the ground, and while starting the takeoff roll, the pilot had to depress a toggle switch under the control column to activate the nose gear steering, to steer the aircraft through the aileron control wheel during takeoff. This was required until rudder pressure took over at about 50 to 60 kts. The problem was, if his switch did not disengage automatically or was released manually, when the gear retracted, the aircraft would perform a mechanical roll to the left. The trick was not to retract the gear with the toggle depressed or the automatic feature in a failed mode. It could make for a 'bad flying day'" (Howard S. Myers, "SAC's First Cold War Super Sleuth," *Klaxon* 4, no. 4 [Winter 1996/97]: 14).

30. The Tornado 8 design study folder was found in the papers of General Willis F. Chapman; the author is indebted to his daughter, Pat Chapman Meder, for making it available.

31. L.C. Craigie to Commanding General, Wright Patterson AFB, 1 April 1948, Case History of the B-45 Aircraft, Vol., 1, Headquarters, Air Materiel Command, Wright-Patterson AFB. He continues: "Again, it is desired to stress the urgent need for determining the effect that high speed with conventional bomb bays has on the accuracy of bombing and the need for expediting development of new methods for carrying, stowing, and releasing bombs, particularly in aircraft which will have even higher speeds than the B-45."

32. "Status of XB-45 Bomb Dropping Program," 6 February 1948, Case History of the B-45 Airplane, Vol. 1; "Flight Test, Incident, and Accident Data on Selected Multi-Engine Bombers," 161: Both Headquarters, Air Materiel Command, Wright-Patterson AFB. General H.A. Craig wrote, "From the meager information now available on the action of bombs when being carried in our present bomb bays and released at speeds of 500 mph or greater, it appears that very poor accuracy may be expected, particularly from the 500 lb. size and smaller" (Bomb Dropping Test with B-45 and B-49 Aircraft, 9 July 1948, Vol. 2).

33. Memorandum for General Vandenberg: The B-45 Procurement Program, undated; Bomb Dropping Test with B-45 and B-49 Aircraft, 9 July 1948: Both Case History of the B-45 Airplane, Vol. 2, Headquarters, Air Materiel Command, Wright-Patterson AFB.

34. Bomb Dropping Tests with B-45 and B-49 Aircraft, 9 July 1948, Case History of the B-45 Airplane, Vol. 1, Headquarters, Air Materiel Command, Wright Patterson AFB.

35. "Recent movies made of bombs dropping from the XB-45 aircraft show that all size bombs will clear the bomb bay. However, considerable wobbling and twisting is evidenced in the fall of the bombs. Tests were conducted up to 500 mph. These preliminary tests indicate the necessity for continued bomb dropping tests from high speed aircraft to determine bomb ballistics and sighting capabilities. Hence a 1-A priority has been established on the scheduled high speed bomb dropping test using the No. 2 XB-45" (Memorandum for Vice Chief of Staff: Bombing Capabilities of B-45 Aircraft, 15 July 1948, Muir S. Fairchild Papers, Box 1, Fld. 1, Manuscript Division, Library of Congress).

36. Bomb Dropping Tests with B-45 and B-49 Aircraft, 16 August 1948, Case History of the B-45 Airplane, Vol. 2, Headquarters, Air Materiel Command, Wright-Patterson AFB.

37. High Speed Bomb Drops, 2 June 1949, Case History of the B-45 Airplane, Vol. 2, Headquarters, Wright Patterson AFB; "The North American B-45: Description and Brief History," 4, Case History, Vol. 1; "B-45 Jets OK'd for Big Bombs," *Air Force Times,* 9 September 1950, 20. "The B-45 also racked up another first during the year by making safe and accurate bomb drops over 500 miles per hour. Prior to the tests with the B-45, the highest speeds at which bombs had been dropped successfully from an operational

airplane were the 350-to-400 mile-an-hour standards of World War II" (*Aircraft Yearbook for 1950,* 106).

38. Quoted in Bodie, "Breaching the Walls," 44; Robert Hoover, *Forever Flying: An Autobiography by R.A. "Bob" Hoover* (New York: Pocket Books, 1996), 193–194. In a telephone conversation with the author, Hoover pronounced B-45s "the Cadillac of jet bombers."

39. Letter to the author, undated. Hunt was not above a little mischief himself. In another communication he relates the following: "We talked a pilot into giving us a low level speed run in the early 1950s. The Long Beach runways were surrounded with bean fields so we could get by with something like this. The B-45 was sweeping low to the east and all we could see was a lot of black smoke. Then he came into view with no sound at fifty feet. As he went by there were vapors appearing and disappearing with long streamers of vapors from the wing tips. He then pulled up in a vertical climb and disappeared into the clouds. I will never forget the thrill of seeing such a large aircraft moving at that rate of speed." Warren Bodie shared Hunt's sense of wonderment in these early days: "I was impressed like crazy with the B-45s in those days. What else was there to compare with it?"

40. Bill Gunston, "North American Tornado," *Aeroplane Monthly* 10 (December 1982): 636; James H. Kindelberger to Muir S. Fairchild, 22 March 1949, Muir S. Fairchild Papers, Box 2, Manuscript Division, Library of Congress. Kindelberger continues: "The new type canopy, incidentally, has very successfully passed all the tests, including a shatter test at very low temperatures, wherein the breaking of one of the subdivisions of the canopy did not result in its complete disintegration, but only in the vicinity of that particular area. In the original type free-blown canopy without reinforcement, the shattering of any one spot would cause the entire plastic form to disintegrate."

41. Service Test (Cold Weather) of the B-45A Series Aircraft and Associated Equipment, 6 May 1949, 6, 11, Copy in B-45 File, National Air and Space Museum Library, Smithsonian Institution.

42. "Tornado," *Skyline* 7, no. 2 (1949): 18; "Jet Bomber Record Claimed," *New York Times,* 13 March 1949, 4. According to test pilot Louis Stokes in communication with the author, "We were comfortable and could handle the worse type of weather that you would see when you went up there to do it. And what it did to the people in that airplane that I'm flying—you get bumped around. It taught them a lot."

43. Functional Test Center (Climatic Hangar Cold) of B-45 Airplane, 29 September 1949, Headquarters, Air Materiel Command, Wright-Patterson AFB.

44. Donald S. Lopez, *Fighter Pilot's Heaven: Flight Testing the Early Jets* (Washington, D.C.: Smithsonian Institution Press, 1995), 191–192. Eglin was also the site of early encounters between B-45s and F-84s training to intercept them. Captain Warren Whitmire relates an exercise whereby altitude was specified, but not speed: "So when he rendezvoused we left them—they couldn't keep up with us. So [squadron commander] Donning is complaining at the meeting, 'Why did you run so fast?' 'We didn't run fast, we were cruising at cruise speed.' 'Well, I was up there with my fighters and I couldn't keep up with you!' 'We could have given you whatever speed you wanted, but we were at cruise speed.' There wasn't a fighter in the world that could catch us."

45. Anthony Leviero, "Air Power Shown to Truman as Bombs and Rockets Roar," *New York Times,* 23 April 1950, 57–58.

46. Roland Beaumont, *Testing Early Jets: Compressibility and the Supersonic Era* (Shrewsbury, England: Airlife, 1990), 29–30. The debut of the XB-45 prototype, while lauded in American aviation journals, occasioned some condescending commentary from their British opposites: "The XB-45

is acclaimed by its makers as 'a significant aeronautical development,' although we are not quite sure wherein the significance lies. The claim is natural enough, no doubt, since all fond parents naturally feel that way about their latest offspring.... Nevertheless, in view of British progress with jet engines, we cannot see much point in British designers following this particular engine layout, for however much we admire the aerodynamic cleanliness, unit by unit, the overall pattern is still only a halfway solution — as viewed through our streamlined crystal ball" (A. Marthason, "The North American XB-45," *Aeroplane* 73 [21 November 1947]: 672–673).

47. "They noted that the plane seemed to have hit the ground virtually in one piece, with both fliers still aboard, which fact was inconsistent with its blowing apart in the air. It was also stated that the plane was carrying ordinary kerosene-type fuel, which is not nearly so volatile as the high test gasoline used in propelleor-driven craft" ("2 Test Pilots Die in B-45 Crash," *New York Times*, 21 September 1948, p. 54).

48. Report of Major Accident, 20 September 1948, Headquarters, Air Force Safety Agency, Kirtland AFB; Status of Crash Investigation, B-45A Airplane, SN 47-1, 30 September 1948, Case History of the B-45 Airplane, Vol. 2, Headquarters, Air Materiel Command, Wright-Patterson AFB. Significantly, "The accident occurred on the second flight with J47s installed" (Allocation of B-45A Airplanes, 11 October 1948 (Case History). It is time to debunk some long-standing misperceptions surrounding this incident. In virtually every printed source pertaining to B-45s examined, myriads of aviation historians list the first prototype, 45-59479, as the culprit responsible for the crash. That vehicle, in fact, was stationed at Wright-Patterson AFB at the time and flew until being wrecked in a belly landing on 28 June 1949. Writers have also bemoaned that Krebs and Piccard died because of the lack of ejector seats. In truth, 47-001, a production B-45A, would have possessed them. However, low altitude, and given the fact that the craft nosed down and ultimately tipped over before crashing, negated any chance of their escape. Equally spurious is the notion that the accident forced North American to redesign and retrofit all B-45s with enlarged tail surfaces. The act of increasing tail plane surface area did, in fact, transpire but came about as the result of flight testing XB-45 No. 1. "The airplane as originally tested was longitudinally unstable in both accelerated and unaccelerated flight. To improve the stability, the Contractor increased the stabilizer span and added an elevator bungee and two elevator spring tabs" (XB-45 Status, 22 March 1948, Case History of the B-45 Airplane, Vol. 1, Headquarters, Air Materiel Command, Wright-Patterson AFB).

49. "North American XB-45," *Air Force Magazine* 30, no. 6 (June 1947): 44.

Chapter Three

1. E.M. Powers, 8 November 1948, Record Group 341, Headquarters, U.S. Air Force, Development Policy Group, Subject Files, 1947–1950, Box 1, Correspondence for 1948, National Archives.

2. C. Lambert, "47th Bombardment Wing (Light)," *Flight* 67 (March 1955): 389.

3. Maurer Maurer, *Air Force Combat Units of World War II* (Washington, D.C.: Office of Air Force History, 1983), 104–105; "America's First Jet Bomb Wing," *Shreveport Magazine* 3, no. 12 (December 1948): 12.

4. Willis F. Chapman file, U.S. Military Academy Archives.

5. Joseph Heller, *Catch 22* (New York: Simon and Schuster, 1961), 185.

6. Robert M. Lee to Commanding Officer, 4th Fighter Wing, 28 February 1950 (copy in possession of Pat Chapman Meder). Captain James Loudon, 85th, was also particularly attached to Chapman: "General Chapman was one of the nicest men I've ever met. I was his public relations officer and he and I were just like father and son." But perhaps Hal Lynch proffers the best evaluation of this gifted leader: "Bill Chapman was the type of man who will never be forgotten by those fortunate enough to have known him. I was one of those who profited from his leadership during the war, and following those years in combat. He set an example of courage and heroism which few of us could hope to emulate. Many of us tried. Bill never selected an 'easy' combat mission during those years we flew over Italy, France, Austria, and Yugoslavia. If it was an especially dangerous mission, Bill Chapman could always be found in the lead ship, first over the target, always" (Hal Lynch to Charlotte Chapman, 26 February 2002 [copy courtesy of Patricia Chapman Meder]).

7. Colonel Neil M. Matzger to Chief of Staff, Air Force, 7 February 1948, History of the Tactical Air Command, 1 January–30 November 1948, Vol. 3, 83, Air Force Historical Research Agency, Maxwell AFB. Despite the hazardous operating conditions at Biggs, Chapman's penchant for thoroughness in training and safety measures resulted in 16,129 hours of flying time, 400 of them in dangerous night formation flying, without a single accident, a significant achievement ("47th Bomb Group, Biggs Base, Completes Year of Operational Flying Without Accident," *El Paso Times* 24 May 1948, 1).

8. History of the 47th Bombardment Group (Light), January thru March 1948, 3, Air Force Historical Research Agency, Maxwell AFB. "Instead of reading long descriptions and studying drawings of the B-45's fuel system, for instance, classes watched colored liquid flow through clear plastic tubes as pumps and valves sent it from the plane's seven fuel tanks to its four engines" (John Stuart, "Air Force Fliers and Ground Men Adapt Their Skills to New Aircraft," *New York Times*, 13 June 1948, X17).

9. History of the 47th Bombardment Group (L) NA, 1 April 1948–30 June 1948, 51; History of the 47th Bombardment Wing (L), 25 August–30 November 1948, 39: Both Air Force Historical Research Agency, Maxwell AFB.

10. History, 47th Bombardment Group, June 1949, 65–66, 69, Captain Raymond L. Fitzgerald knew Cremer well and occasionally flew with him in B-45s: "Typical of Gordon: We wound up somehow in the overcast and flew into a thunderhead — it got black and all of a sudden Gordon says 'Chee-rist, Fritz, who put out the lights?'"

11. History of the 47th Bombardment Group (L) NA, 1 April 1948–30 June 1948, 26, Air Force Historical Research Agency, Maxwell AFB. Captain Warren T. Whitmire, a leading B-45 engineering officer, caught his first glimpse of the jet at Biggs and was totally taken in by the silvery entity: "It was an awesome thing to look at. It was so much different than anything else that anybody had flown, really."

12. History of the 47th Bombardment Group (L) NA, 1 April 1948–30 June 1948, 58, Air Force Historical Research Agency, Maxwell AFB.

13. History of the 47th Bombardment Wing (L), 25 August–30 November 1948, 39; History of the 47th Bombardment Wing (Light), 1 December 1948–31 March 1949, 41. "The physical set up in respect to location and space allotted to the units and the sections in the group is somewhat cramped," the unit historian reported. "The group anticipates some problems upon the arrival of the B-45. The shortage of space will be felt in the maintenance sections, such as engineering, communications, armament, and the radar section. At the present time ... all these sections are being housed in one double hangar" (History of the 47th Bombardment Group, Light, December 1948–March

1949, 4: All Air Force Historical Research Agency, Maxwell AFB).

14. History of the 47th Bombardment Group Light, October–November 1948, 12, 51–52, Air Force Historical Research Agency, Maxwell AFB. At this time in Air Force organization a group consisted of combat formations to an assigned unit; a wing consisted of a group along with the supply, maintenance, and headquarter units attached to it.

15. History of the 47th Bombardment Wing (Light), 1 December to 31 March 1949, 4, 48, Air Force Historical Research Agency, Maxwell AFB.

16. "Bomb Wing Commander Honored," *Shreveport Times*, 19 January 1949, 19; "History of the 47th Bombardment Group, Light," December 1948–March 1949, 110–111, Air Force Historical Research Agency, Maxwell AFB. Throughout a distinguished history, the 47th Bomb Group touted its high morale, exacting standards of performance, and rollicking good times after hours. Chapman himself was not above setting the tone for such matters, off base. Sgt. Claude Riddell fondly remembered one unit picnic by Lake Charles, Louisiana, where all ranks were devotedly in their cups and rank constituted no protection: "They were throwing everybody in the lake — everybody goes — and Col. Chapman happened to be at the location while some of this was going on, so in he went!"

17. History of the 47th Bombardment Wing (Light), 1 December 1948–31 March 1949, 49–50, Air Force Historical Research Agency, Maxwell AFB. Supply Sergeant Jim Sharpe, by his own admission the 47th's most accomplished crap-shooter, gave the author his spin on how the B-45 name contest unfolded: "When they announced it I said, 'Hell, that'll be easy'—I was shooting crap at the time. I said if I were to name a plane like that and it was so powerful and could do such a good job, I'd name it the Tornado. We were having heavy tornados around us, reading about it every day in the paper. I went straight on shooting and that kid went straight to the orderly room, turned it in — and two or three weeks later Captain Louden made the announcement that he had won."

18. History of the 47th Bombardment Group, Light, December 1948–March 1949, 74, 112, Air Force Historical Research Agency, Maxwell AFB; interview with Col. Chapman by his daughter, 30 November 2001 (copy in possession of the author). Whenever possible, the colonel made it his personal policy to fly B-45s whenever the opportunity presented itself. He explained: "During the time I was commanding, I had more time in the bomber than anybody else did. I had to learn all I could about what makes jets work. So I got more flying in than most of them,"

19. History of the 47th Bombardment Wing (Light), 1 December 1948–31 March 1949, 48. "The Group is making history with the receipt of the first jet B-45 bombers to become the world's first jet bomber group. It is felt that adequate planning has been made to make the conversion from conventional to jet as rapidly as possible" (History, 47th Bombardment Group, Light, December 1948–March 1949, 75, 93: Both Air Force Historical Research Center, Maxwell AFB; "First B-45 Jet Bomber for 47th Wing Arrives," *Shreveport Times*, March 24, 1949, 5). Speaking of his own experience during the flight, Captain McDonough told reporters, "It peels off sharply and really pulls up when you pour on the coal. Sure wish we'd had these babies in Africa" (Earl Blount, "Big Bark," *Skyline* 7 [May 1949]: 6).

20. "Tornado Bomber Makes Non-Stop Hop to 'Bark.'" *Skywriter*, 10 June 1949, B-45 File, National Air and Space Museum Library, Smithsonian Institution. "This is in itself not too significant historically but it is significant in that the aircraft was ferried from San Bernadino Air Force Base to Barksdale Air Force Base with no intermediate stops" (History, 47th Bombardment Wing, Light, June 1949, 25, Air Force Historical Research Agency, Maxwell AFB).

21. History, 84th Bombardment Squadron, 1 April 1949–30 April 1949, 12, Air Force Historical Research Agency, Maxwell AFB. Col. Chapman tried his hand at public relations by methodically describing the aerial logic behind the B-45 to a reporter: "When you buy this kind of speed, you pay for it. And you have to have a justification for its use. The justification is this: The faster you go, the more difficult it is to intercept you and the higher your batting average for getting through to your target" (Joseph S. Stocker, "Jet Bomber Jockeys," *Air Trails Pictorial* 33 [March 1950]: 68).

22. On the downside, Major James Story, 85th, told the author, "It had a tremendous pre-flight. When you went RON (remain overnight) somewhere, it probably took you two hours to do it. You had to drop those nacelles and check everything, and they didn't fit that good so you had to have one of those hydraulic jacks that we used to jack up an airplane — put two by fours on it across them and get those clamshells up to where you could get that speed wrench and get the bolt there to hold them up. So it was just a mean and ornery thing to do — but it was a lot of fun to fly."

23. "A 15 minute wire recording of a B-45 flight was made on 26 April from the cockpit of a B-45 by the Wing PIO. Mr. Maurice Wayne, news editor of KTBS, made the recording on the ground in the 47th Bomb Wing radio shop. Piloting the B-45 was Captain Charles E. McDonough, navigator was Major Henry Butler" (History of the 47th Bomb Wing Information Office, 1 April to 30 April 1949, 2, Air Force Historical Research Agency, Maxwell AFB).

24. Blount, "Big Bark," 6; History of the 47th Bombardment Wing, 1 December 1948–31 March 1949, 45, Air Force Historical Research Agency, Maxwell AFB. Chapman was not kidding about fuel conservation. Major James Story, 85th, recounts flying in from Wichita, Kansas, on an early hairsbreadth escape in his B-45: "We were heading out, it was not quite dusk, but it was late in the afternoon. And it was a beautiful night, you could see a million miles and I said to the navigator, 'Is our heading okay?' and pretty soon found out that he didn't have *squat*. He didn't know where we were! And you get real excited in a damn airplane like that, and not know where the Hell you are. And I never got caught in that situation again. We got on the radio right away and got help from radar and they directed us into Wilmington. We landed there and I don't think we could have gone another five minutes — they were dry! The fact is I didn't think we'd have enough fuel to taxi into the line."

25. Colonel Chapman realized that the lack of B-45 repair manuals at airbases around the country meant that pilots were going to have to perform most of the routine repairs themselves. Consequently, he ordered all aircrews qualifying at Muroc to also enroll in the maintenance classes given there. He explained: "I ran all the pilots, co-pilots, and navigators through the same courses that I ran the enlisted men through, and so they came out knowing as much as the crew chiefs did. The first thing you do in the damn cavalry is take care of the damn horse first, then you go eat. So fix the airplane yourself first and be sure it's ready to go. If it isn't, you get on the horn and tell us what the problem is, and we'll see what we can do about it. We could fly something there, you see, almost anywhere in the states. We never had to do it — the guys all learned their lessons and whatever the problems they ran into they could fix."

26. History, 84th Bombardment Squadron, 1 May 1949–31 May 1949, 8, Air Force Historical Research Agency, Maxwell AFB.

27. A detailed account of Louden's life has been aptly captured in Teri Louden, *On God's Wings: A Daughter's Inspirational Story of Her Dad and His Miracle* (Coronado, CA: The Louden Network, 2005). An equally informative Website is www.ongodswings.com. Big Jim's approach to flying was rather philosophical: "Wish for blue skies, fair winds … and great mechanics" (Louden, 207).

28. Louden, *On God's Wings*, 67; "Two Killed, One Injured in Jet Crash," *Shreveport Times*, 10 June 1949, 1; "Two Die in Crash of B-45," *New York Times,* 10 June 1949, 16. Corporal Walter Dackson, a photo repairman, was among those delegated to pick through the aircraft's remains and even after fifty years it left a most vivid impression on him, "There's a particular stench about an aircraft that goes in and breaks up. And you can recognize it instantly. Doesn't matter if it's a military aircraft, commercial, or private — there's this stench about it. It's a mixture of fuel, a mixture of anything that is in the aircraft. And if there are bodies included, it all melds together into this one horrific stench. And every time I see or hear about an aircraft that goes down ... [it comes back]."

29. Written communication to the 47th Bomb Group Reunion, Washington, D.C., October 2001, courtesy of Pat Chapman Meder. Chapman continues: "Thanks to the brains and determination of our personnel we never did lose an aircraft to the same cause as long as I was in command. Out technique of bringing crash parts in and laying them out on the hangar floor for study was adopted as standard procedure by the USAF as well as many airlines."

30. History, 47th Bombardment Wing, Light, June 1949, 20, 35; History, 47th Bombardment Wing, June 1949, 30, 54–58; "Summary of Difficulties Experienced in Operating the B-45," History of the 363rd Tactical Reconnaissance Group, 1 December 1949–31 December 1949, Exhibit 15, 2: All Air Force Historical Research Agency, Maxwell AFB.

31. History, 47th Bombardment Group, Light, July 1949, 22, 24; Exhibit 14, B-45 Combat Crew Training Requirements, Air Force Historical Research Center, Maxwell AFB. Maury Seitz, then an impressionable Air Force cadet, recounts how he caught his first glimpse of a B-45 on 15 April 1949, in a flyover by the B-45, XB-46, XB-47, XB-48, and YB-49: "They put us in the reviewing stand with the colonels and generals. I was standing next to a colonel and the flight came by, and all the great big ones came by and the B-49 was coming up the rear. He turned to me and said, 'There's supposed to be another one, the B-45.' Just about that time up comes this little screaming bird off of Wright — we were at Patterson — and slips right into the diamond in back. And it's the B-45 — and he says, 'I'll give my right arm to fly that thing!'"

32. E-mail from Bruno M. Larsen, 7 October 2002, copy in possession of author; History, 47th Bombardment Wing, August 1949, 12, 18; History, 47th Bombardment Group, August 1949, 22: Both Air Force Historical Research Agency, Maxwell AFB.

33. "Three Barksdale Officers Hurt as Jet Crash Lands," *Shreveport Times*, 13 August 1949, 1; History, 47th Bombardment Group, Light, August 1949, 16; History, 47th Bombardment Group, August 1949, 19–20, Air Force Historical Research Agency, Maxwell AFB.

34. "Two Killed in Crack-up of Jet Plane," *Shreveport Times*, 1 September 1949, 1, 3; History, 47th Bombardment Group, Light, 1 September–2 October 1949, 15, 17; History, 47th Bombardment Wing, August 1949, 17, 24; History, 47th Bombardment Group, August 1949, 22: All Air Force Historical Research Agency, Maxwell AFB.

35. History, 47th Bombardment Wing, Light, 1 September–2 October 1949, 3, 13. "For the transfer of aircraft to Langley it became necessary to fly aircraft to Langley, remove parts, and take them back to Barksdale for installation on aircraft still there. Then it was necessary to take parts from the aircraft at Langley and send them to Brookley AFB to support AIC II" ("Summary of Difficulties Experienced in Operating the B-45," History, 363rd Tactical Reconnaissance Group, 1 December 1949–31 December 1949, Exhibit 15, 3: Both Air Force Historical Research Center, Maxwell AFB).

36. History, 363rd Tactical Reconnaissance Group, 1 September 1949–30 September 1949, 14. For a detailed list of technical failures see "B-45 Operational and Training Difficulties Experienced by Operational Units," 8 May 1950, History, Tactical Air Command, 1 January 1950–30 June 1950, Vol. 3, Item 288, Air Force Historical Research Agency, Maxwell AFB.

37. Herbert B. Thatcher to Willis F. Chapman, 4 October 1949; Willis F. Chapman to Herbert B. Thatcher, 6 October 1949: Both in possession of Pat Chapman Meder, Annandale, Virginia.

38. Joseph S. Stocker, "I Rode a Tornado," *Boy's Life* 60 (January 1950): 5, 32. He elaborated on his experience in a subsequent publication: "And the quiet of it ... the strange whistling quiet that makes you feel as though you are floating through the air detached from anything save the seat you are sitting in. The weird quiet that is such an incredible contrast to that ear-crunching scream of the four big General Electric J-47 jet engines when you sat there on the ramp with the door open, warming up. Now that frenzied, tormented clamor has been shut out. In the whistling stillness only your tachometer tells you that she is responding to the advance of your throttles — there is no sense of acceleration. Only your airspeed indicator lets you know you are within hailing distance of the sonic barrier. There's no sensation of speed in this sealed-in silence. No vibration. No throb of engines. Without your instruments you could not even be sure your engines are running" (Stocker, "Jet Bomber Jockeys," 68).

39. History, 363rd Tactical Reconnaissance Group, 1 October 1949–31 October 1949, 8–9, 18, Summation, Air Force Historical Research Agency, Maxwell AFB.

40. History, 363rd Tactical Reconnaissance Group, November 1949, 1, 20, 22–23,31, Air Force History Research Agency, Maxwell AFB.

41. Ibid., 31, Exhibit 1, Exhibit 18, Air Force Historical Research Agency, Maxwell AFB.

42. History, 363rd Tactical Reconnaissance Group, 1 December 1949–31 December 1949, 15, 23, Air Force Historical Research Agency, Maxwell AFB.

43. History, 363rd Tactical Reconnaissance Group, 1 December 1949–31 December 1949, 33; "Summary of Difficulties Experienced in Operating the B-45"; also Exhibit 15, 1. Chapman concludes his report thusly: "Although the summary paints a rather black picture, we have found that barring mechanical failures and provided that supplies are available in reasonable quantities, the B-45 can be kept in the air day in and day out without undue proportion of time devoted to maintenance" (Both Air Force Historical Research Agency, Maxwell AFB).

44. History, 363rd Tactical Reconnaissance Wing, 1 January–28 February 1950, 16, 37–39, 44–45, Air Force Historical Research Agency, Maxwell AFB.

45. Ibid., 25, Extract AF Form 14, 52, 55; History, 363rd Tactical Reconnaissance Wing, 1 March 1950–30 June 1950, 7: Both Air Force Historical Research Agency, Maxwell AFB.

46. History, 363rd Tactical Reconnaissance Group, 1 March 1950–30 June 1950, 12, 15–16, Air Force Historical Research Center, Maxwell AFB.

47. Ibid., Exhibit, 39, Air Force Historical Research Agency, Maxwell AFB.

48. History, 363rd Tactical Reconnaissance Group, 1 March 1950–30 June 1950, 15–16; also "Automatic Formation Bomb Release Equipment, April 3, 1950," Exhibit 36. The writer continues: "Experience has proved that in formation bombing the circular error is greater than that of single ship bombing. In a formation of B-45 aircraft it is believed that this error will be magnified considerably due to increase in speed, altitude, and position of individual aircraft within the formation. The observer in a wing position cannot see the bomb bay of the lead aircraft, thus making it mandatory for the pilot to release the bombs. The only

means the pilot has to release the bombs is by salvo. To accomplish this the pilot must move his hands from the throttle to the salvo control. This action in itself causes a delay in bomb release and further increases the spread of the formation bomb pattern."

49. "B-45 climbs on the red line at high altitude are extremely successful in rendering fighter attack ineffective. To illustrate, the engines of a B-45 are operating at approximately 93% of full power at 35,000 feet while cruising at 'red' line speed, where the Banshees is utilizing practically full power. B-45s can climb on 'red line' where the Banshee canno," ("High Altitude, High Speed Intercept Exercise," 18–21 July 1950 (History, Tactical Air Command, 1 July 1950–30 November 1950, Vol. 5, Document 872, 3, Air Force Historical Research Agency, Maxwell AFB.

50. History, 363rd Tactical Reconnaissance Group, 1 March 1950–30 June 1950, 32–33; "High Altitude, High Speed Intercept Exercise," 18–21 July 1950, History, Tactical Air Command, 1 July 1950–30 November 1950, Vol. 5, Document 872, 2: Both Air Force Historical Research Agency, Maxwell AFB; "Carrier Task Force Capabilities for Defense by Means of Interception," Enclosure D-III, 148, Record Group 341, Headquarters U.S. Air Force, Air Force Plans, Decimal Files, 1942–1954, Box 30, National Archives.

51. History of the 363rd Tactical Reconnaissance Group, 1 July 1950–30 September 1950, 35. "The performance of the F2H-2 against the B-45A, the later without payload, is marginal to unsatisfactory. The average speed advantage was estimated at 15 knots. When positioning was not advantageous, long tail chases resulted and as much as 8–10 minutes of military power was required before an attack could be completed.... These exercises provide trials which show up the inadequacies of presently modified pursuit course armament. The high speed target leaves only a small tail cone to be protected against attack unless (1) *the effective range of the fighter armament is increased, or* (2) *the limiting mach of the fighter is materially increased*" (*Ibid.*; Exhibit 44: Both Air Force Historical Research Agency, Maxwell AFB).

52. USS *Coral Sea*, Historical Report–Period–1 July 1950–31 December 1950, Archives, Naval Historical Center, Washington, D.C.

53. Marcelle S. Knaack, *Post World War II Bombers, 1945–1973* (Washington, D.C.: Office of Air Force History, 1988), 74–75; Deployment of B-45 Aircraft, 12 September 1949, Record Group 341, Headquarters, U.S. Air Force, Deputy Chief of Staff for Development, Director of Research and Development, Box 36. Puryear notes: "There are presently no projects established for modification of B-45 aircraft with bombing equipment."

54. Ennis Whitehead, 3 January 1950, Record Group 341, Headquarters, U.S. Air Force, Deputy Chief of Staff for Development, Director of Research and Development, Box 36, National Archives.

55. Letter from Leo Hunt, undated; "U.S. Jet Explodes; British Officer Killed," *New York Times*, 25 February 1950; Report of Major Accident, 24 February 1950, from www.accidentreport.com.

56. "Summary, Exercise Swarmer," History, 363rd Tactical Reconnaissance Group, 1 March 1950–30 June 1950, Exhibit 38, 4, Air Force Historical Research Agency, Maxwell AFB; Stocker, "I Rode A Tornado," 32. Sergeant Leonard Satterly gave an eloquent paean to those who, in large measure, were responsible for the B-45's ultimate success: "The aircrews were all wonderful people and they get everything that is due them. But there's a group of guys that were not officers and they were not pilots — they were crew chiefs. Those were the most dedicated guys in the crappiest places, in the lousiest weather, that you can imagine. The air crews got all the credit, but that airplane did not spring from the ground fully loaded and ready to fly — there's a guy who made that son-of-a-gun do that. And they were all *so*

dedicated. I learned early on that if you were going to get around or near an aircraft, you'd better go find the crew chief, you'd better tell him exactly what you're going to do, and until he was totally satisfied that you needed to be in that airplane, you didn't do it. These guys were wonderful people. I never thought or felt that these guys got their due, if you will."

Chapter Four

1. Charles P. Cabell to Hoyt S. Vandenberg, 31 October 1950, Charles P. Cabell Papers, Air Force Historical Research Agency, Maxwell AFB.

2. Charles P. Cabell, Jr., ed., *A Man of Intelligence: Memoirs of War, Peace, and the CIA* (Colorado Springs, CO: Impavide Publications, 1997), 270. According to one authority, "Korea not only presented a different kind of war for military planners and politicians, it also presented a different kind of place for aerial reconnaissance to prove itself" (George W. Goddard, *Overview: A Life-Long Adventure in Aerial Photography* Garden City, NY: Doubleday, 1969), 373.

3. Walter J. Boyne, *Beyond the Wild Blue: A History of the United States Air Force, 1947–1997* (New York: St. Martin's Press, 1997), 88–89; John T. Farquhar, "A Need to Know: The Role of Air Force Reconnaissance in War Planning, 1945–1953" (PhD diss. Ohio State University, 1991), 149–151; Glenn B. Infield, *Unarmed and Unafraid* (New York: Macmillan, 1970), 134–135; Charles P. Cabell to George E. Stratemeyer, 25 July 1950, Charles P. Cabell Papers, Air Force Historical Research Agency, Maxwell AFB. Cabell concludes: "I wish again to stress the importance of this matter and reiterate that General Vandenberg is most perturbed over the inadequacies of reconnaissance in the Korean operation."

4. History of Air Materiel Command Support of the Far Ear Air Force in the Korean Conflict, June–November 1950, Vol. 1, 24, Headquarters, Air Materiel Command, Wright-Patterson AFB; History, 323rd Strategic Reconnaissance Squadron, July 1950, 2, Air Force Historical Research Agency, Maxwell AFB. The only overview of the Tornado in Korea is John C. Fredriksen, "Detachment 2 Goes to War: RB-45C Reconnaissance Activity in Korea, 1950–1953," *Journal of the American Aviation Historical Society* 41, no. 4 (Winter 1996): 282–286.

5. Sgt. William Bombkamp, a jet engine technician with the 85th, also remembered McDonough, although with slightly less affection: "He was strictly Air Force and as far as I am concerned an officer and a gentleman. He used to chew me out. We used to have yellow spots for the nose wheel to be parked on and if I didn't have them perfectly on there I'd get chewed out." Sgt. John Wilkerson, 85th, McDonough's chief mechanic, noted that "As far as the enlisted people were concerned, he was a pretty good guy, he wasn't overly friendly, but he wasn't hostile either."

6. Earl Huggins to author, 1 December 1995. The author had the rare privilege of interviewing Louis Carrington at his home in August 1996, from which the mysterious existence of Detachment A could be vicariously reconstructed. He died in Tyler, Texas, on 25 January 2000.

7. Sgt. Merle Sollars left this interesting anecdote: "Simmons was a different individual. When we landed at Honolulu no one had a dime, our pay records were kind of screwed up. As a matter of fact they became screwed up at Barksdale, so we got there with no money. Simmons went right into the payroll section, threw his records down very loudly, got the payroll officer who Simmons outranked, and got every bit of money he had coming, that he could get. And then turned right around at the payroll office, had all of us people line up — and we borrowed money from Sim-

mons. And that's the way the guy was, but yet you'd call him Captain Simmons, you didn't call him Al or anything like that."

8. History, 323rd Strategic Historical Squadron, July 1950, 3–4, Air Force Historical Research Agency, Maxwell AFB.

9. Daily Staff Digest, 22 August 1950, Record Group 341 Headquarters, U.S. Air Force, Daily Staff Digests, Box 11. Due to parts shortages "readiness date is now set at 20 September"; also 15 September, 1950. This was updated again for a third time. "In order to provide for special reconnaissance missions, FEAF, the first three RB-45 aircraft were diverted from SAC. Three B-45 crews were given intensive strategic reconnaissance training in these RB-45 aircraft under SAC supervision and deployed to FEAF for 90 days TDY on 19 October 1950" (Record Group 341, Headquarters, U.S. Air Force, History of the Directorate of Operations, Deputy Chief of Staff, Operations, Headquarters, USAF, 1 July, 1950–31 December 1950, Box 15: Both National Archives).

10. Jules E. Young to parents, 15 September 1950 (original in possession of Julie Hendrickson, Fairfax, Virginia).

11. History of Air Materiel Command Support of the Far East Air Force in the Korean Conflict, June–November 1950, Vol. 1, 24, Headquarters, Air Materiel Command, Wright-Patterson AFB; "The Continental Air Command and the Korean War," June 1950–December 1950, 99–110, Air Force Historical Research Agency, Maxwell AFB.

12. "Overseas Deployment of Special Project RB-45 Aircraft," 6 September 1950, History, 363rd Tactical Reconnaissance Group, 1 July 1950–30 September 1950, Exhibit 44, Air Force Historical Research Agency, Maxwell AFB.

13. Charles P. Hollstein, Report of Staff Visits, 8 September 1950–13 July 1951, Document 27, 3, Air Force Historical Research Agency, Maxwell AFB.

14. Charles P. Hollstein, Report of Staff Visits, 8 September–13 July 1951, Document 27, 1, Air Force Historical Research Agency, Maxwell AFB.

15. Kenneth W. Price Narrative, 12 February 2004, 3 (copy in possession of the author).

16. In reference to the long-accepted practice of stripping B-45s for parts, Sgt. Sollars emphatically says, "Not at Yokota. That was a *constant* thing at Barksdale, and a *constant* thing at Langley. A couple of airplanes were cannibalized and never flew because they were cannibalized for parts so often that you could not keep them in the air. Like I say we took parts with us — we had 120 days of parts and we never had to scrub a mission or keep an airplane on the ground due to lack of parts."

17. Certain parts, such as the B-9 intervalometer, broke down with alarming regularity and had to be readily replaced through the usual channels. Again, the veil of secrecy raised its ugly head: "Personnel at FEAFCOM revealed that one requisition from their office to supply channels in the United States had brought the reply that FEAFCOM 'could not requisition RB-45 parts because there were no RB-45s in the Far East Theater'" (History, 363rd Tactical Reconnaissance Group, October-December 1950, 21, Air Force Historical Research Agency, Maxwell AFB).

18. A. Timothy Warnock, ed., *The USAF in Korea: A Chronology, 1950–1953* (Washington, D.C.: Air Force History and Museums Program, 2000), 18; "A Day by Day History of Far East Air Forces Operations," Vol. 2, 1 November 1950–28 February 1951, 19, Air Force Historical Research Center, Maxwell AFB; Robert F. Futrell, *The United States Air Force in Korea, 1950–1952* (Washington, D.C.: Air Force History and Museum Program, 1983), 582. Despite the secret nature of Detachment A, word was released within a month of their arrival. See "F-84s Are Going to Far East; Three RB-45s Already There," *Air Force Times*, 21 October 1950, 2. The Air Force did not publicly acknowledge Tor-

nado activity in Korea for another six months, although they conceded that the craft were "being used to take long-distance pictures of Communist airfields and other bases in Manchuria" ("Jet Bombers in Korea," *New York Times*, 15 April 1951, 3).

19. "A Day by Day History of Far East Air Forces Operations," Vol. 2, 1 November 1950–28 February 1951, 23, Air Force Historical Research Agency, Maxwell AFB. One particular flight in late November 1950 caught Sager's immediate attention: "I got the flight report and they were heading north along the main highway along the eastern shore of North Korea. And all the U.S. Vehicles — they were photographing their radiators, not their tail lights. Jules Young, McDonough's co-pilot, was the most interested in the interpretation side and I called him in and said, 'What were you guys doing? You're Your flight report said you were going north?' And he said you're right and I said, 'Then how come all the vehicles are headed this way?' That was our first inkling that our own forces were going in the opposite direction — and one of the first meaningful conclusions that the Chinese had intervened."

20. Robin Higham, John T. Greenwood, and Von Hardesty, eds., *Russian Aviation and Air Power in the Twentieth Century* (Portland, OR: Frank Cass, 1998), 216–217; George A. Larson, "FEAF Intelligence Missions over North Korea," *Combat Aircraft* 2, no. 12 (October–November 2000): 1025; Quote from Yefim Gordon and Vladimir Rigmant, *MiG-15: Design, Development, and Korean War Combat History* (Osceola, WI: Motorbooks, 1993), 129.

21. Quoted from Laurence Jolidon, *Last Seen Alive: The Search for Missing POWs from the Korean War* (Austin, TX: Ink-Slinger, 1995), 205. Sager continues: "And that led to an interesting conflict with the Chief of Intelligence at FEAF Headquarters, Brigadier General Banfill. You knew the guys couldn't maintain the nadir of these photographs on the south side of the river, so every now and then they would inadvertently get a vertical where the airplane was actually over Chinese territory. And that didn't bother me one bit but it bothered General Banfill. So what we had to do with every photo of those 9 × 18 K-35 negatives — we had to cut the negative out of the roll, classify it as Top Secret, stack them together, and we get a stack of Top Secret photos on one side and the rest of the roll on the other! To me it seemed ridiculous that that kind of a restriction would be placed on an aircrew."

22. Kenneth W. Price Narrative, 12 February 2004, 4–5 (copy in possession of the author). Tail warning radars were continually being fitted and refitted on the RB-45s with usually poor results. As late as the summer of 1952 Calvin Pace noted, "Then they put a radar warning device, if anything was on your tail. The only time it ever worked was when you were coming in to land at Yokota and the mountains back there reflected off it."

23. "A Day by Day History of Far East Air Forces Operations," Vol. 2, 1 November 1950 through 28 February 1951, 68; History, 363rd Tactical Reconnaissance Group, October–November–December 1950, 23–24: Both Air Force Historical Research Agency, Maxwell AFB.

24. According to photography expert Goddard, "The Korean War presented us with an aerial reconnaissance problem never encountered before. It was created by the high, jagged mountainous terrain coupled with the fact that so much of our photography was done at night. During World War II the land our recce pilots flew over in all theaters of operations was relatively flat. In Korea it was high flung peaks without clear points of contrast. Our night cameras and illuminating systems were fine at lower altitudes, but with mountains of seven or eight thousand feet we knew we had to get higher. That meant longer focal length lenses, greater illumination, and faster film" (Goddard, *Overview*, 372).

25. History, 363rd Tactical Reconnaissance Group, Oc-

tober–November–December 1950, 22, Air Force Historical Research Agency, Maxwell AFB. For such Top Secret information, the unit historian was particularly well-informed as to the exact nature of Detachment A and continued: "Operationally speaking, the primary mission of the RB-45 detachment is to cover photographically the 490-mile length of the Korean-Manchurian border, including all bridges along this route. Hostile fighters have been sighted on a number of occasions, but no combat encounters have been reported as yet. There is, of course, room for speculation as to the fate of RB-45 48–015, which is missing in action. 015 failed to return from a photo mission to Sinuiju and along the Korean border, and may have been shot down by enemy fighters or by anti-aircraft fire. Sinuiju is in the immediate vicinity of the 'home base' of the Russian-built MiG-15 jet fighter, and it is probable that even though the RB-45 was flying at 40,000 feet 'on the Mach number,' interception may have been made because of the MiG's combat ceiling of 46,000 feet and its speed of 540 knots. In addition, no tail warning radar was installed in the RB-45, increasing the chances of a successful interception."

26. Soviet account is from Korean War Working Group Session of the April 1995 Working Group Sessions, 31–33, Defense POW/MIA Office, The Pentagon. Andrianov continues: "I believe the pilot's primary mission was to perform reconnaissance over Chinese territory to determine if the Chinese were massing forces in support of the Koreans. So, putting myself in his shoes and thinking logically like a pilot, I would have continued into China, confident that there was nothing that could catch me or fly at my altitude, make my run over China and return back to my home base. The pilot made a very unwise decision." Wise or not, McDonough was daring by nature and the decision he made, while implausible given tight restrictions over violating Chinese or Soviet airspace, is consistent with the man. Valuable background information for Russian activity is in Mark O'Neill, "The Other Side of the Yalu: Soviet Pilots in the Korean War" (PhD diss., Florida State University, 1996), 134–136.

27. "A Day by Day History of Far East Air Forces Operations," Vol. 2, 1 November 1950 through 28 February 1951, 109, Air Force Historical Research Agency, Maxwell AFB. McDonough's disappearance lent grist to the usual rumor mill. According to Corporal Walter Dackson, "This is the announcement they gave us: 'We've lost one of our aircraft, we are not sure how it was lost, we think it was shot down, and we think it was shot down by the Navy because they didn't recognize the silhouette.' Put the blame on the Navy the whole time."

28. Jolidon, *Last Seen Alive*, 207–208, 212–213; Paul M. Cole, *POW/MIA Issues*, Vol. 1, *The Korean War* (Santa Monica, CA: RAND, 1994), 150. A wealth of translated information about the RB-45C shootdown may be also reviewed at www.aiipowmia.com. Corporal Walter Dackson left this recollection of Captain McDonough: "He was a good CO but one of his idiosyncracies was that every morning at roll call we would go out there and he would give us this pep talk. And after about the second or third day we knew exactly what he was going to say: 'Okay, men, we have to get out there and cut the mustard, we have to stop spinning our wheels, and we have to touch all bases.' *Every day*. When he got shot down we missed it."

29. Merle Sollars to Louis Carrington, 30 October 1995 (a copy in possession of the author). Sollars goes on to say, "I left some tools laying on a bomb bay door of 015. Regardless of how it happened, I did not do my job properly but you let me off the hook. From that day on, I paid particular attention to your airplane because I was never going to fail at my job again and have a butt-chewing coming from you. I would have noticed any changes in 015 and I saw no provision for a passenger."

30. William E. Burrows, *By Any Means Necessary: Amer-*

ica's Secret Air War in the Cold War (New York: Farrar, Strauss and Giroux, 2001), 122–125.

31. Jolidon, *Last Seen Alive*, 211. See also Robert Burns, "44 Years Later, Families Finally Get Some Answers," *Virginian-Pilot and Ledger-Star*, Sunday, 6 December 1994, A6. Lovell's escapades continues perplexing officials at the highest levels. In the 1990s, Brigadier General James Wold, working with the POW/MIA commission in Moscow, repeatedly inquired of his fate: "I am not sure that he was even manifested on that flight, however, he was on the flight, and the circumstances were never clear in any of the records, at least in our own office as to why he was there."

32. Doris M. Condit, *History of the Office of the Secretary of Defense*, vol. 2, *The Test of War, 1950–1953* (Washington, D.C.: Office of the Secretary of Defense, 1988), 89. Truman was acting strictly in accordance with the norms of international law when he approved the decision for overflights. Because both the People's Republic of China and the Soviet Union had become active players in the ongoing struggle, Chapter VII of the United Nations charter allowed them, as cobelligerents, to be overflown (R. Cargill Hall, "Strategic Reconnaissance in the Cold War: From Concept to National Policy," *Prologue* 28, no. 2 [Summer 1996]: 113).

33. Charles P. Cabell to William A. Adams, 5 October 1950; R. Cargill Hall and Clayton D. Laurie, eds., *Early Cold War Overflights, 1950–1956: Symposium Proceedings*, 2 vols. (Washington, D.C.: Office of the Historian, National Reconnaissance Office, 2003), vol. 2, 438. A General Agee added his comments to the study: "Because of the political implications that are bound to result, the Air Force is not in a position to authorize such missions without reference to the Secretaries of Defense and State. If our past experience with the Department of State on matters of this type still is a criterion, our chances for getting approval on this plan at this time are believed to be zero" (440).

34. William T. Y'Blood., ed., *The Three Wars of Lt. Gen. George E. Stratemeyer* (Washington, D.C.: Air Force History and Museums Program, 1999), 314. A month later Stratemeyer elaborated on his perilous predicament: "In my opinion, the RB-29s would not be able to live for visual or photo reconnaissance unless escorted by prohibitive numbers of fighters. The only other known reconnaissance airplane with any chance of survival and with a radius of action great enough for visual and photo reconnaissance is the RB-45, or the RB-47 if such exists. The lessons of this war so far have shown us that we need almost daily coverage of airfields if we are to successfully destroy the enemy's air capability. Since no additional RB-45s are to be deployed to this theater, I am worried as to just what we should do for this type of reconnaissance" (Telex, George E. Stratemeyer to Hoyt S. Vandenberg, 26 December 1950, Hoyt S. Vandenberg Papers, Box 86, Library of Congress).

35. Cabell, *Man of Intelligence*, 264–265. In December 1950, Cabell arrived in Korea for high-level discussions with General Douglas MacArthur and other ranking leaders and began pushing for overflight authorization: "I raised the question of the desirability from an Intelligence standpoint of permitting air reconnaissance of the airfields in Manchuria. I pointed out that the only element of Chinese Communist power as yet essentially uncommitted is the Chinese Communist Air Force; that these forces had the capability of delivering at least damaging blows to U.N. Forces in Korea; that our intelligence as to the size, deployment, and intentions of the CCAF is inadequately firm, that we need to obtain target data necessary to permit immediate retaliation should air attacks be launched against our ground forces; that we need a datum against which we can apply future changes and so assist in determining their capability and intentions; that air reconnaissance, if discovered, does not carry with it the possible serious consequences as does combat air operations. General MacArthur and General Collins,

while concurring in the desirability of such reconnaissance, did not concur in its accomplishment now, essentially for the reason that even our air reconnaissance might provoke the Chinese Communists to attack our ground forces" (Memorandum for General Vandenberg, 8 December 1950, Record Group 341, Headquarters U.S. Air Force, Deputy Chief of Staff, Operations, General File, Box 54, Fld 2, National Archives).

36. "A Day By Day History of Far East Air Forces Operations," Vol. 2, 1 November 1950 through 28 February 1951, 253, 291. By this time frame, many opinions were solidifying as to the usefulness of the Tornado in this line of work, especially in comparison to RB-29s and RB-50s: "Many people believe the RB-45C is the nearest thing we have to the ideal. This opinion is by no means unanimous, but nearly all will agree the RB-45C is a long step in the right direction, despite the fact it was designed as a bomber" (Photo Reconnaissance with the RB-45C, Air Intelligence Digest, Second Air Force, January 1951, 1, Both Air Force Historical Research Agency, Maxwell AFB).

37. U.S. Department of State, *Foreign Relations of the United States* (Washington, D.C.: Government Printing Office, 1983), *Korea and China*, part 1, vol. 7 (1951), 385; Top Secret Eyes Only, 28 April 1951, Record Group 218, Records of the Joint Chiefs of Staff, Outgoing Messages, Box 9, Fld. 3, National Archives; Far East Air Forces, Bomber Command Provisional, Narrative History, 1 November 1950–31 January 1951, Vol. 1, Book III, 18, Air Force Historical Research Agency, Maxwell AFB; Y'Blood, *Three Wars*, 509. Stratemeyer glowingly concludes: "We have a C-in-C that isn't afraid to make a decision — and he can make it quick. My admiration continues for him — one hundred percent."

38. History, 363rd Tactical Reconnaissance Group, October–November–December 1950, 24, Air Force Historical Research Agency, Maxwell AFB.

39. "A Day by Day History of Far East Air Force Operations," Vol. 2, 1 November 1950 through 28 February 1951, 201, 250, 280, Air Force Historical Research Agency, Maxwell AFB.

40. Carrington continues: "I must have been in at least six good air battles. In the beginning the MiGs would get on the tail of an 86 — they wouldn't bother us. They get on the tail of an 86, or an 86 would get on the tail of a MiG, you'd just see a flurry and a flash and that MiG would be riding that 86. So he'd go straight down, they couldn't dive." According to one official summation, "Interceptions against the RB-45 have been so frequent that F-86 escort is now provided for every mission north of Pyongyang. It is of interest to note that adequate fighter cover is more easily accomplished at 35,000 ft than at 40,000 ft where an economical cruise setting for the RB-45 is uneconomical for the F-86s. Therefore, escorted missions are now being run at 33,000 ft." (Report on Temporary Duty with FEAF, History, Tactical Air Command, 1 December 1950 through 30 June 1950, Vol. 5, Part II, undated, 8, Air Force Historical Research Agency, Maxwell AFB).

41. History, 91st Strategic Reconnaissance Squadron, 1 January 1951–28 February 1951, 13; Report on Temporary Duty with FEAF, History, Tactical Air Command, 1 December 1950–30 June 1951, Vol. 5, Part II, undated, 8: Both Air Force Historical Research Agency, Maxwell AFB. Thanks to unstinting RB-45 activities, "FEAF had completed the Trimetrogon charting photography of North Korea" (Daily Staff Digest, 15 January 1951, Record Group 341, Headquarters, U.S. Air Force, Daily Staff Digests, Box 11, National Archives).

42. According to Corporal Price, "I hate to take away a 'first' from the 452nd Bomb Wing that claims they were the first to wear the new Air Force blue uniforms overseas. They shipped over on 15 October 1950. We shipped over on 16

September 1950. I recall we took the standard 'bus driver' sarcasm but eventually everybody got the blues issue so we were all in the same bus, so to speak" (Kenneth W. Price Narrative, 12 February 2004, 4, [copy in possession of the author]).

43. Kenneth W. Price Narrative, 12 February 2004, 5 (copy in possession of the author).

44. Historical Report, 91st Strategic Reconnaissance Wing, March 1951, 12–13; History, 363rd Tactical Reconnaissance Group, 1 January 1951 to 12 March 1951, 3, Exhibit 6, Air Force Historical Research Agency, Maxwell AFB. In the event of expanded conflict with Communist China, General Ridgway advised the Joint Chiefs of Staff that "your planning provide for the stationing of approx 24 RB-45 with properly trained crews in FEC prior to initiation of such a program. With these acft, recon could be effectively accomplished and would fill a definite need for intelligence data related to air targets, current disposition of enemy air power, capabilities of enemy air defense systems, and location of larger enemy ground force troops and supply dispositions" (Telex, CINCFE to JCS, March 1951, Record Group 218, Geographic File, 1948–1950, Box 21, CCS062 Far East [7-4-50] Sec. 1). Ridgway was subsequently informed that "Additional RB-45 aircraft not available for deployment to FEC prior to initiation of subj reconnaissance program. In view of political implications involved and security desired, JCS believe that program could be accomplished by infrequent flights made by individual aircraft or small formations" (JCS to CINCFE, 27 April 1951, Record Group 218, Records of the Joint Chiefs of Staff, Outgoing Messages, Box 9, Fld. 3, Tab 89627, National Archives).

45. Detachment Report, 19 April 1951, Historical Report, 91st Strategic Reconnaissance Wing, April 1951, Exhibit 19, Air Force Historical Research Agency, Maxwell AFB.

46. "Implications Involved Should Sensitive Items of AF Equipment Used, or Proposed for Use in Korea, Be Compromised or Captured," 8 March 1951, Record Group 341, Head Quarters, U.S. Air Force, Deputy Chief of Operations, General File, Box 55, Fld. 6, National Archives; Report on Temporary Duty with FEAF, History, Tactical Air Command, 1 December through 30 June 1951, Vol. 5, Part II, undated, Air Force Historical Research Agency, Maxwell AFB. The report continues: "The MiG-15 can make passes on the RB-45 at all altitudes, all around the clock, with ease. However, if the RB-45 pilot knows he is under attack he can turn inside of the MiG-15. The MiGs have countered by initiating their attacks from five to seven o'clock low — a blind spot on the RB-45."

47. History, 91st Strategic Reconnaissance Squadron, 1 March 1951 through 31 March 1951, 5–6, Air Force Historical Research Agency, Maxwell AFB; Gordon and Rigmant, *MiG-15*, 130.

48. Detachment Report, 19 April 1951, Historical Report, 91st Strategic Reconnaissance Wing, April 1951, Exhibit 21, VI Operations, Air Force Historical Research Agency, Maxwell AFB. It subsequently states, "The loss of the tip tanks seriously affects the operations of this Detachment due to the lack of parts for the new tanks. This requires that the remaining set of tip tanks has to be transferred from one aircraft to the other. This procedure is also used for the bomb bay booster pumps, replacements for which are non-existent at present."

49. This life or death struggle had a captive audience: "During the time that we were on the ground at K-13, we listened to the radio and caught the air battle over Sinuiji. The 4th Fighter Wing was escorting the RB-45 and during the course of the escort, shot down one Mig and damaged two more. We got away unscathed" (Earl Partridge Diary, Vol. 4, 9 April 1951, Air Force Historical Research Agency, Maxwell AFB).

50. Kenneth W. Price Narrative, 12 February 2004, 4 (copy in possession of the author).

51. Detachment Report, 19 April 1951, Historical Report, 91st Strategic Reconnaissance Wing, April 1951, Exhibit 21, VI Operations, Air Force Historical Research Agency, Maxwell AFB. The report continues: "Photos were taken of the first priority targets but due to aggressive attacks, no further photos could be taken and the RB-45C withdrew to the Southeast and returned safely to base. No hits were sustained. It was found that the RB-45C could out turn the MiG-15 at 40,000 feet but this action is negated when two MiGs attack at once. Also, this evasive action precludes the accomplishment of good photography."

52. Nor was this the first time it happened. According to Carrington, one RB-45C flight consisted of both copilots being allowed to conduct their own first mission: "They were flying straight and level and they started seeing 'pop-pop-pop' in front of them. Neither one of them, well, they knew where third base was and not much else. They couldn't figure out what anti-aircraft was firing at them. So they were looking down and finally they looked up and there was a big red star on their wing tip. The guy had fired everything he had."

53. Detachment Report, 19 April 1951, Historical Report, 91st Strategic Reconnaissance Wing, April 1951, Exhibit 22, VI Operations. High-speed maneuvering exacted its toll on the overworked Tornados: "We looked at one of the B-45s and talked with the crew. The airplane was in good condition except for a bent wing resulting from coming in too close to Mach-1 on frequent occasions. This makes the airplane fly badly at high altitude or at high speed. A recommendation has been submitted that this particular B-45 will be returned to the United States" (Earl Partridge Diary, Vol. 4, 27 May 1951: Both Air Force Historical Research Agency, Maxwell AFB).

Chapter Five

1. Configuration of 32 B-45A Aircraft, 29 June 1951, Record Group 341, Headquarters, U.S. Air Force, Deputy Chief of Staff, Operations, Decimal File, Folder 452.1, "Aircraft," National Archives.

2. Robert D. Little, "Building an Atomic Air Force, 1949–1953," from "The History of Air Force Participation in the Atomic Energy Program, 1943–1953" (internal study, Air Force History Support Office, Bolling AFB, Washington, D.C.), Vol. 3, Part 1, Section 1, 162–164; Bernard C. Nalty, ed., *Winged Shield, Winged Sword: A History of the United States Air Force*. 2 vols. (Washington, D.C.: Air Force History and Museums Program, 1997), Vol. 2, 103.

3. Lee Bowen, "The Development of Weapons," from "The History of Air Force Participation in the Atomic Energy Program, 1943–1953" (internal study, Air Force History Support Office, Bolling AFB, Washington, D.C.), Vol. 4, Part 1, 61–62; History of the Mark 5 Bomb, 8, National Atomic Museum Library; History of the Tactical Air Command, 1 July through 31 December 1951, Vol. 7, 38, Headquarters, Air Force Air Combat Command, Langley AFB; Chuck Hansen, *US Nuclear Weapons: The Secret History* (Arlington, TX: Aerofax, 1988), 128–131; Necah S. Furman, *Sandia National Laboratories: The Post War Decade* (Albuquerque, NM: University of New Mexico Press, 1990), 412.

4. "History of the Mark 5 Bomb," 15, National Atomic Museum Library; James N. Gibson, *Nuclear Weapons of the United States: An Illustrated History* (Atglen, PA: Schiffer, 1996), 91. Sgt. Freeman Cox, a bomb handler, told this author the following: "By today's standards it was extremely crude, mainly because we had to make a physical inspection, in other words we had what we called a 'birdcage' with a nuclear warhead in it. I used gas masks and rubber gloves and

you were supposed to dispose all the clothing after each loading—in three years I used the same gas mask. We did dispose of the rubber gloves but sometimes for weeks at a time we wouldn't be able to change clothes, if we were out on maneuvers, we couldn't change clothes." Within a year of leaving the Mark 5, Cox experienced cancerous growths on his face, spinal compression, vomiting, and headaches—all the symptoms of radiation poisoning.

5. Michael D. Yaffe, "'A Higher Priority than the Korean War!': The Crash Programmes to Modify the Bombers for the Bomb," *Diplomacy & Statecraft* 5, no. 2 (July 1994): 359–361.

6. Memorandum for the Secretary of the Air Force, 21 July 1948, Record Group 341, Headquarters, U.S. Air Force, Deputy Chief of Staff, Special Project File, Box 222, Folder History of B-45 A/C, National Archives.

7. Yaffe, "Higher Priority," 365–367.

8. Configuration of 32 B-45A Aircraft, 29 June 1951, Record Group 341, Headquarters, U.S. Air Force, Deputy Chief of Staff, Operations, Decimal File, Box 21, Folder 452.1, National Archives.

9. History, Tactical Air Command, 1 July through 31 December 1951, Vol. 7, 77–78, Headquarters, Air Combat Command, Langley AFB; "Tactical Air Command Atomic Weapons Project," 16 October 1950, Reel K4336, No. 855, Air Force Historical Research Agency, Maxwell AFB; Frederick A. Alling, "History of Modification of USAF Aircraft for Atomic Weapon Delivery, 1948–1954," 81–82, Headquarters, Air Force Air Materiel Command, Wright-Patterson AFB.

10. Configuration of 32 B-45A Aircraft, 16 August 1951, Record Group 341, Headquarters, U.S. Air Force, Deputy Chief of Staff, Operations, Box 21, Decimal File, Folder 452.1, National Archives; Robert D. Little, "Building an Atomic Air Force, 1949–1953," from "The History of Air Force Participation in the Atomic Energy Program, 1943–1953" (internal study, Air Force History Support Office, Bolling AFB, Washington, D.C.), Vol. 3, Part 1, Section 1, 168, 170–171; Nalty, *Winged Shield*, vol. 2, 103.

11. Frederick A. Alling, "History of Modification of USAF Aircraft for Atomic Weapon Delivery, 1948–1954," 84–90, Headquarters, Air Force Air Materiel Command, Wright-Patterson AFB.

12. Regarding another incident Crowley relates the following: "One of the problems with the B-45, it was the first 3,000 pound system and the accumulators, when you've shot them off and you thought you dumped everything, always had some amount of charge in them depending upon how much air had been applied to it. I was working in the bomb bay on a bomb release problem and one of the guys came up and said, 'Well, maybe I should open up the bomb door a little more,' and I said 'Don't touch it! Don't touch it!' and *boom*! He touched the handle and it caught me right across, just above the knees, and needless to say I don't think I've had as much pain in my life. Fortunately all I got was some really bad bruises."

13. History, Tactical Air Command, 1 July through 31 December 1951, Vol. 7, 45, 65, 98, Headquarters, Air Force Air Combat Command, Langley AFB.

14. "Annex VIII, Light Jet Bomber Tactics," History of the Tactical Air Command 1 July through 31 December 1951," Vol. 7, 305–306; History of the Tactical Air Command, 1 January through 30 June 1952, Vol. 7, 35, 42, 111: Both Headquarters, Air Force Air Combat Command, Langley AFB. Another study warns, "It is recommended that the aircraft not be in the turn at burst time because of the probability of increasing the incidence angle of the thermal radiation on some surface, and also because of the initial structural stresses due to the airloads when the thermal pulse is received" (David C. Knodel and Arthur S. C. Roberts, "Safe Delivery and Escape Conditions in Tactical Atomic Bomb-

ing Operations" (April 1955), 19, Technical Report AD504674, Defense Technical Information Center, Fort Belvoir.

15. "Annex VIII, Light Bomber Tactics," History of the Tactical Air Command, 1 July through 31 December 1951, Vol. 7, 172, 305–306, Headquarters, Air Force Air Combat Command, Langley AFB. According to Captain Don Orr, "Our mode was we were going to be high level bombers, we come in and go over the flak and all that stuff at high altitude. After delivery I think we'd do a 65 degree bank and when you rolled out 135 degrees make a tight turn — and the detonation would be on the tail of the plane, minimum blast coming from the rear, otherwise you went over it — you might almost be above it, get the blast, and do yourself in."

16. History, 84th Bombardment Squadron (Light), 1 January 1951–12 March 1951, 32, Air Force Historical Research Agency, Maxwell AFB; e-mail from Daryle E. Tripp, 6 November 2002, copy in possession of author. According to Captain Donald Orr, "It was pretty intensive — I had no background in that electronics type stuff but we had to learn those fusing and firing circuits from memory and draw them out before they would certify you a bomb commander. Very technical." Major James Story added, "It was a very classified, hush-hush type of thing, they were very specific that you had to be qualified to be a bomb commander and to do that you had to learn by memory the fusing and the firing sequence of the bomb."

17. John D. Hardison, The Megaton Blasters: Story of the 4925th Test Group (Atomic) (Arvada, CO: Boomerang, 1990), 17.

18. Hansen, US Nuclear Weapons, 135; "History of Participation in Operation Buster/Jangle," 1951, 84, 87, National Atomic Museum Library; Richard L. Miller, Under the Cloud: The Decades of Nuclear Testing (New York: Free Press, 1986), 129.

19. Hansen, US Nuclear Weapons, 135; Shot Dog of Tumbler/Snapper, Air Force Special Weapons Center, Aircraft participation in Tumbler/Snapper, 9 June 1952, National Atomic Museum Library; Miller, Under the Cloud, 149. Lieutenant George Roos, who observed Tumbler/Snapper from Control Point, Camp Mercury, told the author that they "had no altitude control by the way of radar like they do now. Everything was time and distance, being at the right place at the right time or you weren't quite sure what was going to happen."

20. A reporter duly noted how "Searchers fighting their way through six-foot sawgrass, swamp and quicksand found the two bodies" ("Bomber Falls in Swamp; 2 Die," New York Times, 7 October 1951, 21.)

21. History of the 363rd Tactical Reconnaissance Group, 1 July 1950–20 September 1950, 25–28; History of the 363rd Tactical Reconnaissance Group, 1 October 1950–31 December 1950, 9–10, 25: Both Air Force Historical Research Agency, Maxwell AFB.

22. History, 363rd Tactical Reconnaissance Wing, September–December 1950, 21; History of the Tactical Air Command, 1 July through 30 November 1950, Vol. 1, 166–167, 278–279: Both Air Force Historical Research Agency, Maxwell AFB.

23. Action on Letter, B-45 Difficulties by AMC and TAC, History, 363rd Tactical Reconnaissance Group, 1 January 1951–12 March 1951, Exhibit 11, Air Force Historical Research Agency, Maxwell AFB.

24. "Combat Readiness of B-45 Aircraft," History, 363rd Tactical Reconnaissance Group, 1 January 1951 to 12 March 1951, Exhibit 23, Air Force Historical Research Agency, Maxwell AFB: "The completely disheartening response and lack of solution to the problems outlined in that letter is deteriorating the entire program for B-45 aircraft. Considering the monetary expense and time concerned to date in the development of this aircraft, it is inconceivable that so many

unsatisfactory conditions can exist and be allowed to continue for so long. A vigorous program of support both administrative and logistical from all levels would aid immeasurably in the development of this equipment" (13).

25. "Restrictions on High Speed Bombardment," 26 February 1951, History, 363rd Tactical Reconnaissance Group, 1 January 1951 to 12 March 1951, Exhibit 28; Air Force Historical Research Agency, Maxwell AFB. The tail guns, when they arrived, would be equipped with the APG-30 radar. According to gunner Don Kinsey, "The specific function of this wetset was to lock on the enemy aircraft and feed ballistics data into the computer. The main problem with this radar set is that it rarely worked properly. If the sensitivity was too acute, it would lock on clouds rather than the selected target and, conversely, if the sensitivity was set too loosely it would not lock on anything. Knowing this I would always turn it off during gunnery missions and use 'Kentucky windage'" (Don Kinsey to author, 1 January 2007, copy in possession of author).

26. In his long association with military aeronautics, Willis F. Chapman went on to enjoy a surprisingly fruitful career. After passing through the National War College and fulfilling a stint at Headquarters, U.S. Air Force, he was sent to Paris in 1956 as the air force representative to the Mutual Weapons Development Plan (MWDP). In this capacity he helped pioneer the concept and development of vertical liftoff and landing (VTOL) aircraft, and was closely involved with the famous Hawker Harrier. A decade later aeronautical engineer Dr. Stanley G. Hooker sent him a telegram stating, "It must be a source of great personal satisfaction to you that the US Marines have ordered a batch of Hawker Harrier aircraft. Without your vision and unstinted support, this aircraft and the Pegasus engine would never have existed" (Stanley Hooker to Willis F. Chapman, 23 December 1969, original owned by Pat Chapman Meder, Annandale, Virginia).

27. History, 47th Bombardment Group, Light, 12 March–30 June 1951, Foreword, 1–6, Air Force Historical Research Agency, Maxwell AFB.

28. History, 47th Bombardment Group, Light, 12 March–30 June 1951, 10, 14, 17–19, Air Force Historical Research Agency, Maxwell AFB.

29. History of the 85th Bomb Squadron, Light, 23 July–31 August 1951, in History of the 47th Bombardment Group, Light, 1 July–30 September 1951, Exhibit 24; Ralph D. Bald, Air Force Participation in Joint Army-Air Force Training Exercises, 1951–1954 (1957), 17, 24: Both Air Force Historical Research Agency, Maxwell AFB.

30. B-45 No. 47–064 Accident Review, History of the 85th Bombardment Squadron, 1 October to 31 December 1951, n.p., Air Force Historical Agency, Maxwell AFB.

31. History, 47th Bombardment Group, Light, 1 October–31 December 1951, 3; History, 47th Bombardment Wing, 1 January–31 March 1952, 1, 11, 27; History, 47th Bombardment Group, Light, 1 January–31 March 1952, 6: Both Air Force Historical Research Agency, Maxwell AFB.

32. "Operations and Training Report," 16 May 1952, History, 47th Bomb Wing, 1 January–31 March 1952," Exhibit 36, Air Force Historical Research Agency, Maxwell AFB.

33. History, 85th Bombardment Squadron, Light, 1 January to 31 March 1952, 17. "The limited parking space for aircraft makes taxiing a very exacting science, especially during hours of darkness. Unused fuel pits continue to dot the parking area. It is known that the weight of the B-45 will break through the metal covers on these pits. It is therefore necessary to 'jockey' even more while taxiing to avoid these pits" (History, 84th Bombardment Squadron, 1 April–30 June 1952, 14: Both Air Force Historical Research Agency, Maxwell AFB).

34. History, 47th Bombardment Group, Light, 1 Janu-

ary–31 March 1952, 6–7, Air Force Historical Research Agency, Maxwell AFB; "14 are Killed in Texas Air Crashes," *New York Times*, 22 March 1952, 29 and "3 Missing in Jet Crash," *Ibid.* 30 March 1952, 3.

35. "3 Killed in Jet Bomber Crash," *New York Times*, 26 May 1952, 18.

36. History, 47th Bomb Group, Light, 12 March–30 July 1952, 14; History of the Tactical Air Command, 1 January through 30 June 1952, Vol. 3, 23–24: Both Air Force Historical Research Agency, Maxwell AFB. The sensitive atomic mission and repeated accidents also resulted in heightened security measures for the ground crews. According to Sgt. William Bombkamp, "They were afraid of sabotage so I got my fingerprints taken three times in four days, and I was in the OSS [CIA] office, I don't know how many times, sitting in front of a desk and an OSS guy trying to explain where I was the night before we worked on it after dark.... I felt like a fugitive but after it was all over I got a Top Secret clearance."

37. Historical Documentation of Major General John D. Stevenson, 11, Air Force Historical Research Agency, Maxwell AFB. Lieutenant Luke Skiles proffers an unusual take on the long-standing rivalry between SAC and TAC: "SAC liked to consider that TAC did not even exist, like an illegitimate cousin, which is fine with me — I don't like to admit that they exist. I left heel marks all the way to Wichita when they sent me to B-47s. They had a different attitude in life, and were totally dedicated to not having any fun. They've taken all the fun out of going on cross country to a strange place — it's no fun. I couldn't wait to get out!"

Chapter Six

1. E.W. Holstrom, "Careful Planning Means Safety," *Strategic Air Command Combat Crew* 2, no. 10 (April 1952): 16.

2. History, 91st Strategic Reconnaissance Squadron, July 1950, 2; Historical Report, 91st Strategic Reconnaissance Wing, July 1950, 25, Air Force Historical Research Agency, Maxwell AFB. The Air Force received initial deliveries of the RB-45s on 2 June 1950; "Air Force Accepts New Jet," *New York Times*, 3 June 1950, 3; Rick Rodrigues, *Aircraft Markings of the Strategic Air Command, 1946–1953* (Jefferson, NC: McFarland, 2006), 131–137. A popular overview of SAC reconnaissance activities during this period is Neil Collins' "America's Jet Cameramen," *Skyline* 9, no. 4 (November 1951): 20–23.

3. History, 91st Strategic Reconnaissance Wing, August 1950, 29, Exhibit 92, Air Force Historical Research Agency, Maxwell AFB; Commanding General's Diary, 30 August 1950, Curtis E. LeMay Papers, Box 103, Manuscript Division, Library of Congress.

4. "Capabilities of RB-45C Aircraft," Historical Report, 91st Strategic Reconnaissance Wing, September 1950, 30, Exhibit 11, Air Force Historical Research Agency, Maxwell AFB; Daily Staff Digest, 22 September 1950, Record Group 341, Headquarters, U.S. Air Force, Daily Staff Digest, Box 11, National Archives; Commanding General's Diary, 28 October 1950, Curtis E. LeMay Papers, Box 103, Manuscript Division, Library of Congress.

5. Howard "Sam" Myers unequivocally states the following: "All told the B-45 was a pilot's aircraft, very responsive on the controls and, like most newly designed aircraft of that era — when a rash of mechanical or structural problems didn't plague it — a super aircraft" ("Big Bodies in Motion: Flying the Best of SAC's Mighty Bomber Brigade," *Wings* 25, no. 4 [August 1995]: 54). He later told the author "It had some dangerous characteristics, like wings falling off occasionally — the center spar was a problem — but as far as doing its task as a recon vehicle for SAC I think it did an outstanding job."

6. Captain Francis Riggs said the following to the author: "The big thing was not to overspeed your gear, get your gear retracted before you got over gear speed and that took some doing the first couple of trips off the field because that thing was a going piece of machinery. Boy, you get that thing off the ground and it seemed like it was going straight up! And it really kept you busy to reach down and retract the gear before you got over the gear speed and it was a tremendous transition to make — but the thing was *smooth*, no vibration, no noise, no nothing — absolutely *smooth*." According to Lieutenant Maury Seitz, "It was so damn fast on take off that you only had a few seconds to get the gear up and get the flaps up before you blew the doors off." Finally, Captain John Keema described his B-45 experience this way: "What impressed me initially was when we started to taxi out, it was just like driving an automobile — so smooth, no jerking, just sheer pleasure, very quiet, no noise, no vibration. You could put your pencil on the table and it would stay there. Of course on takeoff you'd pour the power to it — thrust me right back into the seat — that was great, a real thrilling thing. The only problem was you had no sense of speed once you got into the air because you couldn't see anything."

7. Jay E. Spaulding to author, 20 July 1997, 3; Austin quoted from Wolfgang W.E. Samuel, *I Always Wanted to Fly: America's Cold War Airmen* (Jackson: University of Mississippi Press, 2001), 155. Major Marion Mixon characterized the Tornado's penchant for high flight this way: "It had very good altitude capability. We'd take off and leave 100 percent on for thirty minutes and cruise climb, and we'd end up somewhere in the lower thirties. Then you'd pull back to 92 percent and flew Mach, restricted to .78 because of a flutter back in the tail. To illustrate this we'd fly non-stop from Goose Bay, Labrador, to Sculthorpe, up over Iceland as an alternative if you had a problem, and we'd hit probably close to 46–47,000 feet at Prestwick. If you were a B-47 you'd be ten thousand feet below that."

8. Quoted in Samuel, *I Always Wanted to Fly*, 157–158. Some perilous incidents resulted from the intense heat. According to Lieutenant Jay E. Spaulding, "I remember no attempt to control cockpit temperatures and we cooked for an hour sitting on the ground breathing 100 percent oxygen in an attempt to prevent the bends. I have seen cockpit temperatures of over 160 degrees. On the runway waiting for take off once, Capt. Riggs fainted from the heat one time, the airplane started rolling and I had to pull the emergency air brake handles and hold it until operations could get a pilot out to the aircraft, get into the front seat and shut down the engines. The air was a one shot charge, if released it vented. Only the person in the front seat could stop the engines" (Letter of Jay E. Spaulding, 20 July 1997 [copy in possession of the author]).

9. Regarding cockpit temperature at high altitude, Alvan Barrett told the author "The air was heated, it blew on you, but the whole side panel, rails, and everything would ice up and you couldn't touch anything, you'd get burned by the frost." Jay E. Spaulding echoed these observations: "It was fairly common to have two inches of frost on the cockpit wall beside my right shoulder and a regular ice cone on the toe of my boot in front of the air vent. I still suffer from the results of this treatment. I have constant pain in my right shoulder and have undergone a right hip replacement largely due to flying this aircraft" (Jay E. Spaulding to author, 20 July 1997).

10. Historical Report, 91st Strategic Reconnaissance Wing, October 1950, 24, 30, Exhibits 21, 48, Air Force Historical Research Agency, Maxwell AFB. No matter how rehearsed, the notion of joining two large, fast-moving, heavy aircraft in mid-air by a skinny metal tube was never exactly routine. "Add to this picture of mass and momentum such factors as the dark of night, turbulent weather, and the

prospect of combat, and you have all the elements of a genuine white knuckle drama" (Walter J. Boyne, *Beyond the Wild Blue: A History of the United States Air Force, 1947–1997* [New York: St. Martin's, 1997], 107).

11. Austin quote from Samuel, *I Always Wanted to Fly*, 158; Jay E. Spaulding to author, 20 July 1997, 1. Captain Frank W. Hayslip described his refueling technique this way: "First of all the navigator had to get you to the plane. You drove in behind him and they put the boom down, you drive in underneath and he'd put the boom over your head, stick it in the receptacle, and then all you'd do is fly good, close formation. It was easy."

12. Historical Report, 91st Strategic Reconnaissance Wing, November 1950, 40–41, Exhibit 32, Air Force Historical Research Agency, Maxwell AFB.

13. Historical Report, 91st Strategic Reconnaissance Wing, December 1950, 33, Exhibits 13, 15. On 31 January 1951, SAC headquarters was advised by the 91st Wing that "Speed and altitude of this aircraft is not considered adequate to ensure successful completion of reconnaissance mission in area where jet fighter intercept will be encountered." Major General Thomas S. Power, SAC deputy commander, acknowledged the deficiency, yet advised the 91st that "time is an important factor. The RB-45 is an interim reconnaissance vehicle, with a limited operational life. Therefore the choice of a radar for retrofit should be limited to sets now in stock or production" (Historical Report, 91st Strategic Reconnaissance Wing, March 1951, Exhibit 31: Both Air Force Historical Research Agency, Maxwell AFB).

14. Historical Report, 91st Strategic Reconnaissance Wing, December 1950, Exhibit 12. Air Force Historical Research Agency, Maxwell AFB.

15. Historical Report, 91st Strategic Reconnaissance Wing, January 1951, 51, 52; History of the 323rd Strategic Reconnaissance Squadron, January 1951, 4. As more Tornados arrived at Barksdale, other problems arrived with them. "Parts shortage remains one of the critical problems and during December an average of four aircraft were out of commission per day due to lack of parts. Indications are that the parts problem will become worse in the near future instead of better" (History of the 323rd Strategic Reconnaissance Squadron for December 1950, 8: Both Air Force Historical Research Agency, Maxwell AFB).

16. Historical Report, 91st Strategic Reconnaissance Wing, February 1951, 31–47, Exhibit 17, Air Force Historical Research Agency, Maxwell AFB. Tornado pilots gradually fine-tuned their approach to fuel consumption with greater experience. Colonel Lewis B. Lyle told this author that he "took the RB-45 out to Sacramento and flew it back to Barksdale nonstop, which is the same as going from the Northeast part of the country to Iceland. I decided that I would just climb all the way and when I got to Barksdale I was at 50,000 feet and burning no fuel at all. That was a good lesson — the higher you go the better you are from a range standpoint."

17. Nasby continues about his escapade at Quincy: "I got a statement from Air Force accounting seven or eight years later down in South Carolina, 'Is the following narrative true as best you can remember?' I used this credit card and got like 3,000 gallons of jet fuel that they brought in on a railroad car — enough to get us over to Rantoul. And the guy made trips back and forth with his little truck hauling this and he says, 'Come back anytime, we'd be welcome, it was good business.' It was for $900 for something and I had a bill like that on whatever kind of credit card we used!"

18. "Record Flight," *Time*, 58, no. 8 (20 August 1951): 70.

19. Historical Report, 91st Strategic Reconnaissance Wing, February 1951, Exhibit 41, Air Force Historical Research Agency, Maxwell AFB; "Three Leap as Jet Crashes," *New York Times*, 9 February 1951, 18.

20. Historical Report, 91st Strategic Reconnaissance Wing, March 1951, 43–44, Exhibit 58, Air Force Historical Research Agency, Maxwell AFB; "3 Barksdale Men Die in Jet Crash," *Shreveport Times*, 22 March 1951, 1; "B-45 Crash Toll Rises to Four," *New York Times*, 23 March 1951, 11. Regarding the smoking incident, new regulations were issued forbidding the practice without common sense: "Don't smoke in small, tight or poorly ventilated compartments which can easily trap gasoline fumes or become saturated with oxygen" ("Caution … Fire, When You Smoke," *Strategic Air Command Combat Crew* 1, no. 6 [April 1951]: 27).

21. Historical Report, 91st Strategic Reconnaissance Wing, April 1951, 18–20, 45–46, Exhibits 41, 49, Air Force Historical Research Agency, Maxwell AFB.

22. Curtis E. LeMay to J.H. Atkinson, 23 June 1951, Record Group 342, Records of U.S. Air Force Commands, Entry 1025, Strategic Air Command, Operations Planning Files, 1944–1964, National Archives.

23. Historical Report, 91st Strategic Reconnaissance Wing, May 1951, 43–46, Exhibit 60, Air Force Historical Research Agency, Maxwell AFB.

24. Hal Austin related to this author the following: "One cause of RB-45 mishaps was the placement of bladder tanks in the bomb bays to increase range. Unfortunately, they were hung on bomb racks not designed for the continuous stress of sustained, daily operations. On several occasions metal fatigue broke the racks, causing the heavy bladders to crash through the bomb bay doors. At high speeds the wreckage traveled aft and knocked off the empennage, causing the aircraft to spiral in."

25. Historical Report, 91st Strategic Reconnaissance Wing, June 1951, 20, 37–8, Exhibit 23, Air Force Historical Research Agency, Maxwell AFB. As it turns out, the RB-45C was poorly situated for celestial navigation. According to Captain Thurber Hoyt, "We used to fly celestial flights and shooting celestial was out of a canopy that hadn't been calibrated — that was just a guess, it didn't work out very good. We didn't have a sextant mount, as such, it was hard to hold a sextant going through an uncalibrated canopy so that we were lucky to get within sixty miles of where we should be. We practiced a lot but I do not recall ever having a successful celestial mission."

26. "Development of Evasive Tactics for the RB-45," Historical Report, 91st Strategic Reconnaissance Wing, July 1951, 57, Exhibit 36, Air Force Historical Research Agency, Maxwell AFB.

27. Historical Report, 91st Strategic Reconnaissance Wing, August 1951, 26–27; "Training of RAF Crews," Historical Report, 91st Strategic Reconnaissance Wing, September 1951, Exhibit 23: Both Air Force Historical Research Agency, Maxwell AFB.

28. "Analysis of Operational Problems," 1 September 1951, Historical Report, 91st Strategic Reconnaissance Wing, August 1951, Exhibit 44, Air Force Historical; Research Agency, Maxwell AFB.

29. "RAF Training for October," Historical Report, 91st Strategic Reconnaissance Wing, September 1951, 21–23, Exhibit 66, Air Force Historical Research Agency, Maxwell AFB.

30. Historical Report, 91st Strategic Reconnaissance Wing, November 1951, 21–23, 45, Exhibit 42, Air Force Historical Research Agency, Maxwell AFB. Experiments with tail turrets had been continuing at Long Beach for some time. According to NAA mechanic Leo Hunt, "Two B-45Cs were equipped with radar controlled tail guns. The test crew was testing the response of the radar and were locking on aircraft landing. I drove by on the tow tractor and saw both gun systems lock on me and track me until I was out of range. It was a spooky feeling" (communication from Leo Hunt, undated, in author's possession).

31. Lieutenant David L. Gray also had found reminiscences of starting J47s: "The joke was: If you got four en-

gines in a B-45 started without one hot start, they gave you an instant Air Medal. That wasn't really true, but it was a very rudimentary airplane" (David L. Gray interview, 35, Air Force Historical Research Agency, Maxwell AFB).

32. Historical Report, 91st Strategic Reconnaissance Wing, December 1951, 24–27; "Lost ... One RB-45," *Strategic Air Command Combat Crew* 2, no. 8 (February 1952): 14–15: Both at the Air Force Historical Research Agency, Maxwell AFB.

33. Description of Accident, Historical Report, 91st Strategic Reconnaissance Wing, January 1952, Exhibit 56; History of the 323rd Strategic Reconnaissance Squadron, January, 1952, 4–5, 8; "SAC Flying Safety Year," *Strategic Air Command Combat Crew* 2, no. 9 (March 1952): 9: All Air Force Historical Research Agency, Maxwell AFB.

34. Historical Report, 91st Strategic Reconnaissance Wing, February 1952, 27, Exhibit 59, Air Force Historical Research Agency, Maxwell AFB.

35. Historical Report, 91st Strategic Reconnaissance Wing, March 1952, 23–24, 38, Air Force Historical Research Agency, Maxwell AFB.

36. Historical Report, 91st Strategic Reconnaissance Wing, April 1952, 23, 47–49, Exhibit 28, Air Force Historical Research Agency, Maxwell AFB.

37. Historical Report, 91st Strategic Reconnaissance Squadron, May 1952, 25–27, 28, Exhibit 23, Air Force Historical Research Agency, Maxwell AFB.

38. Historical Report, 91st Strategic Reconnaissance Wing, June 1952, 21–22, 24, Exhibit 11, Air Force Historical Research Agency, Maxwell AFB.

39. Historical Report, 91st Strategic Reconnaissance Wing, July 1952, 5, 18–19, Exhibit 42; August 1952, 5, 18–19, 26, 40–41; September 1952, 18, 38: All Air Force Historical Research Agency, Maxwell AFB.

40. Historical Report, 91st Strategic Reconnaissance Wing, September 1952, Exhibit 86; "Heads Up Flying," *Strategic Air Command Combat Crew* 3, no. 7 (January 1953): 27: Both Air Force Historical Research Agency, Maxwell AFB.

41. Norman Polmar, ed., *Strategic Air Command: People, Aircraft, and Missiles* (Baltimore: Nautical and Aviation, 1979), 30.

42. Historical Report, 91st Strategic Reconnaissance Wing, October 1952, 8, 19, 43, Exhibit 90, 91, Air Force Historical Research Agency, Maxwell AFB; "Jet Crash Kills 4 Airmen," *New York Times,* 21 October 1952, 14.

43. Historical Report, 91st Strategic Reconnaissance Wing, December 1952, 8, 11, 12, 23, 80, Air Force Historical Research Agency, Maxwell AFB.

44. Historical Report, 91st Strategic Reconnaissance Wing, December 1952, Exhibit 80, Air Force Historical Research Agency, Maxwell AFB; "Flier Dies in Jet Bomber Blast," *New York Times,* 15 December 1952, 14. The heavy attrition took its toll on unit morale but occasioned only a few defections. According to Captain John Keema, "In fact, at one point, in each squadron individually, the wing commander came down with the director of operations and squadron commander and said, 'Okay, anyone who wants to get out of the program can do so without prejudice.' That's the only time in my whole military life that I experienced that — and I don't think anyone left."

45. Historical Report, 91st Strategic Reconnaissance Wing, December 1952, Exhibit 90, Air Force Historical Research Agency, Maxwell AFB. According to Major Jim Brownlow, "Every airplane with an even number blew up or crashed. It got to the point where people wouldn't even want to fly in the even-numbered airplanes."

46. Historical Report, 91st Strategic Reconnaissance Wing, January 1953, 29, 31, 39, 45, Air Force Historical Research Center, Maxwell AFB. Regarding flying suits, an official report by the Air Force Office of the Surgeon General unequivocally states, "When nylon melts the small globules may sink into the skin if there is no garment between the nylon and the skin. This is the burn which has been reported. However, cotton or wool will burn at this temperature and the combustion which they support is capable of producing a third degree burn after the flash fire which ignited these fabrics already has been extinguished" (Exhibit 73).

47. Historical Report, 91st Strategic Reconnaissance Wing, February 1953, 55–57, Air Force Historical Research Center, Maxwell AFB.

48. Historical Report, 91st Strategic Reconnaissance Wing, March 1953, 22, 35, 47–48, 73, Air Force Historical Research Agency, Maxwell AFB.

49. Historical Report, 91st Strategic Reconnaissance Wing, April 1953, 23, Exhibit 56; May, 1953, 20–21, 55, 71, Exhibit 6; June 1953, 9, 58–59, 83–84, Exhibit 59: All Air Force Historical Research Agency, Maxwell AFB.

50. Historical Report, 91st Strategic Reconnaissance Wing, July 1953, 61–63, 84–85; August 1953, 71; September 1953, 31; October 1953, 5: All Air Force Historical Research Agency, Maxwell AFB.

51. Historical Report, 91st Strategic Reconnaissance Wing, October 1953, 15, Air Force Historical Research Agency, Maxwell AFB. Many years later Lieutenant Colonel (then lieutenant) Jay E. Spaulding reflected on his experiences with the RB-45C: "The design was a 'tween design. Between props and jets. In a lot of ways it was a rehash of WWII aircraft with a new engine that pushed it into a new era that it wasn't completely suited to. I think, however, that it may have set the stage for the U-2 and SR-71. What it lacked was design knowledge of what the crew needed to live and work in the environment it was entering. I doubt that my being in the unit advanced or assisted the future development of anything, but still I am proud to have been a part" (Jay E. Spaulding to author, 20 July 1997).

Chapter Seven

1. Historical Documentation of Major General John D. Stevenson, September 1966, 21, Air Force Historical Research Agency, Maxwell AFB. General David M. Jones, speaking of his superior, duly noted that "With Commander John Stevenson you could go to a Saturday night party with him and have a roaring good time, go home at midnight, and at three o'clock in the morning the son of a gun would ring the bell."

2. Walton S. Moody, *Building a Strategic Air Force* (Washington, D.C.: Air Force History and Museum Program, 1996), 358. According to General Stevenson, "The decision was made in late 1951 that we would go ahead and create a capability within the Air Force, a tactical air nuclear capability. I had a great part in that decision, and I was really sponsoring the plan within the Air Staff, getting it coordinated, overriding the objections and finally getting it approved. The final event which I think was most decisive, and from which there can never be a returning or turning back, was that day that the late General Thomas White, who was then Deputy Chief of Staff/Operations, wrote off and approved the staff study for the creation of this tactical nuclear capability. I was the one who carried it into his office, over the considerable objections of some people within the Air Staff who wanted to send it back to War Plans for another massaging before I got final approval. But from that day forward nothing could have stopped it, after he signed it off" (Historical Documentation of Major General John D. Stevenson, 1966, 9–10, Air Force Historical Research Agency, Maxwell AFB).

3. Jerome V. Martin, "Reforging the Sword: United States Air Force Tactical Forces, Air Power Doctrine, and

National Security Policy, 1945–1958" (PhD diss., Ohio State University, 1988), 167–168; Matthew Evangelista, *Innovation and the Arms Race: How the United States and the Soviet Union Develop New Military Technologies* (Ithaca, NY: Cornell University Press), 1988, 152; Samuel R. Williamson and Steven L. Readen, *The Origins of U.S. Nuclear Strategy, 1945–1953* (New York: St. Martin's Press, 1993), 168.; Hanson W. Baldwin, "The Russians Can Be Stopped in Europe," *Saturday Evening Post* 22, no. 22 (29 November 1952): 101. A popular overview of this entire episode remains E.R. Johnson, "Operation Backbreaker: Cold War Tripwire," *Aviation History* 15, no. 5 (May 2004): 45–52.

4. Gunston, Bill, "North American Tornado," *Aeroplane Monthly 10* (December 1982): 636; History, 47th Bombardment Wing, Light, 1 April to 30 June 1952, 5–7, Air Force Historical Research Agency, Maxwell AFB; Ray L. Bower, "With the B-45s, 1952–1955: A Memoir," July 1995, 3 (copy in possession of the author); Marcelle S. Knaack, *Post-World War II Bombers, 1945–1973* (Washington, D.C.: Office of Air Force History, 1988), 121.

5. The best overview of this important base is Jim Baldwin, *40 Years of RAF Sculthorpe* (Norfolk, UK: Jim Baldwin, 1986.

6. Michael J.F. Bowyer, *Action Stations* (Wellingborough, England: Stephens, 1990), 177–178; A.R. Sorrells, "Salute to an Old Warrior," *Skyline* 16 (Fall 1958): 17; History, 47th Bomb Group, Light, 1 April–30 June 1952, 8, Air Force Historical Research Agency, Maxwell AFB. Another useful overview of B-45s in England is Michael J. F. Bowyer, *Force for Freedom: The USAF in the UK Since 1948* (Somerset: Patrick Stephens, 1994), 84–125.

7. Historical Data, Headquarters, Third Air Force, January–June 1952, Vol. 1, 15–16; History of Headquarters, 49th Air Division, Operations, 5 June 1952–30 September 1952, 12–15; History, 85th Bombardment Squadron, Light, April–30 June 1952, 11–12: All Air Force Historical Research Agency, Maxwell AFB.

8. E-mail from Daryle E. Tripp, 6 November 2002, copy in possession of the author.

9. History of Headquarters, 49th Air Division, Operational, 1 October 1952–31 December 1952, 12–15; History, 47th Bombardment Wing, Light, 1 July–31 December 1952, Chapter 3, Operations and Training (unpaginated). Back home, the Air Force remained ever-eager to wring out as much range and performance from the B-45s as possible. One study noted how settings of 96 percent greatly extended J47 engine life and promoted greater fuel economy and a faster cruising speed. See "Radius of Action of the B-45A-5 Aircraft," History of the Tactical Air Command, 1 July–31 December 1952, Vol. 5, Exhibit 17: All Air Force Historical Research Agency, Maxwell AFB.

10. History of Headquarters, 49th Air Division, 1 October 52 to 31 December 51, 16; History, 47th Bombardment Wing, Light, 1 July–31 December 1952, Chapter 3, "Operations and Training" (unpaginated), Air Force Historical Research Agency, Maxwell AFB; Moody, *Building a Strategic Air Force*, 369.

11. Telex, Lauris Norstad to Thomas White, 2 February 1953, Hoyt S. Vandenberg Papers, Box 87, Manuscript Division, Library of Congress.

12. History of the Tactical Air Command, 1 January–30 June 1953, Vol. 4, 11–12, 32–33; Vol. 5, 17–19, Air Force Historical Research Agency, Maxwell AFB.

13. History of the Third Air Force, USAF, January–June 1953, Vol. 1, 55–56; History of the 84th Bombardment Squadron, Light, 1 January 1953–31 March 1953, 11; Section C: Description of Accident, History of the 85th Bombardment Squadron, Light, 1 January 1953 through 31 March 1953, Appendix A: All Air Force Historical Research Agency, Maxwell AFB. Regarding the flood, Major Joseph Story related the following: "The 47th came to the rescue because

that was really the only organization around that could do anything and pulled that thing out of the fire. Got those people out of there, housed them, fed them — it was enough that the Queen and Duke came up personally to thank Colonel Jones and invite him to Buckingham Palace for dinner, and the Third Air Force was just furious because none of them got invited!"

14. History, 47th Bombardment Wing, Light, 1 January–31 March 1953, 1; History, 49th Air Division Operational, 1 January 1953–30 June 1953, 1–9: Both Air Force Historical Research Agency, Maxwell AFB. Speaking of the incident, General Jones gave this author the following information: "In fact we were just getting ready for a maneuver and so we called a halt to everything and we literally dropped every engine on every airplane on the base, took every engine into the hangar, we got mattresses from all over the base, the Canadian outfit that had F-86s, the same engine, they came down to help us. We opened every engine, examined the wheels, we hand polished every damn blade on every rotor — that's 160 engines — and we have everybody on the base working. We had the cooks and the bakers and everybody else down in the hangar. We had the whole thing laid out on the damn floor, put 'em all back together in five or six days — a fantastic effort, and we never had another major problem. I don't think we *cured* anything, but we never had another problem."

15. Oral History Interview, Major General David M. Jones, 13–14 January, 1987, 76, Air Force Historical Research Agency, Maxwell AFB. Captain Donald Orr told this author he "was on that classic exercise out of Frankfort with, I think, eighteen airplane from three squadrons, and we took off from Ramstein and went north. And I was wondering, 'Why the Hell are we turning east because we were right next to the buffer zone,' and I was surprised that Colonel Jones didn't know what he was doing. Then we turned around and headed back to England and we dropped all this chaff — this was the chaff drop to see how it bothered their GCI and radars. It went routinely and we read the next day how all the chickens were choking on that stuff in the Netherlands and Belgium."

16. History, 47th Bombardment Wing, 1 July through 30 September 1953, 9–11; History of the 47th Bomb Wing, Light, 1 October 1953 through 31 December 1953, 10–13; History, 84th Bombardment Squadron, Light Jet, 1 October 1953 through 31 December 1953, 4, 14: All Air Force Historical Research Agency, Maxwell AFB. Some of these joint missions did not unfold as smoothly as intended. As Major Everett Walker informed this author, "The Air Ministry wanted to test their capability if bombers approached England from the west — they always expected to get attacked from the east. So we took off in about six planes, we didn't file a flight plan, at night, went out over the ocean west of the U.K., then we came in abreast at 30 or 40,000 — and no one intercepted us, period. There was no activity at all. Come to find out, after we landed and got back home, we found that they didn't intend to do anything. They blew the whistle and everybody was having a party, so they didn't bother to go. I never heard the feedback on that, but I imagine there were a few bent ears."

17. Semi-Annual History of the 49th Air Division (Operational), 1 July through 31 December 1953, 6–7, 22; History of the 84th Bombardment Squadron Light, 1 July 1953 through 30 September 1953, Chapter 3, Operations and Training (unpaginated), Air Force Historical Research Center, Maxwell AFB.

18. "U.S. Flight Tests Atom Retaliation," *New York Times*, 22 January 1954, 7; Security Classification of 3AF regulation 24–16, 2 April 1954, History, 49th Air Division, 1 January 1954–30 June 1954, Air Force Historical Research Center, Maxwell AFB.

19. History, 84th Bombardment Squadron, Light Jet, 1

April 1954 through 30 June 1954, 8; History, 49th Air Division, 1 January 1954–30 June 1954, 7–9, Air Force Historical Research Agency, Maxwell AFB.

20. History of the Third Air Force, USAF, January–December 1954, Vol. 1, 48; History, 84th Bombardment Squadron, Light Jet, 1 January 1954 through 31 March 1954, 13,17; History of the 85th Bombardment Squadron, Light, 1 January 1954 through 31 March 1954, 16: All Air Force Historical Research Agency, Maxwell AFB.

21. History, 49th Air Division, 1 July–31 December 1954, 4–10, Air Force Historical Research Agency, Maxwell AFB.

22. "U.S. 49th AD Is Revealed as NATO's Atomic Punch," *American Daily*, 7 December 1954, 1; Anthony Brown, "Mail Man Tours Atom Base," *London Daily Mail*, 14 December 1954, 1. Regarding the secrecy surrounding the 47th at Sculthorpe, Lieutenant Stephen J. Neile summarized it this way: "The British were very appreciative, really, they didn't know exactly what we were doing but they knew it must be damn important or we wouldn't have been there. That's what it amounts to."

23. History of the Third Air Force, January–June 1955, 13, 30, 34; Preamble to the 47th Bombardment Wing L, History by Colonel David M. Jones, History, 47th Bombardment Wing, Light, 1 January through 30 June 1955, (unpaginated). Jones later stated, "We were there for 3 years and I guess that's the best job I ever had.... We had super troops and we had a helluva lot of work to do. We were on maneuvers all the time. It was great" (Oral History Interview, Major General David M. Jones, 13–14 January 1987: All Air Force Historical Research Agency, Maxwell AFB).

24. History of the Third Air Force, January–June 1955, 123–124, Air Force Historical Research Agency, Maxwell AFB; C. M. Lambert, "At the Controls of the B-45," *Flight* (April 1955): 523. Lambert wrote in an earlier essay: "The wing's flying equipment, the North American B-45 Tornado, is a remarkable aircraft. It has a performance and characteristics in many ways resembling those of the Meteor Mk 8 (with the notable exception that it has far better aileron control), yet in its bomber version it has a normal all-up weight of 85,000 lb and a maximum permissible weight of 110,000 lb" (C.M. Lambert, "47th Bombardment Wing [Light]," *Flight* 67 [March 1953]: 390).

25. History of the 84th Bombardment Squadron, Light, 1 July 1955 through 30 September 1955, 7, 11; History of the 84th Bombardment Squadron Light, 1 October 1955 through 31 December 1955, 13; History of the 86th Bombardment Squadron Tactical, 1 October 1955 through 31 December 1955, Chapter 3, "Operations and Training" (unpaginated); History of the 86th Bombardment Squadron Tactical, 1 July 1955 through 30 September 1955, Mission, (unpaginated); Preamble, History, 47th Bomb Wing, Tactical, 1 July–31 December 1955, (unpaginated): All Air Force Historical Research Agency, Maxwell AFB.

26. History of Third Air Force, USAF, January–December 1956, 2; History of the 47th Bombardment Wing, TAC, 1 January–30 June 1956, 17–18, Air Force Historical Research Agency, Maxwell AFB.

27. History, 49th Air Division, 1 January 1956–1 July 1956, 10–13; History, 47th Bomb Wing, TAC, 1 January–30 June, 1956, 37–38, Air Force Historical Research Agency, Maxwell AFB. Sergeant Freeman Cox a special weapons team chief, was the man actually responsible for the change: "The biggest problem we had when we came over there was removing the doors and it took about two hours and forty-five minutes. I came to work one morning — we had had a pretty good windstorm — and I saw some of the B-45s sitting on their tail skids. Well, we got to talking about it and I got a brainstorm that we could load the weapon if it was sitting on its tail skid. We could back it into the bomb bay and set it down — wouldn't have to take the doors off. This was my idea and I submitted it to the operations officer and

about a week later General Holzapple and a number of officers in three staff cars came out unexpectedly — we were still working on the aircraft. He said he was there to see a demonstration of loading. We ordered a weapon and we started trying to load it, to tip the aircraft. Well, we couldn't tip it — ten men couldn't tip it, so I got talking to the crew chief and I asked him if there was any fuel in the back bomb bay. He said no, there wasn't any it in, so we got an aircraft that did have fuel and it took three of us to tip it. We set it down and I believe they started timing me from the time I started backing the weapon into the aircraft and I finished in thirty four minutes — down from two hours and forty-five minutes. So I ended up with a commendation and a promotion out of it!"

28. "U.S. Bomber Crash," *London Times*, 31 January 1956, 8; "Three Dead After Brandon Crash," *Norfolk Eastern Daily Press*, 31 January 1956, 1.

29. History, 47th Bomb Wing, TAC, 1 July 1956 – 31 December 1956, 18, Air Force Historical Research Agency, Maxwell AFB; "U.S. Observer Killed," *Norfolk Eastern Daily Press* July 13, 1956, 1.

30. History of Third Air Force, USAF, January–June 1957, 29; History, 47th Bombardment Wing, TAC, 1 January to 30 June 1957, 12–13, Air Force Historical Research Agency, Maxwell AFB.

31. History, 47th Bomb Wing, TAC, 1 January to 30 June 1957, 16, 25, Air Force Historical Research Agency, Maxwell AFB. It continues: "The award was given for overall improvement in tactical proficiency in all its phases; higher degrees of accuracy in practice bomb dropping, a greater percentage of aircraft in combat ready status, improvement in navigation procedures and practices, communications improvements, faster reaction time during alerts; and a greater efficiency in maintenance activities."

32. History, 47th Bombardment Wing, TAC, 1 January to 30 June 1957, 34, Exhibit 125, Air Force Historical Research Agency, Maxwell AFB; "Four Bail Out as Bomber Crashes in Norfolk," *Norfolk Eastern Daily Press*, 4 June 1957, 1. Speaking of the operating conditions he encountered, Clete Dold informed this author that "Molesworth had a real short runway. The B-45 did not have anti-skid braking and didn't have a drag chute. So you are at the mercy of two big wheels and two brakes — that's it. You had to learn those and use them right! I can remember Riggs and all the chiefs saying, 'Folks, we're going to ride you more about proper breaking techniques than anything else.' And we blew off Molesworth without any problems."

33. History, 84th Bombardment Squadron, Tactical, 1 July 1957 through 31 December 1957, 112–113, 124; History of Third Air Force, USAF, July–December 1957, 37; History, 47th Bombardment Wing, 1 July through 31 December 1957, 10; History of DCS/Materiel, 1 July 1957–31 December 1957, 27: All Air Force Historical Research Agency, Maxwell AFB. According to Major Everett G. Walker, "The B-66 was no improvement. As a matter of fact, if you tried to go over 35,000 feet in a B-66 you had to give up most of your mission. We cruised the B-45 at 47,000 routinely."

34. "Jersey Man Killed in Crash," *New York Times*, 22 September 1957, 31; "Three Feared Dead in Norfolk Plane Crash," *Norfolk Eastern Daily Press*, 20 September 1957, 1.

35. History of Third Air Force, USAF, January–December 1958, Vol. 1, 41; History, 47th Bombardment Wing, TAC, 1 January–30 June 1958, 12, Air Force Historical Research Agency, Maxwell AFB.

36. Alastair Goodrum, "Flame Out!" *Fly Past* 246 (January 2002): 108; "4 Die in Air Collision," *New York Times*, 13 June 1958, 29. Captain Robert Ashby explains why the aircraft crashed: "One night a mechanic got into the B-45 and the story was that he was angry with his girlfriend and he was going to show her something. At any rate he got into the airplane, started it up, taxied out, and took off. For peo-

ple not familiar with the B-45 it has tremendous acceleration and with that you have to put a lot of forward pressure
as you're climbing out to keep the nose down. Apparently
he was not aware of this or he could not handle it fast
enough and the plane went up, stalled, and crashed."

37. "Air Force Retires B-45s to Fire-Fighting Service,"
Air Force Times (Europe), July 22, 1958, 10.

38. Howard M. Fish interview, 43, Air Force Historical
Research Agency, Maxwell AFB. Lieutenant Alan McLaren
enthusiastically seconded these feelings: "I can't think of a
group of people that I would rather be with than the 86th.
But you know, that's not fair because it's the 47th Bomb
Wing. They were the tightest — not that they didn't have
competition between them because they did. You can still
see they razz each other all the time, but they were an extraordinary group of people. They were the most dedicated
people and there's not a doubt in my mind that most of
them were not coming back from their targets. There's not
a guy there that I wouldn't go to the mat for and I feel quite
sure that they are all the same. Partied hard — real hard —
but when it came to the mission, they got in the airplane to
do what had to be done. They were pretty professional, especially about the fact that they were dedicated to do the
job they were assigned to do. It was the best outfit in the
Air Force as far as I was concerned."

Chapter Eight

1. James Jabara, "Korean Air War," *Air Force* 34, no. 10
(October 1951): 60.

2. History, 91st Strategic Reconnaissance Squadron, 1
May 1951–31 May 1951, 16–23, Air Force Historical Research
Agency, Maxwell AFB.

3. Winton R. Close to Thomas S. Powers, 6 June 1951,
B-11651, Box 198, Curtis LeMay Papers, Manuscript Division, Library of Congress. General Ridgway himself had received authority to permit overflights as of late April: "You
are hereby authorized to use the United States Forces assigned to the Far East Command to conduct air reconnaissance of the enemy air bases in Manchuria and the Shantung Peninsula. Such reconnaissance should, if practicable,
be made at high altitude and as surreptitiously as possible"
(JCS to Ridgway, 28 April 1951, Record Group 218, Records
of the Joint Chiefs of Staff, Outgoing Messages, Box 9, Fld.
3, National Archives).

4. Stacey D. Naftel, "RB-45C Overflights in the Far
East," in *Early Cold War Overflights, 1950–1956,* ed. R.
Cargill Hall and Clayton Laurie, 2 vols. (Washington, D.C.:
Office of the Historian, National Reconnaissance Office,
2003), vol. 1, 61. In my interview with Captain Naftel he
elaborated on his predicament in better detail: "About
twenty minutes after we had coasted in, according to the
sources that we were listening to, they sent up about 300
MiGs in the area. We looked ahead and all we could see was
contrails, the sky was just overcast with contrails! We, of
course, were radio-silenced, but our Ferret aircraft that was
monitoring the mission off the coast came in and gave us
the abort code." Naftel apparently forgot to mention that
he and his crew reported a series of lights following them
on the return leg of the mission, although no damage was
incurred. This fact set off alarm bells at FEAF headquarters
and General O.P. Weyland informed Generals LeMay and
Vandenberg that "Air defense in area overflown are excellent
with enemy on 24 hour alert. Good coordination exists between ground and air. The enemy has the capability of intercepting a high speed acft at 40,000 ft. during the hours
of darkness" (Telex, Weyland to LeMay, 8 June 1951, Box
198, Curtis E. LeMay Papers, Manuscript Division, Library
of Congress).

5. The notion of lights tracking a bomber at night sug-

gests all-weather interception capability in Soviet aircraft,
so naturally it received priority consideration by air intelligence. In a letter to General Cabell, Colonel James H. Walsh
described in detail the matter and systematically ruled out
any such craft being encountered on this mission: "We here
at SAC and Colonel Close, our SAC X-RAY A-3 at Tokyo,
believe the crew was seeing things" (James H. Walsh to
Charles P. Cabell, 7 August 1951, Record Group 341, Head
Quarters, U.S. Air Force, Deputy Chief of Staff, Operations, General File, Box 59, National Archives).

6. History, 91st Strategic Reconnaissance Squadron, 1
June 1950–30 June 1951, 35–36; Detachment Reports, 1
June–15 June and 16 June–30 June, 1951. Historical Report,
91st Strategic Reconnaissance Wing, June 1951, 35–36, Exhibits 13 and 14: Both Air Force Historical Research Agency,
Maxwell AFB. Naftel, author of both reports, insisted, "It
is recommended that actual instrument training be stressed
for all pilots. A combat theater is no place to become
proficient in jet instrument flying."

7. He continues: "After the MiGs fighters broke off,
Dusenberry gave me a revised heading into the target area
of Harbin. We were never told exactly what the target contained, and it was some years later that we learned it was
most probably a medical research center where the Communists were conducting medical experiments on civilians and
prisoners-of-war" (Naftel, RB-45C Overflights. In: Hall
and Laurie, *Early Cold War Overflights,* vol. 1, 61–62).

8. Ibid., 63. Regarding his harrowing encounter with
MiGs, Captain Naftel subsequently told this author the following: "You know we did have a wobble gun in the tail.
We flat-ass forgot about the wobble gun! When you've got
somebody shooting at you, you think 'What's that thing
going to do back there — it might shoot off the tail!' In fact
we didn't even think about it." These sentiments about the
RB-45's defenselessness are echoed by Captain John
Mackey, a subsequent detachment commander, on a flight
to Vladivostok: "We were unarmed reconnaissance which
means if ever one of their MiGs approached us and realized
that, he could play around with us all day — fly wing tip to
wing tip, thumb his nose at us — there was nothing we could
do. We did not have any waist gunners or turret gunners.
So we stuck a couple of broom sticks out the tail to pretend
we had a tail turret, so if anybody intercepted us at least they
wouldn't fly right up the tail and blast us."

9. John B. Henry to Thomas S. Powers, July 30, 1951,
B-12481, Curtis E. LeMay Papers, Box 198, Manuscript Division, Library of Congress. It is easy to see why SAC so coveted this target information: "The resultant photographs
were excellent. Radar scope photographs were taken from
an altitude of 41,500 feet on one mission. These photographs were exceptionally clear, free from spoking, and did
not have the milky appearance sometime found at high altitude. The photographs provided a wealth of information
for photo intelligence, and demonstrated the capabilities of
the APQ-24 at altitudes above 35,000 feet" (Detachment
Report 1 July–15 July 1951, Historical Report, 91st Strategic
Reconnaissance Wing, July 1951, Exhibit 8, Air Force Historical Research Agency, Maxwell AFB).

10. History, 91st Strategic Reconnaissance Squadron, 1
July 1951–31 July 1951, 20, 32; Detachment Report, 1 July–15
July 1951, Historical Report, 91st Strategic Reconnaissance
Wing, July 1951, Exhibit 8; also Supplement, 20; Historical Report, 91st Strategic Reconnaissance Wing, August
1951, Exhibit 35: All Air Force Historical Research Center,
Maxwell AFB. No mention is made in the unit history of
Naftel's highly classified CIA flight past Shanghai the previous June, a distance that could only have been accomplished with the help of tanker aircraft. "When we were
first briefed on this proposed mission, I pointed out that we
could not get there and back without aerial refueling. The
briefer replied, 'That's not a problem. We'll get a tanker

over here.' As I had not formally checked out on night re-fueling, I felt that I would need a little practice before committing to the mission." (Naftel, RB-45C Overflights, in *Early Cold War Overflights*, vol. 1, 61). Exhibit 8, cited previously, mentions that the first KB-29 touched down at Yokota on 2 July 1951; it is not known where the craft that refueled Naftel's June mission originated from or where it was based.

11. Naftel, RB-45C Overflights, in *Early Cold War Overflights*, 63–64; Jim G. Lucas, "Few Secrets of North American B-45 Bared," *Columbus Citizen*, 9 August 1951, 1; "B-45 Recon Men Back from Korea," *Air Force Times*, 22 September 1951, 23. As Naftel afterwards told this author, "They thought they were under armed attack, at least that the impression I had looking at them and I think Ed Kendrex probably felt the same way. These guys were jumping off the sides of the ships and just scrambling for cover. No hostile fire — if there was any it was behind us."

12. History, 91st Strategic Reconnaissance Squadron, 1 August 1951–31 August 1951, 17–18, Air Force Historical Research Agency, Maxwell AFB. Hempen's crew is identified by notes (in possession of the author) provided by his navigator, Captain Vance E. Heavilin. These mention a second flight on 28 August 1951, up to the Soviet-held Kurile Islands that is not recorded in any official history.

13. Robert H. Terrill to Thomas S. Power, 16 August 1951, B-12789/1, Curtis E. LeMay Papers Box 182, Manuscript Division, Library of Congress. He continues: "As a result, FEAF in the person of its Director of Reconnaissance has considerably delayed the much-needed photography, and in one case furnished two photographs within the twenty-mile radius, only one of which was valuable for target prediction. I had a show down a few days ago with [General] Charlie Banfill and believe that arrangements made will allow us to complete the remaining photography and obtain the results in the shortest possible time."

14. Robert H. Terrill to Thomas S. Power, 16 August 1951, B-12789/1, Curtis E. LeMay Papers, Box 182, Manuscript Division, Library of Congress. He continues: "As you know FEAF feels strongly about its D-Day medium bomber bombing forces. Not all of the bitterness which was apparent when you were here has gone as yet."

15. Telex, Weyland to LeMay, 15 August 1951, B-12642; Telex, LeMay to Weyland 23 August 1951, B-12821/2, Curtis E. LeMay Papers, Box 198, Manuscript Division, Library of Congress.

16. Curtis E. LeMay to Hoyt S. Vandenberg, 3 August 1951, B-12453/5, Curtis E. LeMay Papers, Box 198, Manuscript Division, Library of Congress.

17. History, 91st Strategic Reconnaissance Squadron, 1 August 1951–31 August 1951, 33; Historical Report, 91st Strategic Reconnaissance Wing, August 1951, Exhibit 34: Both Air Force Historical Research Agency, Maxwell AFB.

18. History, 91st Strategic Reconnaissance Squadron, 1 September 1951–30 September 1951, 39, Supplement, 22–23; Detachment Report, 1 September–15 September, 1951; Historical Report, 91st Strategic Reconnaissance Wing, September 1951, Exhibit, 31: Both Air Force Historical Research Agency, Maxwell AFB.

19. Pilot's Narrative, Historical Report, 91st Strategic Reconnaissance Wing, October 1951, Exhibit, 51; Alvan Barrett to author, July 23, 1997 (copy in possession of author).

20. History, 91st Strategic Reconnaissance Squadron, 1 October 1951–31 October 1951, 30, 38–39; Detachment Report 15 October–30 October 1951, Historical Report, 91st Strategic Reconnaissance Wing, October 1951, 45, Exhibit 50, Air Force Historical Research Agency, Maxwell AFB. On one routine mission, Lieutenant Barrett recalls trouble reading his altimeter, which was poorly marked for increments of 10,000 feet: "When we came back in we leveled out at the top of the cloud base again and the Tokyo radar

could not find us — we didn't have the sophisticated transponders we have today. And finally it dawned on us that we had leveled out 10,000 feet too high — that is a humongous mistake, because if you made it at the other end you'd be in the dirt. So we realized because of the altimeter and the combination of the instrument not making it clear to you what altitude you were at, and the fact that the base of the clouds had risen 10,000 feet while you were gone — and that's common in the afternoon, cloud bases tend to rise. You heard the expression, Oh, s____! This is where you have to add five 'Atta Boys!' to make up for it. We finally got picked up by the radar and descended to a lower altitude, and when we got debriefed we didn't mention it to the debriefer."

21. History, 91st Strategic Reconnaissance Squadron, 1 November 1951–30 November 1951, 32; Detachment Report 1 November–15 November 1951, Historical Report, 91st Strategic Reconnaissance Wing, November 1951, Exhibit 29: Both Air Force Historical Research Agency, Maxwell AFB. Wilhelm continues: "It is the opinion of this detachment that the RB-45s assigned to this theater of operations are not being utilized are of no further use to this command unless they are assigned operational combat targets that require methods and results that only the RB-45 is capable of acquiring."

22. History, 91st Strategic Reconnaissance Squadron, 1 December 1951–31 December 1951, 31; Detachment Report, 1 December–15 December 1951, Historical Report, 91st Strategic Reconnaissance Wing, December 1951, Exhibit 21: Both Air Force Historical Research Agency, Maxwell AFB.

23. Detachment Report, 16 December — 31 December 1951, Historical Report, 91st Strategic Reconnaissance Wing, January 1952, Exhibit 34, Air Force Historical Research Agency, Maxwell AFB. According to Schamber, "We were taking pictures trying to get photo strips and the winds were so high, it was extremely hard to fly a straight line because they'd keep shifting all the time — and we'd get a 150-knot wind, which was nothing unusual."

24. Detachment Report, 1 January–15 January 1952, Historical Report, 91st Strategic Reconnaissance Wing, January 1952, Exhibit 35, Air Force Historical Research Agency, Maxwell AFB. Schamber continues: "If evasive action is taken and the intercepting aircraft prove to be friendly, the chase has probably carried the photo ship out of practical range of the target. The decision to stay on the photo run or break off and try to escape interception is of course dependent on the area of operation and the presumed odds as to whether the aircraft are friendly or not."

25. History, 91st Strategic Reconnaissance Wing, 1 January–31 January 1952, 5–6, 31–31; Detachment Report, 16 Jan–31 Jan, 1952, Historical Report, 91st Strategic Reconnaissance Wing, January 1952, Exhibit 36: Both Air Force Historical Research Agency, Maxwell AFB.

26. History, 91st Strategic Reconnaissance Wing, 1 February–28 February 1952, 31–32; Detachment Reports, 1 February–15 February and 16 February–29 February 1952, Historical Report, 91st Strategic Reconnaissance Wing, Exhibits 37, 40, 41, Air Force Historical Research Agency, Maxwell AFB.

27. A.W. Jessup, "MiG-15 Dims USAF's A-Bomb Hopes," *Aviation Week* 56 (4 February 1952): 16. The writer states, "Take the RB-45 experience for example; it ran into MiGs above 35,000 ft. and tried diving away to pick up speed. It hits Mach in less than 4,000 feet and had to level off. For the next 150 mi., the MiGs kept 'flying circles' around it. While the MiGs didn't shoot it down, they proved that the MiG at least has no difficulty keeping up with a jet bomber. Granting that the RB-45 is rated below Mach .85, the ease with which the MiG maneuvered leads to the conclusion that it can put on about the same performance against a Mach .85 aircraft."

28. History, 91st Strategic Reconnaissance Squadron, 1 March 1952–31 March 1952, 35, Air Force Historical Research Agency, Maxwell AFB: "Recent intelligence reports indicate the possible existence of a new type MIG with airborne radar installed giving it all-weather day and night potential. Until such opposition is proven effective, night photo is the only method available to obtain necessary intelligence and avoid prohibitive losses if not the complete annihilation of any reconnaissance force sent deep into enemy territory."

29. Ibid., 13; Detachment Report, 15 March–1 April 1952, History, 91st Strategic Reconnaissance Wing, March 1952, Exhibit 27, Air Force Historical Research Agency, Maxwell AFB; "RB-45 Crew Sets Pace in Far Eastern Flying," *Recon Recorder*, 29 May 1952. Apparently Broughton flew a Top Secret mission that was not recorded. According to Calvin Pace, "Tom Broughton and his crew flew this mission and they went up into Russia. The reason I know that they did this is that, as a B-52 crew member, in our target studies, I saw some of the film—it was film that he had taken."

30. History, 91st Strategic Reconnaissance Squadron, 1 April 1952–30 April 1952, 34–35; Detachment Report, 1 April–30 April 1952, Historical Report, 91st Strategic Reconnaissance Wing, April 1952, Exhibit 29, 30: Both Air Force Historical Research Agency, Maxwell AFB.

31. Thomas E. Broughton to Lewis E Lyle, 10 May 1952, Historical Report, 91st Strategic Reconnaissance Wing, May 1952, Exhibit 19, Air Force Historical Research Agency, Maxwell AFB. He then adds as follows: "Such targets as small rail and road bridges in mountainous terrain provide very little if any radar return."

32. History, 91st Strategic Reconnaissance Squadron, 1 May 1952–31 May 1952, 14–18, Supplement, 14; Historical Report, 91st Strategic Reconnaissance Wing, May 1952, Exhibits, 18, 19, 21, Air Force Historical Research Agency, Maxwell AFB. Despite being joined to the 91st SRS, Broughton remained unhappy as to the nature of mission planning. "The people under whom we work in this command are not equipped to direct B-45 operations and of necessity must lean heavily upon our crews for technical assistance in mission planning. In the past mission scheduling and planning was done by individual crews so that in one case our Korean mosaic project was not completed on time and upon investigation it was determined that over half the project had been flown two times, clearly a case of non-coordination between crews. In another instance, a staff officer here envisioned an RB-45 mission going to 50,000 feet over a Korean target, until I pointed out how impossible that was. He expressed real concern because he had been led to believe this was possible by previous crews in the detachment" (Exhibit 19).

33. According to a press release, the RB-45C was in Japan "for testing and evaluation" ("B-45 Crashes in Japan," *New York Times*, 6 June 1952, 2).

34. History, 91st Strategic Reconnaissance Squadron, 1 June 1952–30 June 1952, 38; Detachment Report, 1 June 1952–30 June 1952, Historical Report, 91st Strategic Reconnaissance Wing, June 1952, 35–37, Exhibit 21: Both Air Force Historical Research Agency, Maxwell AFB.

35. Detachment Report, 1 July 1952–13 August 1952, Historical Report, 91st Strategic Reconnaissance Wing, August 1952, Exhibit 33, Air Force Historical Research Agency, Maxwell AFB. Curiously, General LeMay informed FEAF as follows: "In considering the mission assigned this comd and the relatively small number of B-45 type acft assigned, it is not feasible for me to send you additional such aircraft or to replace the one recently lost to you in an opnl acdt" (Telex, Curtis E. LeMay to Wiley D. Ganey, 9 August 1952, Curtis E. LeMay Papers, Box 65, FEAF Fld 2, Manuscript Division, Library of Congress).

36. Historical Report, 91st Strategic Reconnaissance Wing, August 1952, 41; "Jet Flies Pacific, Alaska to Japan," *New York Times*, 8 August 1953, 7. The Air Force withheld information about Carrington's flight for a year before releasing it to the press. As detachment commander, Mackey also instituted a change in flying tactics: "We began to coordinate with the weather. If the weather had a 10,000 foot overcast, that's great—we'd fly in at 10,000, take a picture, and of course they'd scramble and we'd just duck into the clouds. In fact our ground control had such a range and everything that they would tell us when the MiGs were taking off, what their heading was, what altitude they were, and we would just usually make another two or three more passes and go home."

37. Historical Report, 91st Strategic Reconnaissance Wing, July 1952, 41, Exhibit 49, Air Force Historical Research Agency, Maxwell AFB; "Citation to Accompany the Award of the Distinguished Flying Cross to William J. Kristen, Jr." (copy in possession of author).

38. James F. Brady, Reconnaissance Plan for the RB-45, undated, History, FEAF Bomber Command, July–December 1952, Vol. II, supporting documents, Air Force Historical Research Agency, Maxwell AFB. The author continues: "Once enemy fighters (MiG) have been brought within visual range by the GCI net, it is a foregone conclusion that the RB-45 will be in difficulty. Evasion tactics take the plane to the deck under full power until Mach speed (.76) is reached. Then power is held only sufficient to maintain that critical speed. Fuel consumption is excessive and time remaining for return to base is reduced to danger point. But this method is the only possible chance for evading the much faster hostile fighters who have under these conditions an even smaller fuel reserve."

39. The RB-45Cs usually flew in cooperation with the Navy offshore, although with oftentimes unexpected consequences. As Kristen relates, "One flight we were in the clouds, we went over at 25,000 usually, and radar told us they were not passing it to the fleet—we'd identify to them. I looked down through a hole and some guy saw us. And to see four carriers and twelve escort vessels turn simultaneously—oh, what a sight! *Whitewater*! They were leaning over. We didn't get any film of it, of course we should have. It was a beautiful sight, then of course he cleared us."

40. Detachment History 1 August 1952–31 August 1952, Historical Report, 91st Strategic Reconnaissance Wing, September 1952, Exhibit 92; History, 91st Strategic Reconnaissance Squadron, 1 August 1951–31 August 1952, 13–32; Detachment History, 1 July 1952–13 August 1952, Historical Report, 91st Strategic Reconnaissance Wing, August 1952, Exhibit 33: All Air Force Historical Research Agency, Maxwell AFB.

41. Captain Kristen continues: "That's the night we oxygenated the whole crew. We went on oxygen, 100 percent, about a half hour before we pre-flighted, carried around the bottles, pre-flighted at 100 percent with red lenses, got in the airplane at 100 percent, and took the red lenses off. We got over there, I had my cockpit lights on very, very dim, yet they were bright to me. I could look down with starlight and see the ground, see trails, see woods and villages. Pitch black, just star light. When we got down below the bomb line, the 38th, I dropped to 35,000 feet, turned off my oxygen, bled the mask, held some in my lungs, and put a cigarette in my mouth, closed one eye and lighted it. The first puff and the lights went out in the airplane—one puff of a cigarette and I lost my night vision. One puff!"

42. History, 91st Strategic Reconnaissance Squadron, 1 September–30 September 1952, 13–27; Detachment Report, 1 September 1952–30 September 1952, Historical Report, 91st Strategic Reconnaissance Wing, October 1952, Exhibit 51: Both Air Force Historical Research Agency, Maxwell AFB.

43. History, 91st Strategic Reconnaissance Squadron, 1 October 1952–31 October 1952, 14–27; Detachment Report, 1 October 1951–31 October 1952, Historical Report, 91st Strategic Reconnaissance Wing, November 1952, Exhibit 13: Both Air Force Historical Research Agency, Maxwell AFB. Despite the secrecy attending these operations, the government apparently saw fit to make them known to the press two years earlier: "Swift United States jet bombers, in the first appearance of such aircraft in any war, are being used to take long distance pictures of Communist airfields and other bases in Manchuria" ("Jet Bombers in Korea," *New York Times*, 15 April 1951, 3).

44. Quoted from Wolfgang W.E. Samuel, *I Always Wanted to Fly: America's Cold War Airmen* (Jackson: University Press of Mississippi, 2001), 163. Sometimes there was a humorous side to the results gathered from the Kuriles. As Major Fred Sager, now chief of the photo intelligence branch, told the author, "An RB-45 was coming back from a mission upon Sahkalin and there was this strange thing we saw on this island, it looked like a ski launch site, like the V-1s in Normandy during the Second World War except that it was snow covered. And we just got a bare glimpse of it, we sent an RF-80 up later to get it and it showed the same thing, totally snow covered. Later in the spring, after the snow disappeared, we sent an RB-45 back up and the thing had totally disappeared. I think what may have happened — some Russian soldiers up there may have built a little ski lift for themselves during the winter and they tore it down in the summer. But we were also concerned about it — a buzz bomb launching site! But it turned out to be nothing."

45. History, 91st Strategic Reconnaissance Squadron, 1 November 1952–30 November 1952, 13–24; Detachment History, 1 November 1952–30 November 1952, Historical Report, 91st Strategic Reconnaissance Wing, December 1952, Exhibit 41: Both Air Force Historical Research Agency, Maxwell AFB; Howard S. Myers, "Spy Sky: The Life and Times of the North American RB-45C," *Air Classics* 34, no. 3 (1998): 22.

46. Howard S. Myers, "RB-45C Overflight Operations During the Korean War," in Hall and Laurie, *Early Cold War Overflights*, vol. 1, 101; History, 91st Strategic Reconnaissance Squadron, 1 December–31 December 1952, 25; Detachment Report, 1 December 1952–31 December 1952, Historical Report, 91st Strategic Reconnaissance Wing, January 1953, Exhibit 54: Both Air Force Historical Research Agency, Maxwell AFB. Regarding the overflights, Colonel Myers informed the author that he "would say that they were principally strategic reconnaissance missions and there was no intent on the part of the United States to even consider bombing any of those targets at that time, but this was to update the files so that if we ever needed to we had the information."

47. Telex, LeMay to Twining, 23 January 1953; Twining to LeMay, 19 February 1953: Both Curtis E. LeMay Papers, Box 203, Manuscript Division, Library of Congress.

48. History, 91st Strategic Reconnaissance Squadron, 1 January–31 January 1953, 14–29; Detachment Report, 1 January 1952–31 January 1952, Historical Report, 91st Strategic Reconnaissance Wing, February 1952, Exhibit 46: Both Air Force Historical Research Agency, Maxwell AFB; Howard S. Myers, "Midnight Mission: Secret Spy Flights over Korea in the All Black North American RB-45 Tornado!" *Air Power* 23 (July 1993): 44. He continues: "I must add, there is nothing quite as startling when, flying along at 35,000 feet in complete darkness with running lights off and cockpit instruments dimmed, suddenly your whole world is lit up by 800,000,000 candlepower searchlights. To say the least, it's a bit unnerving and requires some quick reaction to keep one's mental gyros from tumbling."

49. History, 91st Strategic Reconnaissance Squadron, 1 February to 28 February 1953, 12–30, Supplement, 15; De-

tachment Report, 1 February 1953–28 February 1953, Historical Report, 91st Strategic Reconnaissance Wing, March 1953, Exhibit 67: Both Air Force Historical Research Center, Maxwell AFB; Myers' account quoted from Samuel, *I Always Wanted to Fly*, 164. Sometimes, the Air Force and Navy would actually cooperate. As Captain Kristen recalled, "The North Koreans or Russians had a radar station off of Wonsan and the navy tried to bomb it out and couldn't. A couple of times we went over there and Joe called and said, 'Kris, I've got a baseball on the scope and it's always in the same spot, right north of Wonsan on that mountain.' 'Okay, Joe, *plot* it.' So he plotted it in from the islands, we gave it to Task Force Jehovah, which was the four carriers, and they went in and *they bombed it out of existence*. So they were no longer reporting in on us."

50. Detachment Report 16 March 1953, Historical Report, 91st Strategic Reconnaissance Wing, March 1953, Exhibit 68, Air Force Historical Research Center, Maxwell AFB. The arrival of armed RB-45s was a welcome development for, in the words of Captain Myers, "We did not have a tailgunner. The tail gun position was not utilized on these aircraft, even though we had two fixed guns back there. They were actually fixed and the pilot had a switch so he could fire these guns, but of course that isn't much of a defense. So we were pretty near defenseless, I would say."

51. History, 91st Strategic Reconnaissance Squadron, 1 March 1953–31 March 1953, 13–35; Detachment Report, 1 March 1953–31 March 1953, Historical Report, 91st Strategic Reconnaissance Wing, April 1953, Exhibit 42, Air Force Historical Research Agency, Maxwell AFB; Howard S. Myers, "We Flew Tornados," *Spyplanes: Air Classics Special Edition* 2 (1988): 31.

52. TDY Mission Report, 23 April 1953, Historical Report, 91st Strategic Reconnaissance Wing, April 1953, Exhibit 45; Detachment Report, 1 April 1953–30 April 1953, Historical Report, 91st Strategic Reconnaissance Wing, May 1953, Exhibit 28: Both Air Force Historical Research Agency, Maxwell AFB.

53. Detachment Report, 1 April 1953–30 April 1953, Historical Report, 91st Strategic Reconnaissance Wing, May 1953, 47, Exhibit 28; History, 91st Strategic Reconnaissance Squadron, 1 April–30 April 1953, Supplement, 15–16: Both Air Force Historical Research Agency, Maxwell AFB.

54. Veron Scott, "My Tour in the Far East," 9–10 (copy in possession of the author).

55. History, 91st Strategic Reconnaissance Squadron, 1 May–31 May 1953, Supplement, 16–17; Detachment Report, 1 May 1953–31 May 1953, Historical Report, 91st Strategic Reconnaissance Wing, June 1953, Exhibit 29: Both Air Force Historical Research Agency, Maxwell AFB.

56. Detachment Report 1 June 1953–30 June 1953, Historical Report, 91st Strategic Reconnaissance Wing, July 1953, Exhibit 34, Air Force Historical Research Agency, Maxwell AFB.

57. Detachment Report 1 July 1953–31 July 1953, Historical Report, 91st Strategic Reconnaissance Wing, August 1953, Exhibit 17, Air Force Historical Research Agency, Maxwell AFB.

58. Fredriksen, "Detachment 2 Goes to War," 286; FEAF Report on Korea, Vol. 2, 43, Air Force Historical Research Agency, Maxwell AFB. One noted Air Force historian dismisses the Tornado as a useful reconnaissance vehicle: "The straight-winged B-45 proved incapable of surviving the Korean air war environment of 1950–1953, when confronted by early MiG-15 sweptwing interceptors. The mistake here, aside from obviously underestimating potential enemy capabilities, was overlooking once again the old truth that an airplane is a totally integrated system; merely adding turbojets to an outmoded aerodynamic configuration did not make an acceptable jet bomber or reconnaissance aircraft" (Richard P. Hallion, "Girding for War:

Perspectives in Research, Development, Acquisition, and the Decision-Making Environment of the 1980s," *Air University Review* 37, no. 6 [September–October 1986]: 54–55). The author disagrees with this assessment. Had the Tornado's strategic overflights even been *attempted* by propeller-driven RB-29s and RB-50s, the toll in men and machines would have been prohibitive, and the practice would have most likely ceased altogether. The fact that only one RB-45C was lost to MiGs in two-and-a-half years of intense reconnaissance activity speaks volumes as to its ability to survive in a combat environment. In sum, the Tornado may have been a stop-gap effort at best, but no viable alternatives were available until the arrival of RB-47s that, in any case, LeMay would have forbidden over Northeast Asia.

59. Perhaps the Tornado's contributions are best summarized not by academics far removed from events being pondered but by a squadron historian whose judgment is contemporaneous with the occurrences in question: "The RB-45C Type aircraft has rendered valuable support in combat operations in the Korean Campaign. This reconnaissance type aircraft has proven to be very effective, particularly in sensitive areas in which Soviet MiG-15 type aircraft operate. It has been successful for procuring aerial reconnaissance of the Yalu River areas adjacent to Manchuria, operating at an altitude up to 42,000 feet. This type of reconnaissance could not have been procured by a lone B-29 operating in the same area. Over the past six months, the RB-45 type aircraft has been successful in evading destruction from enemy aircraft (MiG-15s) due to its maneuverability at altitude, and only in one instance has it been necessary to release the 1,125 gallon tip tanks to evade possible destruction. The RB-45 type aircraft has its limitations under combat operations in the Far East. It requires an ideal runway (smooth and 8,000 feet long when using full tip tanks), special support for the aircraft general, and APQ-24 radar, which is peculiar to the Korean theater of operations. The RB-45 has limited range as far as strategic reconnaissance is concerned, however, this problem can be solved with the use of air refueling. Only the lack of additional aircraft and crews has prevented the Detachment from accepting a greater share of the workload in the Korean theater" (Historical Report, 91st Strategic Reconnaissance Wing, June 1951, 45–46, Air Force Historical Research Agency, Maxwell AFB).

60. Otto P. Weyland interview, 14, Air Force Historical Research Center, Maxwell AFB.

Chapter Nine

1. Ralph A. Cochrane to Sir William Elliot, July 25, 1951, Nathan F. Twining Papers, Box 122, Top Secret File 127, Manuscript Division, Library of Congress.

2. "Jet Bombers Across the Atlantic," *The Aeroplane* 80, no. 2063 (2 February 1951): 130. Nor were American tankers spared the writer's wrath: "Although boom-equipped KB-29s now appear to be in wide-scale service, it is still hard to see how boom equipment can be used in conditions of poor visibility, in the same way as comparable British equipment." Ironically, it took RAF Flight Commander John Crampton to demonstrate to his countrymen just how well the American refueling system performed under duress. However, the writer correctly predicted that the Canberra would soon become the first jet to cross the Atlantic nonstop, for it occurred on 21 February 1951, six weeks after the Tornados arrival in the UK.

3. Historical Report, 91st Strategic Reconnaissance Wing, January 1951, 21, 30–31, Air Force Historical Research Agency, Maxwell AFB. The four Tornados arriving first were 48-019, 48-021, 48-023, and 48-026. The contributions to the unheralded tankers in subsequent RB-45C

operations cannot be understated. In the words of Maury Seitz, "The tanker and the RB-45 were closely tied, because without the tanker the '45 was just another short-range aircraft. And we could have never done the reconnaissance work we did without the tanker" (Maury Seitz Interview by R. Cargill Hall, 23 December 1997, 22 [copy in possession of the author]).

4. Historical Report, 91st Strategic Reconnaissance Wing, February 1951, 25–27, Air Force Historical Research Agency, Maxwell AFB. Captain C.N. "Jack" Price relayed this anecdote about his stopover at Goose: "Trying to get the airplane started in that cold weather is one of the things we were testing. Colonel Lyle couldn't get the thing started. And I said, 'Colonel, I think we're blowing out our igniters with that fuel. It's not vaporizing, it's just solid fuel that's blowing out the igniters. So let's try running it up to sixty percent and then turn on the igniters. Have everything else in a start position.' I said we'll probably get a big ball of flame out the back but I think it will get started. And sure enough we had a big ball of flame but we got the four of them started and off we went. We got to Keflavik and we're waiting and waiting, and we finally got a message sent back to see 'where is everybody?' and they said 'We can't get the engines started!' So I told them how to start the engines and they started coming in."

5. Historical Report, 91st Strategic Reconnaissance Wing, March 1951, 41–43, Exhibit 66, Air Force Historical Research Agency, Maxwell AFB.

6. Historical Report, 91st Strategic Reconnaissance Wing, April 1951, 37–41, Exhibit 66, Air Force Historical Research Agency, Maxwell AFB.

7. Historical Report, 91st Strategic Reconnaissance Wing, May 1951, 31–35, Exhibits, 33, 34, 35; Broemmelsick's flight is in Mackay Trophy Nomination, Historical Report, 91st Strategic Reconnaissance Wing, January 1952, Exhibit 44: Both Air Force Historical Research Agency, Maxwell AFB.

8. Historical Report, 91st Strategic Reconnaissance Wing, June 1951, 32–37, Exhibits 23, 27, Air Force Historical Research Agency, Maxwell AFB.

9. Historical Report, 91st Strategic Reconnaissance Wing, July 1951, 33–36, Exhibits 9, 10, 11, 19, Air Force Historical Research Agency, Maxwell AFB.

10. "How to Prevent an Accident," *Strategic Air Command Combat Crew* 2, no. 7 (January 1952): 5–6; "U.S. Plane Crashes in Labrador," *New York Times*, 6 August 1951, 5. The latter cryptically announces the loss of a "four-engine jet bomber" without describing it as an RB-45 reconnaissance plane. Two weeks after this incident, Captain Hal Austin was letting down into Goose Bay and recalled the following: "I was right over the spot where a friend of mine had crashed only two weeks earlier and my number three engine seized. It flipped us over. I know we were past ninety degrees. It scared the Hell out of me. I rammed the power back up and managed to roll it level. My navigator sitting in the nose of the aircraft, and not knowing what was happening, called over the intercom, 'You son of a bitch, what are you doing up there?' I got her down safely but it was difficult. For a moment, when the aircraft went out of control, I thought I was going to join my friend" (Quoted in Wolfgang W.E. Stephen, *I Always Wanted to Fly: America's Cold War Airmen* [Jackson: University Press of Mississippi, 2001], 157).

11. Historical Report, 91st Strategic Reconnaissance Wing, August 1951, 28–31, Exhibits, 36, 37–42, Air Force Historical Research Agency, Maxwell AFB.

12. Historical Report, 91st Strategic Reconnaissance Wing, September 1951, 33–42, Exhibits 35–39, Air Force Historical Research Agency, Maxwell AFB.

13. Historical Report, 91st Strategic Reconnaissance Wing, October 1951, 34–40, Exhibit 61, Air Force Historical Research Agency, Maxwell AFB.

14. Historical Report, 91st Strategic Reconnaissance Wing, November 1951, 23, 34–39, Exhibits 31–37, Air Force Historical Research Agency, Maxwell AFB.

15. Historical Report, 91st Strategic Reconnaissance Wing, December 1951, 39–45, Exhibits 14–19, Air Force Historical Research Agency, Maxwell AFB.

16. Historical Report, 91st Strategic Reconnaissance Wing, February 1952, 45–47; History of Detachment I, Strategic Reconnaissance Wing for Period 1 February 1952–29 February 1952 (also 3), Air Force Historical Research Agency, Maxwell AFB.

17. Historical Report, 91st Strategic Reconnaissance Wing, March 1952, 36–37, 39–43, Exhibits 41, 42, Air Force Historical Research Agency, Maxwell AFB. Had Detachment I conducted clandestine overflights of Warsaw Pact territory while in England? This cannot be positively ascertained from existing documents, but Captain Howard S. Myers admitted to performing what sounds suspiciously like a penetration mission with RAF crew members in 1952. He stated: "I think once you go over the border at all, that's a penetration. It may not be what you classify as deep. But I think the units before us did probably more deep penetrations, so called deep penetrations than we did. We stayed in the peripheral areas as opposed to a deep, deep, deep penetration. But I would classify what we did as moderately deep" (Howard S. Myers interview with Don Welzenbach, courtesy of Paul Lashmar).

18. Earl Huggins Narrative, 1 December 1995, 3 (copy in possession of the author). Captain Grant Angelus also saw this accident and related the following to the author: "I was in the pattern right behind him, and he came in and they had a snow bank, probably as high as this building at the end of the runway. And he came in and wiped his gear out on that snowbank, landed and slid halfway down the runway on his belly. I had to circle for about half an hour until they got the runway cleared."

19. Historical Report, 91st Strategic Reconnaissance Wing, March 1952, 43–45; History of Detachment 3, 91st Strategic Reconnaissance Wing, for Period 1 March 1952–31 March 1952, 2, Air Force Historical Research Agency, Maxwell AFB.

20. Historical Report, 91st Strategic Reconnaissance Wing, April 1952, 44–46; Supplement, Historical Report, 91st Strategic Reconnaissance Wing, May 1952, Air Force Historical Research Agency, Maxwell AFB.

21. Final Mission Report, 16 May 1952, Historical Report, 91st Strategic Reconnaissance Wing, April 1952, Exhibit 31, Air Force Historical Research Agency, Maxwell AFB.

22. Walter J. Boyne, The Early Overflights," *Air Force Magazine* 84, no. 6 (June 2001): 60–61; R. Cargill Hall, "The Truth About Overflights," *MHQ* 9, no. 3 (Spring 1997): 25–26; Charles P. Hollstein, "Increasing the Capability of Aerial Reconnaissance" (April 1953), 4, Study at the Fairchild Research Information Center, Air University Archives, Maxwell AFB. Hollstein further elaborated on the problem: "Air Defense experts informed the class that the best defense consisted of striking enemy long range bombers on their home bases — yet we do not know the location of such fields inside Russia proper according to the lecturers furnished from Intelligence of the Air Staff. We are further advised by authorities on the Air Offensive that the proper offensive strategy is to strike at the industrial capital of the USSR, of which we know little enough."

23. Duncan Campbell, *The Unsinkable Aircraft Carrier: American Military Power in Britain* (London: Michael Joseph, 1984), 127.

24. Tony Buttler, "Turbojets for Stalin: Some Facts Behind the Sale of British Jet Engines to Russia," *Air Enthusiast* 94 (July/August 2001): 73–77; Quote from Yefim Gordon and Vladimir Rigmant, *MiG-15: Design, Development,*

and Korean War Combat History (Osceola, WI: Motorbooks, 1993), 8.

25. Boyne, "Early Overflights," 63.

26. Paul Lashmar, *Spy Flights of the Cold War* (Annapolis: Naval Institute Press, 1996), 66–68; John Crampton, "RB-45 Operations," in Royal Air Force Historical Society, *Air Intelligence Symposium*. Bracknell Paper No. 7 (1997), 118. Over the course of many years, historian Roy Braybrook mentions that he heard Crampton mention the Tornado only twice in passing: "One was that it had the finest cabin conditioning he had ever encountered. They did the Tornado conversion at Barksdale, Louisiana, with ambients off the clock. A shirt-sleeve operation was therefore essential, although RAF dress regulations insisted that aircrew should always dress on the assumption that the hood would blow off at altitude" (Roy Braybrook, "Let's Hear It for the Hairy Apes," *Air International* 38 [January 1990]: 26).

27. Robert S. Hopkins, III, "U.S. Strategic Aerial Reconnaissance and the Cold War, 1945–1961" (PhD diss., University of Virginia, 1998), 211–212; Ralph A. Cochrane to William Elliot, July 25, 1951, Nathan F. Twining Papers, Box 122, Top Secret File 127, Manuscript Division, Library of Congress; Crampton, "RB-45 Operations," 119. Captain C.N. Rice was one of the pilots who trained the British: "After I came back from the instrument pilot instructor's school at Moody I had not flown the B-45 for 45 days, so I was not current and I had to have a check ride. Crampton, we had made him an IP so he could check other people out if they needed to, he gave me my check ride — and then while we were up I checked him out on air refueling on the same flight."

28. Ralph A. Cochrane to William Elliot, July 25, 1951, Nathan F. Twining Papers, Box 122, Top Secret File 127, Library of Congress; Diary No. 3, 27 September 1951, Curtis E. LeMay Papers, Box B103: Both Manuscript Division, Library of Congress; Lashmar, *Spy Flights*, 70–71; Winston Churchill to Secretary of State for Air, 24 February 1952, in *Early Cold War Overflights, 1950–1956*, ed. R. Cargill Hall and Clayton D. Laurie, 2 vols. (Washington, D.C.: Office of the Historian, National Reconnaissance Office, 2003), vol. 2, 448.

29. Crampton, "RB-45 Operations," 119–120; Sanders quote from Lashmar, *Spy Flights*, 72. Marion C. Mixon subsequently stated, "As for my role in this extremely sensitive and highly classified operation, I was in charge of the planned overflights of the Soviet Union as far as SAC was concerned. To a limited degree I was involved in the mission planning and accompanied Crampton and Sanders to bomber command at High Wycombe near London to sit in on their briefings" (Quoted in Samuel, *I Always Wanted to Fly*, 184).

30. Crampton, "RB-45 Operations," 120; William E. Burrows, *By Any Means Necessary: America's Secret Air War in the Cold War* (New York: Farrar, Straus, and Giroux, 2001), 132–133; Robert Jackson, *High Cold War: Strategic Air Reconnaissance and the Electronic Intelligence War* (Newbury Park, CA: Haynes North American, 1998), 52. Apparently, the Americans were partly responsible for the mission plan. As Captain C.N. Rice notes, "They sent me down to 7th Air Division headquarters to work on flight plans for penetration with British pilots. So I stayed down there for about 30 days and drew up all of these plans and then I briefed the people. I said, 'Now this is tricky, you've got be careful, you got to watch everything.' I was thinking, 'I'm glad it's them, not me!'"

31. Burrows, *By Any Means Possible*, 133–134; Jackson, *High Cold War*, 51–52; Lashmar, *Spy Flights*, 72–74; Norman Polmar, *Spyplane: The U-2 History Declassified* (Osceola, WI.: MBI, 2001), 12. Intelligence historian R. Cargill Hall evaluates the prime minister's contributions this way: "In approving the mission, Churchill took a breathtaking

political risk.... If any of the RB-45Cs had been brought down, the resulting outcry would have led to Churchill's unseating as prime minister. But balanced against this was the need of Western intelligence to acquire radar-scope photographs of specific military installation" (Hall, "The Truth about Overflights," 29). Years later Seitz contacted the British commander: "For all these years I had felt that I had been a part of a history-making flight," he declared. "I saw the '45 turn East after refueling that night and there was only one place he could be going!" (Maury Seitz to John Crampton, 29 January 1999 [copy in the author's possession]).

32. Lashmar, *Spy Flights*, 74–75; Burrows, *By Any Means Possible*, 134–135; Crampton, "RB-45 Operations," 122. He continues: "At Binbrook I quickly settled into the squadron commander's chair and rather less comfortably into the pilot's seat of the Canberra which seemed very small after the RB-45C, not unlike a Ford Escort after a stretched Cadillac."

33. Maury Seitz Interview by R. Cargill Hall, 23 December 1997, 11–13 (copy in possession of the author). Seitz continues: "The resolution was unbelievable. And this was using a radar that had been modified by them and tested in a Lancaster base there. I saw a radar film where they forgot and left the camera on during final approach and they landed and developed the film, and it was 00 fog, and they blew it up and there was a farmer plowing the field, and you could see the reins going from his head to the horse. That's radar. I don't know whether he ever had any children after that, but I actually saw the photograph. That's how good the radar was. Now this was a modified version of the APQ-24."

34. Naftel later wrote as follows: "My assignment upon arrival in England was to re-qualify two Royal Air Force pilots in the RB-45C and then to work with another RAF pilot to check him out completely in that reconnaissance bomber. The two pilots were exchange officers assigned to the 91st Strategic Reconnaissance Wing at Lockbourne and had a fair number of hours in the RB-45C, but the third pilot had no time of experience in this aircraft. He was, however, a well-qualified Canberra pilot. The latter gentleman was one of the sharpest pilots I had ever worked with, and after seven training flights he was fully qualified in the RB-45C, including day and night refueling and emergency procedures" (Stacey D. Naftel, "RB-45C Overflights in the Far East," in Hall and Laurie, *Early Cold War Overflights*, vol. 1, 64). The British officer in question is most likely Flight Lieutenant McAlistair Furze, known to his crewmates as MacFruze.

35. Historical Report, 91st Strategic Reconnaissance Wing, October 1952, 50–51; Historical Report, 91st Strategic Reconnaissance Wing, November 1952, 40–41, Exhibit 48A, Air Force Historical Research Agency, Maxwell AFB. Mixon continues: "Having the detachment split up is not good and being on a Third Air Force base is not like being on a SAC station. The people here don't resent our presence, they are just wrapped up in their own problems and it takes time to get them moving on our projects. All of this plus the fact that we do not have USAF crews makes each problem a little more complex."

36. Earl Huggins Narrative, 1 December 1995 (copy in possession of the author).

37. Final Mission Report, Historical Report, 91st Strategic Reconnaissance Wing, December 1952, 49, 56–58, Exhibit 51, Air Force Historical Research Agency, Maxwell AFB; Mixon quoted in Samuel, *I Always Wanted to Fly*, 187. Hal Austin was present at Lockbourne throughout these proceedings and told the author, "We were aware or became suspicious, I should say, of what happened, not to the point of really asking anybody because we figured it was classified and we weren't authorized to know it anyway. But we had airplanes come back that obviously had new U.S. Markings on them and you could see where something else

had been painted on these and had been taken off."

38. Crampton, "RB-45 Operations," 120; Jackson, *High Cold War*, 52. In 1959, Major John Keema learned about these proceedings in a most direct manner: "We got some really hush-hush, super top secret radar film when I was in the 70th Recon Wing, and I was the intelligence officer; the first roll I opened up and started to look at was by the RAF crews. There it was, bigger than Hell."

39. According to one source, the RB-45Cs employed by the first British overflight were 48–019, 48–034, 48–036, and 48–042; those drawn for the scrubbed mission were 48–023, 48–029, 48–036, and 48–041 (Wai Yip, "Serial Numbers of the Royal Air Force's RB-45Cs," *Small Air Force Observer* 21, no. 4 [December 1997]: 114).

Chapter Ten

1. John Crampton, "RB-45 Operations," in Royal Air Force Historical Society, *Air Intelligence Symposium*, Bracknell Papers, No. 7 (1997), 123.

2. Disposition form, 5 June 1953, History of the Tactical Air Command, 1 January–30 June 1953, Vol. 3, Exhibit 20, Air Force Historical Research Agency, Maxwell, AFB; Maurer Maurer, ed., *Combat Squadrons of the Air Force, World War II* (Washington, D.C.: Office of Air Force History, 1982), 104. Regarding the aircraft, as Colonel John B. Anderson subsequently informed the author of the following: "SAC had them and a good friend of mine, General R.B. Steakley, was chief of reconnaissance in the Pentagon and he thought that it was time that TAC got into the jet reconnaissance business, so he arranged for the fifteen remaining RB-45s to be sent to Shaw."

3. Lieutenant Frank Martin left this vivid description of his old commander: "He was superb. He was very, very quiet, neat, and meticulous, always wanted to do the right thing, good pilot. The people in the squadron would do anything he asked. He was totally different from the people in Lockbourne because the people in TAC wanted to work for Andy, and the people in SAC did it because they were told to. He could get those people to do anything." Enlisted men were also favorably disposed toward "Major Andy." Airman Ray Fritzen remarked, "He was a commander to start with and if you ever got off course he would treat you like a father and put you right back on course." A good indication of Anderson's laid-back nature is also revealed through the following anecdote. Airman Joseph Thernka was once repairing a balky VHF system despite constant interruption by inquiring crewmates. "It was dark and the only lights I had to work with was a little spot light, and I couldn't see around," he recalled. "So into the crawl way comes this guy who says, 'How you doing?' and I blew it. I said, 'If you *bastards* would leave me alone maybe I could find the answer to this problem!' And who was it *but Andy*! He didn't say a word, he just turned around and went out and he never came back in. I never heard another word about it!"

4. History of the 19th Tactical Reconnaissance Squadron Night Photo Jet, 20 July 1953–1 May 1954, 1–3, Air Force Historical Research Agency, Maxwell AFB. "A fantastic organization," Wilbur Stevens assured the author, "tremendous morale, fantastic esprit de corps. Well-qualified individuals that were flying the missions and most of the people that were assigned in as aircraft commanders already had a tremendous wealth of experience in flying hours and so forth." Airman Edwin Carrington proffered an enlisted man's perspective on his old unit: "No. 1, the best outfit. We could out-drink and outfight anybody. We were thicker than thieves. If you hollered 19th, you had men right with you. The APs hated us!"

5. History of the Third Air Force, January–December

1954, Vol. 1, 48, Air Force Historical Research Agency, Maxwell AFB.

6. Hardin continues: "On that flight across the Atlantic, that long flight, something happened in the airplane because we all heard a big *clunk*! back in the bomb bay. I guess one of those really big bladders back there finished out, flexed or something, and made a thumping noise. And the navigator said, 'What's that?' It woke everybody up!"

7. History of the 19th Tactical Reconnaissance Squadron, Night Jet Photo, 20 July–11 May 1954, 3, 12, Air Force Historical Research Agency, Maxwell AFB. Sergeant Russell Stover concurred with Carrington's assessment: "All the guys that didn't drink got sick," he chortled. "If we had trash cans we could have sold them for $5,000 apiece — oh, my God, people were throwing up all over the place."

8. Quoted from Wolfgang W.E. Samuel, *I Always Wanted to Fly: America's Cold War Airman* (Jackson: University Press of Mississippi, 2001), 187; Wai Yip, "Serial Numbers of the Royal Air Force's RB-45Cs," *Small Air Force Observer* 21, no. 4 (December 1997): 114.

9. Crampton, "RB-45 Operations," 123. Apparently, this flight was part of a much larger endeavor conducted by the British and American governments entitled Project Ball Park, a concerted effort to collect target folder radar imagery from a variety of overflights (including the first RB-47 sorties a few weeks later). Its existence and raison d'etre are completely unexplored and unexplained save for a single, oblique reference. See Vance O. Mitchell, "U.S. Air Force Peacetime Airborne Reconnaissance During the Cold War, 1946–1990," in *Golden Legacy, Boundless Future: Essays on the United States Air Force and the Rise of Aerospace Power*, ed. Rebecca H. Cameron and Barbara Wittig (Washington, D.C., Air Force History and Museums Program, 2000), 150.

10. Norman Polmar, *Spyplane: The U-2 History, Declassified* (Osceola, WI: MBI, 2001), 12–13; Robert Jackson, *High Cold War: Strategic Air Reconnaissance and the Electronic Intelligence War* (Newbury Park, CA: Haynes North American, 1998), 52–53; Crampton, "RB-45 Operations," 123–124. He continues: "I thought for a moment of jettisoning our now empty 1,200 gallon wing tip tanks. Their absence might have added a few more knots to our speed but, once found, their maker's name and address would have revealed that they came from America, and there would have been a Devil of a row. Anyway the thought of them bouncing down the High Street of Kiev West at two o'clock in the morning disturbing the ladies and frightening the children did not appeal.... Moreover, General LeMay would not have been pleased at my scattering expensive bits of his aeroplane over Russia."

11. Polar, *Spyplane*, 13; Fritz Krag, "Mysterious Aircraft over Copenhagen in April 1954," *Flyvehistorisk Tidsskrift* No. 2 (June 1999): 13. The author is indebted to Fritz Krag for his English-language translation.

12. History of the Third Air Force, January–December 1954, Vol. 1, 49, Air Force Historical Research Agency, Maxwell AFB.

13. History of the 19th Tactical Reconnaissance Squadron Night Photo Jet, 15 May 1954–30 June 1954, various pagination, Air Force Historical Research Agency, Maxwell AFB. Sergeant Ray Frizten recalls working conditions on the flight lines and a bit of improvisation this entailed: "We didn't have ear protectors like they do now. We took No. 313 light bulbs and they would fit perfectly in your ears, so you always had a pair in your pocket and you'd stick them in your ears whenever we were cranking up the engines."

14. Carrington continues his meteorological tirade: "I can remember going to Norwich where they used to stop the bus, the conductor would get off and walk in front with a lantern, so that the bus driver could see where the road was. That's how bad the fog was — it was terrible." Still, the 19th

TAC did their fair share to help obviate these conditions. According to Captain Robert Altschuler, "Somebody made the remark, 'We had no trouble finding Hunstanton Road because the Americans had been through there and they threw all their beer cans on the side of the road, and they made excellent reflectors'"—another sterling example of Anglo-American cooperation.

15. History of the 19th Tactical Reconnaissance Squadron Night Photo Jet, 1 January 1955–30 June 1955, 5–8, 12; 1 July 1955–31 December 1955, 4–9: Both Air Force Historical Research Agency, Maxwell AFB.

16. According to Lieutenant Francis Martin, AOB on Anderson's plane, "I believe one of the things the Intelligence people were trying to do at the time, other than taking radarscope photography of assigned targets, was to find out what the Russians would do in the way of identifying and stopping us. I think it was important to find out if they would launch night fighters and what radars they would turn on to locate us" (Quoted in Samuel, *I Always Wanted to Fly*, 193–194).

17. Quoted in Samuel, *I Always Wanted to Fly*, 194.

18. History of the 47th Bombardment Wing, 1 July 1956 to 31 December 1956, 12, Air Force Historical Research Agency, Maxwell AFB.

19. History of the 19th Tactical Reconnaissance Squadron Night Photo Jet, 1 January 1957 to 31 March 1957, 3–8, Air Force Historical Research Agency, Maxwell AFB.

20. Quoted in Samuel, *I Always Wanted to Fly*, 194.

21. Richard Hain, a Russian-speaking ECM operator, informed the author of his station: "We flew missions into the Sea of Japan collecting signal intelligence. My position was an addition to the regular crew and I sat on my raft across the aisle to the left of the pilot and copilot, facing the bomb bay. I was supported by straps. I suspect this was some kind of a maintenance crew position as there was both an intercom and an oxygen outlet. We had no practical means to eject in an emergency. I think the navigator had an ejection mechanism which propelled him out the crew entrance door and I was instructed to follow him, but the likelihood for hitting the wing was high. I recall telling the pilot that I would just sit on his lap" (e-mail to the author, 5 September 2004).

22. Earl Huggins narrative, 1 December 1995, 9 (copy in the author's possession). Captain C.N. "Jack" Rice described his Security Service passenger: "A little guy down in the isle of the B-45 and he had a radio and he sat down there and he'd scan all of the frequencies. And if there was anything exciting he'd let us know about it." As Gere Ramsey informed the author, "I was told we carried a fourth man, an operator in the isle, and he would tell us to *run* if he thought it was necessary, other than that I didn't hear any of these transmissions."

23. Bob Gould, "Nighttime Fun Over the Sea of Japan," *Recce Reader* (Summer 2007): 15. Gould continues: "The next morning I was awakened at an early hour and told to report to Ops in a Class A Uniform. FEAF headquarters had read our mission report and wanted us in their office in Tokyo as soon as possible. So off we went in the group commander's staff car. I don't remember who was in the meeting besides our crew (minus the SS sergeant) except for Col. Ed Taylor and a couple of generals and numerous colonels. There were many questions and a general disbelief of our assumptions and some of the staff were genuinely hostile. They didn't believe that the USSR had any radar-equipped night fighters in the Far East. Eventually, the Security Service sergeant was escorted into the room by another colonel. He asked if the story we had told was true. He said it was and he had the recorded radio transmissions between the Russians and could prove it. It's amazing how fast you can be transformed from idiots to heroes. That was the first verbal confirmation we had heard of what the SS people were

doing while riding in the aisle of the RB-45. We were congratulated for not having been shot down, but there weren't any medals awarded."

24. Letter from John P. Corryn, 6 November 1995 (copy in possession of the author).

25. History, 91st Strategic Reconnaissance Squadron, 1 August 1953–14 August 1953, 6A, 13, Air Force Historical Research Agency, Maxwell AFB. Grant Angelus recalled the phenomenal optics of the K-30 set-up: "We had a 100 inch camera that they would mount in the bomb bay and cut a hole in the bomb bay door and mounted it at an angle. And it was a real powerful camera, I think they only made two or three of them. We used to fly along Sakhalin up in the northern islands, Russia, and they scribed a little gunsight thing on the glass canopy, and you'd fly along keeping outside the twelve mile limit, and jockey the airplane and point it at Sakhalin. You could barely see there and we knew where they were. We'd just drive along like that and I've seen some of the pictures in the photo lab and, Hell, you could read the numbers on the Mig's tails—from that far away!"

26. Report of Activities—Detachment Two, 1 August 1953–31 August 1953, Historical Report, 91st Strategic Reconnaissance Wing, September 1953, Exhibit 20; History, 41st Air Division, 1 January–30 June 1954, Exhibit B3. The activities performed by this detachment and its successor unit are described as follows: "During a normal mission the ECM operators collect analysis and direction finding data simultaneously, manipulating complex arrays of electronic equipment. They attempt to gather all possible information which can aid in determining what use is being made of the non-friendly radar. Some of this information takes the form of photographs of radar pulses and recordings of the audio tone created by the pulse repetition rate of the radar signal. Work of this nature entails a great amount of cooperation among the ferret crew members" (History, 91st Strategic Reconnaissance Squadron, 1 February 54–28 February 54, Supplement, 5–6: All Air Force Historical Research Agency, Maxwell AFB).

27. Report of Activities—Detachment 2, 1 September 1953–30 September 1953, Historical Report, 91st Strategic Reconnaissance Wing, October 1953, 50–54, Exhibit 52; History of the 91st Strategic Reconnaissance Squadron, September 1953, Supplement, 16: Both Air Force Historical Research Agency, Maxwell AFB. Speaking of the storm, Captain Charles N. Rice related these details: "We had a typhoon that was approaching and the Base Commander called all crews to the Officers Club for a briefing. He gave the present position and the estimated time it would hit Yokota. He said that all Aircraft commanders should start their engines and keep their planes weather vaned if the winds exceeded our safe crosswind speed. There was only one little hitch in that plan. Our RB-45s had to have an external power unit to start the engines, unlike the B-29s that had an internal power unit for starting. Since the external power units could not be stabilized in a high winds they could not be used. When we pointed this fact out, it was decided that we would remove the wheel chocks and let the aircraft weathervane on its own. That was the darkest night I have ever seen. I kept the brakes set until it felt like the plane was going to be blown over, then I released the brakes and let it weathervane. We were in 110 knot winds and could hear the wind scream outside the airplane" (Addendum to RB-45C Interview with Col. Rice, 16 October 2001, [copy in possession of the author]).

28. Report of Activities—Detachment 2, 1 October 1953–30 October 1953, Historical Report, 91st Strategic Reconnaissance Wing, November 1953, 48–54, Exhibit 23, 24; History of the 91st Strategic Reconnaissance Squadron, 1 October through 31 October 1953, Supplement, 15; Semiannual Historical Data, 6091st Reconnaissance Flight, 1 January to 30 June 1954, 1: All Air Force Historical Research

Agency, Maxwell AFB. Detachment 2 was headed for disbandment but the information it gathered on its many forays was sometimes startling. Captain C.N. Rice related the following: "They had lost a B-29 and they didn't know why but they suspected a SAM had shot it down and they [Bomber Command] wanted the information. So they sent down the order to go up and fly down the coast of Siberia and see what we'd come up with a 100-inch camera. And they said 20,000 feet at 200 knots and I sent word back I go at a minimum of 32,000 feet at a minimum of 400 knots. They said, 'What about the overlap?' I said, 'Would you rather have overlap or no pictures?' They said 'Pictures' and I said, 'Well, do it my way.' 'Okay.' So they mounted on the canopy a peep sight and I controlled the 100-inch camera from it. We flew 110 miles right over the coast because we had to get pictures underneath as well as inside, and in that 110 miles I think we probably had pictures of ten SAM sites on the coast—in addition to those that were inland. And we're going along and this kid from the Security Service reached up and tapped me on the foot—he'd do that and I'd put him on the intercom, and he said they just launched an airplane from base 40 miles away. I said, 'What was it?' He said, 'I don't know, I'll listen in a little bit.' And he listened a little bit more and he tapped me again and said, 'It's a MiG-19.' They didn't have any MiG-19s, we thought. It was a test flight—we didn't know!"

29. Report of Activities–Detachment Two, 1 November 1953–30 November 1953, Historical Report, 91st Strategic Reconnaissance Wing, December 1953, 51–57, Exhibits 19, 58; History, 91st Strategic Reconnaissance Squadron, November 1953, Supplement, 14: Both Air Force Historical Research Agency, Maxwell AFB. Despite the perils involved, Lieutenant Earl Huggins never allowed the stress of work to annoy him, especially on the homeward leg: "There was an Armed Forces AM radio station near Tokyo that played good music 24 hours a day. I would tune in this Tokyo AFRS on the Radio Compass, turn it to automatic, and we would follow the needle home listening to the latest hits. What a life!" (Earl Huggins narrative, 1 December 1995, 10 9 [copy in possession of the author]).

30. The only known unit compilation says it all: "Because of the classified nature of the missions flown by the 6091st Reconnaissance Flight, the normal operational breakdown will be omitted from this history" (Semiannual Historical Data, 6091st Reconnaissance Flight, 1 January 1954 to 30 June 1954, 1, Air Force Historical Research Agency, Maxwell AFB). Major Jim Brownlow, the operations officer, elaborates a little about his unit and its mission: "All the stuff we did was secret, where we were going, when we're going to do it, and even what *we've got* was secret. I remember that even the film we took on pictures was taken out of cameras, packed up, and somebody was selected with handcuffs to bring it back to Washington. Several of my pilots got a free trip for bringing film back! Everything was all kind of at a secret end of the base at Yokota, and nobody was allowed down there except the 91st and the 6091st."

31. History, 91st Strategic Reconnaissance Squadron, 1 December 53 to 31 December 53, 7–8; Supplement, 16: Both Air Force Historical Research Agency, Maxwell AFB.

32. Biography of Bert Beecroft, 22–23 (copy in the author's possession); "U.S. Jets Shoot Down MiG as Reds Attack Korea Patrol," *New York Times*, 1 February 1954, 1–2, and "U.S. Won't Protest Korea Air War Attack," *Ibid.*, 2 February 1954, 2.

33. History, 91st Strategic Reconnaissance Squadron, 1 February–28 February 1954, 5, 13, 44–45; Supplement, 5–6, 18: Both Air Force Historical Research Agency, Maxwell AFB. Speaking of maintenance problems, Harry Pollard, a North American Aviation technical representative on loan to the 6091st, recalls one episode with a J47's balky flow divider: "They were screwing around with it and

we tapped it. We shut the nacelles and the guy fired it up and I started to walk away from the aircraft. I got no more than 35 to 50 feet from it when the engine blew — it was small enough and had a chance to really spread so I didn't get hit. I ran back to the aircraft and I got the guy in the pilot's seat and got him out and he didn't know what the Hell to do. So I turned off the fuel values and stop-cocked the engine. We had fire damage on the side and upon the number three nacelle."

34. History, 91st Strategic Reconnaissance Squadron, 1 March–31 March 1954, 6, 27–28; Supplement, 18–19: Both Air Force Historical Research Agency, Maxwell AFB.

35. History, 91st Strategic Reconnaissance Squadron, 1 April–30 April 1954, 2, 27–28; Supplement, 16–18: Both Air Force Historical Research Agency, Maxwell AFB.

36. History, 91st Strategic Reconnaissance Squadron, 1 May–31 May 1954, 3, 6, 30–31; Supplement, 17–18: Both Air Force Historical Research Agency, Maxwell AFB. Some of these RB-45C flights from Kimpo were observed by Sergeant Wilfred Husted, an aircraft flight controller. He told the author "It was kind of neat because I had never seen one before. It would taxi out and I think eight of our F-86s would go out with it, and they would be gone probably an hour and a half–two hours. They all went out with full tanks and everything. I do recall they came back one time and the 86's gun ports were all smoked up. So this B-45 would come over monthly or twice a month. They'd go out, come back, and the RB-45 would go back to Japan. We just figured they were going up north snooping."

37. History, 91st Strategic Reconnaissance Squadron, 1 June–30 June 1954, n.p., Supplement, 16–17: Both Air Force Historical Research Agency, Maxwell AFB.

38. History, 91st Strategic Reconnaissance Squadron, July 1954, n.p., Supplement, 21–23; August 1954, n.p., Supplement, 24–25: Both Air Force Historical Research Agency, Maxwell AFB.

39. E-mail to author, 5 September 2004. Hain continues: "Major decisions regarding the mission such as flight safety issues remained with the pilot. Once when we were being aggressively chased I told the pilot that my equipment was malfunctioning and to abort immediately. He did so and upon landing at Yokota we were met on the tarmac by a host of officials from Fifth AF and one representative of the AFSS, Major G.I. Mason. I told him what happened, he climbed on board the aircraft, spun the dials on my equipment and announced to all that my equipment was in fact broken. Over the years since that time G.I. and I recalled that incident with laughter each time we met. On a personal note, I became hypotoxic during one sortie and 'tossed my cookies' into my oxygen mask and helmet. The pilot had to execute a rapid descent so I could breathe."

40. General Otto P. Weyland described the activities of the flight this way: "When the armistice was signed we were precluded from overflying North Korea. We had to stay at least three miles offshore, so I used the RB-45 with a long focal length camera, side-looking, and we could fly up and down the two coasts and we got some pretty valuable photographs inland along the lines of communication, what airfields were being reconstructed — they weren't supposed to reconstruct them but we knew they were, we could see them from these pictures — so we were able to keep up pretty much on what was going on" (General O.P. Weyland interview, 14, Air Force Historical Research Agency, Maxwell AFB).

41. For a detailed account of this incident, see "MiG Attack Is Put Off North Korea," *New York Times*, 7 February 1955, 2.

42. Warren E. Thompson, "Close Encounters of the MiG Kind," *Flight Journal* 10, no. 4 (August 2005): 65–68; Bob Stonestreet, "International Incident Over the Yellow Sea," *Sabrejet Classics* 3, no. 2 (Spring 1995): 14–15; "U.S.

Pilots Describe Battle with MiGs," *New York Times*, 8 February 1955, 5.

43. Stonestreet, "International Incident Over the Yellow Sea," 15. Speaking of this skirmish, one reporter blithely exclaimed, "Shooting down another nation's planes these days involves less and less risk of turning the cold war hot" ("If Trouble Is Brought to Us," *Time* 65 [14 February 1955]: 26).

Chapter Eleven

1. Ernest Hemingway, "London Fights the Robots," *Collier's* 114, no. 8 (19 August 1944): 17.

2. Memorandum for General Muir S. Fairchild, January 1950, Record Group 341, Headquarters, U.S. Air Force, Aircraft Division, Director of Research and Development, Box 36, National Archives. Another letter by Colonel J.C. Maxwell insisted that "From a safety standpoint, we believe that it is somewhat premature to place the B-45 in operations along regularly scheduled air carrier routes. The Air Force itself has had, of necessity, limited experience in operations of jet aircraft of this type. We have not succeeded in solving problems such as an anti-icing and all-weather operation for this type of aircraft. While we have evolved a method of de-icing jet engines, this method has not been incorporated on the B-45, or any other jet aircraft" (Memorandum for Colonel Frank Kurtz, 17 April 1950, in the same location).

3. "Jet Airline Tests May Include B-45," *New York Times*, 6 May 1950, 31. It continues: "The experiment would provide various data on jet planes in civilian air traffic, the approximate speed and cost of operating them, and their dependability in all kinds of weather."

4. Teletype, 17 December 1949, Record Group 341, Headquarters, U.S. Air Force, Deputy Chief of Staff, Materiel, Production Engineering Division, Box 11, National Archives.

5. History, 47th Bomb Group, Light, 1 September–2 October 1949, 11, Air Force Historical Research Agency, Maxwell AFB.

6. Don Dwiggins, *They Flew the Bendix Race* (Philadelphia: J.B. Lippincott, 1965), 150–151; "F-86 at 555 M.P.H. Wins Bendix Race," *New York Times*, 19 August 1951, 12; "Tail Wind Speeds Winner of Bendix," *Cleveland Plain Dealer*, 19 August 1951, 8. The B-45s in question were 47-058, 47-084, and 47-035.

7. This biographical information was retrieved from the NASA Dryden Flight Research Center Website, Edwards AFB, California.

8. B-45 accident investigation, 1952, RG 255, Records of the National Aeronautics and Space Administration, Project Correspondence Files, 1918–1978, Box 2–3, National Archives, Mid Atlantic Region, Philadelphia.

9. Rex Hardy letter, 27 January 1997 (in possession of the author). While preparing for one ill-fated test flight, Hardy was going through his check list when he accidentally triggered the B-45's extinguisher system: "I realized my mistake immediately but it was too late! The right side of the airplane was engulfed in extinguishing vapor. The flight was, of course, scrubbed. All the assembled people, who had been working for several hours, disgustedly began to secure their equipment, the other crew members of the plane climbed out, and I took off my helmet and just sat for a long time, deeply humiliated, in my seat. It was certainly my most embarrassing moment and delayed the test program for several days." See also Rex Hardy, "People and Planes," *Aviation* (May 1994): 8–10, 71–72.

10. Kenneth P. Werrel, "The Case Study of Failure," *American Aviation Historical Society Journal* 33 (Fall 1988): 19; History of the Wright Air Development Center, January–June 1955, Vol. 2, IV, Air Materiel Command, Wright-

Patterson AFB. All told, Rex Hardy, as indicated in the following communication to the author, enjoyed his experience with the B-45: "It was a nice airplane to fly. We did a lot of miscellaneous test work on it unrelated to the guidance program. One thing I liked about it was flying with the so called 'formation stick,' which was a small joy stick by the right hand side of the cockpit that allowed you to control the airplane through the autopilot instead of directly through the airplane controls. If you were holding at altitude you could use the stick to climb a little bit or descend a little bit or make it turn if you wanted to, it was all taken care of by the guidance system."

11. History of the 1st Tow Target Squadron, September 1949, 17–18, Exhibit 22, Air Force Historical Research Agency, Maxwell AFB. The public announcement waxed cheerily optimistic: "Another innovation in the B-45 series in 1950 was the development of a special version of the jet bomber to tow aerial targets. The Air Force selected the B-45 to be modified for this work because the versatile airplane provides the high speed and high altitude demanded to give today's fighters a good aerial work out with targets moving at jet speeds" (*Aircraft Year Book, 1950* [Washington, D.C.: Lincoln Press, 1950], 105).

12. History of the 1st Tow Target Squadron, April–May–June 1950, 13–14, 17–18, Exhibit 17, Air Force Historical Research Agency, Maxwell AFB.

13. History of the 1st Tow Target Squadron, July–August–September 1950, 11, 18–20, 35, Air Force Historical Research Agency, Maxwell AFB. The aircraft in question were 47–004, 47–006, 47–007, 47–009, 47–017, 47–018, and 47–019.

14. History of the 1st Tow Target Squadron, October–November–December 1950, 13, 29, 32, Exhibit 15, Air Force Historical Research Agency, Maxwell AFB.

15. History of the 1st Tow Target Squadron, January–February–March 1951, 13, 21, 38; April–May–June 1951, 11, 29; July–August–September 1951, 13, 20; October–November–December 1951, 11, 20, 28: All Air Force Historical Research Agency, Maxwell AFB.

16. History of the 1st Tow Target Squadron, April–June 1952, 19–20, 29–30, 39, Exhibit 10; July–December 1952, 13, 22, Air Force Historical Research Agency, Maxwell AFB. At some point during this period Lieutenant Harry Hutton went aloft in a Tornado for a ride: "It was hot and quiet in the cockpit, but now a noise like a high powered fan interrupted the stillness. Little white flakes started flying through the air in the cockpit. Gad, we've had it, I thought. The thing's going to explode: it's coming apart at the seams, 'Pilot, pilot, something is wrong. There are little white flakes flying through the air and there's a Helluva noise up here. What's wrong?' The pilot calmly told me that he had turned on the refrigeration system and that the white flakes were nothing more than snow created by it. I relaxed and pushed my heart back down into position. Lack of knowledge is certainly the mother of anxiety and fear" (Exhibit 23).

17. A civilian technician accompanied Drain on that flight and laughingly recounts crew reaction to questions posed by the accident board: "Each of us had been asked: 'What evasive action did you take, or observe being taken, when you became aware the rockets had been fired at your aircraft?' We had each demonstrated how we had involuntarily hunched our shoulders and ducked our heads — the total evasive action taken by the highly trained B-45 crew" (O.H. Billman, "Basic Instinct," *Air & Space Smithsonian* 19, no. 3 [September 2004]:17).

18. History of the 1st Tow Target Squadron, January–June 1954, 33–34, Air Force Historical Research Agency, Maxwell AFB.

19. History of the 1st Tow Target Squadron, January–June 1955, 39, 43, Air Force Historical Research Agency, Maxwell AFB. The squadron commander noted how "The

cost of maintaining a B-45 for instrument instruction is prohibitive. It has a fuel consumption rate of approximately 1200 to 1400 gallons per hour. Ground maintenance is extremely costly in man-hours and there are four jet engines to maintain. This is further complicated by a complex, high pressure hydraulic system. In addition, aircraft parts are few, and difficult to obtain."

20. History of the 1st Tow Target Squadron, July–December 1955, 49; July–December 1956, Tab 4; 1 July–31 December 1957, 22: All Air Force Historical Research Agency, Maxwell AFB.

21. History of the 4th Tow Target Squadron, January–February–March 1952, n.p.; July–December 1952, 18–19; July–December 1954, Tab B: All Air Force Historical Research Agency, Maxwell AFB.

22. Roger W. Story, "GE's B-45s, 1950–1957," *Journal of the American Aviation Historical Society* 44, no. 3 (Fall 1999): 232. "The 'flying laboratory' is a North American B-45 bomber assigned 16 months ago by the Air Force to the company for accelerated 'service life' tests of its four J47 powerplants under closely controlled conditions which cannot be attained in normal military operations" (*The Aircraft Yearbook 1951* [Washington, D.C.: Lincoln Press, 1951], 119).

23. See "Engineers Receive Jet Air Test Data," *New York Times,* 19 April 1951, 46, for an overview of flight testing at Schenectady. E.M. Beattie made this relevant observation about runways: "The favorable comparison of the jet to the propeller airplane ceases when the wheels touch the ground. Although the final approach air speed of the B-45 is only slightly higher than that of such airplanes as the B-29, there is a distressing lack of propeller drag for initially slowing down the jet airplane. Bringing the aircraft to a stop with brakes alone is feasible on a wet macadam runway. The more unfavorable braking action on ice or snow renders operation on 5000-foot runways impossible, and even makes operation on wet concrete questionable" (N.N. Davis and E.M. Beattie, "Flying the B-45 Jet Bomber," *SAE Journal* 59 [October 1951]: 23).

24. A.B. Liptak, 15 March 1951, Record Group 255, Records of the National Aeronautics and Space Administration, Box 233, National Archives. Roger Story, who occasionally flew with Beattie as a copilot, recounts a false alarm: "About the time we leveled off at altitude I started to smell a little smoke even with the oxygen mask on, and I was about to get on the intercom with Beattie and I looked up front and he got his oxygen mask off and he was noted for lighting up black cigars. So here we are at 30,000 feet and he'd light up this big black cigar which filled the area with an acrid odor."

25. Story, "GE's B-45s," 234–235.

26. "Jet in Air Unveils Monument to Jets," *New York Times,* 13 May 1955, 11.

27. John F. Smith, "Flights for Proof," *The Bee Hive* 31, no. 3 (Summer 1956): 16.

28. I am indebted to Jim Burridge of Arlington, Virginia, for pointing this out to me in his letter dated 20 June 1996.

29. Only one anecdotal account survives of a B-45 Tornado hauling an Allison J71 engine in its belly. Orville H. Billman was tasked with photographing it at Edwards AFB for the company; ultimately he lay down on the lake bed as the jet made a screaming low pass over him: "The noise was deafening and the jet exhaust nearly lifted me off the ground. The air around me crackled loudly with static electricity. It occurred to me that this whole procedure wasn't a very good idea" (O.H. Billman, "Best Intentions," *Air & Space Smithsonian* 9, no. 1 [December 1994/January 1995]: 24).

30. Earl Huggins narrative, 1 December 1995, 12 (copy in possession of the author). Marion "Hack" Mixon, who was so instrumental in orchestrating RAF use of the RB-45C

over Russia, was equally adamant and told the author "I could go to McDill right now with a model of a B-45, show it to some of the generals, and they won't know what the Hell it is!"

31. Howard S. Myers, "The RB-45C Tornado," *Friends Journal* 23, no. 3 (Fall 2000): 26. Finally, Stephen Neile encapsulates the B-45's predicament with a bittersweet plea for recognition: "I wish the readers of this book and the people in the Air Force would have known, or could have known, or should know what the Hell a B-45 was, because nobody knew that we existed. We spent our four or five years over there until they converted to the B-66. The reason that we were there is because the Strategic Air Command was not combat-ready in the RB-47, so we were filling in the gap, sitting on their targets. They were back in the states, trying to get combat-ready and getting all those spot promotions flying B-47s. And your chances of survival in a B-47 with a refueling capability, if the button were ever pushed, were sure as Hell probably better than ours were."

Bibliography

Primary Sources

AIR FORCE AIR MATERIEL COMMAND, WRIGHT-PATTERSON AFB, DAYTON, OHIO

Studies

Alling, Frederick A. History of Modification of USAF Aircraft for Atomic Weapon Delivery, 1948–1954 (Secret) Case History, B-45, 2 Vols.

History of Air Materiel Command Support of the Far East Air Force in the Korea Conflict, June-November, 1950, Vol. 1.

History of Wright Air Development Center, 1955.

AIR FORCE COMBAT COMMAND, LANGLEY AFB, VIRGINIA

Histories

Tactical Air Command

AIR FORCE HISTORICAL RESEARCH AGENCY, MAXWELL AFB, MONTGOMERY, ALABAMA

Command and Divisional Histories

Bomber Command
Far East Air Force
Fifth Air Force
41st Air Division
49th Air Division
Strategic Air Command
Tactical Air Command
Third Air Force

Group and Wing Histories

47th Bomb Group
47th Bomb Wing
91st Strategic Reconnaissance Wing
363rd Tactical Reconnaissance Group
363rd Tactical Reconnaissance Wing

Squadron and Flight Histories

1st Tow Target Squadron
2nd Tow Target Squadron
3rd Tow Target Squadron
4th Tow Target Squadron
19th Tactical Reconnaissance Squadron

84th Bombardment Squadron, Light
85th Bombardment Squadron, Light
86th Bombardment Squadron, Light
91st Strategic Reconnaissance Squadron
322nd Strategic Reconnaissance Squadron
323rd Strategic Reconnaissance Squadron
324th Strategic Reconnaissance Squadron
6091st Reconnaissance Flight

Manuscripts and Oral Histories

Cabell, Charles P.
Fish, Howard M.
Gray, David L.
Jones, David M.
Partridge, Earl
Stevenson, John D.
Weyland, Otto P.

Studies

"Atomic Weapon Delivery Systems," 1948–1958 (Secret).

Bald, Ralph D. "Air Force Participation in Joint Training Exercises, 1946–1950" (1959).

Beatty, Sherman R. "Potential Capabilities of the B-45 Aircraft as an All-Weather Fighter" (1949).

FEAF Report on Korea, 2 vols.

"Jet Bomber Operations," AU Staff Study on Problems of High Fuel Consumption by Jet Aircraft, 1947–1949 (AU-4740).

Sampson, Raymond D. "Evaluation of B-45 Aircraft for Tactical Air Operations in Comparison with A-26 Aircraft" (1948).

AIR FORCE HISTORY SUPPORT OFFICE, BOLLING AFB, WASHINGTON, D.C.

Studies

Bowen, Lee, and Robert D. Little. "The History of Air Force Participation in the Atomic Energy Program, 1943–1953." 5 vols. (1959).

AIR FORCE SAFETY AGENCY, KIRTLAND AFB, ALBUQUERQUE, NEW MEXICO

B-45 Accident Reports.

DEFENSE TECHNICAL INFORMATION
CENTER (DTIC), FORT BELVOIR, VIRGINIA

Studies
"Comparative Evaluation of Tactical Air Support Aircraft," 15 September 1949 (AD223678).
"Safe Delivery and Escape Conditions in Tactical Atomic Bombing Operations," April 1955 (AD504674).

DWIGHT D. EISENHOWER LIBRARY,
ABILENE, KANSAS
Eisenhower, Dwight D., Papers.
Norstad, Lauris, Papers.

FAIRCHILD RESEARCH CENTER, AIR
UNIVERSITY, MAXWELL AFB,
MONTGOMERY, ALABAMA

Research Papers
Hollstein, Charles P. "Increasing the Capability of Aerial Reconnaissance" (April 1953).

LIBRARY OF CONGRESS, MANUSCRIPT
DIVISION, WASHINGTON, D.C.
Fairchild, Muir S., Papers.
LeMay, Curtis, Papers.
Spaatz, Carl, Papers.
Twining, Nathan, Papers.
Vandenberg, Hoyt S., Papers.

NATIONAL AIR AND SPACE MUSEUM
LIBRARY, SMITHSONIAN INSTITUTION,
WASHINGTON, D.C.
B-45 File.

NATIONAL ARCHIVES, COLLEGE
PARK, MARYLAND
Record Group 218, Records of the Joint Chiefs of Staff.
Record Group 341, Records of Headquarters, U.S. Air Force.
Record Group 342, Records of U.S. Air Force Commands.

NATIONAL ARCHIVES, MID ATLANTIC
REGION, PHILADELPHIA, PENNSYLVANIA
Record Group 255, Records of the National Aeronautics and Space Administration.

NATIONAL ATOMIC MUSEUM LIBRARY,
ALBUQUERQUE, NEW MEXICO

Studies
"History of Air Force Participation in Operation Buster/Jangle," 1951.

"History of Shot Dog of Tumbler/Snapper," 1952.
"History of the Mark 5 Bomb."

NAVAL HISTORICAL CENTER, WASHINGTON
NAVY YARD, WASHINGTON, D.C.
USS *Coral Sea*, Historical Report.

POW/MIA OFFICE, THE PENTAGON,
WASHINGTON, D.C.
Korean War Working Group Session, April 1995.

U.S. ARMY MILITARY ACADEMY,
WEST POINT, NEW YORK
Willis F. Chapman File.

Printed Primary Sources — Books

Beaumont, Roland. *Testing Early Jets: Compressibility and the Supersonic Era.* Shrewsbury, England: Air-Life, 1990.
Cabell, Charles P. *Man of Intelligence: Memoirs of War, Peace, and the CIA.* Colorado Springs, CO: Impavide, 1997.
Goddard, George W. *Overview: A Life-Long Adventure in Aerial Photography.* Garden City, NY: Doubleday, 1969.
Hall, R. Cargill, and Clayton D. Laurie, eds. *Early Cold War Overflights, 1950–1956: Symposium Proceedings.* 2 vols. Washington, DC: Office of the Historian, National Reconnaissance Office, 2003.
Hoover, Bob. *Forever Flying: An Autobiography of R.A. "Bob" Hoover.* New York: Pocket Books, 1996.
Leary, Penn, ed. *Test Flying at Old Wright Field: By the "Wright Stuff" Pilots and Engineers.* Omaha, NB: Westchester House, 1991.
Lopez, Donald S. *Fighter Pilot Heaven: Flight Testing the Early Jets.* Washington, DC: Smithsonian Institution Press, 1995.
Louden, Terri. *On God's Wings: A Daughter's Inspirational Story of Her Dad and His Miracle.* Coronado, CA: Louden Network, 2005.
Samuel, Wolfgang W.E. *I Always Wanted to Fly: America's Cold War Airmen.* Jackson: University Press of Mississippi, 2001.
Y'Blood, William T., ed. *The Three Wars of Lt. Gen. George E. Stratemeyer: His Korean War Diary.* Washington, DC: Air Force History and Museums Program, 1999.
Yeager, Chuck, and Leo Jones. *Yeager: An Autobiography.* New York: Bantam, 1985.

Printed Primary Sources — Articles

Billman, O.H. "Basic Instinct." *Smithsonian Air & Space* 19, no. 3 (August/September 2004).
_____. "Beast Intentions." *Smithsonian Air & Space* 9, no. 1 (December 1994/January 1995).

Crampton, John. "RB-45 Operations. Royal Air Force Historical Society. *Air Intelligence Symposium*. Bracknell Paper No. 7 (1997).

[Dale, Harold E.] "A Product of Teamwork." *Western Flying* 30 (October 1950): 16–17, 44.

Davis, N.N., and E.M. Beattie. "Flying the B-45 Jet Bomber." *SAE Journal* 59 (October 1951): 19–23.

Draper, George T. "I Rode the Tornado." *Saga* 3, no. 4 (December 1951):11–12, 91–92.

Gould, Bob. "Nighttime Fun Over the Sea of Japan." *Recce Reader* (Summer 2007): 15.

Hemingway, Ernest. "London Fights the Robots." *Collier's* 114, no. 8 (August 19, 1944): 17, 80–81.

Lambert, C.M. "At the Controls of the B-45." *Flight* 67 (April 1955): 523–525.

Myers, Howard S. "Midnight Mission: Secret Spy Flights Over Korea in the All-Black North American RB-45 Tornado." *Air Power* 23 (July 1993): 54–61.

_____. "We Flew Tornados." *Spy Planes: Air Classic Special Edition* 2 (1988): 26–31.

Reed, Boardman C. "North American Aviation Bombers I Have Known and Flown." *American Historical Aviation Society Journal* 37, no. 4 (Winter, 1992): 242–263.

Stocker, Joseph S. "I Rode a Tornado." *Boy's Life* 60 (January 1950): 5, 31–32.

_____. "Jet Bomber Jockeys." *Air Trails Pictorial* 33 (March 1950): 22–23, 68.

Stonestreet, Bob. "International Incident Over the Yellow Sea." *Sabrejet Classics* 3, no. 2 (Spring 1995): 14–15.

Newspapers

Air Force Times
American Daily
Cleveland Plain Dealer
Columbus Citizen
London Daily Mail
Norfolk Eastern Daily Press
El Paso Times
New York Times
Shreveport Times
London Times
Norfolk Virginian-Pilot and the Ledger Star

Interviews

All taped interviews and written depositions have been donated to the National Museum of the United States Air Force, Dayton, Ohio, and can be accessed by the public under the call number AR.2008.013.

Altschuler, Robert, 19th Tactical Reconnaissance Squadron.

Anderson, John B., 19th Tactical Reconnaissance Squadron.

Angelus, Grant, 322nd Strategic Reconnaissance Squadron, 6091st Reconnaissance Flight.

Ashby, Robert, 86th Bombardment Squadron.

Austin, Harold, 323rd Strategic Reconnaissance Squadron.

Baer, Leonard, 85th Bombardment Squadron.

Barrett, Alvan, 323rd Strategic Reconnaissance Squadron.

Bass, John M., 19th Tactical Reconnaissance Squadron.

Bastidas, Frank, Pratt and Whitney.

Beecroft, Bertram, 335th Fighter Squadron.

Blair, Hubert M., 85th Bombardment Squadron.

Bodie, Warren, North American Aviation.

Boettcher, Byron, Deputy Chief, Bomber Project Program.

Bombkamp, William, 85th Bombardment Squadron.

Brewer, Paul, North American Aviation.

Brownlow, James, 323rd Strategic Reconnaissance Squadron, 6091st Reconnaissance Flight.

Butts, John, 84th/85th Bombardment Squadrons.

Byrne, Edward, 85th Bombardment Squadron.

Cardenas, Robert, Flight Test Division, Bomber Section.

Carrington, Edwin, 19th Tactical Reconnaissance Squadron.

Carrington, Louis, 85th Bombardment Squadron.

Carroll, Richard E., 86th Bombardment Squadron.

Chapman, Willis F., 47th Bomb Wing.

Chinnock, Earl, 322nd Strategic Reconnaissance Squadron.

Clark, Robert H., 85th Bombardment Squadron.

Collier, Walter, 85th Bombardment Squadron.

Columbus, Michael, 85th Bombardment Squadron.

Corryn, John, U.S. Air Force Security Service.

Cox, Freeman M., 85th Bombardment Squadron.

Crichton, Ted, 86th Bombardment Squadron.

Crowley, William, North American Aviation.

Dackson, Walter, 85th Bombardment Squadron.

Davis, Robert, 84th Bombardment Squadron.

Deakin, Bruce, 85th Bombardment Squadron.

Dold, Cletus, 1st Tow Target Squadron, 86th Bombardment Squadron.

Drain, Jack L., 1st Tow Target Squadron.

Edmonds, Clarence, Northrop Corporation.

Feltus, Donald E., 85th Bombardment Squadron.

Fitzgerald, Raymond L., 84th Bombardment Squadron.

Fleshman, Ray, 84th Bombardment Squadron.

Forsberg, Richard, 323rd Strategic Reconnaissance Squadron.

Fritzen, Ray, 19th Tactical Reconnaissance Squadron.

Gehrkens, George, North American Aviation.

Gordon, George, Pratt and Whitney.

Gould, Robert, 6091st Reconnaissance Flight.

Greenamyre, Vernon, Flight Test Division.

Hain, Richard, U.S. Air Force Security Service.

Hamilton, Dale, 85th Bombardment Squadron.

Hannibal, Nick, 85th Bombardment Squadron.

Hardin, Dick, 19th Tactical Reconnaissance Squadron.

Hardy, Rex, Northrop Corporation.

Hayslip, Frank W. 322nd/323rd Strategic Reconnaissance Squadron.

Heavilin, Vance, 323rd Strategic Reconnaissance Squadron.

Hoover, Robert, North American Aviation.

Hosher, Alfred, 85th Bombardment Squadron.

Hoyt, Thurber, 322nd Strategic Reconnaissance Squadron.

Hunt, Leo, North American Aviation.

Husted, Wilfred.

Jones, David M., 47th Bomb Wing.

Keema, John, 322nd/324th Strategic Reconnaissance Squadrons.

Kirk, James, 85th Bombardment Squadron.

Kristen, William, 324th Strategic Reconnaissance Squadron.

Liptak, Alfred, General Electric.

Little, Terry, 84th Bombardment Squadron.

Louden, Jim, 85th Bombardment Squadron.

Ludlow, Glenn, 86th Bombardment Squadron.

Lyle, Lewis, 91st Strategic Reconnaissance Wing.

Mackay, Hugh, 86th Bombardment Squadron, 19th Tactical Reconnaissance Squadron.

Mackey, John, 324th Strategic Reconnaissance Squadron.

McCann, Wayne, 4211th Armament and Electronics.

McLaren, Alan, 86th Bombardment Squadron.

Mangum, John, 85th Bombardment Squadron.

Martin, Frank, 322nd Strategic Reconnaissance Squadron, 19th Tactical Reconnaissance Squadron.

Menkevich, William, 86th Bombardment Squadron.

Miller, Lloyd, 1st Tow Target Squadron, 84th Bombardment Squadron.

Mixon, Marion, 323rd Strategic Reconnaissance Squadron.

Musser, Glenn, 85th Bombardment Squadron.

Myers, Howard S., 322nd Strategic Reconnaissance Squadron.

Naftel, Stacey, 323rd, Strategic Reconnaissance Squadron.

Nasby, Oliver, 324th Strategic Reconnaissance Squadron, 19th Tactical Reconnaissance Squadron.

Neile, Stephen, 84th Bombardment Squadron.

Nicoloff, George J., 19th Tactical Reconnaissance Squadron.

O'Brien, Sylvester F., 86th Bombardment Squadron.

Orr, Donald, 85th Bombardment Squadron.

Pace, Calvin, 323rd Strategic Reconnaissance Squadron.

Philips, Edward, 85th Bombardment Squadron.

Pollard, Harry, North American Aviation.

Ramsey, Gere, 91st Strategic Reconnaissance Wing, 6091st Reconnaissance Flight.

Ream, Clyde, 86th Bombardment Squadron.

Rice, Jack, 322nd Strategic Reconnaissance Squadron, 6021st Reconnaissance Flight.

Riddell, Claude, 84th Bombardment Squadron.

Riggs, Frank, 323rd Strategic Reconnaissance Squadron, 86th Bombardment Squadron.

Roos, George J., 85th Bombardment Squadron.

Ryall, Zachary, 84th/85th Bombardment Squadrons.

Sager, Frederick, 548th Technical Reconnaissance Squadron.

Sanderson, Edward J., 84th/86th Bombardment Squadrons.

Satterly, Leonard, 85th Bombardment Squadron.

Saunders, Richard, 85th Bombardment Squadron.

Saunders, William, 85th Bombardment Squadron.

Schamber, Robert A, 322nd Strategic Reconnaissance Squadron, 19th Tactical Reconnaissance Squadron.

Schrecengost, Raymond, 19th Tactical Reconnaissance Squadron.

Scott, Vernon, U.S. Air Force Security Service.

Seitz, Maury, 323rd Strategic Reconnaissance Squadron.

Sharpe, James, 85th Bombardment Squadron.

Skiles, Luke, 85th Bombardment Squadron.

Snyder, Eugene, 322nd Strategic Reconnaissance Squadron.

Sollars, Merle, 85th Bombardment Squadron.

Stadille, Robert, 91st Strategic Reconnaissance Squadron.

Stevens, Wilbur, 19th Tactical Reconnaissance Squadron.

Stokes, Louis, Flight Test Division.

Story, James, 85th Bombardment Squadron.

Story, Roger, General Electric.

Stover, Russell, 19th Tactical Reconnaissance Squadron.

Thernka, Joseph, 19th Tactical Reconnaissance Squadron.

Toyeas, Nick, U.S. Air Force Security Service.

Valentine, James, 323rd Strategic Reconnaissance Squadron.

Walker, Everett G., 19th Tactical Reconnaissance Squadron.

Watson, George, 85th Bombardment Squadron.

Wehr, Robert, 19th Tactical Reconnaissance Squadron.

Whitmire, Warren T., 85th Bombardment Squadron.

Whittaker, David, 19th Tactical Reconnaissance Squadron.

Wilkerson, John, 85th Bombardment Squadron.

Wines, Glenn H., 4th Tactical Depot Squadron.

Wiltshire, John B., 85th/86th Bombardment Squadrons, 19th Tactical Reconnaissance Squadron.

Wold, James, 19th Tactical Reconnaissance Squadron.

Yoder, Jack, 19th Tactical Reconnaissance Squadron.

Books

Avery, Norm L. *North American Aircraft*. 2 vols. Santa Ana, CA: Narkiewicz/Thompson, 1998.

Baker, David. *North American/Rockwell Aircraft Since 1928*. Annapolis, MD: Naval Institute Press, 1988.

Borowski, Harry R., ed. *Military Planning in the Twentieth Century*. Washington, DC: Office of Air Force History, 1986.

Bowyer, Michael F.J. *Action Stations*. Wellingborough, England: Stephens, 1990.

_____. *Force for Freedom: The USAF in the United Kingdom Since 1948.* North Yeovil, UK: Patrick Stephens, 1994.

Boyne, Walter J. *Beyond the Wild Blue: A History of the U.S. Air Force, 1947–1997.* New York: St. Martin's, 1997.

Breihan, John R., Stan Piet, and Roger S. Mason. *Martin Aircraft, 1909–1960.* Santa Ana, CA: Narkiewicz/Thompson, 1995.

Brown, Michael E. *Flying Blind: The Politics of the U. S. Strategic Bomber Program.* Ithaca, NY: Cornell University Press, 1992.

Burrows, William E. *By Any Means Possible: America's Secret War in the Cold War Years.* New York: Farrar, Strauss, and Giroux, 2001.

Cameron, Rebecca H., and Barbara Wittig, eds. *Golden Legacy, Boundless Future: Essays on the United States Air Force and the Rise of Aerospace Power.* Washington, DC: Air Force History and Museum Programs, 2000.

Campbell, Duncan. *The Unsinkable Aircraft Carrier: American Military Power in Britain.* London: M. Joseph, 1984.

Cole, Paul M. *POW/MIA Archives Research Project: Ukraine, Latvia, Estonia, and Berlin.* Vol. 1. Moscow, Washington, DC: DFI International, 1994.

_____. *POW/MIA Issues.* Vol. 1, *The Korean War.* Santa Monica, CA: Rand, 1994.

Condit, Doris M. *History of the Office of the Secretary of Defense,* vol. 2, *The Test of War, 1950–1953.* Washington, DC: Office of the Secretary of Defense, 1988.

Crane, Conrad C. *American Air Power Strategy in Korea, 1950–1953.* Lawrence: University Press of Kansas, 1999.

Dwiggins, Don. *They Flew the Bendix Race: The History of the Competition for the Bendix Trophy.* Philadelphia: Lippincott, 1965.

Evangelista, Matthew. *Innovations and the Arms Race: How the United States and the Soviet Union Develop New Military Technologies.* Ithaca, NY: Cornell University Press, 1988.

Furman, Necah S. *Sandia National Laboratories: The Post War Decade.* Albuquerque, NM: University of New Mexico Press, 1990.

Futrell, Robert F. *Ideas, Concepts, Doctrine: Basic Thinking in the United States Air Force, 1907–1960.* 2 vols. Maxwell AFB, AL: Air University Press, 1989.

_____. *The United States Air Force in Korea, 1950–1953.* Washington, DC: Air Force History and Museum Program, 1983.

Gibson, James M. *The History of the U. S. Nuclear Arsenal.* Greenwich, CT: Brompton, 1989.

Gordon, Yefim, and Vladimir Rigmant. *MiG-15: Development and Korean War Combat History.* Osceola, WI: Motorbooks, 1993.

Gunston, Bill, and Peter Gilchrist. *Jet Bombers from the Messerschmitt 262 to the Stealth B-2.* London: Osprey Aerospace, 1993.

Hansen, Chuck. *U.S. Nuclear Weapons: The Secret History.* Arlington, TX: Aerofax, 1988.

Hardison, John D. *The Megaton Blasters: Story of the 4925th Test Group (Atomic).* Arvada, CO: Boomerang, 1990.

Higham, Robin, John T. Greenwood, and Von Hardesty, eds. *Russian Aviation and Air Power in the Twentieth Century.* Portland, OR: Frank Cass, 1998.

Infield, Glenn B. *Unarmed and Unafraid.* New York: Macmillan, 1970.

Jackson, Robert. *Combat Prototypes Since 1945.* Shrewsbury, England: AirLife, 1985.

_____. *High Cold War: Strategic Reconnaissance and the Electronic Intelligence War.* Newbury Park, CA: Haynes North American, 1998.

_____. *United States Air Force in Britain: Its Aircraft, Bases, and Strategy Since 1948.* Shrewsbury, England: AirLife, 1999.

Jolidon, Lawrence. *Last Seen Alive: The Search for Missing POWs from the Korean War.* Austin, TX: Ink-Slinger, 1995.

Kinert, Reed. *American Racing Planes and Historic Air Races.* Chicago: Wilcox and Follett, 1952.

Knaack, Marcelle S. *Encyclopedia of U. S. Air Force Aircraft and Missile Systems,* vol. 2, *Post World War II Bombers, 1945–1973.* Washington, DC: Office of Air Force History, 1988.

Lashmar, Paul. *Spy Flights of the Cold War.* Annapolis: Naval Institute Press, 1996

Mauer, Mauer, ed. *Combat Squadrons of the Air Force, World War II.* Washington, DC: Office of Air Force History, 1982.

McFarland, Linda. *Cold War Strategist: Stuart Symington and the Search for National Security.* Westport, CT: Praeger, 2001.

Miller, Richard L. *Under The Cloud: The Decades of Nuclear Testing.* New York: Free Press, 1986.

Moody, Walton S. *Building A Strategic Air Force.* Washington, DC: Air Force History and Museums Program, 1996.

Nalty, Bernard C., ed. *Winged Shield, Winged Sword: A History of the United States Air Force.* 2 vols. Washington, DC: Air Force History and Museum Program, 1997.

Peebles, Curtis. *Shadow Flights: America's Secret Air War Against the Soviet Union.* Novato, CA: Presidio, 2000.

Polmar, Norman. *Spyplane: The U-2 History Declassified.* Osceola, WI: MBI, 2001.

_____, ed. *Strategic Air Command: People, Aircraft, Missiles.* Baltimore: Nautical and Aviation, 1979.

Rodrigues, Rick. *Aircraft Markings of the Strategic Air Command, 1946–1953.* Jefferson, NC: McFarland, 2006.

Swanborough, Gordon. *North American: An Aviation Album.* London: Ian Miller, 1973.

Tegler, Jan. *B-47 Stratojet: Boeing's Brilliant Bomber.* New York: McGraw Hill, 2000.

Warnock, A. Timothy, ed. *The USAF in Korea: A Chronology, 1950–1953.* Washington, DC: Air Force History and Museums Program, 2000.

Williamson, Samuel R., and Steven L. Rearden. *The Origins of U. S. Nuclear Strategy, 1945–1953.* New York: St. Martin's, 1993.

Articles

"AAF Developing 500 MPH Multi-Jet Bombing Fleet." *Aviation News* 7, no. 15 (April 14, 1947): 7–8.

"America's First Jet Bomb Wing." *Shreveport Magazine* 3, no. 12 (December 1948): 12–13.

Baldwin, Hansen W. "The Russians Can Be Stopped in Europe." *Saturday Evening Post* 225, no. 22 (November 29 1952): 28, 102, 104.

Berg, Paul D., and Christopher Finn. "Anglo-American Strategic Air Power Co-operation in the Cold War and Beyond." *Air and Space Power Journal* 18, no. 4 (Winter, 2004): 50–61.

Blount, Earl. "Big Bark." *Skyline* 7 (July 1949): 5–6.

Bodie, Warren. "Breeching the Walls of Fortress Europe." *Air Power* 3 (September 1973): 36–55.

_____. "XB-45: A Pioneer Among Jet Bombers." *Flight Journal* 10, no. 1 (February 2005): 32.

Boyne, Walter J. "Convair's Needle-Nosed Orphan: The One and Only XB-46 Jet Bomber." *Air Power* 6 (September 1976): 8–19, 66.

_____. "The Early Overflights." *Air Force Magazine* 84, no. 6 (June 2001): 60–65.

_____. "Stuart Symington." *Air Force Magazine* 82 (February 1999): 68–73.

_____. "XB-48: Martin's Pipe Dream." *Air Power* 5 (September 1975): 8–21.

Braybrook, Roy. "Let's Hear It for the Hairy Apes." *Air International* 38 (January 1990): 25–27.

Buttler, Tony. "Turbojets for Stalin." *Air Enthusiast* No. 94 (July/August 2001): 73–77.

Collins, Neil. "America's Jet Cameramen." *Skyline* 9, no. 4 (November 1951): 20–23.

"Eyes of the Air Force." *Flying* 48 (May 1951): 124–125, 168.

Fredriksen, John C. "Detachment 2 Goes to War: RB-45C Reconnaissance Activity in Korea, 1950–1953." *American Aviation Historical Society Journal* 41 (Winter 1996): 282–287.

Goodrum, Alastair. "Flame Out! Some Jet Accidents in England's Fenland." *Fly Past* No. 246 (January 2002): 104–108.

Gunston, Bill. "Martin's Six-jet Bomber." *Aeroplane Monthly* 10 (August 1982): 432–436.

_____. "North American Tornado." *Aeroplane Monthly* 10 (December 1982): 632–637.

Hall, R. Cargill. "Strategic Reconnaissance in the Cold War." *Prologue* 28, no. 2 (Summer 1996): 102–125.

_____. "The Truth About Overflights." *MHQ* 9 (Spring 1997): 24–39.

Hallion, Richard P. "Girding for War: Perspectives on Research, Development, Acquisition, and the Decision-Making Environment of the 1980s." *Air University Review* 37, no. 6 (September-November 1986): 46–61.

Hamilton, Andrew. "SAC's 'Seeing Eye' Jets." *Skyways* 11, no. 6 (June 1952): 10–13, 52.

Hardy, Rex. "People and Planes." *Aviation* (May 1994): 8–10, 71–72.

Holloway, Bruce K. "High Sub-sonic Speed for Air Warfare." *Air University Quarterly Review* 1 (Fall 1947): 42–52.

"If Trouble Is Brought to Us." *Time* 65 (February 15, 1955): 26.

Jabara, James. "Korean Air War. *Air Force Magazine* 34, no. 10 (October 1951): 53, 60.

Jessup, Alpheus W. "MiG-15 Dims USAF's A-Bomb Hopes." *Aviation Week* 56 (4 February 1952): 16.

"Jet Bomber Cockpit." *Flight* 56, no. 2129 (13 October, 1949): 498.

"Jet Bombers Across the Atlantic." *Aeroplane* 80, no. 2063 (February 2, 1951): 130–131.

Johnson, E.R. "Operation Backbreaker: Cold War Tripwire." *Aviation History* 14, no. 5 (May 2004): 46–52.

Krag, Fritz. "Mystiske fly over Kobenhavn, 1 Apal, 1954." *Flyvehistorik Tidsskrift* No. 2 (June 1999): 12–14.

Lambert, C. M. "47th Bombardment Wing (Light)." 67 *Flight* (March 1955): 388–392.

Larson, George A. "America's First Four Engine Jet Bomber." *Friends Journal* 24, no. 2 (2001): 38–41.

_____. "FEAF Intelligence Missions over North Korea." *Combat Aircraft* 2, no. 12 (October-November 2000): 1020–1025.

Marthason, A. "The North American XB-45." *Aeroplane* 73 (November 21, 1947): 672–673.

Mizrahi, Joe. "The Last Great Bomber Fly Off." *Wings* 29 (June 1999): 8–55.

Myers, Howard S. "Big Bodies in Motion: Flying the Best of SAC's Mighty Bomber Brigade." *Wings* 25 (August 1995): 20–24, 54–56.

_____. "The RB-45C Tornado." *Friends Journal* 23, no. 3 (Fall 2000): 21–26.

_____. "SAC's First Cold Warrior Super Sleuth." *Klaxon* 4, no. 4 (Winter 1996/1997): 12–14.

_____. "Sky Spy: The Life and Times of the North American RB-45C Tornado." *Air Classics* 34, no. 3 (March 1998): 12–22.

"NA XB-45, General Briefing Data." *Aeroplane Monthly* 15, no. 10 (October 1987): 511–513.

"The New Look with the RB-45C, Latest Air Force Photo Plane." *Skyline* 8, no. 3, (August 1950): 10–11.

"North American Grooms XB-45 Jet Bomber." *Aviation* 46, no. 5 (May 1947): 71.

"North American Jet Flies at Muroc." *Aviation News* 7, no. 12 (March 24, 1947): 9.

"North American Tornado." *Armchair Aviator* 2 (March-April 1973): 44–46.

"North American XB-45." *Air Force Magazine* 36, no. 6 (June 1947): 44–45.

"Record Flight." *Time* No. 8 (August 20, 1951): 70.

"Recording Test Data on the North American B-45." *Aviation Week* 47, no. 6 (August 11, 1947): 24–25.

Schrader, Richard K. "Douglas XB-43." *Air Classics* 25 (July 1989): 14–20, 32, 37.

Sheehan, John W. "North American B-45 ... The USAF's Tornado." *Air International* 35 (November 1988): 243–250.

Smith, John F. "Flights for Proof." *The Behive* 31, no. 3 (Summer 1956): 12–17.

Sorrels, A. R. "Salute to an Old Warrior." *Skyline* 16 (Fall, 1958): 16–19.

Story, Roger W. "GE's B-45s, 1950–1957." *American Aviation Historical Society Journal* 44, no. 3 (Fall 1999): 232–235.

Thompson, Warren E. "Close Encounters of the MiG Kind." *Flight Journal* 10, no. 4 (August 2005): 65–68.

"Tornado." *Skyline* 7, no. 2 (1949): 17–19.

Trimble, Robert L. "The L.A. Tornados." *Air Classics* 10 (November 1974): 26–32, 64–65.

_____. "New Age Bombers." *Air Progress Aviation Review* 6 (Winter 1982): 34–40, 76–89.

Werrell, Kenneth P. "The Case Study of Failure." *American Aviation Historical Society Journal* 33 (Fall 1988): 190- 204.

Winton, Dave. "Tornado Demise." *Aeromilitaria* 30, no. 117 (Spring 2004): 21–22.

Wolk, Herman S. "First Five Years of the First 50." *Air Force Magazine* 80 (September 1997): 53–58.

"XB-45." *Interavia* 11, no. 4 (April 1947): 14–16.

"XB-45 Completes First Test Flight." *U. S. Air Services* 32 (April 1947): 16.

Yaffe, Michael D. "A Higher Priority than the Korean War! The Crash Program to Modify Bombers for the Bomb." *Diplomacy and Statecraft* 5, no. 2 (July 1994): 358–370.

Yip, Wai. "Serial Numbers of the Royal Air Force's RB-45Cs." *Small Air Force Observer* 21, no. 4 (December 1997): 114.

Dissertations, Monographs, Miscellaneous

Air Force Special Weapons Center, SWO. Aircraft Participation in Tumbler-Snapper. Kirtland AFB, NM: AFSWC, Special Weapons Office, 9 June 1952.

Aircraft Yearbook

Farquhar, John T. "A Need to Know: The Role of Reconnaissance in War Planning, 1945–1953." Phd diss., Ohio State University, 1991.

Hopkins, Robert S., III. "U. S. Strategic Serial Reconnaissance and the Cold War, 1945–1961." Phd diss., University of Virginia, 1998.

Martin, Jerome V. "Reforging the Sword: United States Air Force Tactical Air Forces, Air Power Doctrine, and National Security Policy, 1945–1958." Phd diss., Ohio State University, 1988.

O'Neil, Mark A. "The Other Side of the Yalu: Soviet Pilots in the Korean War, Phase One, 1 November 1950–12 April 1951." Phd diss., Florida State University, 1996.

Recon Recorder

Strategic Air Command Combat Crew

Index

Numbers in **_bold italics_** indicate pages with photographs.